Conspiracy Film

Conspiracy Films

A Tour of Dark Places in the American Conscious

BARNA WILLIAM DONOVAN

To Ilana,

Thank you so much for your help and for all that you have done to keep "V" alive for so many fans. I hope you enjoy the book!

Barna William Donovan

7/27/11

McFarland & Company, Inc., Publishers

Jefferson, North Carolina, and London

LIBRARY OF CONGRESS CATALOGUING-IN-PUBLICATION DATA

Donovan, Barna William, 1970–
Conspiracy films : a tour of dark places in the American
conscious / Barna Williams Donovan.
p.   cm.
Includes bibliographical references and index.

ISBN 978-0-7864-3901-0
softcover : 50# alkaline paper ∞

1. Conspiracy in motion pictures.   2. Motion pictures—
United States—History—20th century.   3. Motion pictures—
United States—History—21st century.   4. Conspiracy theories—
United States.   I. Title.
PN1995.9.C555D66   2011   791.43'658—dc23   2011022796

BRITISH LIBRARY CATALOGUING DATA ARE AVAILABLE

Front cover image: Kevin Costner as Jim Garrison in *JFK*, 1991
(Warner Brothers/Photofest)

Manufactured in the United States of America

McFarland & Company, Inc., Publishers
Box 611, Jefferson, North Carolina 28640
www.mcfarlandpub.com

To my mother, Dr. Eva M. Donovan

Table of Contents

Preface

Prediction

If tonight's news broadcasts show vivid footage of an asteroid streaking out of the sky and destroying the Brooklyn Bridge, by tomorrow the Internet will have at least a dozen webpages and blogs arguing that the bridge, in fact, was leveled by a top-secret missile fired from a suborbital aircraft that had flown out of Nellis Air Force Base's Area 51. A conspiracy reaching to the highest levels of the United States government, funded by an international banking consortium, the heads of which are descendants of royal blood-lines tracing their ancestry to the builders of the Egyptian pyramids, masterminded the attack.

* * *

Over the past five decades, American culture has descended ever further into a shadowy, suspicious world of conspiracy theorizing. The prognostication about the Brooklyn Bridge scenario is actually not as far-fetched as it might appear upon first glance. Nearly every major national and world event, nearly every tragic turn in the lives of the most famous and powerful, has spawned a bounty of lurid, complicated conspiracy theories. For example, many believe that Princess Diana was murdered by the British intelligence services. Others are convinced that Michael Jackson is still alive. There are perhaps more conspiracy theories about the events of September 11, 2001, than theories about the assassination of President John F. Kennedy. Seemingly overnight, conspiracy theories about Hurricane Katrina, the 2010 Haitian earthquake, and the swine flu epidemic spread across the Internet. The number of people who believe that the U.S. government knows for a fact that catastrophic Earth changes are about to destroy much of human civilization on December 21, 2012, grows every day.

But before conspiracy theories found the fertile soil of cyberspace to thrive in, they had Hollywood to keep them alive.

This book is a study of how entertainment has been intersecting with the cultural phenomenon of conspiracy theories over the last five decades. Although fears of conspiracies, misdeeds by the wealthy and the powerful, are as old as human society itself, conspiracy theorizing in the United States has seen a fascinating evolution since roughly the early 1960s. *Conspiracy Films* will examine the history of American culture over that period and see how it gave rise to a unique genre of films and television programs. Decade-by-decade, the book will look at the emergence of the most prominent conspiracy theories in the United States and the entertainment they helped inspire.

1

Films can perhaps be called a true Rosetta Stone of twentieth and twenty-first century America. They reflect society, they reflect everything Americans aspire to, and the fears that keep them on edge. Conspiracy theories, ultimately, are about fear, and that is why conspiracy films deserve study. To truly understand a culture, one needs to understand what it fears the most.

Introduction

It's All a Conspiracy ...
And We Love It!

Here is an interesting experiment to try the next time you're surfing the web: Go to a search engine, select some random words, type "conspiracy" after them and start searching. Try anything from "food" to "water," even something as innocuous as "weather."

So, what did you find?

That perhaps a secret food additive had been developed by a secret organization in a secret lab in the Midwest that will leave you hungrier the more you eat? That it will lead to a further explosion of obesity and diet-related illnesses? That these calamities, in turn, will expand the coffers of drug companies? Which, in turn, will continue pouring more millions of dollars into lobbying the U.S. government and controlling the Food and Drug Administration to keep natural remedies from the bloating masses?

Perhaps you found out that the fluoridation of the drinking water supply is introducing a highly potent drug into the American population that makes them more susceptible to brainwashing.

But all of this is just the tip of the iceberg in a vast, interconnected web of conspiracies, misdeeds and criminality. The United States government, as you will find out upon researching the shocking weather conspiracy, has for decades been developing the High Frequency Active Auroral Research Program. What is it? A vast field of antennae able to concentrate immense doses of radio waves into a single point in the atmosphere to alter weather patterns. This was the technology used to create Hurricane Katrina.

If "food," "water" and the "weather" weren't enough to open your mind to "what's really going on," just keep playing with your search engine. Take any word that comes to mind, append it with "conspiracy," and search for the truth.

And welcome to a glimpse of the modern conspiracy culture!

For over four decades, the American popular imagination has been captured by ever more byzantine conspiracy theories. Extensive subcultures of true believers, those unwilling to subscribe to any idea of a consensus reality, the malcontents, the suspicious and the cynics have been charging that the world is not as it appears to be. The world we live in, according to these suspicious-minded individuals, does not run the way cultural institutions like schools, the government, organized religions and scientists would like us to believe. We are being lied to, we are being duped, we have been brainwashed into a false consciousness. Vast networks of power brokers, shadowy, interconnected cabals of the wealthy, the powerful, and the politically connected have been deceiving us all. Nothing is as it appears to be.

3

In turn, a very lucrative conspiracy industry has been thriving to feed the insatiable appetite of this colorful culture of paranoia. Every major medium, from films to television shows, books, magazines, music and, the most fertile ground for the conspiracy culture, the Internet has to some extent been devoted to helping conspiracy theorists confirm what they, in their heart of hearts, have always known to be true.

In entertainment, the plot device of the conspiracy is now the most reliable lifeline to rescue any sagging story. For example, if a script about a natural disaster feels a bit flat, if the dramatic tension runs out too early, nothing livens the story up more quickly than a sudden conspiracy theory; say, a last-moment revelation that the government knew about the killer earthquake/asteroid/landslide/hurricane/tsunami but kept it hushed up to avoid a panic/win an election/keep developers making money from tourists. In fact, if we look closely enough, we are hard-pressed to find many thrillers, action films, science fiction films or horror films that do not incorporate some sort of a conspiracy in their plots.

This book is devoted to this culture of conspiracy and to the true believers. It will blow the lid off of a tiny fragment of this conspiracy industry and reveal the history of conspiracy theories in film and popular entertainment.

The Big Picture

Before delving into the shadowy world of the Hollywood conspiracy, we must begin like any conspiracy theorist worth his or her salt would. We need to try and understand "the whole truth." The conspiratorial mindset, after all, is about the quest to understand how all things are interconnected. It is a search for The Big Picture.

Just what exactly is the conspiracy culture all about? Where are its origins? Why is conspiracy entertainment hotter than ever today?

To put conspiracy entertainment into a proper perspective, we must follow the conspiracy theorists' modus operandi. We must always dig deeper. We must peel back the onion-like layers of reality and perception. We should first try and understand why conspiracy theories are so attractive to begin with.

What we will find will be as multifaceted and complex as any good conspiracy theory. There are various psychological and sociological reasons for the attraction of conspiracy theories. In many ways, conspiracy theories not so much frighten their believers but put them at ease. Rather than obfuscate and upturn order, conspiracy theories actually try and create order out of the random and unpredictable nature of the world. The search for meaning and predictability is at the core of the quest for The Big Picture. However, by the same token, we will also ask if psychological and sociological explanations for the attractiveness of conspiracy theories necessarily make them untrue.

And attractive conspiracy theories always have been. Although the modern mass media of films and television have latched onto conspiracy theories in the post–Vietnam and post–Watergate eras, conspiracy theories have a very old history. People have always been afraid of how they might be manipulated by forces, by corrupt cabals and secret orders they can not see or understand.

One of the earliest secret orders, and today once again a point of fascination thanks to *The Da Vinci Code* and its plethora of imitation conspiracy thrillers, was the Knights Templar. Originally formed in 1118 and called the Order of the Poor Knights of Christ and of the Temple of Solomon, it was tasked with protecting travelers to the Holy Land. During the Crusades, one of the Templars' main agendas, however, became their extensive archae-ological digs in Solomon's Temple. What they found there remains a mystery to this day and fodder for countless conspiracy theories and imaginative speculation. The fact is that the Templars, far from being poor knights, eventually became one of the wealthiest and most powerful organizations in Europe, enjoying unprecedented favors from the Vatican. Again, the reasons for the Templars' privileged status in relation to the Church continue fueling conspiratorial speculation. Depending on which theorist one listens to, the Templars unearthed vast troves of gold in Jerusalem, sacred relics like pieces of the true cross or the Ark of the Covenant, the bones of saints or ancient scrolls containing heretical texts they used to blackmail the Vatican.[1] The ancient scroll theory, of course, has been in favor of late, dramatized in *The Da Vinci Code* and based on earlier speculation in the books *Holy Blood, Holy Grail* etc., claiming that the Templars found proof that Jesus and Mary Mag-dalene were husband and wife, they had a child and their bloodline founded the Merovingian royal dynasty.

Although the Templars were eventually wiped out by the Church in 1307, on Friday the thirteenth, conspiracy theory claims that many of their members, along with their treas-ures, scattered all across Europe and even to the New World. Some conspiracy theories hold that the Templar treasures were used to found the Swiss banking system and that the descen-dants of the Templar order still use their immense wealth to clandestinely control world affairs today.[2]

Ancient secret organizations like the Bavarian Illuminati and the Freemasons, offshoots of Enlightenment thinking, have also been on the receiving end of many conspiracist accu-sations. Generally, these groups are accused of being secretive, elitist cabals that manipulate politics and control economies. They have been accused of imposing and deposing govern-ments, fomenting revolutions and war, manipulating stock markets, creating economic booms, recessions and depressions, controlling the media and educational institutions, infil-trating religious orders and practicing the occult.

A closer look at the histories and philosophical agendas of both these groups, often closely intertwined, reveals the strange irony of their continued demonization by American conspiracy theorists, however. "Radical" as some of the Illuminati members and Freemasons might have been considered, their so-called radicalism needs to be understood in relation to their times. These were organizations that advocated a quest for rationalism and an oppo-sition to monarchy and theocracy. Basic Illuminati and Freemason ideals espoused science, reason, representative democracy, freedom of speech and the press, and a separation of church and state. While opposed to the theocratic power of the Catholic Church, these organizations, especially the Freemasons, whose members had to profess a belief in God, espoused religious tolerance. For their time, that was a radical idea. At least eight of the signers of the American Declaration of Independence were Freemasons.[3]

While it can be argued that Illuminati and Masonic ideals are the basic ideals of the Declaration of Independence and the U.S. Constitution, American ideals in effect, these groups still continue to suffer the slings and arrows of conspiracy theorists. The two groups' opposition to theocracy has, over the centuries, tarred them with the accusation of opposing religion. Of the two, the Illuminati has generally gotten the worse rap. Conspiracy theo-ries—and a good number of historians as well—have generally charged that the Illuminati were, in fact, made up of the more radical elements of the Freemasons, atheistic elements, some charge, and elements extremely hostile to Christianity while dabbling in occult rituals and seeking ancient, fabled lost rituals of magic that would reveal the secrets of the universe.

The critical view of the groups, and especially the Illuminati, from highly eminent commentators has always been mixed. Edinburgh University professor and Freemason John Robinson, for example, wrote the book *Proofs of a Conspiracy Against All the Religions and Governments of Europe Carried Out in the Secret Meetings of the Free Masons, Illuminati, and Reading Societies*. Thomas Jefferson, on the other hand, remarked that Illuminati founder Adam Weishaupt "seems to be an enthusiastic philanthropist. Weishaupt believes that to promote the perfection of the human character was the object of Jesus Christ. His precepts are the love of God and love of our neighbor."[4] The Illuminati master plan, conspiracy theorists argue, is to take control of all world governments, bring about the New World Order, eradicate all religions and put that new world under the leadership of a single world government.

An offshoot of this theory has been found in the apocalyptic conspiracy theories of fundamentalist Christian groups. The anti-religious conspiracy theory has been dramatized most successfully in the *Left Behind* series of books. The hidden power behind the New World Order, according to the Christian conspiracy theorists, is none other than Satan himself, and the single ruler of the one world government will be the Antichrist. Once the Antichrist ascends to power, much like in the anti–Masonic and anti–Illuminati theories, he will move to outlaw all religion, declare himself god and exterminate all who oppose him.[5]

As old as conspiracy theories are, the one thing they have in common is the insinuation that the lot in life of the average person is troubled and difficult because of some hidden cabal and its shady activities. We could all be better off if not for a conspiracy actively working to keep us down. We could all be wealthier, healthier, and live in peace and safety if some shadowy organization, some rogue arm of the government or unethical business interests wasn't plotting to exploit us and slowly destroy us.

In truth, in his heart, the conspiracy theorist is a supreme optimist. The order of the world is basically good, he argues. Human nature is also good, it is born innocent, it is decent, peaceful and altruistic. Disorder, aggression, hatred and greed are not naturally occurring phenomena, but they are cultivated by a secret order that profits from chaos.

Some of the most active conspiracy theorists have been accusing secret, powerful cabals of orchestrating every world calamity from wars to crime to disease. According to this collection of theories, all conflicts, from both world wars to Vietnam, Gulf Wars I and II and the Cold War itself, were instigated by vast networks of international bankers and industrialists seeking to profit from weapons research and manufacturing.

One grand old World War II conspiracy theory accuses President Franklin D. Roosevelt and the U.S. government of knowing about the planned bombing of Pearl Harbor, but choosing to do nothing. This passive bit of conspiring, the theory says, gave the nation cause to enter the war, in turn enriching the war industries, in turn ending the Great Depression, in turn catapulting the U.S. to the position of a dominant global superpower.[6] Even more intricate theories accuse international financiers and bankers, descendants of the Illuminati, Freemasons and the Templars, of orchestrating the rise of Hitler as well as Communism, the Russian revolution and the Cold War.

Prominent leaders in the African American community, like California Congresswoman Maxine Waters, have forwarded the theory that the crack cocaine epidemic was created by a CIA conspiracy.[7] Not only do moneyed, powerful racists stand to destabilize America's black communities with drugs, but the crime and social disorder created by a drug epidemic will inspire ever more restrictive laws, encroachment on civil liberties, bloating state and federal bureaucracies tasked with combating the drug and crime problems, and put money into the pockets of industries developing anti-crime and anti-privacy technologies. Drugs and crime sustain companies building prisons, they help surveillance and security companies turn tidy profits, and they employ cops, prosecutors, judges, prison guards, border guards, as well as vast armies of bureaucrats running a myriad of agencies in some way responsible for handling the crime "epidemic."

In a similar vein, the blame for AIDS has been placed by some conspiracy theorists on the U.S. government, specifically the CIA and bio-weapons research organizations.[8]

"They live, we sleep" is the catchphrase of director John Carpenter's 1988 alien conspiracy film *They Live*, summing up a major appeal of the conspiracy mindset. At their core, all conspiracy theories try to account for all that is wrong with society. The conspiracy theory is nourishment for all those who, in the words of arch conspiracy theorist Jim Marrs, "look at the daily news, scratch [their] head in wonder, and ask, 'What in the world is going on?'"[9] A true conspiracy is one that is slowly killing, draining, exploiting the individual, all for the gain of the stealthy, sinister conspirators, while its victims are blissfully unaware. Perhaps the best representation of the metaphysics of the conspiracy theory is the science fiction conspiracy epic *The Matrix* (1999). Humanity, asleep and ignorant of a world enslaved by sentient machines, are living batteries used to power the computer matrix that runs their lives. The individual is but food, the exploitable lifeblood of the vampiric conspirators.

The further society advances, the more sophisticated its technologies become, the more rational, orderly, safe and peaceful it should become, we would like to believe. But why is there more disorder, instability, uncertainty and chaos? Someone must be responsible for this, the conspiracy theory argues. The dawn of the twenty-first century should be a world advancing toward utopia. However, it's not. Environmental devastation, disease, terrorism, war and economic uncertainties are the order of the day. There *must* be a hidden hand orchestrating all this misfortune.

Of course, examining the logic of the chaos-creation conspiracy theories will lead to an obvious problem. Just because a party stands to profit from a calamity does not logically mean that said party actually had to have *caused* the calamity. For example, one of the greatest boons for late nineteenth century medical research in the United States was the Civil War. The masses of war dead provided useful cadavers for scientists and doctors to study and experiment on. Therefore, can we say that there is excellent reason to believe that the Civil War was orchestrated by a cabal of politically connected medical researchers?

Perhaps at this point it's even safe to say that conspiracy theories provide a great deal of psychological comfort to their believers. To completely discount conspiracies is to acknowledge frightening chaos, dangerous, threatening complexity, a total lack of order, a lack of purpose, absolutely no value or no cause for fortune and misfortune, pain and suffering.[10] Horror, according to Slovenian philosopher Slavoj Žižek, can be understood through the metaphor of "a ship drifting alone, without a captain or any living crew to steer it. This is the ultimate horror ... there is no plotting agent behind it, the machine just runs by itself as a blind contingent device."[11] The conspiracy theory tries to protect its believers from this sort of horrific realization about the world. Conspiracy theories protect the believers from cruel irony, from having to acknowledge the fact that bad things happen for no reason, or from blind, pointless coincidences. A good conspiracy theory assures us that all the trouble, all the trauma, disorder and tragedies of the world couldn't possibly come from the incompetence of people in positions of power, from clueless stupidity, from irrational, blind commitment to ideology at the expense of common sense. The problems, cruelties, pain, killings and destruction in the world, according to the conspiracy theorist, are not merely random acts of mindless, petty, dumb evil. They are all but a part of greater plots of purposefully orchestrated malevolence. As novelist Dean Koontz observes in his book *From the Corner of His Eye* (a stylistic change of pace after a writing career that produced a remarkably voluminous body of conspiracy thrillers), one of the things many people don't seem to realize about evil is that it's so banal. It is petty, unimaginative, stupid and ugly. True evil is not as suave, brilliant, or darkly seductive as so much popular entertainment makes it out to be. Conspiracy theory seeks to deny this stupidity, this insignificant banality of evil.

Perhaps the conspiracy theory appeals to a part of the human psyche that believes that it's much better to suspect that a cabal of corrupt sociopaths with an epic capacity for evil running the world is much more comforting than knowing that no one is in charge. Even wars, international crises, acts of terror, dictators rising to power somehow feel better when we can attribute them to the grand schemes of international bankers and arms manufacturers than just plain bureaucratic bumbling, bad policymaking, faulty doctrine, miscommunication, incompetent leadership and cruel, ironic bad luck. As critics of the JFK conspiracy canon have said, it's just too painful to believe that the life of a young, virile, popular, charismatic leader of the most powerful nation on Earth could be snuffed out in an instant by one lone deranged loser. It's easier to accept such a tragedy if we believe it to be a part of a grand Machiavellian scheme orchestrated by a coalition of the world's most ruthless villains.

The most creative dramatization of this idea can be seen in the 1997 cult science fiction film *Cube*. The lack of a unified conspiracy makes the plot all the more chilling. The film involves a group of people waking up inside an enormous, diabolically confusing and deadly cube-like device made up of hundreds of identical, interconnected rooms. Many of the rooms are booby-trapped by fiendish death devices, from flesh-dissolving acid to poisonous gas to razor wire that can dismember a body into a pile of bloody cubes. The captives also realize that unless they find a way out, they will eventually die of starvation or thirst. To make the experience all the more complicated, the individual cells of the cube also constantly shift from position to position like a giant, three-dimensional Rubik's Cube. But how the prisoners got inside the sadistic device, who designed and built it and for what possible purpose is the ultimate question they grapple with as they make their way through the machine, slowly unraveling mentally and physically.

The key to *Cube*'s puzzle turns out to be the meekest, most unassuming member of the group. He is an engineer who eventually lets on that he has been working for years designing the outer shell of the giant death device. Through this character, the film delivers its stinging and frightening anti-conspiracy punchline. The engineer himself doesn't know what the Big Picture is and he suspects that no one else who has been working inside that complex, bureaucratic juggernaut of an engineering program knows either. After his fellow captives have spun a series of intricate conspiracy theories—accusing everyone from rogue, sadistic millionaires to foreign powers, the military, and aliens—the engineer explains that there *is* no central planner, no head conspirator, really no single purpose for the cube itself. No one knows who started the cube project or why. No one even knows if the originators of the project are still working on it. Everyone was an individual, isolated member of a cell inside the bureaucracy, the system that created the cube, tasked with doing one, isolated job. No one knew where the component they worked on would eventually go. Their superiors didn't know why they were ordering people to do what they did and these supervisors, in turn, were no more informed of the Big Picture than anyone else. How many individual companies or subsidiaries of companies had been contracted to work on the cube project, no one knew. Companies, of course, merge, are bought and sold or go out of business all the time. Individual workers are constantly replaced, fired, promoted, retired, or they just die one day from quite natural causes or normal accidents. The cube project of this film is Žižek's unpiloted ship metaphor brought to life. And, indeed, contemplating that a massive, complex, powerful, potentially oppressive and deadly system could operate without a central leadership, that in effect a complex system never can have one central leadership who is able to plan and orchestrate and execute any sort of an over-reaching, all-powerful conspiracy, is much more horrifying than naming any kind of a grand cabal of military, scientific or banking conspirators as the true culprits behind the Big Picture.

As the film's director and co-writer, Vincenzo Natali, discussed in the film's DVD commentary, the production team toyed at one point with the idea of using the phrase "Big Brother is Not Watching You" as the tag line for the film's promotional campaign and advertising art.

A Question of Logic

At this point, however, we want to ask if conspiracy theories deserve to be thrown out the window altogether. Sure, they have been the inspiration for a lot of very entertaining pop culture we will shortly examine, but can we believe in them? Are they *real*? Or do conspiracies belong in the fantasy worlds of popular entertainment? Can we still believe that all these multi-faceted conspiracy theories might actually be more than psychological defense mechanisms that help us cope with an overly complicated, chaotic and alienatingly bureaucratized modern world? If conspiracy theories are nothing more than modern empowerment myths that let the believers criticize institutions of power, society's wealthy elites, would so many people be so fascinated by them? Are the masses that gullible and fantasy prone?

Perhaps not.

The fact is that conspiracies are all around us. History has been witness to countless conspiracies. The late twentieth century news media have exposed so many spectacularly audacious and unconscionable conspiracies that, psychologically comforting or not, we cannot rationally discount the existence of far-reaching plots to break laws, subvert governments, deceive the public, or just amass vast sums of wealth by any means necessary.

The United States, after all, is a result of a conspiracy carried out by the wealthiest elites of England's American colonies. The majority of the conspirators were members of the Freemasons. The most spectacular (and often violent) acts of protest against the colonial government were instigated by Masonic lodges. The Boston Tea Party, for example, was planned and carried out by the St. John's Lodge sector of the colonial Freemasons.[12]

Furthermore, today's chroniclers of who America's most influential elites are, where most of the wealth and political power is concentrated and where a disproportionately large number of the country's statesmen and leaders of industry come from, show an infinitesimally small sector of society turning out this country's political and economic leadership. For example, when a mere two percent of America's families control more than half of the nation's wealth and only ten percent of the population controls over eighty percent of the nation's assets, the idea of the greater working of American society being run by a tiny, secretive few no longer seems absurd and fantastic. What's more, when many of the clubs, collegiate fraternal organizations, professional societies and policy organizations of the modern American upper crust have repeatedly been shown to be fanatically secretive, the ideas of a "far-reaching conspiracy" take on ever more believability.[13]

Corruption, abuse of power, and raw, unchecked greed making up most of the news media's headlines today demonstrate that those in power regularly use their positions, their clout, their wealth to hold onto power regardless of laws or morality. The ill-conceived and badly executed Vietnam War, Watergate and all the subsequent "-gates" that have tainted politics over the past thirty years and rampant corporate corruption and thievery have demonstrated time and again that conspiracy is the regular driving engine of modern politics and business. "If your mother says she loves you, check it out," advises the old cliché from the Chicago school of journalism — namely Northwestern's Medill School of Journalism — warning us, just like conspiracy theorists have always implored, that you can trust no one. All people are fallible and prone to corruption, they all lust for power and position. But those who are the wealthiest and most influential have the true power to indulge in all their desires to gain more, to control, to influence and subvert. When we have seen the Catholic Church itself carry on a decades-long "far-reaching conspiracy" to cover up crimes as vile as child abuse, the most rococo of conspiracy theories no longer seems absurd. After so many decades of technical experts and gee-whiz techno-thriller writers telling us that America's intelligence-gathering capabilities were so superb that super hi-tech spy satellites could see the headlines on a newspaper read inside the Kremlin, how can a rogue nation's weapons of mass destruction just vanish into thin air? How come all this ultra-advanced spying hardware couldn't tell us what happened to Iraq's supposed stockpiles of chemical weapons? Or how can those weapons prove to be nonexistent only after another costly and badly executed war? After the debacle of the second Gulf War, one begins to wonder if the military industrial complex conspiracy theories may contain more than just a grain of truth.

Ultimately, one would commit a very basic logical fallacy by saying that just because a conspiracy theory is psychologically comforting, that theory, therefore, must be false. Nothing is further from the truth. In fact, some of the people who have endorsed the secret society-ruling elite theories have not only *not* been the stereotypical wacky conspiracy nuts spinning yarns at the counter of the local bar, or sensationalistic authors touting outrageous plots to shill their books, but people from the highest echelons of society.

As early as 1909, according to conspiracy theory chronicler Jim Marrs, Walter Rathenau, president of the General Electric Corporation of Germany, remarked that "three hundred men, all of whom know one another, direct the economic destiny of Europe and choose their successors from among themselves."[14] Joseph R. Kennedy, patriarch of what is commonly referred to as "America's royal family," stated that "fifty men have run America and that's a high figure."[15]

The very term "military industrial complex" wasn't invented by a wild-eyed, paranoid leftist conspiracy maven either. It was coined by Republican President Dwight D. Eisenhower. In fact, he warned of the detrimental effect this powerful alliance could have on the democratic process.

"Some of the biggest men in the United States, in the field of commerce and manufacture, are afraid of somebody, are afraid of something," wrote President Woodrow Wilson. "They know there is a power somewhere so organized, so subtle, so watchful, so interlocked, so complete, so pervasive that they had better not speak above their breath when they speak in condemnation of it."[16]

President Franklin D. Roosevelt, himself implicated in the Pearl Harbor conspiracy, had remarked that "the real truth of the matter is, as you and I know, that a financial element in the large centers has owned the government ever since the days of Andrew Jackson."[17]

Even when it comes to the most fantastic, most hyperbolic of conspiracy theories, the alleged plots involving UFOs, otherworldly beings and alien abductions, their reality and a top-secret, governmental conspiracy to hide them can't be dismissed out of hand either.

Surely, armies of skeptics and debunkers, hailing from fields as diverse as astronomy, physics, psychiatry and folklore, have argued that we want to believe in aliens and UFOs out of various complex subconscious needs. According to these people, we conjure flying saucers and little gray aliens with big, almond-shaped black eyes out of cloud formations and tricks of light as a need to believe in the supernatural in a rational world that has killed off God, out of a need for a sense of mystery, because of repressed traumas and abuse prompted us to do so, or because we have been conditioned by Hollywood and the mass media.

But are these people right? Maybe. Or maybe not.

Someone possessing both a strong capacity for rational, critical common sense *and* an open mind can listen to equally compelling counter-arguments from equally respectable intellectuals from physics, astronomy or psychiatry about the existence of both extraterrestrials visitors and the government's efforts to keep them hidden.

One of the most eminent scientific names to speak out in defense of the theory of the existence of alien UFOs was Northwestern University astronomer J. Allen Hynek. Hynek had been hired by the Air Force as an investigator and debunker of UFOs in 1952. However, he soon changed his mind about the alien nature of the UFO phenomenon. He publicly declared that there was enough evidence to suggest that UFOs were of an extraterrestrial origin *and* that he believed, based on his experience with the Air Force, that the government never had an intention to publicly endorse the extraterrestrial hypothesis no matter what the scientific evidence would ever suggest. "They wouldn't give UFOs the chance of existing," Hynek said, "even if they were flying up and down the street in broad daylight."[18] In other words, the government would always be likely to actively *conspire* to misinform the public about UFOs.

Hynek subsequently founded the Center for UFO Studies at Northwestern. For decades the organization worked with top scientists to study the UFO phenomenon and fight the fringe, paranoid lunatic stigma the government and skeptics tried to smear UFO believers with.

Some, however, even suggested that many of the wildest, most outlandish conspiracy theories themselves have been, in actuality, creations of a conspiracy. As social scientists have attempted to study the manifestation of the conspiracy theory mindset, the *sociology* of the modern conspiracy culture, they have claimed — quite accurately — that the term "conspiracy theorist" is fast becoming an insult. And what would better serve the purposes of a conspiracy than to have anyone who might publicly hint at their existence immediately dismissed as "just another crazy conspiracy theorist"?

As astrophysicist, Hynek protégé and leading UFO theorist Jacques Vallée has argued for years, the best way to stop a powerful, fast-moving train is not to stand in its way and hope to block its progress. The best way is to speed it up until it runs out of control, jumps the tracks under its own momentum, crashes and destroys itself.[19] In other words, the best way for a conspiracy to wreck a movement of UFO proponents is not by sending out armies of Men in Black in black Cadillacs and black helicopters to harass and intimidate UFO believers. A conspiracy would have an easier and more successful time if they found a way to discredit these believers by making them look like deranged, delusional fanatics. The best way to wreck a UFO community would be to infiltrate it and spread insane-sounding stories of space brothers making telepathic contact with Earthlings, taking true believers on flights to Venusian space bases populated by buxom, supermodel-like female aliens, revealing plots about Denver International Airport functioning as the gateway to a vast underground alien base and letting on that reptilian, shape-changing aliens from an alternate dimension have replaced all the world's leaders with lookalike drones.

In fact, if one were to spend at least an hour on the Internet today, perusing all the conspiracy webpages—including an alarming number of them devoted to the theory that Arnold Schwarzenegger is the third Antichrist—one might be hard-pressed not to come away from the experience convinced that anyone who believes *any* conspiracy theory is a raving, dangerously unbalanced loon.

Ultimately, where does the truth lie? Are conspiracies real? Is the world, in the words of the Wesley Snipes character in the film *Blade*, "nothing more than a sugar-coated fantasy" with evil cabals of criminals, conspirators, secret cult-like orders and alien invaders running everything? Or are conspiracy theories nothing more than modern myths? Are they a psychological defense mechanism we use to make sense out of a rapidly changing, often confusing, alienating, ever corrupt and exploitive modern world? Or is the truth somewhere between these two extremes?

While the truth might be out there somewhere, it is not for this book to find it or definitively endorse any one hypothesis or theory as to what that truth may be. Instead, what it will do is acknowledge the fact that conspiracy theories are a modern cultural phenomenon and it will look at how this phenomenon is reflected in the mass media of film and television. Pop culture has always reflected who we are, how we see ourselves, how we *want* to see ourselves and what we believe in. Today, and for roughly the past forty years, we seem to have believed that we can't trust anyone who is wealthy and influential, we can't trust our government, we can't trust our cultural institutions—and often we can't even trust our neighbors, friends and loved ones either. The theater of the conspiracy theory is a reflection of these times of angst, unease and paranoia.

CHAPTER 1

The Art of Conspiracy
Defining a New Genre

Just like catching a stealthy conspirator who lurks in the corridors of power, identifying a true conspiracy film can be akin to catching smoke. What makes a conspiracy film? What are the boundaries, the traditions, the archetypes that define this genre?

By a strict definition, it could be said that any crime film is a conspiracy film. The intricate machinations of any heist film could be considered a conspiracy. All stories of gangsters and organized crime include a lot of conspiring. The Mafioso of *The Godfather* films (1972, 1974, 1990) conspire, for instance. But neither heist, nor general organized crime films necessarily fall into the "conspiracy theory" film category.

"Conspiracy theory" films may colonize a number of genres—from the police thriller to action-adventure, war films, horror films, or science fiction—but they ultimately have what Leo Braudy calls "the conventions of connection," a very specific set of stylistic threads that link them together and define them as a genre.[1] These conventions can be seen emerging and crystallizing over several decades, borrowing themes, touches of style and characters from various other genres. But from the 1960s to the 2000s, a separate, unique class of film has been forming, a category of film that has been reflecting that particularly late twentieth century fixation on abuses of power, wrongdoing in high places, paranoia and distrust. If genre theory tells us that a film genre's function is to use its limited conventions to comment on a specific social problem, the conspiracy film deals with why we are so afraid today of losing control, of being manipulated by unseen cabals of amoral, even murderous, power brokers.

At its most basic level, a conspiracy film is one that foregrounds the abuse of power, the hidden manipulation of the political, economic or legal systems, the manipulation of the entire country and culture, in effect. These films are about the unseen operations of the powerful few and the effect they have on the lives of the powerless masses. Conspiracy films deal with the use of power to subvert rules, laws for personal gain and the illegal amassing of wealth. But as the genre evolved, especially through the 1990s and the 2000s, it dealt not only with the manipulation of laws, but with the conspirators' very manipulation of social mores, conventions and customs to ensure their positions of unchallenged power and privilege. By these later stages in the establishment of the genre's key conventions, the conspiracy theory film had evolved into a dramatization of the basic ideas behind post-modern social construction. The ultimate aim of a conspiracy is always to redefine reality for its victims. The conspirators always attempt to exploit those victims without the victims being aware of what is being done to them because their understanding of reality has been altered by forces that have the power to shape perceptions and define reality. Conspiracy theory films focusing on these manipulations of perception often lead to plot twists where characters realize that so much of history is not as it appears to be. Major historical turning points are not as they appear to be. There is always a hidden history beyond the "official version" of the truth.

Looking at the timeline of the genre's formation, we can break conspiracy theory films down into three major categories. The first includes conspiracies perpetrated by the government or the military. "Big government," big bureaucracies or corrupt politicians usually turn out to be the most common masterminds behind vast, far-reaching conspiracies. From the earliest appearances of the conspiracy theory as a plot device to the latest conspiracy films, the government is usually the main culprit behind covert wrongdoing and large-scale manipulation. Conspiracies involving big business and multinational corporations are just as common in this genre and they are the second category. Although powerful businessmen in films are usually guilty of some major crime, the corporate conspiracy film first found blockbuster success in the 1970s. The third category of conspiracy theory films crosses genre boundaries into science fiction and fantasy. Conspiracies to cover up alien contact, supernatural creatures and manifestations, and scientific research with the potential to alter the world (or destroy it), are today as plentiful as crooked politicos manipulating the system to stay in power or corporate barons trying to amass ever greater wealth.

When looking at these three categories, one can see how the conspiracies evolve from the plausible to the spectacularly fantastic, if not outlandish and hyperbolic. This evolution of the claims made by conspiracy theory films, we will soon see, also quite astutely mirrors the ever more baroque evolution of real-life conspiracy theory movements.

Politics Unusual

But the first and most basic category of conspiracy theory films deals with corruption in the government and/or military establishment. The greatest power in any society is political power, the ability to have a hand in writing laws and shaping policy. Life and death decisions are always made by the few over the many from the corridors of legislative power. The political conspiracy film is one where the conspiring villains are crooked, power-hungry politicians or candidates for political office. They manipulate the system for their own personal gain. The conspirators, first and foremost, strive to amass unchallenged, unchecked power and hold onto that power by any means. They manipulate the system so as never to be forced to give up power or be held accountable for their actions. The villains of the political conspiracy theory subvert democracy and the "will of the people."

Sometimes the political conspiracy involves the betrayal of America by a conspirator who is manipulating the system because he has been bought off by a foreign power, perhaps brainwashed by enemy agents—as is the case in the classic *The Manchurian Candidate* (1962)—or out of ideological allegiances to a foreign government.

The political conspiracy film's roots reach far back in cinematic history. Its inspirations can be found in political-themed films, from the idealistic *Mr. Smith Goes to Washington* (1939) to the frightening *All the King's Men* (1949). Just like the archetypal plot and character structure of the conspiracy theory films, the classic political films usually involve a clash between idealistic outsiders—or cynical veterans of the political game who rediscover their idealism —and a covert, "back room" culture of crooked insiders subverting democracy for personal gain. Films about politics, just like the conspiracy genre as a whole, warn that so much of what the average person sees of America's institutions of power and influence is in reality a craftily constructed façade.

Archetypal characters who can turn up in the political conspiracy film include the untested, naïve outsider from a small, backwater district who gets his first taste of politics when moving either to Washington or the state legislature. Much like Jefferson Smith in *Mr. Smith Goes to Washington*, this generic hero is most often someone who winds up in big-time politics by the sheerest of accidents. He might get appointed upon the death of a legislator or he runs for office reluctantly as a last resort upon noticing that the state of affairs in his district has gone hopelessly awry. His political career might also be secretly backed by a conspiracy, a political machine that hopes to put the local rube in a position where he could easily be manipulated. The politician heroes of conspiracy films do not seek the spotlight on their own; they are not power-hungry or ambitious. After reluctantly taking the first steps into the political arena, however, their eyes are soon opened to the corruption rotting the system.

Aside from the junior politician, the most likely character to be the hero of a political conspiracy film is a journalist. Reporters, just like the politicians, might either be rookies covering their first stories or grizzled, cynical — occasionally alcoholic — burnouts who have long forgotten their youthful idealism. Both of these characters, however, tend to stumble onto a seemingly insignificant event that slowly makes them aware of a massive conspiracy. At this point, the rookie will put his career in jeopardy to pursue the truth. The drunken burnout will see injustice and criminality so extensive as to feel the last embers of his old idealism reignited, inspiring him on to one last good fight and personal redemption. The aftermath of the Watergate scandal and the nonfiction book *All the President's Men*, as well as the Robert Redford-Dustin Hoffman docudrama (1976) based on the incident, helped cement the image of the idealistic young journalist crusader.

The rookie and the drunk also tend to turn up in conspiracy films in the form of lawyers. The upstart lawyer, trying his first case, or the cynical veteran taking a case no one thinks he has a chance of winning often find conspiracies as well. Some of the best examples of these archetypes can be seen in Paul Newman's *The Verdict* (1983) and Tom Cruise's *The Firm* (1993). John Grisham's novels, like *The Firm*, which served as the source material for the film, generally make extensive use of conspiracy-fighting lawyers.

Newspaper editors, who might either encourage reporters or warn them about the impending collapse of their careers should they insist on digging for the truth, are oft-recurring supporting characters in conspiracy-themed films. These characters may be replaced by the heads of law firms in the legal-political conspiracy.

When the opponents of a conspiracy find themselves isolated, vilified and abandoned by their co-workers and bosses, intimidated by the conspiracy and even pursued by the law, they are usually spurred on to stand by their ideals by a spouse or a lover. These reliable supporting characters are willing to back a conspiracy-busting hero even if it means wrecking their careers or putting themselves in mortal danger.

Typical characters who might also populate conspiracy films are cops and private investigators. Much like the lawyer and the reporter, the cop or the private eye can find himself working on a small-time case that suddenly leads to the uncovering of a vast, shadowy network of corruption. Sometimes they are also backed by world-weary superiors who might warn the heroes about rocking the boat upon the discovery of a conspiracy. Third-act plot twists, however, can often reveal these superiors as traitors. While these superiors and mentors might genuinely care about the hero, they are still stooges in the back pocket of the conspirators. They have often sold out because they realized the futility of idealism (*Mission: Impossible*, 1996), because they have realized that the system and society to whom they gave their best years no longer honors them (*The Recruit*, 2003), or simply for the money to retire in comfort. Post-Cold War thrillers like *The Package* (1990), the first *Mission: Impossible* film and *The Recruit* place extra emphasis on the traitorous superior being partially motivated by the changing world landscape. These superiors have all been legends in Cold War spy skirmishes, but the new world has relegated them to the status of insignificant historical footnotes. Bitterness over this slight turns such characters into mercenaries who sell out the system they fought for in return for a fat retirement check.

The villains of conspiracy films can often be high-ranking politicians, sometimes the president of the United States himself. However, head conspirators can also be the handlers of politicians. Sometimes the political villain might be the upstart legislator who sells out because of his hunger for power, as does Willie Stark in *All the King's Men*. Chiefs of staff (*Murder at 1600*, 1997; *The Shadow Conspiracy*, 1997), advisors or even family members can often be uncovered as the main sources of evil. There is often no one as dangerous as the power broker behind the throne or an ambitious lieutenant. One of the most memorable behind-the-scenes conspirators in this genre is brainwashed assassin Raymond Shaw's power-hungry, sociopathic mother in *The Manchurian Candidate*.

Today's conspiracy films also find a great deal of their thematic inspiration in the shady, hazy worlds of the 1940s and '50s *film noir*. Much like modern conspiracy movies, *film noir* often involves lowly, outnumbered, outclassed loners stumbling onto the crooked, vicious and violent hidden machinery behind modern American government and industry. *Film noir*, to a great extent, functions as a post–World War II counterpoint to a society that was suddenly one of the most powerful, influential and prosperous in the world, and thoroughly in love with itself.[2] While a lot of the 1950s war films and westerns celebrate the conquests, the power and the glorious past of the nation, *noir* delves into the sleazy, corrupt and violent underside of society. It focuses especially on evil within the world of politics and business. The archetypal *noir* heroes — or, rather, anti-heroes — have a lot in common with the people who would emerge as the key players in the conspiracy film. *Noir*'s protagonists are often cynical, emotionally battered veterans who can't quite fit into cheery postwar America. They often function on the fringes of society, mainly as cops or private investigators. They do business out of seedy offices on the wrong side of town and walk the rainy, shadowy city streets at night. Most importantly, a *noir* anti-hero's adventures, foreshadowing the typical conspiracy thriller's plot line, often gets him involved in crimes and corruption leading to the highest levels of power and influence. Small-time cons, thefts or the murder of seemingly insignificant people often lead a *noir* gumshoe to stumble into "something much bigger."[3] He quickly finds himself surrounded by people who are never what they appear to be. This is especially true with women, who turn out to be much more ruthless, amoral and, ultimately, deadly than any man.[4] Ulterior motives, plots, and treachery and corruption at the highest levels of society are all hallmarks of the classic *noir* story.

Armies of Darkness

Similar to the political corruption conspiracy, the genre also often deals with the highest echelons of the military. Just like lawbreakers wielding their power for personal gain, the top military brass in conspiracy theory films is almost always crooked. Generals and Pentagon officials are quick to use their men as expendable cannon fodder on ill-conceived missions and unjustified wars. Military conspirators are especially lethal. They will employ assassins and Special Operations commandos to kill anyone who might expose mistakes in the planning of a mission gone wrong, to cover up the authorization of the use of faulty equipment and weapons systems in collusion with corrupt military contractors, or hide fascistic power plays designed to enact martial law and overthrow democracy following a manufactured national emergency.

This grim view of the military establishment in popular entertainment became virtually institutionalized in Hollywood after Vietnam. Traditionally, though, there has been a certain level of antipathy toward the military felt by artists and writers. Sure, there might have been a period of the flag-waving war films turned out by the studios during and after World War II — thanks in large part to the Motion Picture Production Code that encouraged positive portrayals of the military and organs of state power.[5] But the artistic temperament has never taken well to endorsing the military culture. As Tom Wolfe writes in *The Right Stuff*:

> Immediately following the First World War a certain fashion set in among writers in Europe and soon spread to their obedient colonial counterparts in the United States. War was looked upon as inherently monstrous, and those who waged it — namely, military officers — were looked upon as brutes and philistines. The tone was set by some brilliant novels; among them, *All Quiet on the Western Front, The Journey to the End of the Night,* and *The Good Soldier Schweik.* The only proper protagonist for a tale of war was an enlisted man, and he was to be presented not as a hero but as Everyman, as much a victim of war as any civilian. Any officer above the rank of second lieutenant was to be presented as a martinet or a fool, if not an outright villain, no matter whom he fought for. The old-fashioned tale of prowess and heroism was relegated to second- and third-rate forms of literature, ghost-written autobiographies and stories in pulp magazines on the order of *Argosy* and *Bluebook.*[6]

As we trace the history of military conspiracy films, we will discover the ongoing quest by these evildoers to gain more political clout and more and better weapons systems. The military conspirators are also often dismayed by the civilian leadership of the country and the fact that civilians shape military policy (*Seven Days in May,* 1964). Corrupt generals are often apt to be taking part in the assassination of soft, overly liberal senators (*Enemy of the State,* 1998), Congressmen, or even presidents that can't recognize the true threats the country is facing (*Executive Target,* 1997; *xXx: State of the Union,* 2005).

Military conspiracies also often unfold with the collusion of the intelligence community. Unlike in real life, in the world of the conspiracy theory film, the top military brass and the spies in the CIA or the National Security Agency, or even the agents of the FBI, often work remarkably well together.

When the government conspiracy stories deal with the activities of the intelligence agencies, the archetypal characters and plot devices are borrowed from the spy genre. "Controllers" sending spies on missions to exotic international locales are often involved in the stories, as well as foreign agents who are rarely what they appear to be, and deadly female love interests who can be as duplicitous and ice-cold-murderous as any femme fatale in a *noir* film. However, for a story of espionage and intrigue to truly qualify as a conspiracy theory film, the missions spies are sent on are always a lie and they are little more than pawns to be manipulated by unscrupulous controllers or the conspirators who are likewise manipulating the controllers themselves.

The intelligence-agency-oriented conspiracy film can, basically, be read as an anti–James-Bond-film. These films come more from the literary traditions of John LeCarre and

Robert Ludlum than Ian Fleming or Tom Clancy. Whereas the Fleming and Clancy schools of espionage thrillers are "linear" quests by agents of the government to defend the system from foreign enemies, the conspiratorial approach incorporates the moral ambiguity and cynicism about spying from LeCarre's novels and the labyrinthine plotting of Ludlum. In these stories, secret agents' worst enemies can — and often do— turn out to be the very people they are working for. In a conspiracy theory spy story, intelligence agencies send their spies on missions designed to fail in order to confuse the enemy and supply them with incorrect information. Oftentimes, secret societies within the government organize and supply terrorists in order to justify retaliation, to build up the military and expand fascistic surveillance programs. In the conspiratorial spy films, there are no good guy and bad guy dichotomies. The ruthlessness and duplicity required to play the spy game does not let any one side hold the moral high ground. No matter what ideological claims they make, nations and their governments, these stories argue, are essentially all the same. They are all run by a small, power-hungry elite that conspires, manipulates, kills and uses those with enough naïve idealism to serve their country as disposable tools.

Bad Business

Just as deadly and immoral as the government puppet masters and the military brass are the powerful businessmen of conspiracy theory films. Like the power-hungry who claw and conspire their way to the top of the government on their quest for absolute power, the economic conspirators lie, cheat and kill to amass vast fortunes. In fact, in most suspense and action-oriented entertainment, businessmen tend to outnumber any other profession when it comes to villainous characters. Bankers, high financiers and corporate CEOs have for decades handily outnumbered even terrorists, gang members, drug dealers and serial killers as movie antagonists.

Business conspirators, like the underhanded politicians and murderous military conspirators, are always involved in covert "get *richer* quick" schemes. They attempt to subvert laws that might keep them from increasing their wealth, they plot to increase the size of their empires, and to undermine and take over the competition. Business conspirators are also likely to be found producing faulty, often lethal products. They rely on intimidation to silence crusading journalists and whistle-blowers when not marshalling their private armies of hitmen to simply murder anyone who threatens to expose the large-scale corporate malfeasance.

With their roots in the consumer protection movements of the 1960s and '70s, large-scale business conspiracy plots began turning up in films by the mid– to late 1970s and the 1980s. The corruption and lethality of the business conspiracies can easily rival those of crooked politicians, spies and military men. With a mounting concern and skepticism over corporate ethics, the business conspirator had quickly become a favorite villain for Hollywood films. The gas shortages of the 1970s and the growing environmental movement helped cast big oil companies as convenient villains and conspirators. By the late 1980s, following a series of sensational corporate scandals like illegal insider trading and the collapse of the savings and loan industry, Hollywood was using the culture's souring on the Reagan era success ethic to cast businessmen as some of the most loathsome screen antagonists. In fact, it does not take a lot of effort on the part of a screenwriter, a skilled director or a good actor to stoke an audience's animus toward corporate wrongdoers. Most people can easily hate the wealthy, and class resentment is never too hard to provoke. The most repellent corporate villains already have advantages most can only dream of, yet they will use their power to manipulate the system, to buy off legislators, to maintain their own armies of thugs in an effort to rig the game so they keep profiting at the expense of everyone else. The raw, unchecked greed of those that are already wealthy beyond comprehension can be the most offensive to any moviegoing audience and plots about big business conspiracies can easily be the most successful variation on the genre.

Conspiracy Above and Beyond

Conspiracy theories always tend to grow in complexity, in their claims of nefarious villainy, in the breadth of the conspiratorial web. Arguments for conspiracies all have fairly logical and plausible roots; however, theorists are loathe to sit still or refrain from imagining that the wide reaches of corruption can be "even bigger than previously believed." There is a "can you top this?" aspect to conspiracy theories. While the earliest conspiracies and conspiracy theory films tend to be of the political and business variety, Hollywood soon added otherworldly plots well-rooted in the world of the supernatural and mystical.

The most venerable of the otherworldly conspiracy theories are the alien visitation theories. Films utilizing these theories borrow their "mythology" from the real subculture of UFO enthusiasts and investigators. The modern UFO movement generally traces its genesis to the June 24, 1947, sighting of alleged alien spacecraft by businessman and pilot Kenneth Arnold over Mt. Rainier in Washington State. Arnold described the strange objects he saw as resembling a saucer skipping over water, thus creating the iconic term "flying saucer."[7] Almost immediately, conspiracy theories appeared. Military and scientific debunkers trying to dismiss UFOs as nothing more than mirages, clouds, weather balloons or star formations were accused of conspiring to hide the evidence of alien visitations. This conspiratorial approach to dealing with the UFO phenomenon, however, did not show up in films for several decades. Certainly, Hollywood was quick to catch on to the dramatic possibilities of the alien visitation claims, allegations of experimentations and abductions, but film plots about the government's aggressive efforts to lie about UFOs did not appear until the 1970s.

Science fiction films of the 1950s often dealt with UFO–related storylines, but the vast majority of these films were horrific invasion thrillers. The movies did a close enough job of creating their iconography based on UFO eyewitness accounts—saucer-shaped spacecraft, humanoid aliens, phantom lights in the night sky menacing people caught alone in isolated locales—but the plots were mainly thrillers about evil outsiders. There were only a few rare exceptions. For example, Robert Wise's 1951 classic *The Day the Earth Stood Still* presented a benevolent alien visitor facing hostile earthlings. The film even gave a critique of Cold War paranoia and the arms race. For the better part of the 1950s cycle of flying saucer and space invader films, though, aliens were hostile, infiltrating, brainwashing, body-snatching horrors bent on annihilation and subjugation. As critical consensus—quite accurately— most often argues, the UFO melodramas of this period were a metaphorical reflection on the cultural pressure points of the Cold War era. Americans feared invaders in the 1950s, as they feared a world-annihilating war of nuclear super weapons with the Russians. In turn, the government's own conspiracy theories warned of Communist infiltrators sneaking about in America's heartland, brainwashing those whose patriotic commitment was flagging, replacing loyal Americans with traitors and fifth columnists.

If anything, the original UFO stories presented an endorsement of government conspiracies. Alien infiltrators were hostile, after all. They had come to do the bidding of a rapacious, distant superpower bent on intergalactic imperialism. The only thing standing in their way was the vigilance of the American government, the military and espionage agencies. These governmental protectors, justifiably, had to do their work in secret, behind the scenes, fighting the alien menace without letting the populace in on the horrifying details, lest mass panic and societal breakdown ensue.

The archetypal alien conspiracy film was a true creation of the post–Vietnam and post–Watergate eras. The 1977 Steven Spielberg epic *Close Encounters of the Third Kind* laid down most of what would become the oft-repeated motifs of the alien conspiracy film.

In an alien conspiracy film, a typical crusading Everyman seeks to unearth the truth about an alien presence, but his efforts are usually stymied by a government-military conspiracy. These crusaders often come from the same mold as the generic political conspiracy protagonists. They could be journalists, their investigative instincts about a hot story leading them to keep digging into why the details of the "official version" do not quite make sense. As in *Close Encounters*, they can, in fact, quite literally be the average man on the street who has a UFO encounter that leads him to search for the truth behind the fantastic experience. Small-time members or rebellious elements of local or federal government agencies might also turn into crusaders for the truth, eventually running up against the thuggish minions of the conspiracy.

The purpose for the alien visitations might not be entirely clear to any of the parties in a film like this, but the U.S. government will always be fanatically driven to keep the truth of an alien presence hidden. Among the main reasons for the secrecy is still the fear of alien hostility and their need to prepare to fight an otherworldly menace. In these scenarios of paranoid government agencies covering up alien contact, the military will always have the strongest hand in orchestrating the cover-up, intimidating UFO witnesses, and roughing up or trying to kill investigators seeking to unearth the truth. If there is reason to believe that the aliens are hostile, the government-military conspirators argue, just as they had in the '50s science fiction films, panic will soon follow if the world finds out.

A more recent motivation behind alien-hiding conspiracies, however, can often turn out to be another form of power-grabbing. Especially inspired by the crashed-UFO, retrieved-alien theories first purported in Charles Berlitz and William Moore's 1980 book *The Roswell Incident*, government and military conspirators want to harness alien technology. Crashed alien spaceships, alien machinery or even alien bodies themselves can become useful to the military for "back-engineering" and adoption for military purposes. Non-intelligent (yet highly dangerous) alien creatures or lethal alien viruses are likewise useful in the government's bio-weapons research endeavors.

Combining all three elements of the government-military conspiracy, the alien conspiracy and the business conspiracy, corrupt corporations can just as well turn up in the mix when it comes to hiding the truth about aliens on earth. While the government merely wants to build better weapons systems from extraterrestrial machinery, corporations want to profit from the new technology. Conversely, if this government-business cabal is not seeking to harness new technologies for profit, they may also turn out to by trying to suppress it so as not to upset the current economic status quo. This particular motivation harkens back to the various suppressed-energy-source conspiracies and fuel conspiracies that accused oil companies of hiding the secrets to clean fuel alternatives. As a whole, in the post–Watergate UFO films, large governmental or business organizations are not to be trusted when extraterrestrial contact is made. Their first impulses are always to suppress, to lie and cover up.

In fact, when looking for a greater generic theme that unites conspiracies dealing with the supernatural- or extraordinary-suppressing conspiracies, one finds films that seem to imply the existence of a grand plot to try and enforce a rigid anti-spiritual, anti-religious, and anti-enlightenment worldview. These conspiracy stories suggest that the keys to expanding our breadth of knowledge about the nature of existence, the secrets of the universe, the secrets of alternate realities, enlightenment and growth, in essence, are at hand today but they are kept hidden by secret cabals that profit from our ignorance. Aside from the UFO cover-up conspiracy stories, films involving anything paranormal or mystical are bound to have a plot twist where bureaucratic powers, governmental agencies, elitist intellectuals, or the military leadership suddenly step in and silence eyewitnesses. Attempts to cover up breakthroughs in genetic engineering and cloning (*Parts: The Clonus Horror*, 1979; *Watchers*, 1988; *Universal Soldier*, 1992; *The Island*, 2005), artificial intelligence (*Colossus: The Forbin Project*, 1970; *Westworld*, 1973; *Futureworld*, 1976; *Terminator 2*, 1991, and *Terminator 3*, 2003; *The Matrix*, 1999), time travel (*Time Rider*, 1982; *The Philadelphia Experiment*, 1984; *Time Cop*, 1994) proof of ghosts, demons and the afterlife (*The Entity*, 1981), the existence of God Himself (*Raiders of the Lost Ark*, 1981) or Satan's plot to rule the world (*Damien: Omen II*, 1978; *The Omen: The Final Conflict*, 1981; *Left Behind*, 2000) are all over the place in this type of conspiracy film.

The most famous flip side of this formula, however, comes from *The Da Vinci Code* (2006). Here a conspiracy by the Catholic Church is attempting to keep the superstitious, God-believing, male-dominated worldview in place.

Another recent twist on the otherworldly conspiracy produces storylines where the focus is no longer on corrupt cabals keeping the existence of a larger world, signs of something beyond the conventional consensus reality a secret for their personal gain, but films dealing with the conspiracies carried out by the "others" themselves. Borrowing heavily from the iconography of comic books and graphic novels, delving deeply into the generic traditions of fantasy and horror, these films are about otherworldly beings living side by side with the human world, borrowing the modus operandi of the traditional conspiracy antagonists to keep secrets and to deceive. Films about secret societies of vampires (*Blade*, 1998; *Blade 2*, 2002; *Blade Trinity*, 2004), feuding clans of vampires and werewolves (*Underworld*, 2003; *Underworld Evolution*, 2006), warlocks (*The Covenant*, 2006), European gangs of werewolf punks (*Blood and Chocolate*, 2007), and demons (*Hellboy*, 2004) attempting to stay not only hidden but carrying on centuries-old wars between factions of darkness and light function much like the stories of typical conspirators have always done. These films foreground the concept of layered perception and complex, quasi-bureaucratic efforts to keep much of humanity in the dark about a separate world in their midst.

The Paradox

While the plotlines of conspiracy films revolve around organized deception perpetrated by the corrupt to maintain their power and privilege, the thematic underpinnings of the genre are oddly paradoxical. Conspiracy films are always about an exercise in the manufacturing of perception. A conspiracy's goals are the creation of a worldview, the manipulation of the impressions of reality, the recollection of strategically orchestrated memories.

At the same time, however, just as pop culture researchers Lavery, Hague and Cartwright argue in their analysis of *The X-Files*, conspiracy theory films enact postmodernism, the idea that no reality exists, that all the world is but personal, subjective experience, while at the same time they fiercely oppose it.[8] "The truth is out there," *The X-Files'* catchphrase, screams its defiance of postmodernism, relativism and social-constructionism. Conspiracies in these films might be the manipulation of reality, but the films loudly proclaim that an objective reality exists. Conspiracy-busting heroes are always on a mission to uncover the "truth," and these film believe, more than anything, that a universal set of incontrovertible truths exist.

CHAPTER 2

Enemies Within

The Conspiracy Culture of the 1960s and '70s

The genesis of what can be called the "modern" conspiracy era had arguably taken place in Dallas, Texas, on November 22, 1963. The assassination of President John F. Kennedy almost immediately spawned a plethora of conspiracy theories about "what really happened" in Dealey Plaza that day. The nature of these theories created a whole new atmosphere of paranoia in the United States. While paranoia and conspiratorial thinking were nothing new in American culture — and certainly not just a few years after the McCarthyite witch hunts for Communists in the 1950s — the fear, mistrust, accusation, and insinuations in the aftermath of Kennedy's murder was an entirely new sort of cultural phenomenon. Whereas Americans had traditionally looked for dangerous plots perpetrated by foreign enemies, the post–JFK era focused its fears inward. The real villains, JFK–assassination conspiracy theorists charged, were America's own elites, the nation's institutions of power. Our enemies, for many in this new era, had become the very people and organizations we had trusted the most.

The Kennedy assassination has long been tagged with the popular-culture catchphrase of "the moment American lost its innocence." Understanding what this means is the key to understanding the "modern" era of conspiratorial thinking in the United States. The essence of the modern conspiracy theory that will inspire so much of the separate genre of films and popular entertainment we examine in the following chapters lies in understanding just how exactly the U.S. had supposedly become less innocent that November day.

America certainly had its share of deep, chaotic, culturally divisive problems even before President Kennedy's murder. The period between the end of World War II and the JFK assassination might have been mythologized by popular culture, whitewashed of its simmering social conflicts by sanitized, idealized television shows and films, but it was hardly the carefree land of innocence ingrained in the collective cultural memory today. Sure, coming generations would see a safe, happy time of idealism, naiveté and optimism in endlessly rerun episodes of *Leave It to Beaver* and *Father Knows Best*. They would see rousing Westerns, war films, and crime films from the '40s and '50s about dedicated American heroes fighting for truth, justice and the inherent superiority of the American way of life. But the world that created these images was much darker and much more complicated than its entertainment would suggest. Postwar America, for example, was segregated and racist. This racism, as the Civil Rights movement would witness, was so virulent in some communities that many law enforcement organizations were ready and willing to go to murderously violent extremes to keep African Americans second-class citizens.

Moreover, the Cold War–era America was paranoid and intolerant. In its fear of Communist infiltration and subversion, it had often become as rigid, regimented, conformist, and intolerant of political dissent as the very Communist system it swore to battle. The late 1940s and '50s, in fact, are now as much linked in the popular imagination with Senator Joseph McCarthy, "red-baiting" and the Hollywood blacklist as they are with suburban tract housing, gentle family sitcoms, and poodle skirts.

Even the presidential election of 1960 was the closest in history until that point, and Kennedy's victory would long be shadowed by accusations of underhanded political dirty tricks and vote fraud. The U.S. was a bitterly divided nation at the turn of that decade, with the political left and right passionately hating each other.

Nevertheless, the fledgling Kennedy presidency seemed to inspire something new in the country. Although barely winning half the popular vote, Kennedy's approval ratings shot up to a staggering 92 percent after his inaugural speech. He brought a sort of "star quality" to the presidency heretofore unseen. Supporters and political foes would for decades recall that the youngest politician ever elected to the White House had an uncanny ability to inspire optimism and vision. Many of Kennedy's biographers had, for decades, waxed about the thirty-fifth president in terms that made their subject sound nothing less than messianic.

As historian Stephen Ambrose wrote, "There's a very strong sense that if he had not died, we would have not suffered the 30 years of nightmare that followed—the race riots, the white backlash, assassinations, Vietnam, Watergate, Iran-Contra."[1] As fanciful and unlikely as Ambrose's claim sounds—nothing less than a perfect world would have come about had Kennedy lived!—the JFK presidency did have an aura of hope, promise and energy about it. Most Americans who lived at the time recall that Kennedy made them look forward to a better tomorrow, as if anything was possible. His murder, they recall when speaking about the lost "innocence," seemed to wipe out that hope.

But Kennedy's death will perhaps always be linked to the seemingly endless conspiracy theories that came in its wake. More importantly, the theories the assassination spawned—theories quickly propagated, repeated, debated, and analyzed ad infinitum by hundreds of books, TV shows, documentaries, and movies—are a significant cultural phenomenon because of the accusations the theories made. Most importantly, the very fact that the mainstream culture and the mainstream media accepted these theories so wholeheartedly marks the death of President Kennedy as a crucial turning point in modern American culture, a part of that loss of innocence.

JFK conspiracy theorists made radical, angry charges against the United States itself. They pointed accusatory fingers at American society and charged that the criminals were right here among us. Until the JFK assassination, the people who were in the conspiracy theory business were mainly members of the government. Military and intelligence agencies used to allege that the only conspiracies were the foreign kinds; when Nazi spies and saboteurs tried to undermine the country during World War II or agents of the Soviet bloc tried to subvert our way of life since the start of the Cold War. When massive, organized activities of home-grown criminality were identified, it was the U.S. government pointing the finger yet again. The FBI and police organizations claimed that the Mafia and various other crime rings had grown into vast, immensely powerful shadow empires of vice and corruption since Prohibition. Even Robert F. Kennedy, the attorney general during his brother's presidency, spoke about the organized crime threat to America in decidedly conspiratorial rhetoric. He had said that organized crime was like a shadow government within the United

States.[2] The aftermath of Kennedy's murder changed all this. For the first time, the accusers said the very American system itself had killed the president.

In scores of labyrinthine, convoluted, complex schemes they claimed to have recognized over the decades, conspiracy theorists have charged that the primary culprits in the president's death were the military and intelligence agencies of the U.S. government, all funded, aided, and manipulated by wealthy business elites. At its core, the JFK conspiracy canon is a loud, radical condemnation of modern, postwar America. The vast majority of the Kennedy conspiracy theories imply that the president had been killed because the system had run amok. The military, law enforcement, and intelligence organizations, according to the sum total of all the conspiracies, have slipped their leash. These organizations were no longer accountable to the public, to lawmakers, to the media. They were, instead, a collection of private, uncontrollable little fiefdoms onto themselves, like the paramilitary juntas of Third World "banana republics," all aided by the money of big business interests. Capitalism itself was a failure, according to the JFK conspiracy theorists' position.

But why did these corrupt agencies strike out and murder the president? According to the *gestalt* of the conspiracy movement, these forces all stood to gain from keeping the status quo. These agents of corruption were behind the fractured, paranoid, racist, intolerant darkness that had been plaguing America since the end of World War II. When Kennedy, the charismatic new leader, the man of vision, hope, and progressive optimism, ascended to the presidency, the corruption within the corridors of governmental power, within the financial system, deep within the heart of capitalism, felt threatened. They, in turn, masterminded a perfect assassination plot to remove the threat to their power.

This radical indictment of the American system lies at the core of the modern conspiracy movement that, in turn, shaped and built the conspiracy theory entertainment genre. When the mainstream of American society was willing to give credence to these theories, when it had accepted the fact that the system could have been deeply flawed, that leaders and authority figures could, and regularly did, abuse their power and privilege, America's innocence, in effect, took another blow. It is important to remember, after all, that all major forms of mass entertainment at this time, from movies to television to children's comic books, had been subject to rigid codes of self-censorship designed to reinforce the idea that America was perfect, its leaders were honest, and its institutions could be trusted. In America, these codes of censorship said, law and order prevailed and criminality was always swiftly punished. The Motion Picture Code that had been in effect since 1938 included very explicit rules against depicting police, military, or governmental corruption of any sort. Authority was to be respected at all times in entertainment.[3] A similar code was adopted by the comic book industry in 1954 in the wake of governmental pressure.[4] Furthermore, television had also adopted a similar set of thematic standards that governed all of its programs. Radical criticism and cynicism were not supposed to have been part of the American character. While we can, of course, realistically assume that most adults of the time did not really believe that the American system was so flawlessly perfect, that all public officials were above reproach and idealistic, the JFK assassination and its conspiracy theories put a glaring public spotlight on the possibility that the system really might have been deeply, darkly rotten to its core. It is one thing to suspect the existence of evil; it is quite different to see it confirmed in all its bloody, ugly brutality. Moreover, the victim of the conspiracy, President Kennedy himself, *did* impress so many Americans as being exactly as honest, principled, and committed to public service as the commandments of all the entertainment codes had always said a true American leader would always be.

Interestingly enough, this radically oriented conspiracy movement had virtually become a part of 1960s Americana. When one begins to lay out the basic threads running through most of the Kennedy conspiracy theories, one finds them ensnaring some of the most prominent cultural figures of the era. From politicians to celebrities, from Hollywood movie stars to business titans to gangsters, all of the major figures of the 1960s cultural landscape are alleged to have had ties to Kennedy and have been accused of playing some sort of a role, even if only tangentially, in his demise.[5]

Taking a very brief look at the basics of the JFK conspiracy canon is helpful in understanding how the template for all late-twentieth century conspiracy theories and conspiracy entertainment had been set. This exercise, however, must remain brief and sketched in very broad, general strokes. Within three years of the Kennedy assassination, after all, the *New York Times* was inspired to comment in an editorial piece that "debate on the accuracy of the Warren Commission's work is now approaching the dimensions of a lively small industry in this country."[6] Within those three years, volumes of books charging conspiracy had already cropped up, matched by articles in a number of small, independently published magazines and a growing list of newsletters and journals devoted entirely to the JFK assassination. To recount all of the vast minutia of so many conspiracy theories in a book interested in entertainment and the popular culture's reflection of conspiracies would not only be pointless, but quite an impossible exercise. All that has been written about JFK conspiracy theories to date could, quite literally, fill up a very large library. Entire university courses dealing with JFK conspiracy theories have already been created.

When one sums up the thrust of the majority of Kennedy assassination conspiracies, it sounds a lot like the plot of a standard Agatha Christie mystery. A much beloved, seemingly upstanding man is murdered and it soon turns out that a large, eccentric cast of characters all had a motive for killing him. According to this composite scenario, Kennedy is the scion of a wealthy yet superbly idealistic family committed to public service, who ascended to the highest office in the country out of a drive to make America and the world a better place. The Kennedy clan, in fact, is the picture of the American success story. Their fortunes were made by patriarch Joseph P. Kennedy who, in turn, supposedly imparted a sense of civic responsibility on all his children, instilling in them an unflagging compassion for all those who were not fortunate enough to enjoy the same blessings and opportunities of a great nation. After JFK becomes president, he attempts to realize his progressive, idealistic visions for a better America, only to draw the wrath of scoundrels who stand to lose a great deal if the president's agendas succeed. Eventually, either one or several of these shady parties puts an audacious murder plot into motion, killing the president and making an unbalanced lowlife the fall guy. The authorities tasked with investigating the crime, in turn, collude with the murderers, hiding the truth. All that can now be done is for idealistic, committed amateur investigators to try and solve the crime on their own. After all, much like Kennedy himself believed — and the traditions in standard American heroic stories, books, and films always claimed — a single, committed individual can change the world. In the aftermath of the crime of the century, only the lone, perceptive, dogged, and critical conspiracy theorists remain as the last, best hope of bringing the forces that killed the president to justice.

Ironically, what all the lone, driven conspiracy theorists have achieved by piecing together the "facts" behind the assassination, is to severely tarnish the legend of "America's royal family." But, after all, even in the best mystery stories, the universally beloved murder victim is never what he or she appears to be. Kennedy, as charismatic and inspirational as he might have been, was still a flawed human being. Some of the failings of his character, according to some of the conspiracy theories, might have played a part in his demise.

In part because of his personality quirks and in part because of the sheer nature of politics and power, Kennedy's life and brief tenure in the White House had him embroiled in various plots and caught up in the company of the most unsavory players in Washington, the worlds of espionage, organized crime, and Hollywood and Las Vegas celebrities.[7] Various conspiracy theorists charge that JFK, as much as his brothers would also later do, oftentimes came very close to damaging his reputation and compromising his political career because of his reckless sex life. As legitimate journalists, historians, and his various biographers had repeatedly confirmed, he was a wanton womanizer all his life. Even while president, he had repeatedly been unfaithful to his wife. At one time, he told Clare Boothe Luce that womanizing had been both a norm and an *expectation* in the Kennedy family. "Dad told all the boys to get laid as often as possible,"[8] he admitted. Sexual adventure and infidelity, it appears, were measures of manhood in the Kennedy clan. As JFK was readily embraced by the hippest of Hollywood's liberal entertainers, he had no trouble carrying on affairs with armies of starlets when in California. His brother-in-law, actor Peter Lawford, often procured women when Kennedy visited Los Angeles. As Lawford's biographers unflatteringly characterize him, he functioned, for all intents and purposes, as a pimp working for JFK.[9] But when Lawford was not providing Kennedy with female companionship, the actor's friend and "Rat Pack" leader, Frank Sinatra, took up the slack. Sinatra, as various celebrities still enjoy doing so today, had always been obsessively gravitating toward power. An ardent supporter, he had become a close personal friend of Kennedy as the Senator was rising in Washington and heading toward the presidency. Sinatra, as libidinous a womanizer as Kennedy, had also always been eager to help his friend indulge in the seamier sides of the entertainment scene. In fact, Kennedy's sexual Hollywood escapades are the point where he becomes embroiled in conspiracy theories.

The most talked-about of Kennedy's alleged Hollywood affairs was with Marilyn Monroe. Basically, for the phenomenally popular, young, and handsome president, there was no more fitting a match for a Hollywood dalliance than the woman considered to be the most desirable sex symbol of the twentieth century. According to the volumes of Kennedy-Monroe gossip spread throughout the decades, their relationship quickly became problematic because of Monroe's unstable, clingy personality when it came to sex and romance. As Monroe's biographers often detailed, her childhood of abuse and abandonment left her haunted by too many demons. She was forever searching for stability and love, but using sex as a tool to manipulate Hollywood's predatory legions of producers, stars, and studio moguls for the sake of her career.[10] Kennedy turned out to be yet one more user. The president, after all, could have no more use for Monroe than as a temporary, secret affair. According to lore, Monroe then carried on an affair with JFK's brother Robert, falling for him so hard that she started telling her closest confidants that she would soon be the new Mrs. Robert Kennedy. When RFK broke off the affair, Monroe's already fragile mental state was supposed to have sent her into a destructive tailspin of drug and alcohol binges. She was found dead of a drug overdose on August 5, 1962, by her housekeeper, Eunice Murray. Conspiracy theorists, however, charge that there was much more to the story.

Depending on which theory one chooses to give credence to, Monroe's death was no accidental overdose but murder by one of several factions for one of several reasons. Nearly all the theories tie the Monroe death to yet more theories about who might have *really* killed JFK and to what end.

One version gets the Mafia involved. Before becoming the attorney general under his brother's administration, Robert Kennedy was a member of the Senate Select Committee on Improper Activities in Labor and Management (known commonly as the McClellan Committee), crusading mightily to cripple the influence of organized crime in the labor unions. After JFK's election to the White House, the Kennedy crusade against the mob intensified. One of Kennedy's chief nemeses in organized crime was Teamsters Union boss Jimmy Hoffa. Hoffa, the conspiracy theorists claim, had likewise been obsessed with wrecking the Kennedys' reputation, going so far as to plant surveillance devices in Monroe's house to get solid evidence of her affair with either of the Kennedy brothers. None of these tapes had ever been publicly heard — along with any other surveillance tapes allegedly planted by either or both the CIA and the FBI.[11] At one point, this theory claims, either Hoffa or someone else in the Mafia killed Monroe to spite the Kennedys. If not Hoffa, the Mafia-hit-conspiracy charges, then it could have been Chicago Mafia godfather Sam Giancana, whose girlfriend, Judy Campbell, was also alleged to have slept with JFK.

But the mob's involvement in John F. Kennedy's killing is one of the major schools of thought in what might be called "Kennedy conspiratoriology." Some of the Kennedy involvement with the mob is more than mere unsubstantiated yarn-spinning by conspiracy theorists, though. "America's Royal Family" had been well embroiled in the machinations of the underworld during Prohibition. The foundation of all the Kennedy money had actually come from much more than an ironclad work ethic and the greatness of the American system. Joseph P. Kennedy, by most accounts, even the family's most worshipful biographers, had been a shrewd, ruthless, Machiavellian rogue. He had made the family fortune not just as a real estate investor and through a brief stint as a movie mogul, but through insider trading and stock manipulation while he worked as a stockbroker, then as a bootlegger. His primary agenda was always the amassing of financial power for the sake of eventual political power. All the Kennedy sons had been groomed for political office their entire lives, their positions to be bought by the family fortune.[12]

Once John and Robert Kennedy were in Washington, however, they could afford to be idealistic. Robert Kennedy's assaults on the mob through the McClellan Committee, then as the attorney general, were almost conducted as a private war. Conspiracy theorists suggest that the Kennedy crusade against the mob might have stemmed from an old falling-out between Joseph Kennedy and his organized crime bootlegging partners during Prohibition. In 1973, mobster Frank Costello publicly claimed that the elder Kennedy had been deeply involved in organized crime during the days of illegal liquor. But what Joseph's sons were doing in their anti-crime efforts, conspiracy theorists argue, had gone too far. This view presents that the murder in Dealey Plaza in 1963 was a mob "hit" on the president.

Furthermore, the same theorists also claim that killing Kennedy was not merely revenge for his and his brother's dogged prosecution of the mob, but certain top level Mafioso felt *betrayed* after the *favor* they had done for the Kennedys and the hand they had in putting Joseph's son in the White House. The argument claims that the close presidential election of 1960 was tipped in JFK's favor by Chicago and Texas mobsters who tampered with the ballots. (A long-running joke states that John F. Kennedy was really elected by all the dead people in the cemeteries on the west side of Chicago who somehow got their names on voter registration forms.) The conspiracists argue that the mob had to decide which party to help get elected to the presidency, and they chose to side with the Democrats because the Republicans looked like they were favoring tougher anti-racketeering laws and prosecutions. Yet another faction of the mob involvement school of thought claims that Frank

Sinatra had a hand in convincing Giancana to rig the Chicago election. Sinatra, much like a lot of today's "bad boy" musicians and celebrities, always liked to affect an outlaw image. His biographers insist that he often liked to threaten to have people's legs broken by his Mafia cronies. But, according to conspiracy theorists, Sinatra had supposedly convinced Giancana to tamper with the elections so the mob could have powerful friends in Washington. Sinatra, in his ongoing quest to associate himself with power, also liked to brag about how he lived the most remarkable of all rags-to-riches lives; he was but a poor kid from the streets of Hoboken who grew up to be close personal friends with the president of the United States.[13] Ultimately, conspiracy theorists argue, the mob had various reasons to kill JFK, if not Marilyn Monroe as well, just to strike back at a family that had betrayed them.

The appeal of all the JFK assassination conspiracies stems from the fact that among all the supposition, lies just enough evidence of other *real* conspiracies that it becomes quite easy to consider that perhaps the murder of the president was not what it appeared to be. For example, the 1975 investigations of the Senate Select Committee to Study Governmental Operations with Respect to Intelligence Activities (known as the Church Committee, named after its chairman, Idaho Senator Frank Church) into illegal intelligence-gathering activities by the CIA and the FBI revealed that there was a very real temporary "partnership" between the CIA and members of the Mafia in an attempt to overthrow the Castro regime in Cuba in 1961.[14] The U.S. government did not want a Communist power just ninety miles off the coast of Florida. The Mafioso, in turn, had lost millions when Castro shut down their casinos in Havana. The CIA wanted to be rid of the Communists and the mob wanted to make money again. The partnership was forged in mutual interest. A partnership, of course, is another word for "conspiracy." This conspiracy, in turn, had attempted to overthrow Castro during the Bay of Pigs invasion. But both before and after the failure of the invasion, CIA agents and Mafia hitmen — aided throughout by paramilitary groups of Cuban exiles — made several fanciful attempts to depose or kill Castro. They included failed schemes like using exploding cigars or contaminating Castro with radioactive dust to make his beard fall out and embarrass him in front of his public. Supposedly, a beardless Castro would have lost the support of his followers.[15]

This CIA and Mafia connection, conspiracy theorists assert, would eventually lead to the murder of John F. Kennedy. Blame for the failure of the Bay of Pigs invasion, the theorists argue, was put on Kennedy by the CIA. Kennedy had withdrawn air support for the invasion, leading to the demolition of the invasion force by the Cuban military.

Of course, for those conspiracists who reject the CIA-Mafia theory, the idea that Castro was behind the assassination is a plausible alternative. Castro, they counter, had the most to fear from the U.S. This theory, however, also seems to ignore the argument that Kennedy was seen by conservatives and the military-intelligence establishment as too soft on communism. Or, at least, this specific theory goes, Castro didn't appear to see the same sort of weakling the CIA did and he had Kennedy killed.

Yet another iteration on the Cuban connection asserts that the collusion was really between Castro and the Mafia. As unlikely as this sounds, the purveyors of this particular idea argue that Castro made a deal with the mob to give them their casinos back in return for assassinating JFK.

After one spends enough time navigating the labyrinthine world of Kennedy conspiracies, connections between and variations on just about every motive to murder the president start to emerge. Some theorists search for one link between as many 1960s events as possible. (One of the holy grails of the most hard-core conspiracy theorists is what may be called a sort of unified field theory of conspiracies, where *every* event in history is tied together.) These theorists argue that shortly before her death, distraught over having been dumped by both John and Robert Kennedy, Monroe told several acquaintances that she knew explosive national security secrets. The enraged actress supposedly also said that she was going to go public with this information. The Castro assassination attempts supposedly came up during pillow talk with both Kennedys, especially Robert. Close confidants of Monroe would repeatedly claim that she kept a diary where these secrets were recorded. No diary was found in her house during the L.A.P.D. investigation of her death. Some conspiracy theorists account for this in one set of suppositions that perhaps damns the Kennedys more than any of the other salacious exposes of their sex lives. One school of conspiratorial thought argues that once the Kennedys realized how vindictive Monroe was capable of becoming, they had her murdered. Other theorists, however, exonerate the Kennedy brothers and claim that either the FBI or the CIA killed Monroe without the knowledge of either the president or the attorney general.

The U.S. intelligence and military communities, the conspiracy theorists further argue, were also opposed to Kennedy's foreign policy plans. They opposed Kennedy's planned nuclear test ban treaty with the Soviets and they feared the president's plans for withdrawing troops from Vietnam. The Vietnam withdrawal, according to the conspiracists' charge, was also disagreeable to the "military industrial complex" Eisenhower had warned about. There was money to be made in a prolonged war in Southeast Asia, and defense contractors stood to lose a lot of it if Kennedy's peace plans were put in effect. Essentially, the Vietnam scenario draws big business into the overall Kennedy conspiracy canon here.

The more daring of conspiracy theorists implicate Kennedy's vice-president, Lyndon Johnson, with the military industrial complex–Vietnam theory. Johnson, a liberal Democrat, this theory argues, was still under the control of the war-profiteering defense contractors seeking to escalate the Southeast Asian war.

Whether or not Kennedy would really have completely withdrawn from Vietnam had been debated by historians—disputed by many—but there are enough factual building blocks to the overall conspiracy mythos that a lot of it sounds completely plausible. Many among the top military brass and in the intelligence community did intensely dislike Kennedy. The CIA and the Mafia did engage in a conspiracy to overthrow Castro. Mafia chieftains did feel like they were under siege from the Kennedy administration's war on organized crime. Other factions of the conservative right-wing opposed to Kennedy's social agendas on race and welfare, again, despised Kennedy. Texas was home to many of these wealthy conservatives, some of whom protested Kennedy's visit to Dallas by circulating leaflets accusing the president of treason.

The final and most enigmatic factor in the Kennedy conspiracy lore is the killer—or fall guy, according to conspiracy theorists—and his own background of strange, troubled, eccentric and often inexplicable behavior. Lee Harvey Oswald, the man apprehended shortly after Kennedy's shooting, charged with the murder and assassinated by yet another cipher of a killer, Jack Ruby, has himself been categorized by the conspiracy mythos as a man of so many contradictions, such strange associations and activities that he simply could not have been the lone deranged gunman the government claims he was. Someone who could be categorized as a perennial loser, Oswald appears to have been a man forever stuck on the outside, someone looking for an identity, something to belong to and a place to be noticed. A troubled, underachieving youth, he joined the Marine Corps at seventeen, quickly to be disillusioned by the military life. What has become a point of contention for the conspiracy theorists is the fact that while in the Corps, Oswald had already declared his hatred for America and professed his admiration for Marxism and the Soviet Union. Why would a vocal critic of the U.S. and supporter of the enemy continue serving his time in the Marine Corps with no disciplinary actions or even any extra scrutiny? At the height of the Cold War, someone like this should have been seen as a potential security risk. But Oswald's problems with the Marines stemmed mainly from disorderly behavior. At one point he was court-martialed for accidentally shooting himself with an unauthorized handgun; later court-martialed again for a drunken brawl with an officer; then, while stationed in the Philippines, for firing a rifle into the jungle. In 1959, he got an early discharge under a dependant clause, citing his need to care for his severely ailing mother.[16] Shortly afterward, Oswald immigrated to the Soviet Union, living there for three years and marrying the niece of a colonel in the Ministry of Internal Affairs (MVD).[17] In 1962, claiming disillusionment once again, Oswald and his wife Marina applied for and were granted permission by the State Department to return to the U.S. Oswald's ease of movement back and forth between the two Cold War enemies troubles conspiracy theorists. They point out that not only was Oswald let back into the country, but the government didn't seem to have any particular interest in keeping track of him as a potential spy. This despite the fact that Oswald, while declaring his distaste for Soviet communism, remained a vocal Marxist. While living in New Orleans and Texas, he had become a member of far left-wing organizations supporting Cuba and the Castro regime. At one point he got into a fight in the streets of New Orleans with some Cuban exiles while handing out pro–Castro leaflets. That a leftist troublemaker like Oswald would wind up trying to kill the president, however, becomes too convenient for conspiracy theorists to accept. Others claim that the FBI did keep track of him, knew he was in Dallas before Kennedy's arrival, yet did nothing to investigate whether he was a threat to the president. FBI director J. Edgar Hoover, conspiracy theorists charge, was yet another figure in the very crowded field of passionate Kennedy-haters. This argument, therefore, adds Hoover and the Bureau to the ranks of active conspirators.[18]

Of course, that a troubled, aimless, malcontented anti–American burnout like Oswald should take a shot at the president is perfectly, elegantly plausible for the conspiracy critics. Perhaps the authorities should have kept better track of him, these skeptics counter, yet these points are hardly evidence of the FBI's collusion in the conspiracy, much less evidence that a conspiracy existed at all.

Conspiracists, on the other hand, argue that Oswald was but a wily, deep-cover operative for the CIA since his time in the Marines. His desperate, sad-sack persona was merely a ruse. Upon returning to the U.S., conspiracists argue, Oswald spouted left-wing rhetoric while he consorted with the paramilitary, far right-wing anti–Castro forces in the shadowy bayou training camps and CIA hideouts of Louisiana. In this clandestine, corrupt intersecting-point of intelligence agents, paramilitary extremists, foreign exiles, and racist military-industrialists, Oswald supposedly became a patsy for Kennedy's killers. As the conspiracy canon argues, Oswald never realized that he was set up to be the fall guy for a vast conspiracy until the very end. On November 22, in a moment that would be analyzed, debated, argued about and fought over for decades, Oswald shot at John F. Kennedy's motorcade as it passed through Dealey Plaza in Dallas. Conspiracy theorists to this day, however, charge that Oswald was not the only man doing the shooting. There were sharpshooters, the theorists posit, in anywhere between two and five other spots around the Plaza. The Secret Service detail, of course, was also a part of the conspiracy, providing staggeringly sloppy cover for the president. The Dallas Police Department, conspiracists argue, helped the Secret Service spirit JFK's corpse away to Washington, D.C. before a full autopsy could be performed in Dallas. Among Oswald's final words before being shot down by Jack Ruby, another bizarre figure with organized crime ties among the collection of unsavory, grotesque individuals caught up in the conspiracy lore, were, "I'm just a patsy."[19]

Upon a basic skeleton of confirmed, documented facts, therefore, the first major modern conspiracy industry was built. As many conspiracy theories are wont to do, a foundation of facts led to some tenuous suppositions, connections drawn between people and parties amounting to a great deal of guilt-by-association reasoning, and the overall construction of a massive, convoluted circumstantial case for a murder conspiracy. The Kennedy conspiracy theories are so voluminous that even writers who have been inclined to give the general idea of a conspiracy some credence have pointed out that many of the "believable" theories actually cancel each other out. For example, the idea that the CIA or FBI or Mafia chieftains hostile to the Kennedy administration would keep the Marilyn Monroe affair secret is not plausible. That they would want to go so far as to murder Monroe to keep her silent, and then orchestrate an immensely difficult and intricate murder of JFK himself, is illogical. If the evidence existed that both Kennedy brothers were so reckless and irresponsible as to share national security secrets with a mistress they never seriously considered to be anything more that a cheap tryst, would not making this information public be the easiest option to destroy JFK's tenure in the White House, his chances for reelection, as well as any political future Robert Kennedy ever had beyond the attorney general's office? Furthermore, of all the various parties that had an interest in Kennedy's murder, it is impossible to argue that they all had a hand in one massive conspiracy to kill him. The most obvious example would be that it was either someone inside the U.S. that murdered Kennedy, or someone on the outside. There could be no conceivable link between conspirators in the U.S. and those abroad. The foreigners would have to be either the Cubans or the Russians. These foreign communist powers would obviously not be in collusion with fringe right-wingers in the U.S.

By the same token, vocal conspiracy theory critics, like former prosecutor Vincent Bugliosi, argue that political rivalries would make the second phase of most conspiracy theories implausible. According to the conspiratorial view of the JFK killing, the plot did not merely involve the shooting. They argue that the subsequent Warren Commission's investigation, including each of its seven members, the general counsel, the 14 assistant counsels, including the large staffs of those 22 people, were all part of the conspiracy as well, cleaning up behind the murderers, covering up the crime with a fraudulent report concluding that Oswald acted alone. As Bugliosi counters in his immense, 1612-page refutation of all the major Kennedy conspiracy theories, the idea that an investigative commission headed by an arch liberal like Supreme Court Justice Earl Warren would collude with an ultra right-wing conspiracy is completely implausible.

Furthermore, the conspiracist speculations about Oswald's "real" role in the assassination easily turn contradictory. On the one hand, he is categorized—given the requirements of the theory—as either a shrewd, deep-cover operative for the CIA, infiltrating the Soviet Union, perhaps acting as a double agent and giving up secrets that led to the 1960 shoot-down of the U2 spy plane, or perhaps acting as a triple agent and working to further the agendas of American intelligence. On the other hand, to serve the needs of other theorists, Oswald, the CIA spy, is presented as a clueless stooge, a patsy, a puppet and fall guy manipulated by the CIA and its own right-wing millionaire industrialist string-pullers to put his head in the noose and present himself to the world as the lone gunman responsible for the Kennedy murder. These same theorists, however, never discount the fact that this stooge-version of Oswald, the clueless patsy and loser, was nevertheless a part of earlier spy missions to Russia. The most zealous conspiracy theorists like to tie many major events together into one interconnected web of influences and manipulations. But oblivious, unstable losers are hardly reliable espionage agents. The U.S. government, from military special operations units to intelligence agencies, employs psychologists and psychiatrists to very carefully handpick and train their operatives. Hollywood films and spy novels about "rogue agents" aside, mentally unstable, impulsive loose cannons are the worst possible field operatives for dangerous missions. People like that are weeded out long before they are anywhere close to actual field training. Furthermore, it's difficult to imagine that a conspiracy as intricate and careful as what would be required to pull off the assassination of the president would risk putting a wild card like Oswald in the middle of its operation.

It is also remarkable that for so many conspiracy theorists who have weaved and shaped and cobbled together a murder scenario so large that it would have truly been the crime of the century in scope and complexity, it is not difficult to place at its epicenter an intelligence-gathering organization that seems to have spectacularly bungled much less complicated operations. A CIA that would need to go into a partnership with the street hoodlums of the Mafia to try and assassinate a tin-pot revolutionary like Fidel Castro should have found it nearly impossible to pull off a coup like the murder of the president of the United States. What's more, the fact the CIA *failed* to kill or depose Castro should inspire much more skepticism about the labyrinthine, massive, flawless operation the conspiracy theorists charge the agency with. Those who seriously considered, then failed, to pull off schemes like murdering Castro with exploding cigars and radioactive dust would have been facing an infinitely more daunting task when attempting to kill the president in front of hundreds of eyewitnesses. In such a light, the idea that the same people who wanted to blow Castro up with exploding cigars could perfectly orchestrate a conspiracy so complex as to involve the various branches of the military, the Secret Service, the FBI, the Dallas police department, the criminals of the mob, Chief Justice Earl Warren, Senator Gerald Ford and the other 22 people on the Warren Commission stretches logic and believability past all breaking points.

While the pros and cons of the believability of the conspiracy theories or the weight of anti-conspiracy debunkings have long been debated and will be debated for decades to come, it is important to understand these theories in their historical and cultural context. Furthermore, the JFK assassination mythos also helps put the focus on the inherently political nature of conspiracy theorizing. Not only are conspiracy theories mainly a product of the social anxieties of any given moment in history, but people usually accuse their political and ideological enemies of orchestrating sinister and dangerous plots.

The theories of John F. Kennedy's murder having been a result of an intricate right-wing conspiracy found traction in the 1960s because of the cultural pressure points building up in the early half of that decade. Again, conspiracy theories have always been a part of American culture even before November 22, 1963. Fear of the Freemasons and Illuminati go back to colonial America. Fears of the "international bankers" and "moneyed interest" and "institutions of power and influence" have always been around. Just like Walter Rathenau and Woodrow Wilson and Franklin D. Roosevelt voiced concerns over these clandestine forces, as discussed in the first chapter, Americans, to a degree, have always feared the rich and the powerful. The centuries-old Masonic lodges have always been the private clubs of the wealthy and the politically influential. Many conspiracy historians have argued that certain fears of the "institutions of power" have also been founded in rather disturbing beliefs and attitudes themselves. The original financial conspiracy theories have been rooted, for instance, in anti–Semitism. The term "international bankers" has for decades been a code word for Jews. The nightmarish scenarios of powerful banking institutions manipulating governments are actually founded in the centuries-old anti–Semitic conspiracy theories of powerful cabals of Jews using their wealth to enslave the world. In 1930s Germany, the Nazis pinned the country's economic woes on conspiracies of wealthy Jewish bankers. Conspiracy theories, in essence, usually point a finger at those groups and institutions that most people are afraid of or hate at any given time. In the early 1960s, the intense cultural conservatism of postwar America created the left-wing backlash of the Kennedy conspiracy movement.

The rigid, paranoid, and conformist culture of the late 1940s and '50s had slowly transformed from something dull and banal, to overbearing, to suffocating, and it had all been enforced by the power of the law and government. From the late 1940s through the early '50s, political dissent had been pursued and punished by the law, radicals and outsiders attacked by the full force of Congress, Joseph McCarthy, and the House Un-American Activities Committee. When the country faced the insidious Communist enemy in Europe, right-wingers argued, patriotism and absolute unquestioning loyalty to the status quo were the only defenses against foreign subversion. As the 1950s progressed, however, to many it felt like this stultifying cultural uniformity had evolved from a uniformity in politics to uniformity in tastes, culture, art, and *thought*. The distasteful impression lingered that a true American had to look, talk, dress a certain way; he or she had to cut their hair the correct way, they had to listen to the proper music, read the proper books, and *live* the correct lifestyle. Although the national crisis of the degenerating state of the war in Vietnam by the end of the 1960s would help fuel a full-scale youth revolt against an older generation's paranoid conservatism, the Kennedy assassination and the possibility of a right-wing conspiracy behind it was the spark to ignite a preliminary, small-scale version of a cultural revolt by some in the early half of the decade. A believer in the Kennedy conspiracy could, in effect, condemn the right wingers, the status quo, the military, the intelligence community, the super patriots, big business and the capitalist system. The idea of a conspiracy behind Kennedy's murder is the strongest repudiation of conservative powers that be. The sort of conspiracy alleged by the true believers turned the tables on the self-appointed guardians of patriotism, law, order, of everything all–American. If a conspiracy killed JFK, these patriots were proven to be the worst kinds of traitors in the country. The murder of the president is the ultimate act of treason.

As Bugliosi documents in his timeline of the birth and growth of the Kennedy conspiracy movement, the first conspiracy advocates came from the far left. Although the conspiracy movement has spanned several generations so far and has included many vocal theorists and critics of the Warren Commission report who were completely apolitical and free of ideological dogma, the roots of the movement are firmly embedded in the ultra-leftist political-activist circles of the early 1960s.

In May of 1964, the first book alleging a conspiracy in JFK's murder was written by Thomas Buchanan, a Communist Party member living in London. Titled *Who Killed Kennedy?*, it laid out one of the basic arguments of the *conspiratoriology*; that Kennedy was killed in a crossfire of several snipers firing at once. The main impetus for Buchanan's writing of the book, though, was to counteract the few right-leaning arguments for a foreign conspiracy. If someone other than Oswald murdered Kennedy, some anti–Communists have argued, then it had to have been either the Cubans, getting revenge for the Bay of Pigs and the CIA's attempts at deposing Castro, or it was the Russians, striking back at Kennedy for forcing them to remove their missiles from Cuba. Buchanan's work was conceived as a defense of the Soviets and Cubans, an attempt at exonerating them and shifting the blame to a massive, far-right-wing cabal of all the elements of American society the left despised the most.

On September 24, 1964, Joachim Joesten published *Oswald: Assassin or Fall Guy?*, questioning Oswald's official biography. Joesten, a German immigrant and former member of the German Communist Party, argued that Oswald was really a deep-cover operative for both the FBI and the CIA. Oswald's pro–Cuban activism and vocal Marxism were but a ruse, Joesten's book posits, and all a part of the right-wing conspiracy's ploy to set him up as the perfect patsy for the presidential assassination.

In 1965, Harold Weisberg self-published *Whitewash*, arguing that the conspiracy researchers and critics of the Warren Commission were being targeted by a government conspiracy of misinformation and character assassination. Weisberg had at one point worked for the State Department, but he was fired for having a "known association with agents of the Soviet Union."[20] In 1938 he had also been fired from the La Follette Civil Liberties Committee for giving information to a communist newspaper. Weisberg had to go the vanity press route for his book because it was rejected by sixty publishing houses in the U.S. and eleven publishers in eight foreign countries. His difficulty in getting his book before the public, Weisberg argued, was in itself a proof of the massive, well-orchestrated plot between the government and right-wing media elites to silence those attempting to uncover the truth.

Weisberg's tome, however, did well enough to be bought and published by Dell, a major New York publisher, a year later. In fact, the issue of the media disseminating some of the most dramatic and provocative conspiracy theory literature is worth mentioning very briefly. Perhaps what can be counted as a strike against many conspiracy theorists is the fact that so many major book publishers, magazine publishers, newspapers, TV and film production companies have given them a forum to air their theories. Some of the most enthusiastic conspiracy theorists usually claim that the mass media are but the propaganda arms of the conspirators. The right-wing cabals perpetrating great conspiracies, after all, are headed by business tycoons, billionaires whose vast holdings usually include media outlets. As ever greater numbers of media companies have merged or been bought up by global corporations— the trend growing since the 1970s and '80s—for conspiracy theorists, along with leftist media critics and academics, the media consolidation has been a cause to rally around. The media conglomerates, they charge, are run by members of the conspiracies that have done everything from killing the Kennedys, Martin Luther King, and Malcolm X, concealing clean-air technologies, hiding aliens, creating diseases, and starting profitable wars. The truth, the theorists contend, can never come out, because the conspirators control the channels of communication throughout the world. Nevertheless, the fact is that the mainstream media have been more than receptive to some of the most radical and whimsical of conspiracy theorists. All of the major New York publishing houses have released a plethora of conspiracy theory books over the decades. One of the most imaginative conspiracy theorists, former Texas journalist Jim Marrs, had a number of his most successful conspiracy books published by major New York houses. Marrs' book *Crossfire: The Plot That Killed Kennedy* was published by Carroll & Graff in 1989. Aside from being a leading Kennedy assassination conspiracy proponent, Marrs also wrote *Alien Agenda: Investigating the Extra-*

terrestrial Presence Among Us and *Rule by Secrecy: The Hidden History That Connects the Trilateral Commission, the Freemasons, and the Great Pyramids* (both published by Harper-Collins). In these books he argues that ancient secret societies are still running the world, hiding the truth about UFOs, and that they control the conspiracy that killed John F. Kennedy. Interestingly enough, *Rule by Secrecy* is described in a cover blurb as "the underground bestseller." What makes the book "underground," published and promoted by a major house like HarperCollins, is not quite explained. Since September 11, 2001, he has published *PSI Spies: The True Story of America's Psychic Warfare Program* (2002), *The War on Freedom: The 9/11 Conspiracies* (2003), *Inside Job: Unmasking the 9/11 Conspiracies* (2004), *The Terror Conspiracy: Deception, 9/11, and the Loss of Liberty* (2006) — albeit with the smaller presses of (respectively) New Page Books, ARES Publishing, Origin Press and The Disinformation Company — and *The Rise of the Fourth Reich: The Secret Societies That Threaten to Take Over America* (2008) and *The Trillion Dollar Conspiracy: How the New World Order, Man-Made Diseases, and Zombie Banks are Destroying America* (2010). *The Rise of the Fourth Reich* and *The Trillion Dollar Conspiracy* were both put forth by William Morrow, yet another of the New York corporate publishing giants. In *Fourth Reich*, as the title suggests, he argues that a fascistic cabal of government right-wingers led by George W. Bush and Dick Cheney, in league with the corporate media, either orchestrated the September 11 attacks or knew about it but did nothing to prevent them, all in an effort to turn the United States into a Nazi-like super dictatorship. *Fourth Reich* even has the audacity to include the jacket copy, "Close the approved textbooks, turn off the corporate mass media." For some reason, the global corporate media conspiracy that has been publishing Marrs' books has not noticed how he has been working hard to reveal all their evil secrets.

The point, however, is that when any one party is being accused of masterminding a far-reaching, sinister conspiracy, it is interesting to check who is pointing a finger at them. One might find that most often the conspiracy theorists are the political and ideological enemies of the accused. The earliest Kennedy conspiracy theorists all had very solid and very far left political credentials. Perhaps the most successful of what has been called the "first generation" of conspiracy theorists was lawyer Mark Lane, the author of *Rush to Judgment*, published in 1966 by Dell. His book was one of the earliest attempts at not merely picking one of the several parties from the conspiracy theory roster of possible JFK assassination masterminds but tying *all* of them together. As Bugliosi writes, "it accuses the Warren Commission of so many misdeeds and suggests so many things (e.g., one or more shots came from the front, Ruby knew Oswald, Oswald may have been framed) that a gullible reader has no choice but to infer the existence of a conspiracy."[21] Lane has also always been a champion of far-left causes and a member of such Communist Party front organizations as the National Lawyer's Guild and the Abraham Lincoln Brigade. Nonetheless, the bestselling success of Lane's *Rush to Judgment* has led a number of anti-conspiracy advocates to credit his work as the most influential foundation of the ongoing JFK conspiracy theory cult, for convincing an entire generation that a conspiracy of some sort simply had to have taken place. *Rush to Judgment* was the basis for the first Hollywood film about a JFK assassination conspiracy, *Executive Action* (Warner Brothers, 1973), produced by and starring Hollywood liberal icon Burt Lancaster.

Ultimately, the John F. Kennedy conspiracy theory phenomenon can be understood in its historical context as more than a mere examination of and debate over the events of November 22, 1963. It has profound political import. The conspiracy movement was an act of political protest, a way for the liberal left, so viciously vilified and attacked by establishment conservatives of the late '40s and '50s, to strike back at some of the bedrock institutions of American society. Throughout the massive, labyrinthine, convoluted theories, they had the opportunity to try and demonize the military, law enforcement, the intelligence community, big business and capitalism itself, all the while wrapping themselves in the flag and claiming they were doing their patriotic American duty to bring the murderers of the president to justice.

But the Kennedy conspiracy theories took a foothold in the greater American consciousness because of the increasing turbulence of the decade. Distrust of the establishment had become mainstream with every passing year. Suspicion about the motives of the military, the intelligence services, the police and the FBI was no longer for fringe anti–American radicals.

Fueling this cultural atmosphere of suspicion and distrust were more assassinations and the escalation of the Vietnam War. With the deaths of Malcolm X in 1965, then Martin Luther King and Robert Kennedy in 1968, it looked like every liberal who advocated a profound, radical overhaul of the system was suddenly shot down before he was about to affect change. For the conspiratorially inclined, this was all too much of a coincidence. But nothing pushed America into disillusionment and suspicion more than the state of the war in Southeast Asia. Within a year of Kennedy's death, the Johnson administration dramatically increased the country's involvement in Vietnam. Although never declared by Congress, for all intents and purposes, the U.S. was at war. This fueled the suspicions and inspired ever more spectacular theories by those conspiracists who believed that Johnson himself was a part of the plot against Kennedy. Indeed, the conspiracy theorists charged, the military industrial complex had made a pact with Johnson, who was ready to do their bidding, and conspired to kill JFK, who was too pure and idealistic to ever go along with the designs of this cabal. The longer the Vietnam involvement wore on, the more opposition to the war increased. The opposition came from the very large generation of Baby Boomer teenagers and 20-somethings: The kids who stood the greatest chance of being drafted into the war had become its most outspoken and angry critics. These young people were the kids of mainstream Middle America. These were the kids of the average citizen growing outraged with the apparent failures of foreign policy and not a radical minority screaming "down with America" on the edges of society. The Baby Boomers, angry with the apparent failure of their parents' world, were open and receptive to the tenets of the new conspiracy movement that said that the real enemies of America were not on the outside, but within the system itself. Those among the Baby Boomers who were old enough to embark on careers in the media (journalism, the arts, TV and film) became conduits for the conspiracy theories to reach further into popular culture.

If the seeds of conspiracy theories are actual, *proven* instances of criminality and collusion in the highest corridors of power, then second to the Kennedy assassination, the Nixon White House did the most to inspire the conspiracy culture we still live in today. The Watergate scandal, the "Pentagon Papers" affair, and the subsequent Church Committee hearings proved to the country that men in positions of immense power (the military, the FBI, the CIA, all the way to the White House) had always regularly colluded and attempted to manipulate, obfuscate, bypass, and subvert laws in order to maintain power and further their own social and ideological agendas.

As most historians and Richard Nixon's numerous biographers have argued, Nixon's most self-destructive flaw was his overwhelming paranoia. Nixon had always believed that forces were allied to tear him down, to tarnish his reputation, to deny his accomplishments.

Even critics of his policies have conceded that Nixon might have gone down in history as one of the most successful presidents had he not allowed a series of paranoid decisions and secret programs initiated to protect himself from perceived enemies culminate in the Watergate burglary. It is almost darkly ironic that Nixon's undoing was rooted in the fact that he was nothing if not a supreme conspiracy theorist himself. In a mirror image of the conspiracy theory movement that had its genesis in the Kennedy assassination, Nixon also felt that there was a vast, organized "system" plotting to destroy him. Whereas the Kennedy conspiracists were always looking for evil right-wingers in positions of business and governmental power, Nixon saw himself besieged by the "Eastern liberal establishment." He believed that liberals in the media and old-moneyed, East Coast liberal political machines were conspiring to wreck his career and tarnish his legacy. His first vice-president, Spiro Agnew, in fact, had made media-bashing one of his standard talking points. Agnew argued that the media liked to foster cynicism and pessimism in the country by focusing only on the bad news and the failings of the government — particularly those of the Nixon administration. Labeling the media the "nattering nabobs of negativity" became his memorable catchphrase.

But, in many ways, Nixon did have legitimate grievances against the media and its liberal practitioners. Since 1960, when he ran against John F. Kennedy for the presidency, Nixon was always characterized as the dark, old-guard, old-fashioned counterpoint to the young, handsome, optimistic and glamourous Kennedy. The standard media template for the race between the two men had always been a comparison between the young, exciting, and charismatic Kennedy and the old, awkward, paranoid Nixon. Nixon's service on the House Un-American Activities Committee in 1948 had made him a figure of disdain for liberals in the news media. Nixon had been cast as a figure of the establishment, everything paranoid, repressive and reactionary, whereas Kennedy was youth, change, and hope personified. Some of the media's disdain for Nixon hurt him badly when an erroneous suggestion for his preparation for an NBC-televised debate with Kennedy amounted to nothing less than the sabotage of Nixon's performance. A leak from NBC had suggested to Nixon that he wear a light-colored suit for the debate so he could be seen well enough against a dark background. The set decoration, in fact, turned out to be light in color, causing Nixon to nearly vanish off most TV sets. Kennedy, on the other hand, had been given proper information about how to dress to look his best for the cameras. This, compounded by the fact that Nixon looked stiff and uncomfortable before the cameras, had decimated his impression and the content of his message for an overwhelming majority of TV viewers. Opinion polls suggested that a vast majority of TV viewers believed that Kennedy had won the debate. Most of those who listened on the radio, however, concluded that Nixon had given the more substantive answers, made the better arguments, and won the debate. From 1960 and onward, though, television had fundamentally altered the rules of politics. In Nixon's calculation, however, this new medium had provided a new outlet for the East Coast establishment to use a new set of tricks and image-manipulations to hurt him. What had stung Nixon throughout most of his political career, however, and certainly during his contest with Kennedy, was the fact that he embodied much more of the populist values liberals purported to champion. If the liberals said they understood the little guys and the working people, Nixon, the son of a grocery store and gas station owner, growing up in poverty, had a truer connection to those working people than the debonair Kennedy, born to status and privilege. Nevertheless, history and timing had repeatedly dealt Nixon bad cards. His first attempt at the presidency had been undone by the emergence of the image and charisma politics of the television age. During his second run, he had been categorized as a representative of the conservative, reactionary old guard again, someone who had merely lucked into the White House after Robert Kennedy's assassination. Some liberal pundits characterized Nixon's 1968 victory as something akin to the Nazis marching into Paris. For the insecure Nixon, these slights by the media were signs of a larger, more insidious conspiracy by the Eastern establishment to yet again deny him his true place in history.[23]

Perceived conspiracy, however, begat real conspiracies. They were founded on Nixon's compulsion to stop leaks to the press by his administration, as well as leaks about government problems, scandals and failures at all costs. His administration, Nixon was convinced, after all, was under siege by the media and the liberal establishment. Secret funds had been set up by the White House to employ investigators, many of them former as well as acting intelligence agents, to hunt down and suppress all unauthorized communication between government officials and the media. Many have charged that the hunt for government whistle blowers included intimidation through threats of blackmail and threats of violence.[24]

The first time this war between the Nixon White House and whistle blowers came to public attention was during the court battle over the attempted publication of the Pentagon Papers by *The New York Times* in 1971. What had been characterized by free-speech and media scholars as a constitutional crisis over a battle between the First Amendment and national security secrets was initiated by whistle-blower Daniel Ellsberg.[25] An analyst working for the Rand Corporation, Ellsberg had attempted to leak copies of a secret 1968 Defense Department study of the U.S. involvement in Southeast Asia between the end of World War II and 1967. The report, formally titled *United States-Vietnam Relations, 1945–1967: A Study Prepared by the Department of Defense* and dubbed the Pentagon Papers during the ensuing scandal, detailed a series of miscalculations and mistakes in policy-making that had blown up into the ongoing Vietnam quagmire. The study revealed that many in the military believed a full-scale involvement in Vietnam would turn into a war the U.S. could not win. Nevertheless, the escalation of the fighting continued. Moreover, the study also made embarrassing revelations about the Pentagon's disdain for public opinion and a callous belief that a gullible country could be manipulated into supporting the war no matter how long Washington chose to be involved. What would further fuel the outrage of anti-war activists was the report's detailing of how cavalierly unconcerned the Pentagon was with the immense body count American forces were bound to suffer during a protracted war. Ellsberg, who had initially supported the war and even served a two-year tour of duty in Vietnam as a Marine, also became convinced that the war was an enormous, deadly folly. He decided that the official Defense Department study spelling out this fact needed to be made public. Ellsberg, however, then incurred the wrath of the Nixon administration.[26]

White House lawyers sued to have the *Times* stopped from publishing the Pentagon Papers. They then threatened Ellsberg with prosecution. At one point, Ellsberg went on the run to evade arrest. On June 30, 1971, however, the Supreme Court ruled in favor of the *Times* and allowed the publication. Ellsberg, after turning himself in to authorities, did not have to serve any prison time and he was not charged with any crimes. During the time the *New York Times* lawyers and the government's prosecutors fought in the courts, the Nixon investigators were out to wreck Ellsberg's reputation. At one point, they stole medical records from his psychiatrist in an attempt to paint him as mentally unstable and unreliable.[27]

But these clandestine operations against Nixon's enemies—carried out by a group of "Plumbers" tasked with fighting the leaks and whistle-blowing—turned out to be much bigger and more extensive than Ellsberg's pursuit and harassment. People on Nixon's enemies list — including prominent figures in the media, Washington legislators, and even entertainers — had been routinely spied on. Wiretapping laws had been broken trying to keep track of, blackmail, silence, and intimidate Nixon's "Eastern liberal establishment" conspirators. In fact, other than the select inner circle of White House Plumbers, FBI and CIA agents had often been recruited into the domestic spying activities against Nixon's enemies.[28] Conspiracy theorists have charged that CIA agents, paid from the White House's secret funds, had contracted Cuban expatriates to hunt down and kill Ellsberg at one point.

The irony of the Pentagon Papers scandal, and yet another testament to Nixon's irrational, impulsive paranoia, was the fact that the Defense Department study was much more critical of the Kennedy and Johnson administrations than his own. For one, the study detailed how ill-conceived and unrealistic John F. Kennedy's plans for getting the U.S. involved in Vietnam were. It also detailed how the Johnson administration repeatedly deceived the American public about military operations The documents fully disclosed how Johnson had ordered bombings in Laos and Special Forces incursions into North Vietnam before admitting these operations to the public. The Pentagon Papers also described detailed plans drawn at Johnson's behest for a full-scale invasion of Vietnam. Again, publicly he swore that the U.S. role would never go beyond the advising and assistance of the South Vietnamese. A full invasion, Johnson also told the American public, was never even considered and never planned for.[29]

Nevertheless, Nixon's war on leaks attempted to suppress the Pentagon Papers, even if it took the fight all the way to the Supreme Court. As Oval Office tape recordings would later show, however, Nixon's fervent motivation was in great part spurred by the national atmosphere of cynicism and distrust that had been building throughout the 1960s. Even if the Pentagon Papers were greatly critical of his predecessors, including the most popular president of the 1960s, the publishing of the Defense Department study stood to have a general corrosive effect on the public's trust in the government. In one of the tape recordings, Nixon's chief of staff, H.R. Haldeman, pinpoints the greatest effect on the national psyche Ellsberg's whistle-blowing stood to create:

> To the ordinary guy, this is a bunch of gobbledygook. But out of the gobbledygook comes a very clear thing: You can't trust the government; you can't believe what they say; and you can't rely on their judgment. And the implicit infallibility of presidents, which has been an accepted thing in America, is badly hurt by this, because it shows that people do things the president wants to do even though it's wrong, and the president can be wrong.[30]

But if Richard Nixon's driven campaign against critics of the government, the military, and the war in Vietnam was spurred by a misguided attempt to counter a national mood of distrust and cynicism, its results were pure irony on an epic scale. When Nixon's fall came, its true cultural impact was a disillusionment Americans would feel for decades to come. The Kennedy assassination had merely gotten many to start considering that all might not have been well in America. Whether Kennedy was actually killed by a conspiracy or a left-wing conspiracy culture merely trumpeted an erroneous and whimsical theory, the fact remains that November 22, 1963, made many Americans just a little more suspicious and wary. But the Nixon administration's demise just confirmed that they were right to have been suspicious. Enemies, the country concluded in the wake of Nixon's downfall, truly were within.

The interesting fact to this day, however, is that the motivation behind the burglary of the Democratic National Committee's offices in the Watergate complex is not quite clear. Nixon's 1972 reelection appeared to be all but a sure thing and there was very little strategic information to be gained by breaking into the Democrats' headquarters. Historians conclude that it was but a part of the rampant criminality of the "Plumbers" and investigators spying on and discrediting Nixon's enemies. Just as they had burglarized the offices of Ellsberg's psychiatrist, so they were determined to keep tabs on Nixon's opponents, even if it meant going after the very top of the Democratic Party.[31] This time, however, they got caught and the results were catastrophic not just for the Nixon administration, but the country's self-image.

As a result of the Watergate scandal and the resultant revelations of the widespread misuses of the powers of the country's various investigative and intelligence agencies, in 1974 Frank Church convened the Senate Select Committee to Study Governmental Operations with Respect to Intelligence Activities. For conspiracy theorists, its findings were a boon. A long history of the CIA's assassinations and assisted coups in foreign countries was made public. The agency's anti–Castro activities under the Kennedy administration were also exposed. Furthermore, the use of the FBI to systematically spy on, infiltrate, and damage domestic radical organizations was laid out for more public scrutiny. The Commission detailed the Bureau's Counter Intelligence Program (COINTELPRO) project where agents were tasked with gathering information on, then disrupting and damaging, these extremist political movements. Groups like the Black Panthers, the National Association for the Advancement of Colored People, Students for a Democratic Society, the Weathermen and various left-wing anti-war and anti-government organizations had been targeted between 1956 and 1971 for such surveillance and disruption. Officially, the program was justified as an attempt to monitor potentially violent and anti–American domestic groups. To be even-handed in the assessment of COINTELPRO, it had also monitored and infiltrated the Ku Klux Klan, the American Nazi party, and various other hate groups.[32] But the program's primary thrust had always been the left. One of the most bizarre revelations of the Church Committee, however, was the CIA's MK ULTRA program. A study of mind-control and consciousness-altering drugs, MK ULTRA was a partnership between the CIA and various universities where student subjects were unknowingly given doses of LSD.[33] But for the post–Kennedy conspiracy movement, forever on the lookout for the right-wing master plan to destroy all progressive challenges to the status quo, the findings of the Church Committee were but a reaffirmation of their deepest suspicions. For the average American, on the other hand, the entire Watergate affair was merely a lesson in the fact that no one in a position of power could be trusted. As the demise of the Nixon administration reverberated through the culture, the old-fashioned notions that America's civil servants were idealistic heroes and *servants* of the people had become a quaint fantasy.

For those given to skepticism of a different sort, the lessons of Watergate and the Church Committee might have been quite different. For some, the wild conspiracy theorizing still appeared to be unfounded. The anti-conspiracy skeptic could always point out that even with an examination of the CIA's and FBI's clandestine activities throughout the Cold War, no evidence of the Kennedy conspiracy turned up. What Watergate and the Church investigation proved, the anti-conspiracists argue, was the fact that no secret in Washington can stay hidden for long. If the sort of epic cabals the Kennedy conspiracy theorists usually posit exist, how could the Nixon administration come apart so thoroughly? Why weren't the president's two most dogged pursuers, *Washington Post* reporters Bob Woodward and Carl Bernstein, simply assassinated and made to look like the victims of some type of accident? How could one man like Daniel Ellsberg deal such a tremendous blow to the government? Furthermore, logic would also dictate that if shadowy forces running everything could eliminate a president, they could surely do away with a threatening senator like Church. Corruption is the dark side of power, certainly, conspiracy critics always argue, yet there is a difference between common criminality and the sort of operatic-scale reality-manipulation that conspiracy theorists are always looking for. The Cold War had seen plenty of zealotry, conspiracy critics contend, and those who hunger for power will always break rules and abuse their positions of privilege. Yet Watergate, the Pentagon Papers, and the Church Committee episodes merely demonstrate bad judgment, bad policy-making, and common criminality. For the anti-conspiracist, there is hardly a smoking gun proving the existence of "one grand cabal that runs everything."

Naturally, for these skeptical counter-arguments the conspiracy theorists have an even more suspicious response. Certainly the Church Committee didn't find any hints of the Kennedy conspiracy, they argue, because JFK's killers were too powerful, too well funded, and too well organized to be discovered. An even more grandiose iteration of this theory is the one that states that Watergate and the discoveries of the old domestic spying and COINTELPRO secrets were just tidbits released by the grand cabal *on purpose*. Perhaps COINTELPRO had to be discovered, Nixon had to be destroyed, and Church had to run his investigations to discredit the conspiracists and hide that fact that there was something "much bigger" being hidden by the government.

As far as the rest of the 1970s were concerned, paranoia lingered and conspiracy theories found many minds to be fertile grounds for growth and nourishment. Then in 1979, Congress once again gave conspiracy theorists a reason to celebrate when it reopened the John F. Kennedy investigation with the House Select Committee on Assassinations (HSCA). The results were different from the findings of the Warren Commission and just as controversial. Using state-of-the-art audio analysis equipment to listen to the recording of a police channel left open during the assassination, the HSCA's investigators concluded that a fourth shot might have been fired in Dealey Plaza. Since only three bullets had left Oswald's rifle, this could only suggest a second shooter and a conspiracy. Ultimately, the conspiracy theorists were not entirely satisfied with this official endorsement of their position. The HSCA also concluded that there was no evidence to prove that the CIA, the FBI, the Secret Service, or the Dallas Police Department were a part of any conspiracy to kill Kennedy. Essentially, what was left by the HSCA was the opportunity for the conspiracy culture to keep growing and fostering more and more theories. The HSCA didn't really provide any answers, only more questions.

The ongoing state of cynicism and paranoia would be seen for decades in entertainment where the most common politicians were the crooked ones, where corruption reigned, everyone was out for themselves, and idealism by the wealthy and powerful was merely a public façade that only the most gullible would every believe. Such cynical entertainment, writers, producers, and filmmakers would explain, was merely a reflection of the real world.

Something Much Bigger

Although assassinations and political chicanery fed a new era of conspiratorial thinking in the 1960s and '70s, this was also a time when unexplained phenomena became entangled in all the accusations of government lies. The UFO cover-up movement flourished, with believers claiming that secret military and intelligence organizations were hiding the truth about ongoing contact with extraterrestrials. A closer look at the history of the UFO movement, however, reveals a phenomenon of conspiratorial thinking that is actually much older and more complex than that of assassination theorists.

UFO historians generally point out that on June 24, 1947, "flying saucers" entered the popular lexicon with Kenneth Arnold's sighting of nine unidentified flying objects over Mount Rainer, Washington. The story became a worldwide media sensation less than a month later, on July 3, with the alleged crash of an alien space craft in Lincoln County, New Mexico, close to the town of Roswell. But alien visitations, "UFOlogists" contend, is much older. Contact with otherworldly beings, they argue, has been going on for much of human history. At least as they could be observed in the late nineteenth and twentieth centuries, alien appearances have always been coming in waves, with time periods spanning several years when UFO sightings are disturbingly abundant; they call these periods "flaps." One of the earliest media-documented flaps happened in the late nineteenth century. A more recent one took place in the 1950s and 1960s, when Hollywood and television was ready to take advantage of it.

The first flap, starting in the 1880s and lasting roughly until the turn of the twentieth century, seems to have been concentrated around the West Coast and the southwestern states, although not *all* the sightings were confined to those areas. Hundreds of eyewitnesses in California, Arizona, New Mexico, and Texas reported mysterious "airships" that scarcely resembled the hot air balloons of the time. People as far away as Nebraska and even Kansas made the same types of sightings. The eyewitnesses described flying machines that sound in line with the sort of advanced, mechanized dirigibles in Jules Verne's novels, or perhaps today's steampunk science fiction. While most of the mystery aircraft were said to have a general balloon-like or cigar-like shape, they were also said to have been outfitted with mechanical devices that sound decades ahead of their time. The craft were said to have been able to emit powerful rays of light and they were highly maneuverable by propellers and loud, humming, throbbing and buzzing engines. Many airships, according to the witnesses, were entirely made of metal and they had round portholes through which human crews could be seen surveying the ground. Other airships were fitted with wings, fin structures and stabilizers. Decades later, such structures would be standard on large, metal-skinned, hydrogen-filled dirigibles. In the 1880s and 1890s, however, the appearance of such machines is unexplainable.[34]

Modern UFOlogists generally tend to explain the Victorian-era airship sightings as an early UFO flap. The culture of the time, they argue, had no conception of space travel and extraterrestrial life, so they would not attempt to explain these mystery machines as interplanetary visitors. In fact, most of the theorizing at the time argued that the airships were the products of various reclusive inventors and lone geniuses working in hidden labs and secluded factories constructing these fantastically advanced machines. At the height of world industrialization, the lone inventor theory was a perfectly fitting product of the culture. Jules Verne's own pioneering science fiction literature employed similar plots. His most iconic creation, Captain Nemo, was a reclusive genius, withdrawing from civilization and planning on unleashing his wrath on the rest of the world with the aid of highly advanced marine technology. In his 1886 novel *Robur the Conqueror*, Verne created the enigmatic inventor Robur, who stirred fear when unwitting people caught glimpses of his mystery aircraft flying through the night sky. Verne's descriptions of Robur's heavier-than-air flying machines sounded uncannily like the real eyewitness descriptions of the unidentified airships. When the mystery airships began appearing in the skies over Europe in 1913, some speculation claimed the craft were experimental war machines of aggressive countries and political regimes. Often suspicious fingers were pointed at Germany. Some UFO researchers today, though, argue that the rogue inventor theory was the most fitting explanation in a culture that could not conceive of realistic interplanetary travel. These researchers point out that the elongated dirigible or cigar shape of the airships is very similar to the elongated UFOs that so many witnesses claim to see today. The powerful spotlights on these ships also resemble modern UFOs, and some of the airships were reported to have flown through the air at hundreds of miles per hour. Clearly, no propeller-driven balloons have ever been capable of flying that fast. There could have been no Earthly genius in any hidden lab anywhere in the world in the late nineteenth century who could have built the devices the eyewitnesses reported seeing.

The mystery of the steampunk UFOs lingers because the vast majority of the sightings do seem to describe devices that sound low-tech to modern sensibilities. While some of the reports detail aircraft traveling at the speeds of modern jets and rockets, many of the witnesses give clear descriptions of rattling propellers, airships floating about rather slowly, and the craft clearly bolted and riveted together by individual segments of metal plates. If UFOs are, as their believers claim, interplanetary spacecraft, the UFOs of the airship era appear to be the Model-T forerunners of today's sleek, high-end sports-model UFOs. While these turn-of-the-century machines are indeed something out of the ordinary, they are clearly not the same type of flying machines reported by late twentieth and twenty-first century UFO eyewitnesses. If, as believers claim, the flying saucers Kenneth Arnold saw or the machine that crashed in Roswell, New Mexico, are real, the airships of the Victorian era are not the same class of aircraft. The steampunk UFOs, again, *if* they are real and not figments of people's imaginations, mistakes, misidentifications, or simple puckish practical jokes, are entirely different devices constructed by different parties for much different and ultimately inexplicable ends.

Perhaps the only theory that might reconcile the slow, sputtering, propeller-driven Victorian airships and the sleek twentieth century UFOs might be the argument advanced by a small handful of anomaly-researchers like French astrophysicist Jacques Vallée and American writer John Keel for a "psychosocial" explanation of the UFO phenomenon. This point of view argues that UFOs are much stranger and much more fantastic than interplanetary spacecraft. Vallée expounded on this theory in four books, *Passport to Magonia* (1960), *The Invisible College* (1975), *Messengers of Deception* (1979), and *Revelations* (1991). He argued that it was highly unlikely, if not impossible, that aliens from another planet could bridge the vast distances of space to travel to Earth. This argument is in line with the most basic of skeptical retorts to the possibility of UFOs being spacecraft from alien planets. Vallée, however, does believe that the UFO phenomenon is real and that it represents contact with extra*dimensional* entities rather than extra*terrestrial* ones. Keel, most famous for his examination of the 1966 "Mothman" phenomenon of West Virginia, concurs with this theory in his books *The Mothman Prophecies* (1975) and *UFOs: Operation Trojan Horse* (1970). UFOs, according to Vallée and Keel, involve contact with beings from alternate dimensions. Mankind, the theory argues, has always had contact with extradimensional phenomena, except in the past it was interpreted as contact with faeries, demons, and such supernatural entities of folklore and legend. Reality is but a creation of language, and language is but a reflection of cultural perspectives and experiences. The extradimensional beings always seem to manifest themselves in ways that any culture would be capable of comprehending and talking about. For a society steeped in superstition, the extradimensional beings might appear as angels, demons and faeries. For a society in the middle of mass industrialization, the phenomenon looks like the kind of propeller-driven airships that rogue geniuses could have cobbled together in some secret lair; and for the people of the twentieth century, capable of understanding the concept of alien planets and alien civilizations, the phenomenon becomes interplanetary spaceships and extraterrestrial aliens. Moreover, both Vallée and Keel point out that the extraterrestrial hypothesis has always been founded on rather tenuous logic. Basically, adherents of this hypothesis have argued that UFOs are *probably* spaceships from another planet because they *have* to be. The first articulation of the hypothesis came from one of two factions of scientists working on the first government-sponsored research project on the UFO phenomenon. Convened on December 30, 1947, and code-named Project Sign, it was a study group ran by the U.S. Air Force out of Wright Field in Dayton, Ohio. Quickly enough, the project members fell into two camps, with one advocating the position that UFOs were either misidentifications of natural phenomena or hoaxes and lies. The other camp argued that the strange craft had come from other planets. This extraterrestrial hypothesis was founded on the reasoning that if the unexplainable saucers, balls of light, cigars, anomalous triangles, and phantom lights were unlike technology anyone could construct on Earth at that time, then the only other logical explanation for their existence was that they *must* have been constructed on another planet.[35]

But it's also interesting to note that even the Victorian-era airship flap has some of the vague shadings of conspiratorial thought. The mystery craft are the products of some secretive cabal that works alone and in seclusion. The cabal is headed by some sort of a genius inventor who commands vast resources that let him run an enterprise producing technology far ahead of the rest of the "open" and accountable scientific establishment of the time. Moreover, the secret-inventor theory has a built-in suggestion that this cabal could possibly exercise immense power over the rest of society if it chose to do so. This power, of course, need not always be benevolent. But conspiracy theories are almost always founded on the notion that conspirators, those who work alone, in silence, in the shadows, are up to no good. Someone who can fly about the sky in ultra-advanced aircraft, reason would argue, can just as well turn those aircraft into weapons. Jules Verne's secret-inventor fiction articulated the fear lurking just beneath the airship origin theories. His Nemo character, for example, was a megalomaniac who used his genius, wealth, and power to turn his advanced technology against the world.

As the anomalous aerial phenomena of the late nineteenth and twentieth centuries gained vast legions of followers, so too did conspiracy theories get enmeshed in the theories of where these phenomena came from. Not only were the mystery aircraft real and of fantastic origins to phenomena believers, but there were always people in positions of power who know about them and kept quiet. Those who knew the secrets, according to the airship enthusiasts and the budding UFO communities, always stayed mum for some sort of personal gain. The mystery machines, many conspiracy theorists argued, were controlled by a secretive brotherhood that operated clandestinely to amass wealth, rule the world, maintain the status quo, and control and exploit the masses.

Another notable pre–1947 UFO flap was said to have taken place during World War II, when numerous American fighter and bomber pilots claimed their aircraft were being routinely tailed by mysterious flying objects. Many of these UFOs were described as either fitted with multicolored lights or they appeared to be made entirely of glowing balls of light. The mystery flyers could also travel at speeds impossible to achieve by any aircraft of the time and they often executed turns and complex maneuvers that no human being could have survived. The UFOs were dubbed "foo-fighters" (some attribute the origins of the term to a tag-line from a pre-war comic strip). As impossible as their maneuvers seemed, the Army's 8th Air Force soon tried to determine their exact nature. Since any mysterious flying object showing an interest in American planes could have been a secret Axis weapon, the investigation was warranted and critical. Unfortunately, the Army Air Force study could produce no conclusive answers. Hypotheses for the nature of the strange phenomenon ranged from ball lightning to St. Elmo's fire to illuminated ice crystals in the high atmosphere to airmen's combat fatigue and hallucinations.[36] For the most suspicious of conspiracy theorists, this was just the beginning of the government's sleight of hand and official policy of obfuscation when it came to anomalous aircraft.

The UFO phenomenon, however, produced its most significant flap in the postwar period. In the 1940s and '50s, the time was ripe for the mass media to latch onto the flying saucer craze sweeping the nation. But the most interesting aspect of the postwar UFO period involved the people who first started making charges of conspiracies and cover-ups. The backgrounds of these conspiracy theorists complicate the political aspects of the UFO movement. Far from being anti-establishment outsiders and radicals, the first UFO conspiracists came from within the system. The first people to accuse the government of hiding the truth about the UFO phenomenon were in the military.

In 1947, the U.S. government decided to be quick in responding to the UFO phenomenon because in the wake of the Kenneth Arnold sightings, a proverbial army of other UFO witnesses were emboldened to go public with their own tales of encountering mysterious saucer-shaped, triangular and cigar-shaped aircraft. Moreover, the media were quick to listen to these people and give them a forum for their bizarre tales. The sum total of these stories, Washington decided, was not good for the national psyche during the height of the Cold War, when the nation was already on edge over the looming threat of the Soviet Union and communist infiltration. Moreover, the government was not happy with the fact that all the UFO sightings basically suggested that extremely advanced foreign aircraft were invading America's skies—aircraft so hi-tech as to render anything in the U.S. military's arsenal completely useless against the intruders. More than just defense, the U.S. government and the military in the late '40s and '50s saw itself as being in the business of *reassurance*. Not only did the government build and operate fighters, submarines, nuclear missiles and tanks, but they needed to convince Americans that its military machines were the best in the world, its soldiers were the most competent, honorable and brave. For the U.S. to weather the Cold War, its citizens needed to feel certain that their system was superior, its defenses strong and impenetrable. One of the most important jobs of Washington in this period, therefore, was to make sure that Americans could sleep well at night. Lurid and paranoid tales of strange aircraft that the American military machine could never hope to match undermined this mission of reassurance. To deal with the problem, the Army Air Force instituted Project Sign.[37]

The investigators of Project Sign had their hands full as the sightings increased through the latter years of the decade. One of the most spectacular incidents appeared to produce the first death related to a UFO sighting on the early afternoon of January 7, 1948. It involved Kentucky Air National Guard pilot Captain Thomas F. Mantell, Jr., whose plane crashed during the pursuit of an unidentified object. Mantell and two other Guard pilots had been asked to try and follow an object that had been reported throughout several towns in Kentucky and even the control tower at Godman Air Force Base. Mantell's group eventually found what they described as an enormous metallic object ascending higher and higher into the atmosphere. The pilots quickly gave chase; Mantell's companions eventually broke off their pursuit as the UFO appeared to climb past 30,000 feet. The F-51s flown by the Guardsmen were not equipped with oxygen. As a result, Mantell eventually passed out and his plane spiraled downward into a fiery crash.[38]

The Air Force's accounting of the event and Project Sign's official conclusion was that Mantell and his group were chasing the planet Venus, distorted by atmospheric optical conditions. UFOlogists skeptical of the official conclusion would for years dispute that explanation, countering with the argument that it's hard to believe so many ground observers could mistake a star in the daylight sky with a saucer-shaped metallic object. The UFOlogists, in fact, would quote various witnesses, including former Air Force Captain James F. Duesler, who claimed to have seen an aircraft that resembled a "rotating inverted ice cream cone" with a glowing reddish light on its underside. Moreover, several of the eyewitnesses had reported that the UFO often changed directions, as if under intelligent and deliberate control, and even stopped in a midair hover. Duesler claimed to have seen the object hovering over Goldman Airfield. To further damage the Venus explanation, UFO researchers proved that at the time of Mantell's death, Venus was no higher than 33 degrees above the horizon. Thus, they argued, it would have been impossible for Mantell and the other pilots to see the object climbing high above their heads. In 1948 already, Project Sign investigators felt that the UFO proponents' dismantling of the Venus explanation was so well-argued and backed by data that they revised their conclusion. Their new conclusion: What witnesses on the ground and Mantell saw were Skyhook balloons, devices used by the military to conduct high altitude atmospheric testing. The reflection of the sun off the silvery balloon's surface could give the observer the impression of a large metallic sphere. Although the Skyhook balloon stands as the explanation for the Mantell crash, UFOlogists continue retorting that even the balloon reflection argument does not account for the maneuvers reported by eyewitnesses, or the very specific description of the UFO as an inverted ice cream cone with a glowing red light.[39]

It should be added, however, that one major UFO incident of 1947 — if not *the* major UFO incident — was actually not a point of interest for Sign. The Army Air Force's dismissal of the Roswell crash had immediately let it disappear off the media's radar. Over three decades later, authors Charles Berlitz and William Moore wrote a book about the incident, and the question of crashed flying saucers became a central issue for UFOlogists.

But work for the Project Sign members quickly became divisive and controversial. All agreed that among the hundreds of UFO reports, a large majority proved to be nothing more than the misidentification of mundane atmospheric phenomena, stars, or conventional aircraft seen under adverse conditions; but a small yet significant number of cases defied explanation. In fact, the unexplained cases had been so well documented — usually by multiple reliable eyewitnesses, ground traces left by the UFO, or radar confirmation by civilian and military radar operators — that they caused a contentious rift among the Sign investigators. One group remained convinced that all UFOs, even the unexplained ones, were *probably* either cases of misidentification or — as a worst-case national security scenario — advanced Soviet spy planes. The opposing camp, however, argued the case for extraterrestrials.

Before Sign was shut down in 1949, its findings, and the state of the opposing conclusions reached by the pro-extraterrestrial faction of the investigators, had to be reported to the Air Force chief of staff, General Hoyt S. Vandenberg. In a move that galvanized conspiracy theorists for decades, Vandenberg reportedly ordered the extraterrestrial hypothesis section of the Top Secret report burned. The U.S. government, Vandenberg allegedly declared, would never go public with the conclusion that alien spacecraft were invading its skies and that these aliens possessed technology above and beyond anything the military could guard against. These allegations, again, did not come from the sort of radical fringe of conspiracy theorists inspired by the Kennedy assassination. They were written by Air Force intelligence officer Edward J. Ruppelt, a former investigator for Project Sign and the temporary head of what would be the third major government investigation into UFOs, Project Blue Book. In 1956, Ruppelt wrote the book *The Report on Unidentified Flying Objects* about how he had become convinced of the alien nature of UFOs and how he has seen the military and the U.S. government trying to discredit the extraterrestrial hypothesis.

In total, between 1947 and 1969, the Air Force had conducted or commissioned six separate studies of UFOs, or at least six they publicly admitted to. Most of the criticism of these efforts would claim that the studies were an attempt by the Air Force to prove that UFOs were no more than lies, mistakes or hallucinations. In other words, the government was going out of its way, according to the critics, many of whom were members of these projects, to cajole and force its investigators *not* to be objective.

Once Project Sign was closed, it was replaced by Project Grudge, which, critics like Ruppelt and astronomer J. Allen Hynek claimed, was as far from an objective, scientific investigation of the phenomenon as one could get. According to Hynek, one of the most prestigious scientists associated with the government's UFO investigations and the Air Force's *chief scientific adviser*, Grudge was less science and more of a public relations campaign by the government. Its real objective was to convince the media that UFOs did not exist. As Hynek had publicly explained, Project Grudge was so disingenuous in its research methodology that all of its investigators were told that if any UFO eyewitness ever used words and phrases like "similar to a balloon" or "looked like a star" or "resembled a cloud," or "lightning" or "plane," their stories immediately needed to be categorized as being nothing more than a balloon, or star, and so forth.[40]

Although Project Blue Book started out as an objective assessment of UFO reports under Ruppelt, the endeavor quickly turned into a Grudge-style PR campaign soon after his departure in 1953. That year, a panel of five scientists—usually referred to as the Robertson panel after its chief, physicist H.P. Robertson — was convened to analyze the Blue Book data and issue recommendations for further action. Openly hostile to the extraterrestrial hypothesis, the Robertson panel recommended an aggressive debunking campaign aimed at convincing the media not to give any more credence to the stories by UFO witnesses.[41]

A somewhat more extraterrestrial-hypothesis-friendly report came in 1952 when the Air Force commissioned a study of more Blue Book data by the Columbus, Ohio–based think tank, the Battelle Memorial Institute. The report, named Project Stork, used the statistical chi-square test to present that all the UFO reports classified as "unexplained" could not possibly be the same as the "explained" reports. Thus, UFO–debunkers to the contrary, the Stork conclusion was that there was no statistical probability that the unexplained sightings could still be expected to be no more than mundane atmospheric phenomena. To the chagrin of UFOlogists, the Stork conclusions were used to write and release *Project Blue Book Special Report 14*, yet another argument against extraterrestrials. According to scientists like Hynek, who called the report "utterly incredible," *Report 14* was a blatant misrepresentation of the Stork report and a "manipulation" of its data. Again, the most noteworthy aspect of *Report 14* was how loudly and thoroughly it was denounced by every independent scientist that examined it. As the scientific and academic worlds are notoriously conservative and reluctant to ever endorse any claims of revolutionary, paradigm-altering claims, their unqualified criticism of *Report 14*, which argued, in the words of Donald A. Quarles, secretary of the Air Force, that "no objects such as those popularly described as flying saucers have overflown the United States," is quite remarkable.[42]

But the most damaging report for the extraterrestrial hypothesis came in 1969 after the Air Force had contracted with the University of Colorado to assemble an independent study to analyze UFO data. Most of the project's outspoken critics, including Jacques Vallée and J. Allen Hynek, felt that the endeavor should not have carried the label "scientific." The project's top echelon, including its director, physicist Edward Uhler Condon, was openly hostile to the extraterrestrial hypothesis. Condon, in fact, had no qualms about publicly speaking of his opinion and what could only be described as a lack of objectivity when studying the UFO issue. When asked by the media about what he expected the study to find, he said, "It is my inclination right now to recommend that the government get out of this business. My attitude right now is that there is nothing to it." He then added, reportedly with a wry smile, "But I'm not supposed to reach a conclusion for another year."[43] Just as with the original Project Sign, the Condon committee's members had quickly formed hostile, contentious camps. While the group had its own extraterrestrial hypothesis camp, the project management, according to its critics, had been bound and determined from the outset to avoid giving the existence of aliens any credence. According to Hynek, the study's most grievous error was the use of a tiny data set, looking at only 90 UFO reports out of the thousands collected by the Air Force. Moreover, Hynek added before he was finally dropped by the Air Force as a consultant for his ever more outspoken endorsement of the extraterrestrial hypothesis, Condon and his like-minded colleagues had started the study with the predetermined notion that UFOs were nothing more than natural phenomena. "Scientific method!" Hynek wrote, "What sort of a scientific investigation is it that assumes the answers before starting?"[44] When two pro-alien members of the group had become too vocal in their position — and criticism of Condon — they were immediately fired. The end result of the Condon committee, however, was the cancellation of the military's only ongoing UFO study. On December 17, 1969, the Air Force used the committee's recommendation to cancel Project Blue Book.[45]

The ongoing public controversy and infighting among government officials tasked with studying the UFO phenomenon naturally fanned the flames of conspiratorial speculation. But again, the important twist to the UFO conspiracy movement is the fact that some of the most vocal conspiracy theorists are government, military, and scientific figures who were at some point members of these investigative efforts. For example, one of the most suspicious of conspiratorial assessments of all the contentious government UFO study projects came from Marine Corps Major Donald E. Keyhoe. Keyhoe, a UFO investigator and author of *Flying Saucers from Outer Space* (1953) and *Aliens from Space* (1973), said that all the blatantly biased negative reports from so many of the government's studies might be but a front, with all the serious investigations taking place in secret. While the government conducted rigged projects in public and aired conclusions debunking the extraterrestrial hypothesis, Keyhoe argued, it was also conducting secret studies because they knew full well that the unidentified flying objects were quite real and they were coming from another planet.

As for the reason for the cover-up, Keyhoe, like many UFO conspiracy theorists, believed that the government was afraid of a panic. At a time of Cold War posturing and the military's ongoing mission of *reassurance*, nationwide (or perhaps global) fear and panic would have ensued if the government admitted that it knew UFOs were of an alien origin. One of the reasons the government came to this conclusion, according to the conspiratorial point of view, was the previous panic in the wake of Orson Welles' 1938 *War of the Worlds* broadcast. In 1938, the country was, after all, in another state of high tension because of the global war. If such a moment of international tensions could cause so many people to come unhinged after listening to Welles' radio show, a world where two nuclear superpowers were poised for yet another world war could have had catastrophic effects on the national psyche.

As the decades passed, UFO conspiracy theories grew in complexity. The accusations of the theorists got more intricate, the threats they saw more gruesome, and the criminality of the conspirators more unconscionable. If aliens were behind the UFO phenomenon, it is logical to ponder the reasons for their interplanetary trip. Moreover, it is logical to wonder why the aliens never make themselves known, why they hover in the night skies, why they behave like ghostly, sneaky intruders and not make contact after traveling what must have been incredible distances through space. As UFO skeptics generally ask, why don't these aliens just land on the White House lawn or on top of the UN building and put an end to all the mystery? The more reasoned of the UFO believers generally argue that the UFO phenomenon represents something like an interplanetary version of an anthropologist conducting unobtrusive social research. They are hiding behind the proverbial bush, observing a primitive, hostile, warlike planet and taking notes for their extensive field reports. A great number of UFO sightings, after all, are close to military facilities. Some UFO theories suggest that the aliens, especially after the two world wars and the nuclear arms race of the Cold War, were curious about the levels of aggression and destruction humans are capable of. An interesting counterpoint to the alien-as-unobtrusive-social-scientist explanation was advanced by Jacques Vallée. Arguing that the alien beings are from a parallel dimension and not another planet, Vallée likens them to interdimensional psychologists. In his book *Revelations*, he argues that the beings behind the UFOs are hardly elusive. While they might not land on the White House lawn and make open contact, they do appear over crowded skies, they tail aircraft and they hover over military facilities. If anything, these beings might be conducting experiments in perception and mass planetary psychology. They very much *want* to be seen, they want to expose people to the unknown and study how we react when there is no clear, tangible explanation our current scientific theories and technology can offer. For other, more fearful UFO believers, however, the reason behind the alien visitations appeared to be much more sinister. Especially after the 1950s, they claimed that evidence was slowly emerging that the UFOnauts were up to something ghastly. When the evidence was not quite so solid to back the theory, many believers argued that the U.S. government and the rest of the world governments were conspiring to conceal the truth.

Aside from all the witnesses of anomalous lights and flying saucers in the skies, by the early 1950s people had come forward and claimed they made contact with UFOnauts. This soon turned into the next major phase of the UFO debate. Just like the very issue of UFO sightings, the contact phenomenon — or a "close encounter of the third kind" in J. Allen Hynek's classification of UFO experiences, with a close encounter of the first kind being a sighting and a close encounter of the second kind involving the discovery of some sort of a physical trace left by an alien craft[46] — would soon turn contentious and invite plenty of conspiratorial accusation of government lies and cover-ups. By the 1960s, the nature of the stories told by UFO contactees would start taking on a dark, menacing edge.

The first tale of a close encounter of the third kind was told in 1952 by George Adamski, a former hamburger stand operator and occult enthusiast. Overall, it was a whimsical story of meeting friendly, attractive, quite human-looking emissaries of peace and interplanetary brotherhood from Venus.[47] Adamski's story, on the one hand, very quickly built up a small community of UFO believers and people claiming similar experiences (the "contactee" movement) who enthusiastically spoke of the phenomenon as something positive for humankind and something the governments of the world should be embracing rather than hiding. On the other hand, Adamski's accounts of his experiences sounded so absurd to anyone with even the slightest critical-thinking abilities that just as many, if not more, criticized him as embraced him. For researchers like J. Allen Hynek and others within the scientific community who insisted that the UFO phenomenon needed to be studied according to the strictest empirical methods, Adamski actually did more harm than good. His tales, after all, sounded like they could have come from any pulp science fiction magazines of the time. He told of being visited by flying saucers from Venus and meeting human UFOnauts who looked like they could have been employed by any Earthly modeling agency. These Venusian men were all tall, athletic, and handsome. The women were all gorgeous, leggy, buxom blondes. Furthermore, these people repeatedly took Adamski on flying saucer rides to their home world, a spiritual and technological utopia. The aliens, part of an interplanetary community Adamski called the "Space Brothers," were supposedly unhappy with Earthlings' warlike ways. As Adamski explained, the aliens usually showed up around military facilities because they were concerned about the Cold War arms race and worried about the planet being destroyed in a nuclear holocaust. By the time the space race between the U.S. and the U.S.S.R. would be rushing ahead at full speed in the 1960s, contactees would claim that the peaceful aliens were worried about Earth people finally traveling into space and taking their hostilities and nuclear weapons with them. Contactees, Adamski claimed, were to be used by the aliens to spread the word of intergalactic brotherhood and to prepare the world for the time the extraterrestrials would make themselves known to all.

The logical holes in a story like this are obvious. If the Space Brothers were afraid that the Earth was on the brink of annihilation, why didn't they make themselves known right away? Would these aliens, who claimed to have studied human society for centuries, not realize the sort of skepticism Adamski's tales, as well as those of his fellow contactees, stood to inspire in the general population? Moreover, if the aliens were worried about the shock their appearance might have on the people of Earth and chose to use spokesmen instead of appearing in the open, why would they not use emissaries who could inspire a bit more confidence than a hamburger cook? In fact, some of the other "celebrities" of the contactee movement, people like Orfeo Angelucci, Truman Bethurum, Daniel Fry, Howard Menger, George Van Tassel, and George Hunt Williamson, came from equally unimpressive backgrounds. Angelucci worked on an assembly line in a Lockheed aircraft plant; Bethurum used to work on a road crew; Fry used to work various odd jobs before getting a position setting up instrumentation at the White Sands testing grounds; Menger was a sign painter; Van Tassel worked in a garage at one point, then at the same Lockheed plant as Angelucci; and Williamson used to be employed by a small publication dedicated to occult subjects. Why could these aliens not contact a prominent physicist or any other respected scientist, an intellectual of some type, a noted academic, a politician or a media figure?

To the chagrin of the very few scientists who did believe the UFO phenomenon represented the possibility of a very real contact with otherworldly intelligences, the contactee movement quickly degenerated into a circus sideshow throughout the '50s. The tales of travel to alien bases on the moon and other planets in the solar system sounded ever more incredible. After a while, many contactees did not even claim direct physical contact with the aliens, but told stories of psychic communication and information gleaned from cosmic spirits and spiritual guides.[48]

To those sociologically inclined, including UFO skeptics and debunkers, the contactee movement had all the aspects of a true, newly emerging religious and spiritual movement.[49] The aliens had replaced the gods of traditional religions, taking over as the new inscrutable, all-powerful deities who promised an afterlife in the cosmos for those Earthlings who had faith and lived correctly. Contactees like Adamski had become the new prophets. They gave their followers a set of commandments in the form of descriptions of the alien world, the alien laws and social structures the aliens lived under. If Earthlings could just live more like the aliens, the contactees claimed, they could ascend to a higher level of consciousness, live more fulfilling lives, and stand some chance of avoiding a horrifying future of global cataclysm. As a matter of fact, when it came to the issue of global catastrophes and nuclear wars that the aliens were so interested in, the contactee movement showed remarkable similarities to all the traditional apocalyptic fundamentalist religious movements throughout history. Much like fundamentalist Christian sects organized around the concept of the Rapture, Judgment Day, and Christ's return to Earth, the contactees preached a similar gospel of global destruction and the salvation of a faithful elect. While the Rapture–oriented Christian sects were waiting for a world cataclysm initiated by God to cleanse the Earth of sin and evil, the contactees were preparing for the day the world's shortsighted, self-destructive stupidity, aggression, and evil destroyed everything in a nuclear holocaust. As pollution, environmental damage, and global warming would start emerging as new threats to life on Earth by the later '60s, '70s, and beyond, contactees would tell tales of alien worries over environmental devastation rather than nuclear war. But in further parallels with apocalyptic religious movements, the contactees' dogma was also concerned with the salvation of the faithful and the destruction of the non-believers who refused to change their ways and adopt the commandments of the alien gospel. Whereas the Christian Rapture believers preached the importance of being born again and accepting Christ as the one and only savior, the contactees stressed the importance of belief in the aliens and the adoption of a new social system based on the alien's otherworldly societies. Those who can change their lives, the contactees preach, will soon be contacted by UFOs and spirited away from the Earth just before its destruction. This is a near-perfect parallel to the End of Times scenario advocated by the Rapture movements of fundamentalist Christianity. Interestingly, only about two decades after the contactee movement, Rapture — and end-times— oriented Christianity would also find a strong, mainstream surge in the United States. With the popularity of born again Christian fundamentalism, authors like Hal Lindsey and Carole C. Carlson in their best-selling *The Late, Great Planet Earth* (1970) warned against an imminent nuclear holocaust that only Fundamentalist Christians had a chance of escaping. This belief system also stressed an absolute acceptance of Christ as the savior and the exclusive salvation of the faithful. Just before the coming apocalypse, born again Christians, just like the faithful contactees, were going to be whisked away to the everlasting kingdom of God.

For those frustrated enough with the transformation of the UFO phenomenon into a New Age apocalyptic religious movement, the subtle handprints of conspiracy were all over the place. They claimed the absurdist contactee stories might just have been the result of a far-reaching government conspiracy to paint all UFO witnesses as unbalanced, fantasy-prone lunatics, and to make the phenomenon completely toxic for anyone in the mainstream scientific community. Many UFO believers had already told tales of threats and intimidation from government investigators. With the contactee movement, conspiracists claimed that the Washington and Pentagon attempts to discredit UFOlogy had shifted tactics from denial and intimidation to discrediting witnesses. By secretly funding and organizing one outlandish, over-the-top group of contactees after another, the conspiratorial argument goes, the government had efficiently crippled any serious chance of the world's scientific communities taking the UFO phenomenon seriously.[50]

Whereas UFOlogists and conspiracy theorists always claimed the authorities knew much more about the alien nature and agenda of the UFOs and Washington's chief modus operandi in dealing with the public was vigorous denial and the silencing of witnesses through threats and public ridicule, a declassified Central Intelligence Agency document paints an entirely different picture. According to this memo, the CIA — which had also started investigating UFOs in 1952, following a much publicized flurry of flying saucer reports over Washington, D.C. between July 13 and July 29 of that year — recommended that the government could use the phenomenon to its advantage when it came to keeping the research and development of hi-tech military hardware and weapons programs secret. The agency suggested that the military actually *spread* stories of UFO sightings in the vicinity of top secret aircraft and weapons testing sites. The reasoning was that the UFO reports could be effectively crazy-sounding smoke screens when it came to deceiving foreign spies trying to keep track of U.S. weapons tests. Any time a new, top-secret aircraft might be spotted by civilians, the CIA suggested, the military should immediately start leaking phony eyewitness testimonies of UFOs. The more outlandish these phony stories, the better, the agency suggested. The logic of this policy must have been assuming that the Soviets put no more credence into the existence of alien visitors than Washington. If so, Soviet spies operating in the U.S. would have been less likely to pay attention to top secret aircraft reports if said reports were veiled in the high absurdity of alien contact stories.[51]

The CIA report carries interesting implications for UFOlogy. It does give credence to some of the logic behind the accusations that the contactee movement was really manufactured by the U.S. government. The CIA, after all, recommended high strangeness when it came to UFO sightings going public. Perhaps the ultra-high strangeness of Adamski's contactees could have been seen as being useful in not just thwarting mainstream science from taking UFOlogy seriously, but also in thwarting the Soviets who were looking for certain experimental aircraft and weapons systems. What is also interesting in the report is the fact that the CIA acknowledges the UFO phenomenon and the agency does not seem to understand the nature of UFOs any better than anyone else in the world. The report implies that the CIA is completely clueless about the origins of these mystery craft, but, at most, they feel this phenomenon, whatever it may be, can still be exploited for counter-intelligence purposes. The report is an effective response to the most militant anti–UFO skeptics who have long claimed that the entire UFO phenomenon was but a government creation to cover up the development of top secret aircraft. According to the report, the UFO phenomenon clearly came *first* and the U.S. government took advantage of it.

If Adamski, the contactees, and the Space Brothers were but the garish, kitschy roadside attraction of the UFO phenomenon of the 1950s, the '60s ushered in tales of contact that were often harrowingly nightmarish. The 1960s brought forth the "abductees," people who claimed to have been taken aboard alien spacecraft against their will and subjected to painful, traumatizing medical procedures. The abductee phenomenon would eventually cement the popular culture's iconic image of alien visitors. These visitors, unlike Adamski's Venusians, did not look anything like fashion models. These aliens were small, spindly, fragile-looking, gnomish creatures. Somewhat humanoid, they were usually described as having parched, grayish skin, thin arms and legs protruding out of tiny bodies, and strikingly large heads with a thin slit of a mouth, no ears, tiny nasal openings, and enormous, black, often hypnotic, almond-shaped eyes.[52]

Although the abductees are still highly controversial, even among researchers who believe in the alien nature of the UFO phenomenon, they can be credited with *sounding* much more realistic than Adamski and his colleagues. The abductees' stories of being forcefully taken by strange-looking creatures sound much more like what one might reasonably expect an alien kidnapping to be like. Perhaps the most plausible aspect is the idea that these people are being forced to undergo something traumatic. If such inconceivably advanced creatures could travel to Earth from either across the gulf of space or through the barriers of dimensional reality, they might consider humans to be little more than lab rats to be used for observation and experimentation. The examination processes described by abductees often sound like their captors are treating them like the least complex of lab specimens squirming around in a petri dish. This certainly sounds a lot more believable than the contactee allegations of highly advanced aliens sitting down for friendly banter with the same Earthlings they found childishly primitive and uncivilized.

This is not to say that there are no similarities between some of the contactee claims and those of the abductees. To the chagrin of the most conservative UFOlogists, however, these similarities tend to be the most lurid and salacious of both categories of alien-contact stories. In both the tales told by contactees *and* abductees, the extraterrestrials seem to have a pointed interest in human reproduction and interspecies sexual experimentation. Several contactees, including such "luminaries" as Truman Bethurum, Elizabeth Klarer, and George Van Tassel, claim to have had sex with aliens. Bethurum said he carried on an extensive relationship with a beautiful female UFOnaut who regularly took him on flights throughout the solar system. Klarer said that her human-looking alien lover was a man named Akon and that she gave birth to his son while visiting his home world of Meton. Van Tassel, who claimed that he received regular psychic communications from a council of aliens ruling the solar system, said the aliens had revealed that Earth humans were the result of an intermarriage between Venusians and Earth apes. For those seeking to elevate UFOlogy to the level and respect of a scientific discipline, stories like these gave the phenomenon even stronger shadings of sensational pulp science fiction stories. Unfortunately, even the more plausible-sounding abductees had their own tales of alien sex.

The first account of a modern alien abduction came from Brazil. There, a twenty-three-year-old farmer name Antonio Villas-Boas claimed to have been taken by several small, humanoid creatures that emerged from a UFO he ran across while tilling his field. While on board the craft, he claimed to have been stripped naked and forced to have sex with a woman who looked almost entirely human, but for her slightly angular face and cat-like eyes. Villas-Boas claimed that after the copulation was finished, the woman left him, but not before pointing to her stomach and indicating that she had been impregnated with his seed. Villas-Boas, who later completed his education and earned a law degree, has never changed his story. He has also never profited from it in any way.

The first major abduction story to be publicized in the U.S. involved Betty and Barney Hill, a New Hampshire couple who had a run-in with the unexplained on their way home from a Canadian vacation on September 19, 1961. In what would become a recurring motif in abduction accounts, the Hills had no initial memories of their experience. All they could recall on their own was having driven through the desolate New Hampshire countryside at night and noticing a glowing object in the sky that might or might not have been following them. In fact, the Hills' last recollection of the event was a mild disagreement over whether it was a flying object of some sort or merely a star in the sky. Betty thought the object looked unusual, arguing that it appeared to be following them. Barney, on the other hand, preferred the more logical star hypothesis. Their memories ended there. The strangeness, however, began afterward. Upon arriving home, the Hills realized that they arrived two hours later than they should have. They could not account for the missing time. This phenomenon would be one of ongoing interest, debate, and contention for UFO enthusiasts for decades. Some of the more byzantine speculation about the missing time experiences has ranged from time warps to the abductees being snatched into alternate dimensions. The most "likely" explanation is that the kidnappings and experimentations had been erased from the memories of the victims.

Several other abductees have claimed to have been removed from their cars while en route to some destination. Usually people waiting for them are the first ones to notice that the abductee had taken a lot longer to get to the place they were going. But the Hills' experience following the discovery of the missing time included the discovery of unexplainable silver spots in their car, including the interior of the trunk. These spots would set compasses wildly spinning. Suspecting that something out of the ordinary had happened to them, the Hills filed a UFO report at Pease Air Force Base in Portsmouth, New Hampshire. Years later, UFO researchers discovered that radar operators at the base had tracked an unidentified object at exactly the same time the Hills believed their missing time experience occurred and in the same general area. Furthermore, both Betty and Barney began suffering a series of stressful mental and physical maladies in the weeks following their strange drive. Betty was plagued with nightmares of being abducted by small, non-human entities, and Barney developed elevated blood pressure problems and ulcers, and a strange ring of warts appeared in his groin area. After meeting UFO researcher Walter Webb in October, the Hills were introduced to psychiatrist Benjamin Simon. Simon, an expert in hypnosis, subjected the couple to a series of sessions, eliciting what appeared to be repressed memories of those two missing hours. According to the stories told by the Hills while hypnotized, their car had come to a dead stop after they realized that the object following them was a strange, pancake-shaped aircraft. The craft then landed in front of them and a team of small humanoid creatures in black uniforms emerged and took them aboard their ship. Betty had a long needle inserted into her abdomen in a procedure the creatures described as a "pregnancy test." Barney had a probing device attached to his groin.[53]

In the decades to follow, according to abduction experts like freelance researcher-artist Budd Hopkins, Penn State University historian David M. Jacobs, and Harvard professor and psychiatrist John Mack, a pattern of experiences similar to what the Hills described emerged from tens of thousands of abductees the world over. The missing time, the physical exams with a strong emphasis on the reproductive system, the nightmares and repressed memories would be a standard staple in most of these stories. Even more disturbing additions to this template, according to Hopkins and Jacobs, would come from female abductees who claimed to have been impregnated by the aliens, then abducted at some point during the pregnancy and their fetuses removed. Some of these women then said the abductions would go on for years and sometimes they would be shown their children. Many of these children would appear to be human-alien hybrids. Physically the hybrids seemed to be mostly human, but they had slightly enlarged heads and eyes that resembled the almond-shaped alien eyes.

Not surprisingly, the human-alien hybrid stories had inspired most of the controversy and some of the furor even among UFOlogists. To many they smacked of the pulp fiction absurdity of the contactee stories. Others were troubled by the fact that a lot of abductees started recounting messages and instructions given by the aliens. These instructions also sounded like echoes of the contactee New Age homilies about cosmic peace, brotherhood, and transformation. Some abductees claimed to have been given instructions to persuade the world of coming cataclysmic events, environmental destruction, and nuclear apocalypse, just like Adamski and his followers. Many of the abductee parents believed the hybrid children were a sign of an imminent, worldwide contact with the aliens, where the hybrids would stand as a symbol of universal brotherhood.

Not all UFOlogists interpreted these allegations in such positive terms. The strongest reaction has come from historian David M. Jacobs, articulated in his book *The Threat*. Jacobs, who has interviewed numerous abductees, argues that the vast majority of the alien contact stories are not these glowing, positive visions of hope and interplanetary peace and love. He believes the hybrid program, if it indeed is real, is more likely some kind of a breeding experiment to replenish or transform an alien race. Perhaps, he hypothesizes, it is a colonization experiment where alien invaders are preparing to infiltrate the world with these armies of hybrids. He does end his book on the most ominous note of any of the works written by the abduction scholars: "We now know the alarming dimensions of the alien agenda and its goals. I could never have imagined it would turn out this way. I desperately wish it not to be true. I do not think about the future with much hope. When I was a child, I had a future with much hope. When I was a child, I had a future to look forward to. Now I fear for the future of my own children."[54]

But whether the alien abductions, experimentations, and hybrid programs are ultimately positive or negative, many believe that the U.S. government, its intelligence agencies, and the upper echelons of the military services are most likely to know the full story. They, of course, are not talking. The ever more suspicious and disaffected culture of the 1960s and '70s, however, had been open to all this speculation. The media of films and publishing were eager to incorporate storylines of cover-ups, secret plots, and hidden truths into archetypal science fiction and horror stories about monsters and alien invaders.

Among the UFO conspiracy theories of the '50s, '60s and '70s, speculation about the extent of the government's knowledge about abductions was in the minds of the conspiratorially inclined. These ideas were also the most likely to be adapted by filmmakers during this period. However, these were not the only otherworldly conspiracy theories of the time. One other UFO–related phenomenon emerged in the late 1960s, but this one has subsisted on a more cult-like level of UFOlogy. Only the most hard-core UFO enthusiasts followed this issue through the decades and it has not yet inspired a significant number of films.

Starting in 1967, anomaly researchers were drawn to the animal mutilation phenomenon, supposedly taking place in the rural areas of the upper Midwest and stretching down into Northern Texas.[55] It usually involved farmers finding slaughtered livestock — most often cattle, but sometimes horses as well — in their fields, the animals having been killed with various body parts removed. According to the mutilation lore, much of it discussed in the works of documentary filmmaker Linda Moulton Howe, one of the leading mutilation researchers, the animals always displayed signs of having been dismembered with careful, deliberate precision, most often their eyes, tongues, and reproductive organs removed with what had to have been high-quality surgical instruments.

According to several mutilation investigators, however, some of the slaughtered animals were dispatched with instruments that appeared to have been *too* high-quality. Several of the earliest cattle to have fallen victim to the mystery killers displayed flawlessly straight cuts on their hides, with the edges of the cuts seemingly cauterized by an extreme heat source. According to veterinarians familiar with the state of the art in both existing and experimental surgical instruments, the only way such cuts could have been inflicted would have been through the use of a laser. Unfortunately, the experimental surgical laser equipment of the late 1960s was so large that it would have been impossible to take to a remote location like a Midwestern farm, be powered up and put to use without anyone noticing.

Adding to the strangeness of the mutilation phenomenon, and making it tempting for many to attribute paranormal involvement, was the way so many of the animals appeared to have been thoroughly drained of blood. According to Howe, it would have been impossible to remove so much blood; the animals' veins and arteries would have collapsed long before all that blood was gone. Quite literally, some of the animals appeared to have been bled dry. What was left at that point was the question of where, exactly, all that blood went. Farmers would report that there were no pools of blood. It appeared as if the killings and the exsanguinations had taken place elsewhere, then the bodies dumped back on the owners' fields.

Soon the UFO reports started coming in. UFO researchers and mutilation investigators would draw strong correlations between UFO sightings and mutilations throughout the Midwestern farm country. As the number of mutilations would usually increase in any area, so would the UFO sightings. In some farm communities throughout the '70s, the numbers of reported mutilations would reach the hundreds. Local media would often report on farmers organizing modern-day vigilance committees and patrolling their fields at night with pickup trucks full of heavily armed men. Not one of these patrols ever even came close to seeing, much less capturing, any of the mutilators. Several of them, however, have seen UFOs appearing and disappearing over farms and herds of animals. Throughout the '70s and '80s, eyewitnesses had come forward claiming they saw cattle being levitated into the air and pulled inside hovering UFOs.

Adding conspiracy theories of government involvement into the strange mix of animal mutilations and UFOs, numerous farmers have also come forward and claimed to have seen unmarked black helicopters and airplanes flying over their fields immediately after fresh mutilations.

Two schools of thought have formed over the decades. One group claims that mutilations are tied to UFOs and the perpetrators are aliens. This faction believes that the genetic testing of and experimentation on cattle is some sort of an extraterrestrial project carried out parallel to the human abductions. The opposing faction, taking a cue from the CIA and its recommendation to manufacture phony alien-sighting stories, lays the blame entirely on the military. For this faction, the key is in the unmarked aircraft, planes, and helicopters that are unmistakably terrestrial but possibly a part of some clandestine operation. For the government conspiracy faction, the mutilations might represent the government checking the livestock in areas where secret chemical spills, chemical weapons tests, or any other such illegal environmental pollutants might be affecting animals. The UFO reports, these conspiracists argue, might be fake, planted by the military to keep anyone from taking the mutilations seriously.

The most interesting counterpoint to both mutilation-theory camps comes from Jacques Vallée. In his book *Revelations*, he lays out an elegant argument against the positions of both groups. Although Vallée feels that the animal mutilation phenomenon is real, he believes that neither the alien genetic testing theory, nor the government chemical testing theory is adequate to explain it. Aliens whose science and technology would be centuries ahead of those of Earth people, he argues, would hardly need to keep taking simple blood and tissue samples from animals for decades. What conceivable reason would aliens have for conducting these experiments for so long? If there was something these creatures needed to know about animal life on Earth — or human life, for that matter, Vallée adds since he is also highly skeptical of the abduction phenomenon — their ultra-advanced medical, cloning, and genetic engineering technology would have let them learn it a long time ago and without a need to mutilate thousands of cattle and horses. Furthermore, Vallée deflates the "secret" government chemical testing argument by pointing out that if the government was worried about contaminated livestock, rather than stealing the animals, they could simply buy them and test them in government research laboratories. Afterward, they would quietly dispose of the carcasses in those same laboratories. It would make no logical sense for these government operatives to dump the mutilated animals back on the same farms they stole them from. Vallée, instead, makes the argument for a mass psychological and sociological experiment. In fact, it is similar to the Victorian airships' "psychosocial" interpretation. The parties doing the mutilating, he writes, are most certainly not trying to keep their activities secret. The purpose behind the mutilations might be the reactions they elicit. The forces behind this gruesome study, for some reason, want to know how the farmers, how the media, how the authorities, how *society*, essentially, is reacting to the unknown.

But again, interestingly enough, the animal mutilation phenomenon has not been adapted into popular entertainment as freely as alien abduction or invasion scenarios. Given the grisly nature of the phenomenon, one might have expected horror films to take full advantage of the mutilations, perhaps touting their blood-and-guts shockers with screaming taglines like "Based on Terrifying True Events!"

Broken Machines

While the political assassination and alien visitation conspiracy theories spanned a wide spectrum between the somewhat plausible and the highly fantastic, the 1960s and '70s also witnessed the emergence of theories reacting to an increased concern over the environment, the effects of technology and industrialization, and fears of big business and industry abusing their wealth and political clout. In some respects, environmental and industrial conspiracies could even, on occasion, bridge the gap between the plausibility of the assassination theories and the credibility-stretching speculation of the UFO conspiracy movement. The environmental conspiracy theorists, after all, had often claimed that wondrous technologies that could change the world and improve the quality of life for everyone existed, yet they were being suppressed. In political orientation, though, these theories had more of the overtly left-wing slant of the Kennedy–Vietnam–political assassination theories. Very much like the original JFK murder conspiracy theories, the environmental and technological conspiracies were actually pointed attacks on capitalism.

Among the major social changes and attitude shifts in the 1960s, American society had started rethinking its views of the environment, technology, and consumerism. Until then, much like patriotism, support for the military, religion, and law and order, business and technology were sacrosanct concepts. It was simply un–American to attack business and industry. But from the earliest days of the country, after all, American folk heroes had been pioneers, settlers, hunters and woodsman who "tamed" the wilderness. This had been a nation that believed it had a *manifest destiny* to take over, transform, and use land exactly as it saw fit. While expansion, industrialization, and colonization had been policies of the world's major powers since the nineteenth century, by the end of the twentieth, the United States had been the most successful at it. As surprising as it is in today's images and celebrity-obsessed world, in the earliest decades of the twentieth century, inventors were among the most admired public figures. Men of technical savvy who could transform the world with their science and machines were lauded and fawned over by the media much the same way today's movie stars and supermodels are haunted by the paparazzi. By the end of the second World War, the U.S. was the most powerful, most affluent and comfortable industrial power in the world. Men who invented, perfected and successfully exploited technology created this affluence, won the two major wars of the century, and made the country a world leader.

But once American society began taking a more introspective look at itself, once it allowed itself to acknowledge the racial and social injustices that better machines, better cars, better washing machines, and TVs could not alleviate, it began considering that perhaps all of its progress had not really brought about a flawless society after all. There was more to a good society than living well, ever more social critics had started to argue. The most radical of these critics charged that all the good life in America was sowing the seeds of a worldwide environmental apocalypse.

In the later days of the 1960s, the mainstream media and ever larger segments of Middle America had become aware of the potentially negative impact all the technology and industrialization it took to keep such a highly affluent consumer culture in the goods it required to live a comfortable life. By 1970, with the advent of the first Earth Day, the warnings of a growing number of environmental scientists about potentially irreversible ecological damage wrought by our hi-tech society were being heeded. Phenomena like acid rain, smog over big cities, and polluted lakes and rivers had made it onto the national list of concerns and fears. Although various movements of conservationists had been advocating the protection of wilderness areas throughout the twentieth century, by the '60s and '70s a fear of the looming extinction of entire species of animals had also gone mainstream. The biggest threat, however, was only fully realized in the early 1970s. With the oil embargo of the Middle Eastern OPEC cartel in 1973, Americans had been painfully awakened to the fact that they were slaves to a natural resource without which the entire industrial system would collapse. And if modern society could not live without oil, it was also warned that it could not live *with* it for too long, either. The oil and gasoline it took to power all the high technology of the modern world was also its chief pollutant, perhaps the most pernicious threat to the environment and life on the planet in the long run.

But America was a country that had never met a national emergency it could not overcome. Perseverance and success seemed to have been woven into the very fabric of the American character. If the country now faced an environmental problem, it could surely meet it head-on and triumph just as it had *always* triumphed through wars, depressions, and national and global emergencies. Could it not? Unfortunately, in the 1960s and '70s, it appeared as if the country had become entrenched in its environmentally self-destructive ways. An immense, ever more global industrial system appeared to be simply too large and too complex to suddenly and completely overhaul itself. The infrastructure in place to drill for, refine, and distribute oil could not be dismantled and refitted overnight into more eco-friendly technologies no matter how dire scientists' warnings about air pollution, water pollution, and a depleting ozone layer were becoming. Furthermore, the factories building the technologies, the consumer goods enjoyed by Americans, as well as consumers the world over, also employed millions of those same consumers. The problem, it appeared, wasn't simply in the technology, but in the social structures that needed those factories running if they didn't want to collapse into mass unemployment, poverty, and a catastrophic global economic meltdown. For the conspiratorially inclined, however, the problem was more complex, while at the same time much simpler.

The conspiratorial view of environmental damage and business corruption generally tended to function according to the sort of reductionist logic that propels much of conspiracy theories ever questing to connect everything. If instances of white-collar and governmental criminality are regularly uncovered by the courts and the media, it is logical to assume that crimes immensely more complex are being committed every day and going unpunished, this thinking argues. If it is logical to assume that a vast conspiracy of business interests had some hand in the murder of the president of the United States—and for many during the 1960s and '70s it indeed was logical to make that assumption—then it's not a stretch of the imagination to see business interests killing inventors and innovators to keep revolutionary clean-air and free-energy technologies from reaching the market and making the world better.

Most of the environmental and business conspiracies of this era had, in effect, functioned according to the murdered/intimidated/suppressed lone genius template. Theorists had charged that everything from an electricity-driven car, a water-driven car, longer lasting light bulbs, and clean-burning fuel, all the way to the more fantastic technologies like cold fusion, have all existed for decades. These innovations, sure to make the lives of so many people better, not to mention avert future environmental crises, had all been suppressed because they would have hurt the profits of power companies, the Arab oil cartels, auto makers, and the big oil corporations. According to the conspiracy theorists, inventors working outside of the corporate system, unencumbered by bureaucracies, had been able to solve so many of the looming environmental problems of the world. Innovation, invention, and marketing are in the hands of corporate titans in the modern world, however, and these lone geniuses, according to the conspiracy theories, have all been found and crushed before their discoveries could have changed the world. Theorists, for example, argue that inventor Stanley Meyer, who had been working on water-powered automobile technology until his death in 1998 from an aneurism, was really murdered by "big oil interests." The charges of foul play are not deterred, however, even by the fact that Meyer was successfully sued by two investors in 1996 for bilking them out of money spent on a water-driven car engine. The engine, the court decided, was little more than flim-flam and none of Meyer's claims about a water-powered perpetual motion machine could ever be verified by independent investigators.[56] Conspiracists likewise blame the September 29, 1913, death of Rudolf Christian Karl Diesel, looking like an apparent suicide, on oil companies.[57] These same conspiracists argue that the entire scientific establishment and its ultra-cautious, ultra-conservative system of peer reviews is but an industry-controlled ploy to keep innovators marginalized and ridiculed. Many of these theorists point out that most physicists would agree that the concept of cold fusion and its promise of cheap, abundant, and clean energy is theoretically possible. Yet very few respectable scientists want to stake their careers, sources of funding, their very professional reputations on extensively pursuing and developing cold fusion technologies. The conspiracy theorists argue that the selection committees of the top academic conferences and the heads of universities, departments, and tenure boards have all written cold fusion off as ridiculously unrealistic science fiction. To further pursue its research is tantamount to career suicide.

The appeal of these suppressed-genius conspiracy theories can be seen on a fairly obvious psychological level, as well as through a certain all–American, rugged individual framework. Looking at the theories through a strictly psychological framework, one can see the attempt at bringing order to a world becoming increasingly chaotic, dangerous, and oppressive. It simply does not make sense that if the world is facing environmental catastrophe, that the most brilliant minds in the world could not successfully avert this dark future. The simplest explanation that becomes attractive to the conspiratorially inclined is that those same brilliant minds and powerful industries simply do not *want* to address the problem. Hence, if they do not want to address the problem, any number of conspiracy theories argue, it is because those intellectual, governmental, and industry power players have something to gain from the status quo. Profits are to be made from keeping everything the way it is. Changing the world economy would be too expensive and it would interrupt the cash flow of too many of the wealthy elites; therefore, these elites are carrying on a massive, oppressive conspiracy to hold onto their positions of power and wealth.

The most colorful of 1970s conspiracy theories takes this idea of a wealthy elite plotting to allow the destruction of the world straight into the fantastic realm of the UFOs and aliens. The Alternative 3 conspiracy of the late '70s, which even inspired a mock documentary on British TV in 1977, argued that the ruling elites had realized that all the environmental devastation and exploitation of the twentieth century would soon leave the planet uninhabitable. As a result, this shadowy cabal had for decades been planning and developing secret technologies to leave the planet and set up moon-based, Mars-based, and space station-based colonies. Of course, the conspiracy theorists argue, only the elites and their progeny will be able to enjoy these space colonies. Or the elites and a small number of slaves who will be catering to their luxurious needs while the rest of humanity will die out or revert to chaotic primitive societies on a poisoned and defiled Earth.[58]

Aside from offering the psychological comfort that someone, no matter how greedy, sociopathic, and evil they may be, is at least in charge, the environmental and industrial conspiracies have a sort of populist, grass-roots American appeal. Most of the industrial conspiracy theorists are firmly in the camps of the anti-capitalist far-left; in fact, most of the conservative retorts to their big-business-is-knowingly-killing-the-planet arguments usually point out that the environmental records of the former Soviet bloc countries had always been abysmally worse than those of the U.S. and Western Europe, a fact conspiracy theorists like to ignore in their vehement bashing of American institutions. But there is a certain "rugged individualist" appeal to these theories that even a right-wing conservative can embrace. At the metaphysical core of the suppressed-genius conspiracy formula, one finds a lamentation of how the world is ever more bureaucratized, controlled, regulated and regimented. The heroes— or perhaps the unlucky, praiseworthy victims— of these conspiracy theories are the little guys with nothing but a dream, talent, and determination in the best tradition of the classic Horatio Alger success myths. The villains are the big corporations where everyone is under the control of one monolithic, inflexible "system." All these conspiracies essentially argue that the world could be changed for the better by the lone thinker, but instead we are heading toward an apocalypse created by giant bureaucracies that suppress dissent and vision.

The chief conspiracy theories of the 1960s and '70s grew out of a society that started taking a more critical, introspective look at itself. When Americans were willing to admit that abuses of power and privilege were not only possible but perhaps the norm from the highest offices of the government to the board rooms of big business, conspiracy theorists argued that enemies as dangerous as any hostile foreign power were lurking within the system. In this newly suspicious and cynical age, conspiracies about anything, even the fantastic and extraterrestrial, suddenly seemed plausible. To what extent these theories are correct, Americans have debated for decades and they are likely to keep debating for decades to come. But these theories have been attractive to Hollywood as well, and the allegations of nefarious plots and shadowy villains have made for some of the most entertaining films of that era.

CHAPTER 3

From Nuclear
Apocalypse to Conspiracy
Conspiracy Films of the 1960s and '70s

Just as American society began to take a more critical look at itself, Hollywood film-makers working with military, espionage, and science fiction stories could be seen cautiously stretching, testing, and reshaping genres that were optimal for conspiracy plots. A careful look at these films reveals an apparent attempt at reimagining conspiracies as threats from within the system rather than the traditional tales of threatening outsiders, foreign invaders, or radical subversives acting on behalf of a foreign power. Furthermore, such an analysis also reveals unexpected trends when it comes to film genres turning their conspiratorial accusations inward. Specifically, it's not the science fiction and alien-invasion-oriented films that are the first to indict American institutions for being corrupt nests of conspirators, but rather military and spy thrillers. Movies jumping on the '50s and '60s UFO bandwagons, for instance, were not dealing with the sorts of cover-up conspiracies that real-life military and scientific figures like Donald Keyhoe, Edward Ruppelt and J. Allen Hynek were accusing the government of. If anything, these films actually turn out to be tacitly endorsing government secrecy when it comes to UFOs. This apparent lack of interest in conspiratorial plots is remarkable since one might expect storytellers who can work with fantasy and allegory to be more willing to critique government institutions and policies. The first accusations of conspiracies, misguided policies, and corruption started showing up in Cold War thrillers, however.

Nukes and Mad Generals

Aside from the political corruption films that trace their roots as far back as the 1930s and classics like Frank Capra's *Mr. Smith Goes to Washington*, the modern conspiracy film is also shaped by a post–World War II series of nuclear threat and nuclear war films. While these films are not always openly critical of the government, a number of them do offer warnings about the dangers of the arms race, bellicose patriotism in a world full of atomic weapons, and the threat of military and governmental bureaucracies that might subvert the checks and balances of democracy.

Popular entertainment has always reflected the tenor of the times, even when unquestioning loyalty and the support of the patriotic party line were insisted upon by the government. As much as the McCarthyites and the censors enforcing the Motion Picture Code might have wanted Hollywood to be a good team player at the start of the nuclear arms race, to support the military, the authorities, and Washington's policies, Americans had been getting ever more nervous about the state of the world in the late '40s and the '50s. Nuclear weapons, radioactive fallout, and the mass extinction of the human race had become the national nightmare. Patriots and the military attempted to be reassuring about the superiority of the U.S. armed forces, while demagogues threatened to mark anyone too critical and skeptical of the arms race as communists and subversives. Americans could all too clearly remember what atomic weapons did to Hiroshima and Nagasaki. If a bomb apiece leveled both of those cities, people could picture what could happen in a world where two warring countries unleashed hundreds of atomic weapons, each nuclear bomb immensely more powerful than the ones dropped on Japan. Preparation for war with the Soviet Union, civil defense drills, and the building of bomb shelters in backyards had also become a part of 1950s Americana. Popular lifestyle and culture magazines like *Life* had regularly run articles on how to build, furnish, and stock one's own fallout shelter. While Americans wanted desperately to stay optimistic, they were also realistic enough to know they had plenty of reasons to be very afraid. This sort of free-floating anxiety could not stay out of Hollywood films. Movies about the outbreak of a nuclear war, accidents involving nuclear weapons, etc., had become a product of the times. All was not as safe as the government was assuring the public, these films insisted. Policies and personnel in place to control this power could be highly flawed and unstable. Before conspiracy theorists aimed their criticism at the nation's most esteemed institutions, these nuclear weapon and military thrillers suggested that the road to Armageddon was being built by America's own military, political, and scientific establishments.

Filmed in 1946, just one year after the bombing of Japan, and released in 1947, the MGM docudrama *The Beginning or the End* depicted the development of the A-bomb. A historical curiosity, the film is an example of a series of contrivances and compromises in favor of audience expectations and political sensitivities of the time. While the filmmakers appear to have endeavored to mimic a newsreel documentary, presenting something like a chronological timeline of the development of atomic technology and the decision to use it on Hiroshima and Nagasaki, the end result is a sentimental, romantic melodrama supported by a great deal of patriotism and a few lines of concern over the dangers of atomic weaponry. Much of the plot involves a young scientist named Matt Cochran (Tom Drake) working on the Manhattan Project; he is the only member of the team harboring doubts about the development of the weapon. All his time at work is severely straining his marriage to Anne (Beverly Tyler). He's away from home too much and Anne can't deal with it any more. Matt, however, is eventually able to quell his personal doubts, realizing that men much higher above him in the project — not to mention the military leadership — are in a position to make informed decisions about the need for the bomb. In essence, he realizes that the right thing to do is trust authority. If he can put his doubts aside and do his job to the best of his abilities, he can go home to his wife as soon as possible. The ending of the film turns out to be a sort of inspirational tearjerker as Matt sacrifices his life when a technical glitch almost causes a premature detonation of the bomb. Taking a lethal dose of radiation, he nevertheless is able to stop the explosion and save all of his colleagues' lives. The final scene takes place at the Lincoln Memorial, where Matt's farewell letter is read for his widow. With his face superimposed over the screen, the audience hears Matt tell of his hope that in the future, atomic energy will be used for the betterment of mankind.

Although the film's very title seems to suggest a dialogue about the positive and negative implications of atomic power, the story is very much in line with the World War II and postwar era cheerleading style of filmmaking. *The Beginning or the End* gives a vague hint at "some who might say" that atomic power is a danger that cannot be controlled and that even the U.S. government cannot be trusted not to bring about Armageddon. However, the overall film is a celebration of American victory and a declaration of faith in the scientific and military establishments to always do what is right. Matt Cochran, the film's only representative of the skeptical or cautious approach to atomic power, learns his lesson, after all, well before the end of the film. Once he puts his opposition aside, he helps bring about a positive end to the war and assures U.S. supremacy in the world. In fact, he is so convinced of his mission and the rightness of the Manhattan Project that he gives his life to make sure the work is completed and the military can use the bomb.

But, again, in the greater trend of postwar entertainment, this sort of film was standard. While Hollywood made combat films during World War II to bolster Americans' support and morale, after 1946 and throughout the '50s it made films celebrating and commemorating the country's success in the war. Where audience dollars left at the box office might not have been enough to convince filmmakers to continue the trend, the increasing paranoia and censorious atmosphere of the McCarthyite Red Scare sent a clear message to Hollywood that patriotism was the formula for films. Plus, if the red-baiters didn't intimidate filmmakers enough to toe the party line, the Motion Picture Code remained unyielding in its demand that only positive depictions of the government and authority figures be shown in films.[1]

Nevertheless, nuclear war films would continue making it onto screens in the next two decades. While most of them retained the elements of the sort of high melodrama seen in *The Beginning or the End*'s doomed love story, the genre became darker (appropriately enough, given the subject matter), pessimistic and apocalyptic.

In 1951, former radio writer Arch Oboler wrote and directed *Five*, where all of the Earth's population is wiped out in a nuclear war, save for five people living in a lodge in the California wilderness. While the film performs an important genre-establishing function, argues analyst Ernest F. Martin, setting down the archetypal theme of humanism being incapable of coexisting with technology, it, too, is but ultimately a love story.[2] Here, a young couple finds love and hope amidst the ruins of a nuclear war. They become a latter-day Adam and Eve, promising that humanity might still go on after nearly wiping itself out. Although the optimistic note is still present at the end of the film, *Five* does not wave its flags and instruct its audiences to trust America's "experts" and patriots. There are no experts in this film's view, there is no one worthy of unquestioning faith and trust. All of the men who had built the bombs and unleashed the nuclear apocalypse, be they Americans or Russians, were equally stupid or mad.

While *Five* was a low-budget affair and is generally unknown outside of cineaste circles, in 1959 United Artists released director Stanley Kramer's *On the Beach* with loud promotional fanfare. Based on Nevil Shute's acclaimed post-nuclear holocaust novel, the film boasted an A-list Hollywood cast, including Gregory Peck, Ava Gardner, Fred Astaire, and Anthony Perkins. It was not only generally well-reviewed by the entertainment press, but it got several ringing endorsements from scientists and peace activists. Skirting hyperbole, scientist Linus Pauling declared, "It may be that some years from now we can look back and say that *On the Beach* is the movie that saved the world."[3] The film faithfully follows Shute's source material and presents a surprisingly grim and downbeat post–World War III scenario. Not only is it darker and more fatalistic than films like *The Beginning or the*

End and *Five*, but its hopeless conclusion was a surprise given that fact that the film was so lavishly financed by a major company. The basic plot involves a group of Australians and American Navy personnel awaiting their death from radiation poisoning with quiet resignation. The U.S., the U.S.S.R., and the entire northern hemisphere have been destroyed in a nuclear exchange, with only Australia avoiding direct hits from the bombs. That country, however, will not escape the approaching clouds of lethal radiation. Once Australia is engulfed in the fallout, its citizens will all die, wiping out the rest of the human race. The film then follows the lives of a handful of people as they try to cope with the fact that they are all really dead, that there is no hope and no salvation. Since even *On the Beach* does not forgo some of the romantic melodrama seen in the previous nuclear war films, including a subplot of a tenuously budding romance between Peck's Navy captain and a beautiful Australian admirer played by Gardner, the overall effect of this device is much more powerful than the one in *Five*. Whereas *Five* presents its romance as a symbol of hope — or the somewhat trite convention of love as a redemptive force — *On the Beach*'s love stories are hopeless and ironic. All of these people are going to die. As glamourous and attractive as they may be, played by stars the audience has been conditioned to count on to see a happy ending, there is no happy ending. In *On the Beach*, the doomed lovers are an even more effective device for the film to deliver its angry indictment of blind, insane politics and war. As the nuclear war films usually do, *On the Beach* forcefully denies that anyone's expertise can help avert a mass holocaust as long as nuclear technology exists. Political systems, be they American or Russian, are all just as mad, short-sighted, and unworthy of trust by their citizens if they are willing to risk wiping out all life on Earth for the sake of ideology. But, then again, the film, just as Shute's novel, accuses all mankind of being stupid and insane in the late '50s. We are all obsessed with national honor, patriotism, and pride, even at the risk of Armageddon.

The aftermath of a nuclear war turned up as the plot of more movies in the late '50s and early '60s. As critics agreed, however, these apocalyptic offerings were generally a mixed bag of elements. MGM's *The World, the Flesh, and the Devil* (1959) was, once again, heavier on the romantic sentiment than on the realistic depiction of an atomic war or the details of the political maneuverings and failures that led to the final destruction of the world. As Frank W. Oglesbee writes, "In this cinematic wasteland, an absence of science and an abundance of fiction prevailed."[4] It appears that the world of this film fell victim to the tidiest nuclear holocaust yet. Here radioactive dust — from what must have been early "dirty bombs" — blanketed the Earth and killed and instantly dissolved all humans. From the standpoint of logistics, budget, and production design, this scenario left the filmmakers to merely clear and shoot a lot of empty streets instead of creating expensive special effects shots of ruined cities. The plot of the film involves an interracial love triangle between a black and a white man (Harry Belafonte and Mel Ferrer respectively) and a white woman (Inger Stevens) in the desolation of the new world.

In *The Day the Earth Caught Fire* (1961), the end of the world appears to be looming because of excessive nuclear testing. If *The World, the Flesh, and the Devil* was weak in its scientific foundations, *The Day the Earth Caught Fire* moved almost entirely into the territory of the sort of scientific hyperbole seen in giant bug movies. The film posits that simultaneous nuclear tests conducted by the Americans and the Russians tilted the Earth toward the sun and threatened to make it "catch on fire." If the film is not entirely convincing in its science, it did successfully exploit another nuclear paranoia of the times. *Fire*, in fact, works quite well on the metaphorical level. If an all-out nuclear war did not bring about the end of the world, many feared at the time, then all the atomic testing and radiation in the air, radioactive contaminants, and pollutants would surely do the job. The cycle of the 1950s giant mutated-monster movies, after all, usually blamed atomic testing for giant ants, spiders, mantises, grasshoppers, and even a rampaging, crazed giant man. What makes *The Day the Earth Caught Fire* noteworthy is its use of the government conspiracy and cover-up device. In the course of the film, the cataclysm soon to be unleashed by the disturbed Earth tilt is not known by the public for quite a while. Only an increasingly deadly series of natural catastrophes signal that something might be terribly wrong. The authorities, of course, know all along what their reckless tests have produced. In a far-reaching conspiracy of silence, they try to avoid a worldwide panic by covering up the results of the atomic testing while a solution can be sought and implemented. The only person who is able to ferret out the truth is a burned-out, divorced, alcoholic reporter (Edward Judd) and the beautiful government switchboard operator (Janet Munro) he falls in love with. The film ends on an edgy and pessimistic tone, even after the world powers have learned to put their differences aside and attempted to solve the problem they created. The final scene involves a shot of two newspaper headlines printed just before a nuclear bomb at the equator has been set off to try and knock the planet back to its proper position. One of the headlines reads "Earth Saved!" and the other "Earth Doomed." The film, however, does not reveal which of the headlines is the one that needs to hit the streets. It leaves it up to the audience to decide whether or not the catastrophic nightmare nuclear technology has created can be undone.

In *Panic in Year Zero!* (1962), nuclear war becomes the catalyst for a study of human behavior once all the trappings of civilization have been stripped away. The film focuses on the "typical" all–American Baldwin family and their ordeals once World War III has come and gone with a rain of nuclear missiles while they were taking a vacation. The major problem for the family —comprised of father Harry (Ray Milland), wife Ann (Jean Hagen), and teenagers Rick (Frankie Avalon) and Karen (Mary Mitchel)— is the collapse of law, order, and civility. From one moment to the next, they pass from the world of buttoned-down, conservative, well-mannered early '60s America to a wasteland of marauding thugs, killers, and rapists. Where the law of the jungle suddenly rules, the Baldwins must fight for survival while holding on to some remnants of their humanity. This sort of character arc was also fast on its way to becoming popular at the same time on television in Rod Serling's *Twilight Zone* series. In fact, some of that series' most memorable episodes involve this same theme that the order, control, manners, and genteel civilization Americans had come to believe were bedrock foundations of their character were but parts of a fragile, unstable façade. Once the "all–American" routine is even slightly disrupted, even the best-behaved Middle American suburbanites could degenerate into anarchic maniacs.

The most anti-authoritarian of the nuclear disaster films, however, came in 1963 from Stanley Kubrick, the acclaimed director of films like *Paths of Glory* (1957), *Spartacus* (1960), and *Lolita* (1962). *Dr. Strangelove, or: How I Learned to Stop Worrying and Love the Bomb* took the premise of an accidental instigation of World War III and turned it into an absurdist black comedy. Its condemnation of the arms race, the military mentality, and superpower brinksmanship has made it one of the classic films of that era. *Dr. Strangelove* further set the stage for mainstream Hollywood's suspicious, conspiratorial mindset that would produce a crop of films over the following two decades where threats, corruption, and evil all originate within the American system.

Dr. Strangelove's plot could make for a straightforward military thriller. It begins with a mentally unbalanced general (Sterling Hayden) at an American air base in England sending the nuclear launch command to a B-52 bomber flying over Europe. True to their training and professionalism, the crew of the plane heads for the Soviet Union. Back in England, the general has locked down his base and, at first, attempted to arrest the only man (Peter Sellers) — a British liaison officer — who realizes what is going on, then attempted to kill him. Meanwhile, the American Joint Chiefs of Staff and the U.S. president (Peter Sellers, in a second role), who have been alerted to the imminent attack on Russia, try to defuse the situation before the bomber reaches its target and the Russians retaliate with an all-out attack from the "Doomsday Weapon."

Again, this rudimentary plot would be perfectly at home in scores of thrillers, spy novels, and James Bond films to come. In most of these other venues, the story would race toward a breathless conclusion where Armageddon is averted in the last moment. In Kubrick's hands, however, the film becomes an assault on the Cold War and all the concepts of deterrence, military capability, and official expertise. *Dr. Strangelove* ends with a barrage of mushroom clouds as the failure of the massive, complex nuclear weapons system destroys the world. Or, perhaps, more chillingly, according to Roger Ebert, *Dr. Strangelove* really shows what happens when the nuclear deterrent system works perfectly.[5] Once the launch command is given, the rest of the film proceeds as a series of falling dominoes. All of the immense, complicated nuclear weapon program's myriad components kick in exactly as they are supposed to. The system performs flawlessly and logically, carrying out an attack on the U.S.S.R. The Soviets' own "Doomsday Weapon" then also activates and destroys the world. One can quarrel with the fine points of Ebert's analysis, countering that a ranting, unstable madman like General Jack D. Ripper is hardly part of the logical defense equation — or if an unhinged lunatic like him could ever go unnoticed, let alone have the opportunity to single-handedly issue launch orders. But Kubrick's point is not without merit. Accidents or various out-of-control emergencies could have happened — as the Cuban missile crisis of 1962 demonstrated — and once the scenario had gotten past a point of no return, the defense apparatus would have been left on its own to carry out the Apocalypse. The defense system itself was the enemy even more so than the Russians in Kubrick's view. Men in charge of the machinery could make mistakes and trigger a process which, thanks to the monumental stupidity of the Cold War architects, could never again be turned off.

Furthering Kubrick's subversive agenda of charging that the enemies are really within, is the over-the-top comedy. Although the comic approach of the film had been given a great deal of academic and critical treatment, often through discussions of the deftness or subtlety of the satire, *Dr. Strangelove*, in fact, is *not* subtle in its comedy. Of course, this is not to say that the absurdity of the humor is not effective and doesn't help further Kubrick's statements. The comedy often gets outlandishly broad, as in the name of characters like Jack D. Ripper, General Turgidson (George C. Scott), President Muffley, Major T.J. "King" Kong (Slim Pickens), Premier Kissoff, Colonel "Bat" Guano (Keenan Wynn) and, of course, the titular Dr. Strangelove (Peter Sellers yet again); it's a representation of a mad world where an uncontrollable nuclear apparatus can start a countdown to Armageddon with no way of turning back.

However, the origins of the film are in a very serious, very straight military thriller novel called *Red Alert* by Peter George. When Kubrick was hired to adapt and film the book, he and co-author Terry Southern first intended to do a faithful adaptation. The more the work progressed, however, the more Kubrick was tempted to interpret the scenario through absurd gallows humor. By most accounts, Southern wasn't comfortable with Kubrick's comedy intruding on the nuclear war theme. Kubrick reportedly joked more and more about doing the film as an unrestrained farce, all to Southern's frustration. It was only after Southern departed the project — but with enough input on the script to retain a co-writer credit — that Kubrick made the radical turn to outright comedy.[6] As Kubrick saw the project, comedy was the only way to truly deliver an effective critique of a system as massive, powerful, and monstrously flawed as the "Mutually Assured Destruction" (MAD!) concept behind the arms race. Such a policy, in Kubrick's reckoning, was unrestrained insanity. In his film, therefore, a cast of ranting, driven, out-of-control maniacs hurtle the world into complete nuclear annihilation.

An interesting note about direct references to conspiracy theories in *Dr. Strangelove*: In a few key scenes, the film actually proves to be a *critique* of conspiratorial paranoia. Of course, the critique is aimed mostly at *right*-wing paranoia and conspiracy theories and not the sort of anti-government, anti-establishment leftist theories that would take flight in the aftermath of the Kennedy assassination. General Jack D. Ripper, a conspiracy theorist in the far-right-wing mold, believes that the U.S. is weakening in its resolve to combat the spread of communism because subversives have destroyed the health and morale of Americans. He fears that the fluoridation of America's drinking water supply is a communist plot to poison "the purity and essence of our natural fluids." Before the country can be completely weakened and the world overrun by communism, Ripper decides to launch his own first strike against the U.S.S.R. and nip the problem in the bud. Furthermore, the Dr. Strangelove character, a transplanted Nazi psychopath, is referencing the post–World War II relocation of former German scientists in the U.S. This program, code named Project Paperclip, would also become a fertile source for a number of conspiracy theories.[7] According to conspiracists, the relocation of the Nazis gave the U.S. military access to a number of advanced technologies Germany had been experimenting with and perfecting before the end of the war. One school of UFO conspiracy theorists claims that many of the Foo Fighters were experimental German aircraft. This theory disputes the extraterrestrial hypothesis, claiming instead that UFO sightings are really glimpses of experimental military aircraft powered by antigravity drives first invented by the Nazis. A number of post–9/11, Nazified America theorists of the Jim Marrs school of thought argue that the relocated Nazis of Project Paperclip were the first wave of a Fourth Reich secret society taking over America.[8]

Interestingly, the fall of 1963 also offered another accidental-nuclear-launch film with *Fail-Safe*. Whereas *Dr. Strangelove* did the comedy interpretation of the end of the world, *Fail-Safe* is the film *Dr. Strangelove* might have been had Kubrick followed Terry Southern's advice and written a straight adaptation of *Red Alert*. In *Fail-Safe*, too, bombers are accidentally sent to launch a nuclear attack on Moscow. Just as in *Dr. Strangelove*, the president (Henry Fonda), the Joint Chiefs, and scientific advisors quarrel and struggle to stop an immensely complicated nuclear attack system from launching World War III once it has been set in motion. Although the ending is not as apocalyptic as that of *Dr. Strangelove*, *Fail-Safe* does, nevertheless, conclude with an extremely chilling final note of its own. Just as in *Dr. Strangelove*, the bombers finally reach a point past which they cannot be recalled. This is the titular "Fail-Safe" point. Knowing that the destruction of Moscow cannot be averted, the president and his advisors try to convince the Russian premier that the attack was a mistake. The plea, they hope, will avert retaliation and the complete destruction of the world. The Russians, however, cannot believe this. Or even if the premier does not strike back at the U.S., the aftermath of the bombing might get him deposed and his successor could go ahead with a counterstrike. The only way an all-out Russian retaliation can be averted, the only way the Russians can be convinced that the bombing of Moscow was an unintentional mistake, is by the Americans destroying one of their own cities. The president then orders a nuclear launch on New York City to avert a full-scale war with the Soviets.

Both films, released in the immediate aftermath of the JFK assassination, helped foment the mood of national disillusionment that would birth the modern conspiracy theory movement. They put the exclamation point on the sentiment that would motivate all the conspiracy theorists. The enemy was among us, these films, just like the other nuclear war films, argued. The threat was the system. The threat was the military machinery, the Cold War doctrine, the dogma, the intellectuals who created policies from the sterile, sheltered think tanks removed from the real world and the lives of real people.

The Conspirators

While the increasingly bleak, pessimistic and angry nuclear war films helped cement a mainstream popular cultural atmosphere that would be receptive to conspiracy theories, by 1963 films that dealt directly with hidden cabals and their clandestine power plays began showing up in theaters. These films would go beyond vague suggestions of an imperfect system and build their plots around actual criminal conspiracies.

One of the key pioneering films in this genre was 1962's *The Manchurian Candidate*. The audacity of this film is remarkable since not only did it premiere before such angry Cold War–critique films as *Dr. Strangelove* and *Fail-Safe*, but it was the first film to openly address and condemn McCarthyism. Opening just months before the Kennedy assassination, its message of corruption within the system would be a foundation for many of the real assassination theories soon to come.

The Manchurian Candidate, based on Richard Condon's wry novel satirizing the 1950s political culture, is focused entirely on the fears and speculations of all manner of Cold War conspiracies and subterfuges. While enacting its plot of spying, foreign agents, double agents, and assassinations as effectively as any straight political thriller, *The Manchurian Candidate* is ultimately a darkly comic satire about the fears of conspiracies. It deftly balances a plot of a very real conspiracy while simultaneously condemning McCarthyite right-wing paranoid fantasies for being nothing more than an unscrupulous attempt at ruling through fear.

The Manchurian Candidate is the story of Raymond Shaw (Laurence Harvey), a Korean War hero and the stepson of up-and-coming U.S. Senator John Iselin (James Gregory). But Shaw is also an unwitting communist agent, his platoon having been captured and brainwashed in Korea. His acts of heroism have been hypnotically implanted in his mind, as well as in the minds of his fellow soldiers. Once Shaw returns home, his battlefield exploits are quickly taken advantage of by Iselin, a hard-line McCarthyesque anti-communist crusader. Masterminding Shaw's exploitation, in turn, is his very own mother (Angela Lansbury). She sees a way to parlay the heroism into a political career not just for Iselin, but for Shaw himself. All this opportunism, of course, plays well into the hands of the communists who hope to one day have a high-ranking Washington politician — perhaps even the president of the United States — under their complete hypnotic control.

Up to this point, the film is entirely in line with any number of other standard Cold War espionage potboilers. But then, just like Condon had done in his novel, it unleashes a major plot twist that makes the conspiracies more complex, as well as setting the story up as a tool for criticizing far-right-wing McCarthyite conspiracy-mongering. The plot is turned on its head when it is revealed that Raymond Shaw's own mother is in on the brain-washing conspiracy. She is a communist collaborator who had married the dimwitted right-wing zealot Iselin because she saw his red-baiting as a sure-fire way to rise to power in the Cold War political culture. Moreover, Iselin was the best way to give her soon-to-be-brainwashed son an entrée into politics. Of course, the marriage is also the best way to position herself as the manipulating power behind the future president. Ultimately, Shaw's mother is neither right-wing nor left-wing, neither capitalist nor communist, but a power-hungry sociopath who allies herself with whomever can put her into the greater position of influence. Once Shaw is to become president, she doesn't so much envision him as a tool to put the government under the control of communist ideology, but to turn the country into an iron-clad, Draconian dictatorship where she will pull all the strings from behind the throne.

The plot twist functions well as both a critique of far-right-wing McCarthyite paranoia, as well as an uncanny prediction of what would, by the late 1990s, emerge as a sort of post-political meta conspiracy theory. *The Manchurian Candidate*, first and foremost, delivers the standard liberal retort to McCarthyism. The superpatriots and zealots who had been so obsessed with defending freedom and democracy from communist subversion had done the most to erode freedom, independence, and the right to dissent, protest, or debate with their paranoid accusations and police state intimidation tactics when it came to ferreting out all the suspected communists. Freedom, this argument claims, is not real freedom if you are only free to go along with the party line. In one scene, a chief target of Senator Iselin's accusations and harassment declares that no communist subversive could have done more damage to America than the Senator's witch hunts. But *The Manchurian Candidate*'s treatment of Raymond's conniving, power-crazed mother brings to mind a sort of uber-conspiracy theory that would find fans in the 1980s and the '90s, and among the secret society theorists of the turn of the millennium. Just as Raymond's mother had no real politics other than raw power, these theorists claim that there never really was any natural evolution of a global right-wing and left-wing, capitalist and communist rivalry. There were only powerful economic interests that always sought to sow the seeds of conflict, hatred and war. There has always been one hidden cabal, this theory argues, that bankrolled everyone from the Nazis to Lenin and the Bolshevik revolution. The ultimate goal of the global conspiratorial cabal, theorists argue, is to create conflict and use it to seize power and turn a profit. The cabal operates much like Raymond's mother who works for communists, yet manipulates a rabid communist-baiter to exploit Cold War fears and seize power.

Whereas *The Manchurian Candidate* (much like *Dr. Strangelove*) approached its subject by way of wry satire, 1964's *Seven Days in May*, produced by and starring Burt Lancaster, presented its conspiracy plot of an attempted military *coup d'état* with turgid, straight-faced seriousness. Such seriousness turned out to save the film, perhaps. Although based on a book written before the John F. Kennedy assassination — and reportedly a book Kennedy read and took seriously — the movie premiered while the country was still in mourning. The plot presents a liberal president contemplating a historic nuclear test ban treaty with the Soviets. Just as in the JFK conspiracy theories, the proposed treaty is loathed by the military hawks. Unlike in Kennedy's case, the film's President Lyman is highly unpop-ular with the country at large because of his stand on nuclear weapons. But while Lyman's political opponents are eagerly awaiting the next election to pounce and drive him from office, a cabal among the Joint Chiefs of Staff cannot wait that long. Led by General James Mattoon Scott (Lancaster), the conspirators plot to assassinate Lyman during an upcoming military preparedness exercise. If Lyman, in his naïve blindness and unrealistic trust of the Soviets, is about to wreck the country's defenses by signing the treaty, Scott and his cohorts will strike first and remove him from power before the damage is done.

Seven Days in May unfolds its story arc in what would become the classic conspiracy film plot-sequence. As discussed in Chapter 1, the rudimentary plot of these films most often follows a dogged investigator who unwittingly stumbles onto a large, complex, and immensely dangerous plan put into action by a clique of criminals. In *Seven Days in May*, Scott's trusted aide, Colonel Martin Casey (Kirk Douglas), slowly starts to suspect that a betting pool among a number of high-ranking members of the Joint Chiefs is not all that it appears to be. Messages being passed back and forth about horses, jockeys, and odds in upcoming races appear to be a code of sorts. As much as it might disturb Casey, he soon needs to consider that the coded notes might be covering up some kind of a criminal, if not treasonous, activity. Doing so, however, is not easy for Casey. He is a decorated soldier and a political kindred spirit to Scott. Casey admires Scott's war record and believes that military men who have seen combat have a much more realistic view of war, defense, and international diplomacy than civilian political hacks like the liberal Lyman. Although not as vocal in his opposition to Lyman's policies as the bombastic, flamboyant Scott, Casey also worries that the president is taking the country down the wrong road. Ultimately, however, even as Casey realizes what Scott is up to, he still remains faithful to his oath to uphold the law and defend the Constitution. As distasteful as Casey might find Lyman, Scott's coup, he knows, is ultimately tantamount to the overthrow of democracy.

Although *The Manchurian Candidate, Dr. Strangelove*, and *Seven Days in May* would eventually attain the status of "classic" films in the Cold War, political, and conspiracy genres, conspiracy theory films would only really turn into a regular staple of Hollywood filmmaking in the 1970s. While the Kennedy assassination, the escalation and eventual deterioration of the war in Vietnam, and a growing counter culture movement helped spread a more critical worldview into the mainstream media, it took the Watergate scandal and the exposure of the depth of institutionalized corruption in Washington and the Nixon administration to disillusion most of America like it had never been disillusioned before. The extent of the disillusionment had reached the mainstream media by the end of the entire Watergate debacle. Adding to the impetus to turn out darker, more suspicious, cynical, and conspiracy-oriented entertainment in the 1970s was the demise of the Motion Picture Code in 1968. The country's liberalized social attitudes and the proliferation of TV sets in the vast majority of American homes helped kill the Code. Religious and socially conservative forces like the Catholic Church that had forced the Code on Hollywood had lost their political power by the end of the '60s. Hollywood's need to compete with television, in turn, forced the film industry to push the envelope of complex — often angry, violent, and explicitly sexual — themes into areas never before seen. The cynicism of the conspiracy theories was tailor-made for the post–Watergate '70s. In films, authority figures, the wealthy, the powerful, the government, the military, and the intelligence services would never look quite the same again.

In 1973, the first Hollywood film took on the Kennedy assassination in the semi-documentary-style *Executive Action*. Nearly ten years after *Seven Days in May*, Burt Lancaster again produced and starred in a passionate indictment of paranoid right-wing conspirators overthrowing an administration they disagree with. Just as in *May*, the democratic system, in the eyes of these plotters, can no longer be trusted. The bitter irony of *Executive Action*, just like that of *May*, is that the villains are superpatriots. They believe they are fighting for freedom and democracy while, in truth, they are subverting and destroying both.

Executive Action, although largely forgotten outside of a few of the most die-hard conspiracy movie buffs, is also one of the most remarkable conspiracy films because of its plot structure. It focuses entirely on its conspirators. *Executive Action* is an inversion of the classic thriller formula. Here, the audience is not cheering a group of heroes racing to uncover the secret identities of the conspirators and trying to stop a fiendish plot from being put into action. As a matter of fact, there *are* no heroes in *Executive Action*. Just as the film's plot is about a twisted inversion of patriotism, the movie itself gets rid of the generic thriller plot arc. Here, the viewers watch a step-by-step unfolding of the plans to assassinate John F. Kennedy. It's much like watching a faux documentary on how to orchestrate and pull off the killing of the president.

Executive Action is based on Mark Lane's blockbuster JFK conspiracy theory book, *Rush to Judgment*. Just like the book that birthed much of the Kennedy conspiracy culture, the film endeavors to dramatize the "everyone was involved" theory of so much of that culture. The head plotters, Foster (Robert Ryan) and Farrington (Lancaster), are business titans and cast-iron traditionalists. They are appalled by Kennedy's social, economic, and military agendas, primarily Kennedy's quest to secure treaties with the Russians, downgrade the Cold War, and pull out of Vietnam. For the sake of clarity throughout a 91-minute running time, *Executive Action* does not mix quite as many motives and conspirators into its plot as Lane does into his book. But the movie does convey the point of Lane's thesis. The JFK murder, the film argues, did not have a single motive. The killing was but a representation of a war within American culture before the catchphrase "culture wars" came into vogue. The killing of President Kennedy was ground zero in a war between the old elites, a cultural, economic, and ideological old guard, and young reformers who attempted to change America.

Close on *Executive Action*'s trail, Warren Beatty produced and starred in *The Parallax View* (1974) about a fictional political assassination. The lynchpin of JFK assassination theories is the argument that all that we have been told about the shooting itself was a lie. Even more so than the supposed motivations of wealthy industrialists and warmongering military figures, how Lee Harvey Oswald was created and used as a stooge was the key to the success of the entire murder plot. *The Parallax View* is specifically about the making of an Oswald-like patsy for a political killing.

In true genre fashion, *The Parallax View* involves a tarnished, yet ultimately capable and idealistic hero who stumbles onto a mystery that is just part of a much bigger, much more sinister crime. Here, the hero is boozy, womanizing reporter Joe Frady (Beatty) who begins to suspect that there is much more to the killing of an up-and-coming Senator than suggested by "the official version" of the events. Years ago, Charles Carroll (Bill Joyce), a popular centrist moderate, was shot while making an appearance at Seattle's Space Needle. Soon afterward, however, the authorities accosted his shooter and in the scuffle the murderer fell to his death. Mirroring the fate of Oswald, Carroll's killer is dispatched before his true role in the killing can be unraveled. All that remains afterward is the "government version" of the events.

Frady, much like the rest of America, has been content to accept the official conclusion and go on with his life, such as it is. The once promising journalist has been mired in bouts of alcoholism. His affliction, in effect, is but a metaphor for all Americans who are duped by powerful governmental conspiracies and are comfortable in their oblivious ignorance. Just like Frady is asleep and blind in his alcoholism, so, too, are Americans blind when they willingly accept convenient explanations from powerful institutions. Soon enough, however, Frady is wrenched out of his ignorance and he needs to find the truth behind Carroll's assassination.

Frady's awakening begins with a visit from an old friend, Lee Carter (Paula Prentiss). Lee is also a reporter and, unlike Frady, was never satisfied with the findings of the government's official investigation. Not only are there discrepancies in the facts, but Lee claims that a number of the witnesses to Carroll's murder have died under "mysterious" circumstances. People who could have disputed the official conclusions of the investigation might have been killed off before they could talk. As in the "accidental" killing of Senator Carroll's shooter, this plot point directly mirrors one of the major allegations of JFK conspiracy theorists: They claim that in the years following the assassination, various people who witnessed the event or might have had ties to the conspirators died under suspicious circumstances. In *The Parallax View*, Frady's first reaction to this claim is incredulity and dismissal. Again, as a surrogate for the "average American" who is content to accept the government's explanation of major world events, crises, and assassinations, Frady quickly labels Lee a paranoid conspiracy nut. His illusions are shattered once Lee joins the witnesses who have died suspicious deaths. After Lee is found dead from a drug overdose, Frady realizes that she might have been right about a conspiracy behind Carroll's killing, inviting retaliation by the conspirators.

Frady's investigation eventually leads him to the Parallax Corporation and their peculiar hiring system where applicants are subjected to extensive psychological tests. Realizing that the tests are designed to pinpoint psychopathic personalities who are capable of murder on command, he infiltrates the organization and tries to hunt down an individual he believes is another assassin. He eventually follows the killer to a stadium where rehearsals are underway for a speech by Senator George Hammond (Jim Davis). Trying to catch up to the assassin among the girders and catwalks of the stadium, Frady realizes only too late that he had been duped. He finds a rifle planted in one location and security guards waiting for him to show up. In the meantime, Hammond is shot and Frady is in the convenient location to look like the killer. In an attempt to escape the trap, he is shot dead. The final scene is the nightmare vision every conspiracy theorist has of the Warren Commission. An investigative commission declares that all the best evidence shows that Joe Frady was Hammond's lone assassin and there is no reason to believe that a conspiracy was involved.

The Parallax View—which is a term in optical physics where an object can appear to be at various distances, depending on the angle of observation—is an effective, chilling film because so little is known about the nature of the conspiracy, the identity of the conspirators, or their agendas. Unlike *Executive Action*, which lays everything bare about the plot to assassinate Kennedy, *The Parallax View* shows everything through Frady's limited point of view. The audience never knows more than he does. Why Carroll and Hammond had to die is never revealed. What the Parallax Corporation had to gain by these killings is never explained either. The film is a perfect demonstration that no fear is greater than the fear of the unknown. For conspiracy believers, the unknown goals, the agendas, or ideological motivations of shadowy cabals who might suddenly kill people is the most horrifying aspect of conspiracy theories.

But for conspiracy films in the '70s as a whole, the years 1974 to 1976 were a boon. By 1974, the ongoing Watergate investigation had captured the attentions of most Americans. What had started out as a sloppy burglary that no one, in *Washington Post* reporters Bob Woodward and Carl Bernstein's estimations, really cared about, had become a daily headline-making scandal. Watergate was a part of the popular culture by 1974. The systematic destruction of Richard Nixon's image in particular, and a greater faith in politics in general, had become the daily fodder for cartoonists and comedians everywhere. Hollywood, in turn, as a cultural mirror, fashioned some of its most successful thrillers around cynical plots of conspiracies and corruption.

Francis Ford Coppola's *The Conversation* (1974) and Roman Polanski's *Chinatown* (1974), both earning several Oscar nominations and attaining long-standing reputations as classic thrillers, built their plots around the concept that corruption is the most basic foundation of business and politics. *The Conversation* focuses on a professional wiretapper who has a crisis of conscience over the nature of his work. Harry Caul (Gene Hackman) prizes his dispassionate professionalism when it comes to surveillance work. His personal code, he explains, is not to question the use of the information his bugs and listening devices uncover. He is but a provider of information, well-removed from the worlds, agendas, and decisions of his employers in big business and politics. The private Harry Caul, however, is tormented by guilt. Several people were killed as a result of his wiretapping several years back. Because of his lingering guilt, he at least tries to intervene when he comes to suspect that his current employer (Robert Duvall), the director of a high-powered corporation, will kill his wife (Cindy Williams) once Caul's recordings show that she appears to be having an affair *and* the fact that she suspects her husband capable of committing a murder. The film's conclusion is ironically tragic. Because Caul failed to properly interpret the inflection of one word in the wife's conversation with her lover, he didn't realize that the people plotting murder all along were the wife and the lover. But a disturbing final note of the film, for Watergate-era audiences certainly, is Caul's realization that now he himself is under surveillance. In a frenzy of paranoia, he rips his entire apartment to splinters, trying to uncover the listening devices. Surveillance in the modern world, after all, is everywhere and it's perfectly foolproof and perfectly invisible.

The Conversation's Watergate tie-in, according to Francis Ford Coppola's DVD commentary, appeared to be much stronger than it really was. Watergate parallels are obvious in hindsight, he explains, but they were not as intentional as they might appear. The script was originally written in the 1960s and filmed *before* the most damaging evidence against Nixon's complicity in the burglary had become public. Nevertheless, the overall theme of paranoia and corruption had been the new American fear since the Kennedy assassination theories took flight. In *The Conversation*, it is a given that all powerful businessmen and politicians use underhanded and illegal methods to get their way. This theme, in the midst of the Watergate scandal, just a few months before Richard Nixon resigned the presidency, was a perfect reflection of the mood of the mid–1970s.

Chinatown reflected Watergate era cynicism, as well as the roots of the conspiracy film in film noir. Set in 1930s Los Angeles, it involves one of the quintessential plots of film noir: the cynical private investigator getting caught up in a case that turns out to be much more complex and dangerous than he could ever imagine. Jake Gittes (Jack Nicholson) is a sharply dressed, tough-talking private eye who quietly nurses old disillusionments and shattered idealism. He is hired for what looks like a simple surveillance of a cheating husband. Soon he gets sucked into the dirty dealings of politicians and the moneyed upper crust of Los

Angeles society. He finds out that what will turn out to be the grandest construction project in Southern California history, an irrigation system that will provide Los Angeles enough fresh water to turn it into a world-class metropolis, has all been arranged through bribery, fraud, and murder. The grander and more powerful the system is, the film hints, the darker and dirtier the secrets about the people who helped establish it all.

Even in much lighter entertainment of 1974, like the all-star, big-budget action film *The Towering Inferno*, a disaster of epic proportions is brought about by a conspiracy of greedy high-rise developers. One of the key pictures in the 1970s cycle of disaster sagas, it builds its plot on corporate malfeasance and a conspiracy to cover it all up. The grand opening of the luxurious Glass Tower (disaster films usually involved grand openings or maiden voyages of ships and planes that were doomed to spectacular destruction) turns into a conflagration because of the builders' corruption. The company that built the Glass Tower, the tallest building in the world, secretly tried to maximize profits by ignoring safety codes and using cheap, substandard materials. On opening night, of course, a fire breaks out and a catastrophic blaze engulfs the building. The Glass Tower might as well be a symbol of America in this film. It's the biggest, most advanced, and most glamourous building of its kind, it's the standard for the world to emulate. However, true to the sensibilities of the early '70s, the massive edifice has been badly compromised. The Glass Tower is more like a Tower of Babel, doomed to failure because of the treachery of its builders. The film's angry subtext is punctuated by Paul Newman, playing the Glass Tower's conscientious architect whose careful designs had been ignored by the greedy developer (William Holden) and his sychophantic son-in-law (Richard Chamberlain). "They should just leave it," Newman says of the burned-out hulk on the end. "Kind of a monument to all the bullshit in the world."

Nineteen seventy-five saw the blockbuster success of a film that would change filmmaking and exhibition practices to this day. *Jaws*, a sort of nature-run-amok thriller, not only created Steven Spielberg's career as an A-list director virtually overnight, but its success as a summer release created a new model for the summer blockbuster film that would turn enormous profits from repeat viewings by vacationing teenagers and audiences looking to escape the heat with an old-fashioned action and adventure fantasy. While *Jaws* might have had plenty of suspense and thrills in its story of three men battling a great white shark, the film's subplot of small-town politics and business was a pure Watergate-era allegory for corruption. Spielberg readily admitted that the thematic inspiration for his adaptation of Peter Benchley's novel was the Watergate scandal.

Jaws' Amity is a tranquil all–American small town where everything is running exactly as it should. It is the perfect community for families, law and order are respected, and business is vigorously promoted by the mayor and the chamber of commerce. A mortal danger, however, lurks *literally* beneath the surface. An almost preternaturally enormous shark has invaded the local waters and it begins picking off unsuspecting swimmers. While the presence of the shark is known to the audience from the film's opening, and its true destructive force is suspected by several characters— namely the conscientious Sheriff Martin Brody (Roy Scheider)— most of the citizens of Amity seem to be, for the longest time, almost willfully ignorant of the threat. The Amity mindset, the film suggests, is similar to the public's initial attitude toward Watergate. The threat is but an inconvenience they'd rather not know about. Ignorance really *does* seem to be bliss in this town. Once it seems like the shark can't be ignored any more, the mayor and the local businessmen still do their best to downplay its threat. Scaring people about a man-eating shark would be bad for the summer tourist season. Much like crusading journalists Woodward and Bernstein, Brody seems to be carrying on a futile fight to get someone to take the danger seriously and do something about it.

The same year, espionage thrillers like *The Eiger Sanction* and *Three Days of the Condor* touched on similar paranoid conspiratorial themes. The former, directed by and starring Clint Eastwood, accuses the world of intelligence-gathering of corruption and conspiratorial maneuverings in a plot about a former government operative who is in as much danger from his vicious and duplicitous employers as he is from spies from "the other side." *The Eiger Sanction*'s main problem, though, is its pulp fiction origin, having been adapted from an "airport paperback" potboiler written by the enigmatic novelist Trevanian. The film's condemnation is hard to take seriously when so much of it is so cartoonish. The unscrupulous spy agency Eastwood's character used to work for, C2, is run by an ex–Nazi albino named Dragon. Dragon, by the way, is also hypersensitive to light and runs his organization — staffed mainly by sociopaths or hulking thugs who look like Mafia bodyguards— from a darkened, sterilized room. The Eastwood character, an assassin who only works occasionally for the payment of rare paintings, or when he has been blackmailed, also goes by the distracting name of Dr. Jonathan Hemlock. While all of this is taken fairly faithfully from the novel, the true intentions of the author's work have been in some dispute among fans and critics. Trevanian's real name was Rodney Whitaker, and he was a professor of Communication and media at the University of Texas. His spy novels, like *The Eiger Sanction*, according to fans, were but a clever intellectual's parodies of the spy genre, particularly Ian Fleming's James Bond books. To critics, these claims are much too generous, especially given the fact that Fleming's books were already parodies themselves. A truly perceptive writer, critics argue, would hardly spoof a spoof. To Trevanian-Whitaker's detractors, his books were merely an academic's hobby of (not very skillfully) imitating popular literature. Author-screenwriter Warren Murphy, who co-wrote the *Eiger Sanction* script, had at one point parodied Trevanian in one of his own books, characterizing the one-named author's work as "embarrassingly illiterate."[9] But despite the story's intentions or the film's merits as art, *The Eiger Sanction*'s angry message is well in line with the popular mood of the '70s. The shadowy C2 organization is so corrupt that its best operatives need to be threatened and blackmailed into doing their jobs. The one operative who truly seems to be motivated by patriotic idealism, a young African-American named Jemima Brown (Vonetta McGee), is portrayed as hopelessly naïve. But the film's most critical outrage at the government and the military-intelligence-industrial complex is delivered by its assassination plot. Hemlock needs to kill an enemy agent before he delivers a highly lethal chemical weapon formula to "the other side." The formula, however, was stolen from an American government research lab. If the American government is ethically superior to the other side, Hemlock tells the innocent Jemima, then why does it possess this weapon to begin with? Why would the Americans be working with a weapon that had been outlawed by all the international treaties?

In tones a lot less pulpy, director Sydney Pollack's *Three Days of the Condor* likewise presents an intelligence community riddled with corruption. While *The Eiger Sanction* created fictitious spy organizations and maneuvered its story around the hoary plot device of the secret-formula-falling-into-enemy-hands, *Three Days of the Condor* is a more sedate assassination mystery founded in the very real international and financial concerns of the day. *Condor*'s main character and unwitting conspiracy-fighter Joe Turner, is a low-level CIA analyst (Robert Redford) getting caught up in the efforts to keep top-secret war and invasion plans from being made public. Echoing the Nixon administration's battles against Daniel Ellsberg and the Pentagon Papers, Turner's character is marked for death because he could possibly reveal CIA plans for the invasion of Middle Eastern oil fields. The plot, in fact, is a radical inversion of the traditional secret-that-must-be-kept structure of espionage films. Unlike in the generic spy film where the hero is a member of the system — even if an unwilling and disaffected member like Jonathan Hemlock — who is trying to keep some vital government secret from slipping out, *Condor*'s Turner must fight to expose the CIA's secrets. For just as the Pentagon Papers affair, the Watergate scandal, and the Church Committee's investigations revealed, government secrecy could just as well hide plans to wreck democracy and put the world in danger of unnecessary wars. Perhaps even a decade before, a character like Joe Turner, heading off toward the offices of *The New York Times* at the end of the film, would have been seen as a traitor. By the 1970s, of course, American audiences had reasons to feel different. Nonetheless, the film, to handle this issue safely — and to maintain suspense throughout — does not reveal the reason Turner has been targeted for assassination until the finale. Until his relentless hunter (Max Von Sydow) lays out the reasons for Turner's pursuit at the end of the movie, he remains a sympathetic character because he is an apparently innocent man who is being wrongly pursued. In a Hitchcockian approach to the plot, Turner is someone who seems to have done nothing wrong, broken no rules and no laws, yet he finds himself running and fighting for his life. This wrongful persecution helps ensure that most audiences, no matter what their views about Washington, intelligence, the CIA, and the Middle East, will sympathize with Turner's plight enough to cheer him on and eventually see the importance of revealing potentially damaging government secrets to the world.

But perhaps the most important conspiracy film of the 1970s made its impact because it was a true story. In 1976, producer-star Robert Redford and director Alan J. Pakula dramatized Bob Woodward and Carl Bernstein's investigation of the Watergate break-in with flawlessly precise and detailed accuracy in *All the President's Men*.

The most interesting — and, in hindsight, astonishing — fact about the production is that it was not an easy sell to Hollywood's studios. Redford had been interested in the Watergate break-in from the time the story started appearing in publication, but even after the affair's metamorphosis into a full-blown scandal and Constitutional crisis, none of the studios were particularly keen on making the film. Even after President Nixon's resignation, many had deemed the story as not quite right for a big-screen adaptation. The affair was something akin to Vietnam in Hollywood's reckoning. Watergate was a national nightmare Americans had no choice but to see day in and day out on their TVs. There was no reason to believe those same Americans were about to pay money to see it again in the movie theaters. Moreover, cooperation from the story's principals, Woodward and Bernstein, had been slow in coming, according to Redford. The reporters had been reticent to deal with filmmakers. Redford approached the two as the scandal had been slowly unfolding, telling them that he had been fascinated with the affair since their first stories appeared in the *Washington Post*. At first, however, it was decided that the Watergate hearings had to reach legal closure for the complete story to be told. Afterward, Woodward and Bernstein decided that they would write their final account of the investigation in a book before the film could be made.[10]

All the President's Men seems to follow the standard conspiracy theory story arc that had already been developed in films throughout the previous decade. Since this is all based on real people and real events, this coincidence is astonishing. Moreover, since the film has withstood over three decades' worth of critical and historical scrutiny, its exacting details and accuracy establish it as a standard-setting work in honest docudrama filmmaking. Whereas Hollywood had a spotty track record when it came to accuracy in historical films, *All the President's Men* aimed for the truth over Hollywood high drama and embellishment. The fact that the film, nevertheless, feels like any fictional investigative thriller is surprising.

In *All the President's Men*, true to generic form, the lowliest of crimes has a connection to the highest corridors of power in the government. Covering the arrests in a botched burglary at the Democratic National Committee's offices in the Watergate hotel, rookie *Washington Post* reporter Bob Woodward (Redford) is surprised by the fact that all of the culprits have backgrounds in espionage and covert military operations. Pursuing the case based on this peculiar detail, and discovering that all of the men have well-paid attorneys, Woodward stumbles onto a convoluted trail of payments and bank accounts financing the burglars and their legal representatives. When the payments seem to repeatedly originate from the Republican party and the White House's Committee to Reelect the President, Woodward — soon joined by the more seasoned Carl Bernstein (Dustin Hoffman)—can't help but conclude that a scandal is sure to break if he just does a little more digging and gets a few more Washington insiders on the record.

What is surprising about the film, according to Redford on the film's DVD commentary, is how restrained it ultimately remains in its treatment of institutionalized corruption in Washington, D.C. As Redford explains how he became interested in the case in 1972, shortly after stories of the burglary showed up in the *Post*, one realizes that the film could have been a lot more cynical and damning of not only Nixon and the Republicans, but the entire Washington political culture. As Redford recalls, he first started asking questions of political figures about their take on the burglary while doing research for his film *The Candidate* (1972). Astoundingly, most of the people he spoke to already suspected that the burglary was sanctioned by the White House and that Nixon knew all about it. The prevailing Washington attitude, however, seemed to be that Watergate was yet another example of the usual practice of illegal political dirty tricks. Nixon, many suspected, could possibly be caught for doing something everyone —*both* parties— engaged in routinely. The reason no one, including Democrats, considered doing anything about it was the fact that Nixon's reelection seemed assured. In turn, if Nixon held on to the White House with landslide numbers, they didn't want to be on his enemies list. Nixon, Redford explains, was roundly feared and loathed for being vindictive and mean. Making an issue of Watergate in 1972 was in no one's interest.

Nonetheless, *All the President's Men* is not a film of rage; it does not condemn Washington or the political system. There are no indictments of "institutionalized corruption." The film is about an earnest search for the truth, a quest to root out corruption so the system can go about functioning properly. The sort of cynicism Redford reportedly heard about from the insiders of the Washington culture does not make it onto the screen. If anything could be quarreled with in this film, it's the relationship between Woodward and Bernstein, radical opposites in personality, temperament, and political ideologies that could have put more of a probing focus on the issue of how endemic corruption is in the American political system. In real life, Woodward and Bernstein had, for quite a while, a contentious working relationship. Bernstein had been working at the *Post* longer than Woodward and he was considered a better writer. Woodward, though, was a more methodical journalist, while Bernstein was more flamboyant and confrontational. Woodward was a conservative

Republican whereas Bernstein was a liberal Democrat. There are tiny, fleeting hints of these fundamental differences between the two men. There is, for example, a scene where Woodward appears to be quietly resentful of Bernstein's rewriting of one of his stories. There is a glimpse of some counter culture posters on the walls of Bernstein's office. How these two reporters personally interpreted the larger significance of the scandal unfolding in front of them, given their radically different worldviews and ideologies, could have added several more layers of complexity to the film. In defense of *All the President's Men*, however, the film is already 138 minutes long. Its meticulous details of the investigative reporter's daily routine of phone calls, paperwork, and interviews, not to mention the complicated details of the financing behind the burglary, are complex enough.

The impact of *All the President's Men* is ultimately fascinating to ponder. It is an example of a film no one wanted to make attaining critical and commercial success no one could believe. But, perhaps the film's greatest power had been ascribed by President Gerald Ford. He personally believed that its 1976 release was a factor in his loss to Jimmy Carter. The film's success, he had often said in interviews, dredged up memories of Watergate. The film just might have reignited whatever ill will Americans harbored for him in 1974 for pardoning Nixon.

All the President's Men also became a template film for a sort of public service-oriented conspiracy film, the likes of which would often be seen in environmental and business conspiracy movies. Functioning a lot like latter-day versions of 1930s and '40s journalism films, these films present dogged heroes fighting for the welfare of citizens about to be lied to by their elected officials or cheated and hurt by crooked and predatory big business. In 1979, dedicated (if not underestimated and small-time) journalists played by Jane Fonda and Michael Douglas exposed the cover-up of potentially catastrophic flaws in the safety systems of nuclear power plants in *The China Syndrome*. *Silkwood* (1983), based on the true story of nuclear power plant whistle-blower Karen Silkwood's mysterious death, likewise pointed an accusatory finger charging conspiracy in the nuclear industry.

Perhaps one of the most complex and prescient films of the decade that can be fit into the conspiracy theory category was Sidney Lumet's *Network* (1976). The focus of the MGM film, from a screenplay by multiple award-winning screenwriter and playwright Paddy Chayefsky, is the world of network television and its brutal politics and machinations to win an endless race for ratings and advertising dollars. Indicting corporate control, the film laments the fact that modern TV programmers, and mainly news producers, are losing their profession's traditional set of ethical principles oriented toward civic duty, social responsibility, and service. Much like media critics and academic commentators on the news industry usually claim, the biggest problem of corporate control over news broadcasting has been the increased push to run news divisions just like any other profit-earning department of a TV network. This phenomenon has been taking shape since the 1970s. Traditionally, however, TV and radio networks have always looked at their news divisions as prestige departments. News was where a network did its civic duty to its viewers and to democracy itself. The bottom line was never the chief driving factor for a television network's news department.

When news needs to turn a profit just like entertainment programming, *Network* argues, the end result will be news that is more entertainment than serious reporting, yellow journalism for the airwaves. The film demonstrates this through a storyline steeped in absurd black comedy. The plot involves the on-air nervous breakdown of the aging, fading news anchor Howard Beale. Beale had once been a well-respected, award-winning star journalist, a crusader in the tradition of Murrow and Cronkite, the jewel in the crown of the successful UBS television network. Times and the business environment changed, however. The over-the-hill Beale is no longer exciting and relevant, a younger generation of viewers can't relate to him, and the once-powerhouse UBS is faltering in the ratings. A corporate takeover and new management, in turn, want to shake things up. News, just like everything at UBS, needs to start earning its keep. The irrelevant Beale, as a result, is about to be fired. The pressure is slowly getting to him. Eventually, he snaps and goes into a series of incoherent, rambling tirades on the air. Within his ramblings, however, are words that touch something in the few remaining members of the UBS audience. His outrage at the disintegration of his career and the unfairness of life speaks to the general frustration of modern Americans. At the core of Beale's rants is a not-so-quiet outrage at the forces of modernity, of big bureaucracies, big government, big business, the powerful, the elites, everyone who is taking advantage of, cheating, and lying to everyday, average Americans. The answer, Beale screams, is to push back at all these forces, to get up and yell at the system and announce that all this unfairness and abuse will no longer go on. In the film's iconic scene, Beale urges all his viewers to get out of their seats, snap out of their complacency, open their windows and shout, "I'm as mad as hell and I'm not going to take this any more!" Surprisingly, people do just that. The shouting not only becomes a cathartic release for audiences, but its powerful message proves contagious. People all across the country start screaming that they're as mad as hell. Seemingly overnight, the burned-out, insane Beale is a star once more. Since audiences, attention, and ratings are the building blocks of all broadcast networks, not only does UBS let Beal scream his outrage as much as possible, but they fill the rest of their time slots with equally shocking and bizarre programs in the quest to draw audiences and garner ratings.

The impact of *Network*'s message can be interpreted in two ways. On the one hand — along the lines of what critics and media scholars usually say — the film is almost shockingly prophetic. On the other, looking at the film's depiction of network television's jockeying for ratings and attempts at audience manipulation, it casts the idea of media conspiracies in an entirely new light. In fact, this second approach to *Network*'s meaning might just find and effective *critique* of media conspiracies.

Most media commentators point out that all one needs to do to appreciate *Network*'s power of prediction is to take a look at the tabloid-like nature of so much of today's TV entertainment. From reality shows to Jerry Springer, the myriad of lurid crime and courtroom reenactment programs, pontificating political pundits and endless entertainment and celebrity gossip, modern television is the world of *Network* come true. In fact, *Network* had already been referenced by media critics as early as the 1980s when daytime television was transformed from a landscape of soap operas and game shows to ever-more confrontational, shocking, and perverse talk shows. When former ABC correspondent Geraldo Rivera started hosting one outlandish prime time special after another, focusing on everything from Al Capone's secret vault to a nationwide network of Satanic cults, to many, the world of *Network* had come to pass. Then, if Al Capone and the Satanists were not enough, Rivera went on to host a daytime talk show (1987–1998) whose highlight was a brawl between white supremacists and black militants (Rivera got his nose broken by a flying chair). While daytime TV might have appeared to be sinking further into the gutter in the 1990s, perhaps the purest "*Network* moment" came in 1997 on the Chicago NBC affiliate, WMAQ Channel 5. To boost ratings, NBC executives wanted to give talk show host Jerry Springer a spot to deliver daily commentaries. Emmy award-winning anchors Ron Magers and Carol Marin quit in protest.[11] While tabloid sensationalism in the mainstream media is certainly not new, wary critics have argued that in the last three decades it has only been getting worse. In the 2000s, one-sided political pundit shows are more influential than straight news reports, and gossip and scandal have their own cable networks.

But how the world of *Network* can come about bears a bit of scrutiny, and the film itself does have some interesting things to say about it. In fact, in many ways, the film dismisses the notion that the debasement of entertainment and the news is some sort of a deliberate, orchestrated conspiracy for the sake of social control. As *Network*'s UBS flounders, its programmers scramble to try and air *anything* that will win ratings. Howard Beale's breakdown boosts ratings, so he gets his own show to keep on ranting and pontificating as much as possible. Then in Beale's wake, anything that might work gets on the air. At one point, an SLA-type Marxist domestic terrorist group is given its own reality show. Audiences can tune in every week and see the gang plan bank heists and strategize how to overthrow the system.

This sort of uncoordinated opportunism is where the film pointedly disagrees with much of the media conspiracy theories. For the most imaginative theorists—and left-wing academic media-critics *à la* Ben Bagdikian[12]—the media is but a part of the grand conspiracy to control everything. The ultimate media conspiracy is to maintain the status quo and keep elites in positions of power, the argument goes. As the academic critics usually charge, from the European Marxists of the "Frankfurt School" in the 1930s to their modern-day disciples in the "critical theory" school of thought, all forms of entertainment, all forms of media content that might undermine a right-wing, corporate-capitalist system will never make it onto the airwaves. *Network*—although made by a creative team with solidly left-leaning liberal credentials, like writer Chayefsky and director Lumet—begs to differ with this point of view. Something as complex as network television cannot be controlled so easily. In fact, it is the UBS network itself that is perpetually riding a chaotic rollercoaster of failure and prosperity, always at the mercy of the unpredictable whims of the audience. If anything, *Network* is an early dramatization of Žižek's unpiloted ship metaphor. Should one put stock in the power of the media being able to shape society, the UBS network's seat-of-the-pants programming schemes look much more disturbing that anything an organized cabal could dream up in its most malevolent moments.

The 1970s turned into more and more of a cultural landscape of cynicism, and disaffection, corruption, and mass-scale criminality reigned as a favorite theme for filmmakers. Few government figures, high-ranking intelligence operatives, military leaders, business tycoons, or media moguls were above suspicion of conspiracy. This trajectory into dark territory would continue in the science fiction genre as well.

Fantastic Conspiracies

While the worlds of politicians, cops, spies, and soldiers were getting embroiled in the moral gray areas of conspiracies and corruption on film, science fiction took longer to reflect this darkening mood in America.

In the beginning, however, fantastic films, especially films about UFOs and their alien occupants, had often tried to frighten audiences as much as possible. Outer space travel, alien visitation of the Earth, and the contact with extraterrestrial beings seemed to almost always inspire artists with dread fear before anything else.

The first science fiction motion picture, French filmmaker Georges Méliès' 1902 comic space adventure *A Trip to the Moon*, might have started on a humorous tone, but a sinister, paranoid subtext quickly turned up. The story, very loosely based on Jules Verne's concept of space travel via a giant artillery shell, involves a group of scientists taking a trip to the moon and encountering its inhabitants. Much of the film (before the moon dwellers turn up) is light comedy and sight gags. The arrival on the moon is the iconic image of the man in the moon getting hit in the eye by the cannon shell. But once the inhabitants of the moon meet the Earthlings, things become a lot darker. From that point on, the moon creatures might as well be the stand-ins for all the "unfriendly natives" in scores of pulp fiction adventure stories of clean-cut, civilized American or European adventurers menaced by the simple-minded aggressiveness of the "primitives" of Darkest Africa. The moon dwellers, looking something like miniature devils with horns and long, pointy noses, react to the friendly Earth visitors with mindless violence. They take the scientists hostage and present them to their leader. The leader appears to be a king on a high throne. The moon, obviously, has not yet discovered the superiority of Western democracy. Subsequently, another slapstick chase ensues. The Earth scientists flee back to their cannon shell, with the moon men in hot pursuit.

A near remake of this story would be made by British director J.V. Leigh in 1919. Crediting H.G. Wells' *The First Men in the Moon* as source material, the film involves another group of scientists traveling to the moon (this time by way of a spaceship made of an anti-gravity metal), running afoul of hostile moon-dwellers, and escaping back to Earth in the nick of time.

From the early days of science fiction film, extraterrestrials had, more often than not, been convenient villains and monsters. The creatures were the ones to be feared, not government agents who tried to protect the world from the aliens' hostile intentions. Even if these G-men might have, on occasion, resorted to subterfuge, they were on the side of right and we could trust their underhanded tactics because it was all well-intentioned. But it must be added that this sort of xenophobia was not just the creation of filmmakers, or only the creation of American artists. Science fiction's literary roots had often used aliens as dangerous "others" or symbolic representatives of the worst impulses of the human race. H.G. Wells, laying the archetypal foundation for alien invasion stories with *War of the Worlds* in 1898, used aliens as a metaphor for colonialism. The book was designed as a consciousness-raising tool for Victorian England. How would the citizens of one of the world's great colonial powers feel, the book asks, if the tables were suddenly turned and they were the ones being overrun by the forces of an implacable, unknowable, and supremely advanced invading army? Although the book's cerebral core offered social critique, its aliens were, nonetheless, merciless monsters. As science fiction traveled west, European writers like Wells and Jules Verne finding favor among the purveyors of American popular literature, these evil "others" had, more often than not, remained the dominant image of aliens. Especially as science fiction became popularized in the pulp magazines like *Argosy, Amazing Stories*, and *Astounding Stories*, aliens would continue turning up in the forms of grotesque invaders. Moreover, when early films turned their attention to borrowing themes from science fiction, as Melies had done, the evil alien always seemed to be more attractive than the friendly alien, than the enlightened role-model for a more peaceful and rational society.

When the benign aliens did show up, one might find an interesting comparison to the alien-as-threat stories. Side by side, these two types of films reveal an interesting dialogue between isolationist cultural and political impulses and a more liberal openness to the foreign, the alternative, and cultural influences challenging the status quo. Both of these themes, however, originate in early European silent films. In 1913, the British film *A Message from Mars* was about a Martian named Ramiel sent to Earth to save a lost soul. Rescuing a depressed, despondent man, Ramiel fulfills his mission and can return home. The film, it has been noted by critics, is actually a lot like the angel-on-a mission plot Frank Capra would later use in *It's a Wonderful Life*. In 1917, Dutch director Forest Holger-Madsen made *Heaven Ship* (*Himmelskibet*), about an expedition to Mars finding an intellectually and morally superior society living in harmony with the environment, and given to frequent ethical contemplation. The popularity of these films in Europe during and after World War I is obvious, reflecting that continent's yearning for peace. But not all of the peaceful-alien films showed *only* gentle and admirable extraterrestrials. In turn, their messages were not entirely works of enlightened acceptance of alternative cultures. Many films from the silent era and the late 1920s through the '50s infused their stories with a sort of paternalistic message of intervention. For example, the 1924 Russian film *Aelita*, and the American films *Just Imagine* (1930), *Rocketship X-M* (1950), *Cat Women of the Moon* (1954), *Fire Maidens from Outer Space* (1955), *Queen of Outer Space* (1958), and *Voyage to the Planet of Prehistoric Women* usually involved astronauts from the Earth finding alien planets in the grip of some kind of a war or oppressed by dictatorial rulers. The visitors from Earth then quickly aid the side of freedom — represented by the alien race trying to live according to a social structure most resembling that of the country producing the film — overthrowing the oppressors and making this alien world more Earthlike. While the American films end with the establishment of a new order akin to liberal democracy, the Russian *Aelita* sees the overthrow of an oppressive system resembling the most stultifying example of industrial capitalism and the establishment of a socialistic, proletariat-ruled society. American cliffhanger serials of the 1930s, like *Flash Gordon* and *Buck Rogers*, exemplified this tradition. In the *Flash Gordon* serials, a blonde, all–American hero (Larry "Buster" Crabbe) travels to the planet Mongo and gives a helping hand to a besieged coalition of states resisting the dictatorial emperor Ming. Likewise in *Buck Rogers*— once again with Crabbe — an astronaut from contemporary America gets transported to an exotic world — this time the future — and helps remake that world in the image of the one he left.

In essence, a great deal of early science fiction cinema was a product of filmmakers attempting to extol the virtues of their own countries. These films, for the most part, did not attempt to show alien worlds and extraterrestrial creatures as something wondrous and worth knowing on their own terms. These stories reflected the strongly nationalistic, imperialistic flavor of the early twentieth century. Any place different from the Earth needed to be conquered, made more Earthlike, and their inhabitants converted to "our way of life." By the time Hollywood embraced science fiction in the '50s, in the wake of the flying saucer craze, the paranoia of the Cold War helped insure that a great deal of the chauvinism of early science fiction remained intact in the new saucer movies.

The earliest alternatives to the evil alien invader came in 1951, a landmark year for saucer cinema. Robert Wise's *The Day the Earth Stood Still* presented an alien invader as an urbane gentleman named Klaatu. The fully human alien (played by British actor Michael Rennie) lands his flying saucer in the middle of Washington, D.C., and comes with a peace offering for the Cold War–era Earthlings. Unfortunately, a jittery soldier shoots Klaatu. While recovering in a hospital, Klaatu explains that his shooting just bears out the necessity of his visit. The people of Earth are not only a violent and primitive lot, but they have gotten too technologically advanced for both their own good *and* the safety of the rest of the cosmos. The alien wants to address all the leaders of the world about the need for peace and disarmament. When this request is refused — dismissed, actually, as being hopelessly naïve — Klaatu flees the hospital and attempts to learn the ways of Earthlings by living among them. During his "undercover" work, the alien realizes that many people of the Earth do have the capacity and the yearning to live in peace. He is especially taken by the widowed Helen (Patricia Neal) and her son (Billy Gray). Helen's husband had been killed in World War II and she turns out to be the most receptive to suggestions that there can be a better way of running the world and a more productive way in which countries can deal with their problems. The world's governments, however, are much too entrenched in their bellicose, aggressive ways. The *system*, or *all* of the world's systems, are so stuck in the status quo that things can never change on their own. The only way the Earth can change is under a threat from Klaatu and his big, hulking bodyguard robot, Gort. Before departing for space, Klaatu, essentially, warns the people of the Earth that they *must* find a way to do away with their atomic weapons and aggressive policies or face annihilation from space. All the other technologically advanced civilizations of the universe, Klaatu explains, have elected to live under a sort of intergalactic enforcement system. This system is run by robots like Gort. Should any one of the planets threaten any other, the robots would instantly annihilate the aggressor. None of the planets has control over the enforcers. Gort and his kind cannot be manipulated or subverted in any way.

"Our way of life," the film argues, is not only dangerously unstable, but it is certainly no role model for any other societies in the cosmos to emulate. The film is a quiet yet forceful repudiation of the old Saturday matinee serial fantasies that used to endorse Earthly imperialism for the rest of the universe. If anything, the irrational aggression of all of the world's countries — with the United States being no better than any other system in the world — needs to be contained by a strong, benevolent, and paternalistic outside force. The call for a paternalistic benevolent force that had the ability to bend any of the world's nations to its will marked *The Day the Earth Stood Still* with its lingering controversy. The film's critics accused the end of the film of endorsing a fascist message. Despite all of the film's good intentions and Klaatu's Christ-like love and patience with the childishly backward and bellicose Earthlings, the argument that the world must be under that watchful eye — and the thumb — of an autonomous, non-representative body like the enforcement-robots is basically tantamount to an endorsement of a totalitarian rule. Certainly, director Wise and his screenwriter, Edmund H. North, had often countered that their true intentions were to advocate for a strong United Nations. But a critic can easily argue that the Gort peacekeeping system is not an accurate metaphor for the U.N. While ultimately the film historian needs to give Wise and North the benefit of the doubt that their intentions were good and they were not a pair of crypto fascists, the film's final moments still have a mildly disturbing aftertaste.[13]

A more interesting influence of the film, in terms of tracing the development of conspiracy theories in science fiction, is the way it showed that audiences were receptive to stories of benevolent aliens and dangerous, wrongheaded, and repressive U.S. government operatives. An audience can accept the premises and the warnings of conspiracy theory films when they do not accept the complete infallibility of their government. More importantly, *The Day the Earth Stood Still* was able to pull off its social critique at the height of the Red Scare and while the HUAC hearings were still attempting to unearth communist agents within the film industry.

Nonetheless, the success of *The Day the Earth Stood Still* did not birth as many stories of benevolent aliens as subversive, threatening aliens for the rest of the '50s. In 1951, *Earth* followed on the heels of another Cold War alien film, Howard Hawks' *The Thing from Another World*. Considered as much of a classic as *Earth*, *The Thing* is the diametrical opposition to Wise's film. Whereas *Earth* was a liberal call for a global governing body, *The Thing* was a warning against naïve blindness to foreign threats. In Hawks' film, a group of soldiers and scientists at a North Pole base accidentally unleash an alien creature (James Arness) whose spaceship had been embedded in the ice. The alien quickly goes on the rampage, fulfilling its instinctive drive to dominate and colonize. There are two approaches to dealing with the Thing and, of course, only one can be correct. The scientists want to communicate and reason with the creature, hoping to appeal to its peaceful impulses. The monster, they believe, cannot be a destructive, evil savage by nature. The soldiers, on the other hand, believe it's safer to assume that the creature is hostile than to let their guard down and be sorry later. In this instance, the soldiers' more "conservative," pessimistic mindset wins out. The one scientist attempting to initiate a conversation with the Thing is quickly crushed by the vicious monstrosity.

Ultimately, both *The Thing* and *The Day the Earth Stood Still* are excellent examples of Americans' warring instincts during the Cold War. Coming from talented directors and writers, both films well-represent the left-wing and right-wing attitudes during that period. In a way, both stances were right in their hopes and fears during a time when the country — and the world — was facing real villains and threats, *and* it needed to solve its problems without resorting to an all-out nuclear war.

For much of the flying saucer cycle of that decade, however, *The Thing From Another World* remained the standard setter. Aliens were, more often than not, threats, and government agents were heroes when they fought a clandestine battle against them and covered their tracks, doing their best to deceive the American public about the dangers in their midst. An interesting glimpse at this sort of *de facto* conspiracy to hide any tracks of monstrosities can often be seen in the giant mutated animal films of that decade. That science fiction subgenre is a complex form of entertainment because it also warns about the dangers of atomic power and the giant rampaging bugs and mutated grotesqueries are metaphors for the weapons of the Cold War getting out of hand. Nevertheless, when these weapons do get out of hand, the heroes of these films, usually scientists who work with the government or government agents, first try their best to keep everything secret and the populace blissfully ignorant. For a good example of this, one should take a look at the film considered the best of the "giant bug" movies, 1954's *Them!* Here, atomic testing in the desert Southwest has mutated ants, causing them to grown to the size of cattle. Part of the government's efforts of containing the threat is to avert the mass panic that is sure to sweep the country, especially the West Coast as the ants quickly take shelter in the Los Angeles storm drains. The film's most noteworthy scene where government cover-ups and conspiracies are casually endorsed for the sake of national security takes place in a hospital's mental ward. A pilot, who has seen one of the flying queen ants, has been locked up here for ranting about giant flying monsters. The film's stalwart hero, Robert Graham (James Arness), comes to interview the man, listening to his story impassively and giving no hint to the hapless pilot that his sighting is indeed accurate. Once the interrogation is over, Graham calmly tells the pilot's doctor that the man is, in fact, as sick as he appears to be, and there is no truth to his rants of airborne monsters. While Graham and his government team goes on to try and find a way of containing the ants, the pilot is left locked up indefinitely in the hospital.

The most noteworthy and well-remembered alien contact films of the decade include

The Man from Planet X (1951), *It Came from Outer Space* (1953), *Invaders from Mars* (1953), *This Island Earth* (1955), *The Creeping Unknown* (1955), *Invasion of the Body Snatchers* (1956), *Earth vs. the Flying Saucers* (1956), *It Conquered the World* (1956), *Enemy from Space* (1957), *Invasion of the Saucer Men* (1957), *I Married a Monster from Outer Space* (1958), *The Blob* (1958), *The Mysterians* (1958) and *The Space Children* (1958). Of this lot — again, representing the slightly higher caliber of alien contact films — *It Came from Outer Space*, *Invasion of the Saucer Men*, and *The Space Children* are the only ones where the aliens are not one-dimensional monstrosities that need to be vanquished without a second thought.

The two films with forceful anti-paranoia or anti-war themes are *It Came from Outer Space* and *The Space Children*. In *It Came from Outer Space*, the aliens are not even invaders but mere space travelers making a pit stop on Earth to fix their ship. They hide out in a mine in Arizona; complications arise when they need to be protected from primitive Earthlings who are apt to react to their repulsive appearance with fear and hostility. The aliens are capable of assuming human form and controlling human minds, but despite these potentially dangerous powers, one of the townspeople (Richard Carlson) learns to trust in life forms that do not look like he does. In fact, his trust is never betrayed and the aliens leave in peace once their repairs have been made. Peace begins, the film argues, when people are capable of ignoring surface differences and abandoning their prejudices against those who do not look like they do.

With an even more forceful anti-arms race message, *The Space Children* has an alien brain assume control of the minds of the children of scientists and military leaders involved in weapons testing and development. Using the children as a tool, the alien consciousness sabotages various missile launch attempts. By the end of the film, however, it is revealed that the alien is not interfering with weapons development in an attempt to weaken the world and pave the way for an invasion. The creature is merely trying to stop the ignorant, self-destructive humans from killing themselves with their own weapons.

The most important film in the development of the science fiction conspiracy canon, however, is *Invasion of the Saucer Men*. This is ironic since the film is largely uneven in its tone, more slapstick and juvenile humor than speculative science fiction, straight drama, or even frightening thriller. In fact, in his essay on the early conspiracy theory mindset among UFO enthusiasts and Hollywood's adaptation of the UFO themes, Lyndon W. Joslin calls *Invasion of the Saucer Men* a "crummy little movie" and an "inconsequential B-film."[14] Although the film might be low-budget, and often embarrassingly inept in its storytelling, pacing, and direction, it is not quite inconsequential. *Saucer Men* is the first film to use the theme of a special clandestine saucer-recovery military unit of the government and a team of agents tasked with silencing and discrediting UFO witnesses.

In part, such figures were integral to the UFO conspiracy theorists' claims since Edward Ruppelt and Donald Keyhoe charged that the Air Force and the U.S. government had been covering up the truth about alien spaceship sightings. There was very little conclusive physical evidence of alien visitations, conspiracists claimed, since the government's foot soldiers have always been quickly dispatched in the wake of a saucer landing. These agents allegedly stole or destroyed all the evidence when not intimidating and harassing witnesses into either staying silent about their experiences or recanting their stories of alien contact.

The most interesting — and sinister — twist to the claims of UFO witnesses being intimidated into silence surfaced in the Men in Black (MIB) companion-phenomenon to UFO lore. Starting in the 1950s, UFO researchers claimed that eyewitnesses to particularly convincing close encounters had been visited by men wearing black suits, sporting black hats and sunglasses, and driving large black sedans. These MIBs were very circumspect about what agency they represented, but allegedly claimed U.S. government affiliation and took several tacks at persuading the witnesses not to discuss their UFO experiences with anyone. The MIBs' attempts at persuasion ran the gamut from the most innocuous of suggestions to frightening and violent intimidation. Usually the witness would first be told that the strange objects they saw were not alien spacecraft but either easily mistakable weather phenomena or terrestrial aircraft. The MIBs would often "helpfully suggest" that the witnesses recant whatever public statements they might have made about UFOs. The suggestion would often be along the lines of concern for the witnesses' reputation. People telling crazy stories about alien spaceships were liable to have their public reputations destroyed. If this sort of concerned paternalism did not work, the MIBs, according to UFO researchers, might appeal to the witnesses' sense of patriotism. Until the deep cultural disillusionment and pessimism of the post–JFK assassination and Vietnam and Watergate eras, a simple appeal to patriotism by government agents would usually work on large segments of the American population. In rural and conservative areas of the country, people tended to support the military, law enforcement operatives, and national defense projects quite staunchly. But when even an attempt at flag-waving would not dissuade a vocal UFO witness, the MIBs are purported to have become aggressive. Witnesses were allegedly warned that people talking too much about their UFO experiences tended to fall victim to unfortunate accidents, their families were known to have gotten killed, or the witnesses have often just simply disappeared.[15]

To the conspiracy theorists who believed that the U.S. government and all of its military, police, and intelligence agencies were nests of festering criminality, this sort of thuggish MIB behavior made perfect sense. Government agencies, after all, were ready to go to any lengths to protect the status quo that kept their corrupt masters in power. But then the UFO conspiracy movement took yet another colorful turn in its claims about the nature of the Men in Black. The idea that MIBs were working with the government, some argued, was yet another lie, designed to hide the fact that aliens had already established a presence on Earth, had been able to assume human identities, and infiltrated governments. Allegations had surfaced that while real government agents had, in fact, visited many UFO witnesses and attempted to convince them that they saw nothing more incredible than cloud formations, airplanes, and unusual optical phenomena, some of the MIBs looked and acted suspiciously inhuman. For example, some witnesses claimed that when MIBs would show up at their front door, there would be an eerie silence all around, as if the world outside of the encounter had somehow disappeared or been turned off. Other witnesses said that while the MIBs appeared to have been driving large sedans, these cars would likewise look somehow "off." The vehicles appeared to have been nothing more than simulations of the general shape of a large black car. Upon closer look, the MIBs' conveyances didn't really resemble any make or model of automobile. But the physical appearance of the Men in Black themselves was the most disturbing of all. Some witnesses said that the movements of these men appeared strangely stiff and robotic. Others claimed that their skin appeared to be completely hairless, their texture strange and not quite human. Some witnesses claimed to have seen parts of the MIBs' skin exposed where several electrical wires protruded from the flesh. According to conspiracy theorists fascinated by these peculiar tales of the Men in Black, these strange individuals were either aliens themselves or nearly lifelike androids controlled by the aliens. Since UFO witnesses numbered in the thousands and relatively few of them received visits from these MIBs, the theorists have reasoned that the Men in Black would only make an appearance when a witness was about to disclose the shocking "real truth" behind the UFO phenomenon.[16]

Invasion of the Saucer Men is not quite imaginative enough to compete with any of the claims of the real UFO witnesses or conspiracy theorists. What this low-budget, farcical little movie does present, however, is a clumsy explanation for why so little physical evidence exists. In this movie, not only are the extraterrestrials actively trying to hide their presence on Earth, but a secretive and paranoid special branch of the military is hard at work discrediting eyewitnesses. *Saucer Men*'s convoluted plot, reeling maniacally back and forth between a conspiracy thriller and broad slapstick, presents an intersection between a UFO landing, a pair of teenagers cruising lover's lane, a drunken con man, and a top-secret government saucer-recovery team on one night in the small town of Hicksville. In the course of the film, teenagers Johnny (Steve Terrell) and Joan (Gloria Castillo) borrow Johnny's father's car for a night of romance. Unfortunately, they also run into a UFO landing on the outskirts of town, and accidentally run over one of the aliens. Horrified by the sight of the dead creature, they leave their car and run home, telling their father and the local police what happened. The UFO was also seen by drunken con artist Joe Gruen (Frank Gorshin, the future Riddler of TV's *Batman* bringing equally manic comic capering to this small role). Running into the remainder of the alien team, Joe gets killed when the creatures inject a serum of pure alcohol into his bloodstream. The aliens then place Joe's body under Johnny's car. The government agents also show up, wise to what has been going on. True to the claims of countless conspiracies, the government does its best to cover up the truth about the UFO landing, perpetuating the story that a couple of careless teenagers accidentally hit a drunken drifter on a country road.

While the UFO conspiracy movement had been growing ever more vocal in its claims of government cover-ups, flying saucer-themed films actually saw a marked decline by the beginning of the 1960s. Paul Meehan's history of UFO films, *Saucer Movies: A UFOlogical History of the Cinema* (1998), credits the beginning of space exploration as one of the reasons for the dip of interest in alien invader films. Once unmanned probes were sent into space, it was quickly proven what a harsh and inhospitable place the cosmos really was. Pictures and data sent back from planets like Mars and Venus revealed barren, toxic environments incapable of supporting even the simplest of life forms, much less superior civilizations capable of interplanetary travel and colonization. At least as far as our solar system went, Earthlings appeared to have been completely alone. Even in entertainment, it was no longer possible to suspend disbelief and watch movies of invaders from Mars or flying saucers from Venus.

While this is a perfectly plausible explanation, we can also add that entertainment genres usually thrive and stagnate in cycles. What is a box-office powerhouse one year might be out of style by the next. After a decade of flying saucers, body snatchers, alien blobs, bug-eyed monsters and mind-controlling invaders, audiences might just have gotten their fill of formulaic invasion potboilers. Moreover, the fact is that the vast majority of the UFO films were hardly among the studios' A-list efforts. Aside from a few serious attempts at making thoughtful and artistic alien and UFO-themed science fiction films (features in the league of *The Thing from Another World, The Day the Earth Stood Still* and *Forbidden Planet*), most of these films were B-level exploitation pictures. These were films aimed at teenagers in drive-ins. While kids might enjoy being scared by the alien monsters a few times, they, too, can grow tired of the same stale formula after a while. Or, most importantly, the teenagers of the '50s had grown up by the '60s and graduated to more thoughtful, speculative or socially relevant science fiction like *2001: A Space Odyssey* and *Planet of the Apes* (1968).

The one noteworthy UFO film of the latter half of the decade was *The Bamboo Saucer* (1968). Not only did this movie take its subject seriously, but its theme prophesized the crashed flying saucer controversy that would take center stage in UFOlogy in the 1980s and '90s. The film's plot involves teams of government operatives from the U.S., the Soviet Union, and China racing to recover an alien spacecraft found crashed in China. Although the film's heroes are the American team members, it does not end on the sort of pro-conspiracy note the paranoid invasion films and giant bug films did in the 1950s. The Americans might be racing to get to the saucer before the Soviets and the Chinese, but the film ends with its American protagonists forging an uneasy alliance with the Russians and flying the reactivated alien craft to neutral Switzerland to reveal the existence of aliens to the world.

By the 1970s, conspiracies would reappear in science fiction with greater frequency, but the plots of most of these movies would not be dealing exclusively with UFO cover-ups and aliens. Instead, the genre would address more immediate social issues and concerns, just like other Hollywood films had started doing during that decade. The impact of technology on society, genetic experimentation, worldwide disease epidemics, environmental problems, and the misuse of governmental power were issues addressed in some of the most noteworthy conspiracy theory films of the '70s. If humanity continues on its present course, if current trends in technological advancement and social attitudes continue, the genre has always wondered, just where exactly will we end up sooner rather than later?

In 1971, screenwriter Nelson Gidding and director Robert Wise adapted *The Andromeda Strain*, Michael Crichton's breakout 1968 novel, to the screen. The film examines a major concern of the early days of the space program: If astronauts, satellites, and space probes spend enough time in space, could they find life in the form of microscopic germs, bacteria, and viruses? Could an alien menace not come to Earth in the form of a disease that no one can cure? In *The Andromeda Strain*, a space probe crash-landing in a tiny Arizona town unleashes a disease that appears to be airborne and able to infect nearly all terrestrial life forms it comes in contact with. The only hope of studying the virus and developing a cure lies in the resources of the government's most top-secret subterranean infectious disease research facility. The secrecy behind this research facility, however, once again, nearly turns out to be as much of a threat as the disease itself. Technology is unpredictable, the film argues, and the most secure and most advanced facilities could have dangerous flaws, accidents, and glitches. If the whereabouts of these facilities are shrouded in Cold War military paranoia and secrecy, the flaws and accidents are just as likely to grow exponentially out of control until the outside world itself is threatened. Furthermore, once the alien virus of *The Andromeda Strain* escapes its containment area, the scientists scrambling to find a cure discover a more disturbing secret. Their job, they realize, wasn't just conceived to find a way to contain and cure the alien virus. Their laboratory is also a bio-weapons research facility. Had they been able to completely understand the nature of the virus, they would have been expected to turn it into a weapon for the military.

But the most assertive fusing of science fiction and the archetypal conspiracy theory film came in the 1973 Charlton Heston thriller *Soylent Green*. The film is an entry in the Heston dystopian science fiction trilogy begun by *Planet of the Apes* (1968) and *The Omega Man* (1971). In *Apes* and *The Omega Man*, the world's destruction is presented in symbolic stories of the passage of one ruling class and the emergence of a new one. In those films, intelligent apes and mutants, respectively, stand in for the world's minorities and under-classes who have, at last, turned the tables on their oppressors and established a new world order. In *Soylent Green*, however, the downfall of mankind is only looming just over the horizon. Here, the cause of the destruction is damage done to the environment by over-population and pollution. Moreover, a massive conspiracy of the wealthy, government elites, and big business is attempting to keep their hold on privilege while hiding the truth about a coming global catastrophe.

The world of *Soylent Green* is eerily in line with the sort of doomsday future being predicted by many climate scientists today. Pollution and greenhouse gasses have raised the planet's temperatures until only a perpetual heat wave persists night and day. But what is even more difficult to manage is the ever-increasing size of the world's population. Mega-cities are teeming with millions of people, most of who are living in shanty towns, in aban-doned cars, on the streets, and in just about any tiny space they are able to lie down for a night's sleep. The housing crisis is so bad that the government encourages programs of assisted suicide for the sick and the elderly. The higher the death rates, the more space is freed up for others. What is even more difficult is feeding them all. The only hope of averting worldwide starvation is the farming of the oceans for plankton. The marine life forms, in turn, are being turned into nutrient-rich wafers by the technology of the Soylent Corporation. These wafers come in various colors, denoting lesser or greater nutrient content. The latest line of wafers, Soylent Green, is the healthiest of all. But even this food-manufacturing process is not perfect, as a cop pursuing a routine murder investigation soon finds out.

Detective Thorne (Heston) is the archetypal, put-upon everyman hero of the conspiracy genre. He is a rank-and-file New York City cop assigned to investigate the murder of a lawyer (Joseph Cotten) working for the Soylent Corporation. Thorne quickly begins to sus-pect that all is not as it seems with the scientist's death (conspiracy and corruption are the driving engines of this desperate society). In this world, everyone uses whatever extra lever-age they can to survive from one day to the next, mainly by getting their hands on extra food or a better place to live. Thorne himself usually takes the opportunity to rob the apart-ments of murder victims. The lawyer's home provides an extra boon since he was one of the New York upper crust, living in a plush apartment that came with its own round-the-clock prostitute (Leigh Taylor-Young). But trying to unravel the motive for the man's death — which soon becomes obvious was something other than robbery — puts Thorne at odds with his bosses and the city's political power brokers. The more he suspects that it was something the lawyer knew that led to his death, the more pressure he feels to end his investigation. Thorne's investigation eventually reveals what the Soylent Corporation has been doing to avert global starvation: since the world's plankton has almost died out from all the pollution and global warming, what's left to feed all the billions of people is mankind itself. Those who just died — or have been encouraged to take their own lives at one of the city's assisted suicide centers — are being processed for the new line of Soylent Green wafers. The film's most effectively chilling moment comes as Thorne lies dying after a fight and shootout with a Soylent Corporation hitman (Chuck Connors) and he wheezes his final words. His dying gasps let the viewer extrapolate a gruesome future for mankind. If global cannibalism is the only way for humans to survive, and suicides are already encouraged because natural deaths don't provide enough food, then the wholesale harvesting of humans for food will follow. Then, if the world is already stratified along classes of power and socioe-conomic positions, soon the advantaged will be the ones feeding off of the lower classes and the powerless.

This theme that a society's progress is secretly founded on vicious, homicidal criminality reappears in several other notable 1970s science fiction conspiracy theory films. For example, the kitsch classic *Logan's Run* (1976) presents a future world that has apparently been transformed into a carefree, hedonistic Nirvana by high technology and some careful social engineering. In the twenty-third century, following periods of war, disorder, and environmental devastation, humanity has moved into massive domed cities. Here life is perfect, no one knows want or fear or sickness or violence, and everyone lives for the pursuit of pleasure. Of course, the number of people living in these cities need to be strictly regulated, so procreation is done artificially and no one lives past the age of 30. But the fact that everyone must die on their thirtieth birthday in a public suicide ritual called Carousel is not a bother. Everyone has been raised to believe that after their death in Carousel, they will be "renewed." The renewal process is a vaguely implied cross between cloning and reincarnation. The cities are policed by squads of "Sandmen"—black-clad assassination teams that hunt down and kill the occasional dissenter.

Dissenters, dubbed "runners," are really few and far in between, even as they try and maintain a small network futilely trying to escape the cities. People raised in this society are conditioned strictly to pursue nothing more than pleasure and fun. Intellectual pursuit and independent thought are never engendered in these people. In an echo of Ray Bradbury's *Fahrenheit 451*, pleasure, entertainment and unbridled hedonism are the engines of any effectively totalitarian system and the hidden conspiracies that run them. As long as people are having a good time, they will not question the status quo, their leaders, or the value systems their society has been founded on. As Robert Tinnell argues in his essay on the film, even more than repeating the usual missives of anti-totalitarian literature like *Fahrenheit 451*, *Logan's Run* very specifically indicts some of the social trends of 1970s America. The hedonistic domed cities are but the "anything goes" ethos of the Me Generation taken to its extreme. Furthermore, the world of *Logan's Run* is a prophetic metaphor for the Internet-, online dating—and reality TV—addicted twenty-first century where instant consumption and instant gratification has become the only value and belief system.[17]

But as one of the Sandmen, Logan 5 (Michael York), discovers, this entire system is a sham. For once in his life, he is forced to begin thinking critically when confronted by Jessica 6 (Jenny Agutter), a beautiful resistance movement member. The Carousel and renewal system is all a lie and people are merely murdered for the sake of maintaining a system whose members aspire to nothing more than vapid pleasure and consumption.

In 1976, Columbia Pictures made *Futureworld*, a sequel to *Westworld*, Michael Crichton's thriller about artificial intelligence-controlled theme parks running haywire. Superior to *Westworld* in its social commentary, *Futureworld* offers a newly refurbished theme park whose controllers are now masterminding a conspiracy of political manipulation. Both films are set in hi-tech, Disney-style theme parks for adults, separated into several "worlds" where vacationers can live out exciting fantasies of visiting historic places. They can travel to the Old West, to a world of castles and knights in the Middle Ages, or into a simulated futuristic space station via a passenger rocketship. Instead of actors playing the roles of knights, cowboys and spacemen in these worlds, fully lifelike robots interact with guests. But the heads of the park have managed to make their artificial theme entertainers even more lifelike. This time they are able to replicate people with flesh-and-blood clones they are able to fully control and manipulate. The only thing missing from each clone is the ability to think independently. Given the enormous price tag of the park, most of their visitors are the wealthiest people in the world. This clientele includes men of immense economic and political power. Some are heads of state. As a pair of investigative reporters (Peter Fonda, Blythe Danner) find out, the park managers have been cloning some of their most powerful guests in a plot to replace the world's leaders with duplicates. Similar to what the New World Order conspiracy theorists of the 1990s would warn against, the *Futureworld* conspirators are attempting to put all the nations of the world under the command of one small, elite cabal. Individuals, the conspirators argue, cannot be trusted to run their own lives and make decisions that have the potential to impact millions of other lives. The most chilling villains, the film presents, are the ones that cheat, steal, murder, and subvert democracy and the rule of law because they believe they have the best intentions of the world at heart.

In a similar vein, *Futureworld* producer Paul N. Lazarus III, along with screenwriter-director Peter Hyams, produced 1978's *Capricorn One* about the best of intentions behind a conspiracy to fake a NASA mission to Mars. The good intentions of these conspirators are so strong that they believe they are justified in murdering anyone who gets in their way.

As the first manned mission to Mars, Capricorn One, is about to take off, the heads of the space program are still stung by the quickly eroding public support for space exploration. According to opinion polls, most Americans feel that all the billions being poured into the space program would be better spent on Earth. As a result, NASA needs to fight Congress for every dollar of funding. As Capricorn One is about to blast off on its historic flight, the president won't even make the time to attend the event. The heads of the space agency know they can't make any mistakes or give Washington any reason to shut down the Mars mission. A successful flight to Mars is the only thing that can keep the agency alive. However, they have long realized that they can't make the mission on Congress' tight timetable and ever smaller budget. A costly flaw has been discovered in the spacecraft's life support system. Had Washington — and the American people — gotten wind of this problem, they would have forced the cancellation of the entire Capricorn project. The only thing left to do is to fake the mission. Unfortunately, the three astronauts (James Brolin, Sam Waterston, O.J. Simpson) don't know anything is amiss until moments before liftoff.

Having been secretly spirited away from the ship before the launch and flown to an abandoned base in the middle of the desert, the three men are told why the biggest lie in history needs to be told for the good of the country. The space program is more than exploration and more than just scientific advance. It is a symbol of America's strength and standing as a world superpower. But that standing has been fast eroding. At home, pessimism reigns. Americans feel that their nation's best days are behind them. A successful Mars mission would give Americans a reason to be proud of their country, a reason to believe that only the best country in the world could accomplish a feat like sending men to another planet. Despite the sales pitch, the astronauts eventually rebel against the conspiracy, escaping into the desert to be hunted by hit squads in black helicopters.

In *Capricorn One*'s parallel storyline, a stalwart archetypal conspiracy genre character, a nosy investigative journalist named Robert Caulfield (Elliott Gould), gets a nagging feeling that something is not quite right with the Mars mission. He had been contacted by one of the NASA engineers (Robert Walden) who was exasperated by his bosses' lack of concern with a faulty computer in the mission control center that keeps giving inaccurate data about the location of the space capsule's radio transmissions. According to the computer, the transmissions could not be coming from somewhere more than a few hundred miles away. Once Caulfield, a showboat with a penchant for pursuing sensational stories, thinks the engineer's story might be worth checking out, the assassins try to put him out of commission permanently.

Capricorn One is an effective amalgam of post–Watergate fears of government conspiracies and what could be termed a Carter-era theater of malaise. This is the only conspiracy theory film where the villains are attempting to manipulate the national psyche.

The origins of the film, however, are rooted in a conspiracy theory that had taken shape immediately after the Apollo 11 moon landing. Although not as well-known as the UFO cover-up theories or the assassination conspiracy theories of the 1960s, the theory that NASA had faked the moon landing did, in fact, have a small but avid following. The staying power of the theory on a sort of cult level was witnessed in 2001 when FOX television devoted an hour-long documentary to the subject, the program heavily biased in favor of the theory. At the time of this writing, one can find roughly 2,860,000 hits on any Internet search engine query on the topic of a faked moon landing.

Propagated in large part by conspiracy theorist Bill Kaysing in his self-published 1974 book *We Never Went to the Moon: America's Thirty Billion Dollar Swindle,* the theory states that the U.S. faked the landing on the moon to win Cold War political points by not only beating the Soviets to the moon, but by proving that John F. Kennedy's vision of a successful lunar mission was not an unrealistic, naïve pipe dream. The theory bases most of its motives on the political symbolism of the space race between the U.S. and the U.S.S.R. As Kaysing argues, the space programs of the two countries were primarily about political posturing, rather than actual strategic and scientific advantages to be gained. Whoever made the biggest gains in space simply stood to look the best in the eyes of the world. A moon landing, of course, was the holy grail of space exploration. The country that accomplished this could lay claim to possessing the superior political system. As the Russians had made the first moves of the space race, being the first to put a satellite in orbit, an animal in orbit, and a man in orbit, they missed no opportunity to announce that these historic gains proved the advantages of communism over capitalism. For capitalism to score a PR move that could trump all of the Russians' victories, they could only succeed with a coup like putting the first men on the moon. In 1961, John F. Kennedy tasked NASA with not only accomplishing this feat, but he gave the space agency less than ten years to do it. According to Kaysing's charges, this was not possible.

As Kaysing argues in his book, NASA soon realized that they simply did not have the time to perfect the technology for a moon landing. They worked as fast as they could on building the rocket to get the astronauts into orbit, on building the space capsules and the moon lander. However, they ultimately decided to fake a moon landing and images of astronauts walking on the moon inside of giant sound stages in a hidden production studio. Kaysing further charges that intimidation and murder were a part of this conspiracy. Several NASA members had been vocally skeptical about whether Kennedy's deadline could be met. Astronaut Edward H. White publicly criticized NASA and charged that the agency was putting lives at risk by cutting corners on safety for the sake of politics. White and astronauts Virgil Grissom and Roger B. Chaffee died in their Apollo 1 space capsule on January 27, 1967, during a pre-launch training exercise. According to the NASA explanation, an accidental spark had ignited the pure oxygen that filled the capsule. According to Kaysing, the accident was staged to silence one of the Apollo program's critics.

Kaysing goes on to argue that the photos of the moon landing, as well as the existing video footage, is full of inconsistencies and clues that hint that they were taken somewhere other that the lunar surface. Kaysing claims that shadows can be seen falling at incorrect angles, completely unlike the way shadows should fall when illuminated by only the sun. He argues that the Lunar Roving Vehicle's dimensions are far too large to have been carried in the lunar module's cargo sections. He takes issue with the amount of rocks brought back from the moon, claiming it would not have been possible to return with so much weight in a spacecraft the size of the Apollo vehicles. Kaysing also claims that the computers on the space capsule and the lunar lander in the 1960s did not have the computation power to do the sort of advanced calculations needed to control the movements and trajectory of the craft in space. But ultimately, Kaysing writes that his case-winning argument is the issue of solar radiation. The Apollo spacecraft, according to Kaysing, was not built well enough to shield the astronauts from the high doses of solar radiation they would be bombarded with on the way to the moon and back. In fact, to this day, radiation shielding remains one of the most difficult problems NASA engineers contend with when designing manned vehicles for a future Mars mission. According to Kaysing's argument, the astronauts should have been exposed to lethal doses of radiation from the Van Allen belt encircling the earth. But not only did all the Apollo astronauts survive their missions, but none of them has ever shown any signs of any radiation-related illnesses.

If a phony moon landing could be pulled off, the plot would eclipse even the Kennedy assassination in sheer boundless corruption. Counterarguments to Kaysing's claims, of course, are voluminous. Many scientists have devoted webpages and blogs to debunking the fake moon landing argument, their online projects sometimes long enough to fill books in their own right. They point out that there really are no anomalies in the position of the shadows in the moon photos, that, in fact, such shadows can easily be reproduced on Earth with an ordinary camera and the sun as the only source of lighting, and that the lunar lander and the Roving Vehicle are on display in museums where their dimensions can be compared and a disassembled rover can be seen fitting into the lander. The counterarguments explain that the Apollo capsules and lunar modules did not need large computers because the computations were done on Earth and relayed into space by radio. One of the most effective replies to the moon hoax theory, however, came in response to its seemingly airtight solar radiation claim. James Van Allen, the discoverer and namesake of the Van Allen belt, shot down the radiation argument. Although there is a large concentration of radiation in the belt, Van Allen explained, it would not be lethal to astronauts inside a spaceship if they just passed through it. Moreover, while their spacecraft might not have been protected from radiation well enough to keep them healthy on a very long flight, say a trip to Mars, the protection of the space capsule and the lunar lander were enough to do the job during the time spent in space by the Apollo astronauts.[18]

While the moon landing hoax theory had its legions of critics from the beginning, writer-director Peter Hyams did feel it would make for an exciting fictional film. He wrote the story of a fake Mars mission soon after hearing of the theory in the early '70s. He started pitching his screenplay to studios in 1972. At that point, there were no takers. Most studios and producers told him that it was inconceivable that such a massive conspiracy could ever be pulled off. By the end of the decade, however, after the full implications of the Watergate affair had permeated throughout the culture and Americans believed their government was capable of anything, *Capricorn One* went before cameras at Columbia Pictures.

By the late 1970s, another theoretical advance in medical science had captured science fiction writers' imaginations. The cloning of cells and the exact duplication of living beings— theoretically as complex as humans— offered the very real confirmation of technology that had only existed in the most outlandish, most pulpy science fiction epics. In an era wary of conspiracies and large-scale corruption in every industry and organization, however, Hollywood imagined cloning being used in the most exploitive and unethical way possible. In 1979's *The Clonus Horror*, a secret cloning laboratory functions as a harvesting facility for wealthy clients who clone themselves and have their own aging, failing organs replaced by the young, healthy organs of their clones. The clones, however, are fully functioning, self-aware, individual human beings. The use of their body parts is nothing less than murder.

In the course of the plot—which would be almost completely duplicated in director Michael Bay's big-budget action epic *The Island* (2005)[19]—one of the clones living on the farm begins to suspect that his idyllic life is not all that it appears to be. The small community of people on the farm, constantly supervised in an endless regime of fitness, sports, and health by a cadre of doctors, is told that they will regularly compete in races and contests to win a chance to go to "America." "America" is a distant utopian concept for the clones, a promised land of wealth, comfort, and opportunity. Once a person is selected to go, they are never seen again. But Richard (Tim Donnelly), one of the clones, accidentally stumbles into one of the compound's restricted areas, finding the latest winner of a trip to America (Frank Ashmore) hanging in a plastic bag in a meat locker. It looks like he had been recently killed and his eyes removed. Like all true victims of conspiracies, Richard must painfully accept the fact that his entire life has been a carefully programmed lie. Escaping the compound, he stumbles into the middle of the real America. Here Richard tracks down his own double, the man whose DNA had been used to create him, the man he was supposed to eventually become an organ donor for.

Perhaps the most radical of these science fiction conspiracy theory films, *The Clonus Horror* raised a concern about cloning at the theoretical phase of the science that would be echoed by some of the leading medical ethicists decades later. As screenwriter Bob Sullivan explains in the film's DVD documentary, his initial agenda for including any sort of a message in his film was to raise alarms about how the unchecked power of wealth stood to corrupt and exploit any society. He hedges his statements to a degree, arguing that he never wanted to condemn all of the United States as an exploitive system with his plot device of the clones walking off to their deaths when they think they've won a trip to a mythologized, perfect "America," but to warn against the potential abuses in modern capitalism. He does admit that his own political orientation has been greatly shaped by parents who were active in the far-left-wing political movements of the '50s and '60s. In the 1970s, in the aftermath of Watergate, the politics of *The Clonus Horror* were not so far from mainstream sentiments any more. But politics aside, it is still remarkable that by the late 1990s and early 2000s, when scientists were cloning sheep, the fear of exploitation had again been raised in the debates over the ethics of genetic engineering. Some of the most respected scientific ethicists were warning of a very real future when new life would be created in a human harvest just so those who could afford to buy the latest fruits of medical technology could strive to live into eternity with an endless supply of body parts coming from living, feeling, thinking human beings.[20]

The 1970s also offered more revisions of the UFO and alien visitor conspiracy theories. One of them, Steven Spielberg's 1977 blockbuster *Close Encounters of the Third Kind*, became one of the highest grossing films of all time. The conventions of the UFO conspiracy films of the '70s helped shape what would be standard generic plot devices and archetypes to come for decades.

The first of these alien conspiracy films, however, actually came from television in 1974: *The Disappearance of Flight 412* with Glenn Ford and David Soul in the lead roles. It is an extremely lean drama about the aftermath of a UFO sighting by the crew of a military radar aircraft. While on a training mission, the men of Flight 412 spot several mystery aircraft neither they, nor their ground controllers, can contact. Moreover, the flight characteristics of the unknown craft look completely unlike those of any conventional airplanes. But before Flight 412 can return home, it is suddenly ordered off its routine flight path and forced to land at an abandoned air base. There the crew is detained by intelligence agents from Washington and relentlessly grilled over what they saw. In the meantime, Flight 412's base commander (Ford) gets into a jurisdictional tug of war with the intelligence men, fighting to get his plane back and his men released, all the while trying to determine Washington's reason for detaining the crew.

The Disappearance of Flight 412 is a highly remarkable and impressive little TV production. It is unfortunate for UFO fans and conspiracy entertainment buffs that no high quality DVD copies of the film exist so far. The DVDs available from several used film vendors suffer from truly shoddy transfer attempts. As the film is already very spare in its production values, the grainy, hazy picture quality and poor soundtrack might dissuade impatient viewers from sitting through the entire film, letting them think the bad picture and sound is a sign of a poor story. This is certainly not the case as *Flight 412* is a very effective psychological thriller, ratcheting up its tension as the crewmen are being made to endure ever more extreme and sadistic interrogation attempts while their boss is facing a true nightmare scenario of bureaucratic infighting and backstabbing. *Flight 412*, for the first time, takes a serious look at the repressive intimidation tactics an intelligence unit might use to keep evidence of a UFO encounter secret. If the claims of reputable military figures like Edward Ruppelt and Donald Keyhoe are true, or the allegations of the Men in Black proponents hold any merit, a government conspiracy to intimidate UFO witnesses into silence could possibly unfold like this. Audiences who read about the Pentagon Papers affair in the newspaper could imagine a paranoid government cover-up of an alien encounter unfolding like the scenario of *Flight 412*. There are no special effects to speak of (the UFOs are never seen as anything other than blips on radar screens and the aerial shots of the planes look like stock footage) so the film has a terse, documentary feel to it, further underlining the fact that its producers are taking its issues very seriously and are using every storytelling device at their disposal to avoid hyperbole, camp, or the suggestion of sensational exploitation.

What is even more remarkable about *Flight 412* is the very fact that it aired on television. Despite 1974 seeing the Watergate scandal come to a head, television is not the medium where forceful system- and status quo-challenging entertainment first shows up. A film this hostile to the intelligence community, depicting its UFO-suppression agents as little more than common thugs, and a downbeat ending of the conscientious Ford character seeing his career derailed, seems a very ill fit for what has long been perhaps the most cautious mass medium in America.

But the themes of *Flight 412* would remain oft-recurring archetypes of the UFO conspiracy film. True to the general plot structures of the conspiracy genre, the UFO-oriented films are quests for the truth by characters who have suddenly become lone outsiders by the virtue of something they accidentally witnessed. A UFO encounter in a film like this rips the main characters out of their comfortable places within society. The men of Flight 412 have been committed Air Force officers, patriotic and professional in their duties in every way. They have invested their lives in the system and they follow all of its rules and codes of conduct. But once they have an encounter with the unexplained, that system suddenly forces them to make a difficult choice. They must either deny they had the UFO experience or be punished and forcefully silenced. Since these characters also have a personal commitment to the truth — a characteristic that had served them well within their organization — they must now face the unpleasant prospect of being lone, ostracized, and ridiculed crusaders for a truth that no one wants to hear. The system, in fact, is so averse to hearing that truth that it will often violently turn against the UFO witness protagonists. In *Flight 412*, the intimidating intelligence goons from Washington show up, threatening the heroes' careers, lives, and families. In more UFO-oriented conspiracy films to come, the government agents will often be completely indistinguishable from organized crime hitmen. In a realization of the most nightmarish scenarios out of Men in Black lore, UFO witnesses and various conspiracy-busting heroes will be targeted for assassination by cold, calculating, implacable murderers working for the government.

Since a television film like *Flight 412* put such an edgy, sinister conspiratorial twist on UFO films, a theatrical film like *Close Encounters of the Third Kind*, coming fours year later, becomes interesting to look at because its own vision of a conspiracy becomes so mild and, basically, *soft*-edged by the end of the story.

Close Encounters is among the very few films Steven Spielberg scripted himself. As he explained in numerous interviews, the story was a product of his own long-standing fascination with UFOs. After ascending to A-list Hollywood power-player status in the wake of *Jaws*, Spielberg had the ability to get the sort of financial backing and technology available to realize his vision of a film that would be his all-encompassing, summary statement on the topic of the UFO phenomenon. The end result strives to balance the mystery, awe, inspiration, as well as conspiratorial intrigue that have become the staples of UFO lore. Ultimately, though, while a conspiracy propels the story forward and toward its spectacular conclusion, the overall tone of the film is more wondrous and awe-inspiring rather than unsettling and sinister the way *Flight 412* was.

In *Close Encounters* we see a great deal of the story through the eyes of a "typical," all–American everyman. The protagonist is Roy Neary (Richard Dreyfus), a linesman for the electric company who lives almost literally in Middle America (Muncie, Indiana). He has an average house with an average family. He has three loud, rambunctious kids and a loving and good-hearted — if somewhat unimaginative and dull-witted — wife, Ronni (Teri Garr). His home might be somewhat crowded and messy, but it's crowded and messy in a good way; they are a close family and spend all their free time together. However, Roy also has a quality that sets him up as a questing hero, someone who soon finds himself ripped out of this comfortable existence following a UFO encounter. Unlike the military men in *Flight 412*, Roy stumbles across the UFO on a deserted road in the middle of the night by accident. Almost as if taken right out of the countless reports of purportedly real alien encounters, Roy is the "average" person UFOlogists usually talk about when demonstrating how eye-witnesses come from "all walks of life." Roy, however, is just slightly different from that proverbial "average Joe" because of his childlike curiosity and imagination. In the first scene in which we get a glimpse of Roy, we see an odd sort of a duality about him. He is playing with his children and a large model train set. While he is an adult and a father (even giving one of his sons a quick math lesson in fractions like any dutiful dad concerned with his kid's grades), he is just as engrossed in the pretend world of the elaborate train set as any of the kids. Unlike his wife, Roy has the capacity to imagine a bigger, more complex, more mysterious world than the one he lives in. It is this quality that will motivate his quest for the truth and drive him toward a head-on confrontation with a government conspiracy.

Once a wave of sudden blackouts hits the Midwest, Roy is one of the many linesmen called on to go on the road in the middle of the night and attempt to track down the problem. He instead encounters an alien spacecraft. From that point onward, he is incapable of turning away from the strange phenomenon. Unlike the men of Flight 412, who are swept up in the conspiracy through no fault of their own, Roy does everything in his power to inject himself into the world of other UFO witnesses, activists, and public meetings where condescending, dismissive public officials do their best to debunk the phenomenon. But, quite similarly to the characters of *Flight 412* who are given the choice of going along with Washington or facing retribution, Roy is also given an ultimatum by his wife. He must stop this obsession with aliens, Ronni tells him, or he will lose his family. Ronni is incapable of dealing with any sort of a disruption to the norm. She is a part of her world and she is terrified of that world's censure if she breaks any of its rules of propriety. Simply, Ronnie can't stand being the wife of the guy who says and believes in weird things nobody else believes in. True to form, however, Roy also makes the decision to pursue the truth, to pursue a bigger world and the answers to bigger mysteries outside of his average, Middle-American life.

Possessed by visions of the Devil's Tower mountain in Wyoming, Roy heads across the country, eventually joining forces with Jillian Guiler (Melinda Dillon), a single mother whose son was abducted by a UFO. This quest leads him toward a confrontation with a government conspiracy.

This film's conspirators are perhaps some of the most laid-back ones in the entire genre. They are a collection of top scientists from around the world, working for the U.S. government, and they do their work in secret because they honestly worry about adverse effects on the culture if the truth of extraterrestrials gets out before the entire nature of the phenomenon can be understood. *Close Encounters'* conspirators are neither evil nor power-hungry. In fact, the conspiracy seems to be quite factional, comprised of scientists who are not even comfortable with all the secrecy, and military men given to paranoia and subterfuge. One of the head scientists, a Frenchman named Lacombe (François Truffaut), was based on UFO researcher Jacques Vallée. J. Allen Hynek even makes a brief cameo appearance as a scientist at the moment the alien mother ship lands and the UFOnauts reveal themselves. The military, to the quiet dismay of the scientists, however, runs the operation, and the soldiers usually go to extraordinary lengths to hide the truth about the UFOs. When it looks like contact might be made with the aliens in the Devil's Tower area, a chemical spill is faked as an excuse to evacuate all the nearby towns. Nevertheless, even the military branch of this conspiracy would never resort to lethal force or physical threats to carry out their plans. When Roy, Jillian, and other UFO hunters are about to sneak onto a hidden government base at the foot of Devil's Tower, helicopters are dispatched to stop them, but without resorting to violence. The trespassers are merely sprayed with gasses that knock them unconscious.

Although the conspiracy of *Close Encounters* is curiously benign, the success of the film did serve to cement the concept of official secrecy into the template of most UFO films that would be made for decades to come. Just the very topic of UFOs and alien encounters would nearly always be coupled with a government plot to cover it all up. In the wake of *Close Encounters*, filmmakers would make it a given that governments would always be dishonest about the nature of aliens, that they always knew more about an alien presence on Earth than witnesses could ever imagine, and extreme — if not lethal — measures would always be taken to cover up the truth.

That by the end of the 1970s conspiracy themes should be appearing in films in ever greater numbers can be considered inevitable when analyzing film history. Two decades of national tragedies, the uncovering of governmental corruption and cynicism, and the aftermath of a long, ill-conceived and badly executed war had left Americans questioning much of what they had assumed to be true about their country. For most of those Americans, it had become natural to suspect that much of the world was being run by secretive and often unscrupulous power players who were above scrutiny and above the law. Nothing could speak to these suspicions better than the cinema of conspiracy theories. Since the cynicism engendered by the aftermath of the Kennedy assassination, the Vietnam War, and the Watergate scandal would prove to have permanently killed America's "innocence," this form of entertainment would remain a part of Hollywood filmmaking for decades to come.

CHAPTER 4

Everything Is Connected
The Conspiracy Theories of the 1980s

Since conspiracy theories constantly need to grow and become more complex, the early 1980s saw a dramatic revitalization of the UFO movement. New information had surfaced about the purported alien crash near Roswell, New Mexico. This offered tantalizing new hope for UFO researchers and alien buffs that tangible proof of an extraterrestrial presence might be available at last. This proof, of course, was hidden by a government conspiracy.

In general, some of the major conspiracy movements of the 1980s offered theories that were becoming more and more baroque. Much of the conspiracy culture was embracing claims that offered to prove that individual events were orchestrated by some hidden cabal, and that much of what we "know" of history, political affairs and reality itself is all but an intricate lie. "Everything is connected" became the new philosophy of conspiracism. During the 1980s, conspiracy theorists feared hidden organizations and secret societies more than ever. The "everything is connected" school of thought felt that such massive, all-encompassing plots could only be hidden by large, well-funded organizations that had existed for decades, if not centuries. While much of the mainstream culture had actually taken a significant right turn in the early years of the decade, as evidenced by the election and lasting popularity of Ronald Reagan, many conspiracy theorists started revisiting old suspicions about the existence of multigenerational dynasties of business conspirators. These theorists rekindled the idea that malevolent families of bankers and industrialists were secretly steering world events. These bankers and industrialists, in turn, did not merely bribe and corrupt legislators for simple, immediate gains, but the criminality was always tied to events in the past that had also been a part of one long, ongoing master plan. For example, conspiracy theorists would now argue that the Vietnam quagmire wasn't merely bought and paid for by defense contractors, but all of the Cold War had been orchestrated by banking and industrial conglomerates. The bankers and industrialists of the West, conspiracy theorists argued, had originally funded and supported Lenin and the Communists in Russia to give capitalism an enemy to fear and a threat the military and armaments manufacturers would need millions of dollars to defend against. Although there were still theories charging that government conspiracies had been in effect to cover up bad policies and blunders, the scope of conspiratorial thinking in the '80s tended to get larger and larger.

But alien conspiracies would take center stage in the world of UFOlogy when in 1980 Charles Berlitz and William Moore published their book *The Roswell Incident*. Although the alleged crash of an alien spaceship in the New Mexico desert had made headlines around the world in 1947, news of the affair had disappeared almost as quickly. Literally within one day of word reaching the media that the U.S. military had its hands on a UFO, all media interest in the incident evaporated. The Army Air Force declared that nothing more than an ordinary weather balloon was found in the desert wilderness and the story, as far as the media were concerned, was effectively dead. Berlitz and Moore claimed that the disappearance of the original story was largely a result of the times (a more trusting era when the government could say almost anything and most of the American people were willing to listen and believe). The story of the century, according to Berlitz and Moore's book, was still hidden away in secret military installations and a vast conspiracy was still hard at work covering it all up.

The Roswell tale started on July 3, 1947, when, according to Major Jesse A. Marcel, intelligence officer of the 509th Bomb Group of the Roswell Army Air Base, local rancher W. W. "Mac" Brazel found some strange wreckage strewn across his range. In an area about three quarters of a mile long and two or three hundred feet wide, Brazel found unusual metallic shards and some plastic-like beams. Eventually the wreckage would get to the Roswell Air Base where public relations officer Walter Haut released a bombshell of a press report. The U.S. military finally got its hands on one of the mysterious flying discs that had been all the rage in the media, Haut's release explained. As the world was in the grip of a full-blown UFOmania, for one fleeting day the tiny, dusty town of Roswell would be the center of attention of the media from as far away as London and Hong Kong.

The fact that the Roswell incident would vanish from the public spotlight as quickly as it did is remarkable since the summer of 1947 appeared to have been the summer of the UFO. Coming close on the heels of Kenneth Arnold's June 24 sighting of the mysterious, boomerang-shaped objects flying over Mt. Rainier like "saucers skipping across the surface of a lake," the last days of June and the beginning of July witnessed waves of UFO sightings across the country. On the very same day as Arnold's sighting and iconic description, a prospector in the Cascade Mountains watched a fleet of five or six disc-shaped UFOs fly overhead. As the strange craft flew by, the man's compass needle started spinning wildly. On the following day, more mystery craft were seen as far away as Kansas City, Missouri, Pueblo, Colorado, in Utah, in Oklahoma, and in Glens Falls, New York. On June 26, UFO sightings were reported and written about in local newspapers across Utah, Arizona, Oklahoma, Texas, and New Mexico. In Capitan, New Mexico, witnesses saw a shiny unidentified object hurtle out of the sky and land in the nearby hills. On June 27, UFOs were seen in Michigan and in several provinces of Canada. Then reports came in from Australia and New Zealand. In fact, the interest in UFOs by the media had been energized to the point where scientists were sought out for expert opinions. Many of them did not dismiss the possibility that the witnesses might have actually seen something unusual in the skies. Several opined that people might have gotten a glimpse of top-secret military aircraft being tested.

Some scientists though, not surprisingly, soon offered such ungenerous hypotheses as delayed war hysteria causing people to imagine weird flying objects that did not exist. Yet others argued that people who had accidentally stared into the sun too long were mistaking afterimages of the glare as flying objects. But on the Fourth of July weekend, fighter pilots on air bases in California and Seattle were placed on alert to intercept any reported UFOs. In Oregon, fighters had been sent on patrols with gun cameras, looking to document any of the mystery aircraft. During that same weekend, the crew of a commercial airliner reported watching a fleet of four sleek, elongated UFOs for about forty minutes while in flight.

In July, after having kept pieces of the unusual metal wreckage in a shed, Mac Brazel headed into Roswell to talk to Sheriff George A. Wilcox. Brazel had apparently been struck by the number of UFO stories his friends and family were talking about and he got to wondering what the wreckage in his shed might really be. As Jesse Marcel would tell authors Berlitz and Moore three decades later, the metallic debris was unlike anything anyone had seen at the time.[1]

After meeting Sheriff Wilcox, Berlitz and Moore's book recounts, Brazel was urged to get in touch with the Army Air base. Apparently Wilcox wasn't ready to say what Brazel's metallic debris might have been, but he wasn't impressed by it enough to speculate about its paranormal or extraterrestrial origins. As a result of the call from the rancher, however, Jesse Marcel and a civilian Counter-Intelligence Corps agent were sent out to Brazel's ranch to take stock of the situation. Marcel was so impressed by the unusual nature of the wreckage — which he described as being lighter than tin foil, yet being so incredibly strong that it could neither be torn, cut, burned, nor permanently misshapen by blows from a sledgehammer — that he went home and showed his wife and son some of the pieces. Once back on the air base, Marcel presented his story to his superior, Colonel William Blanchard. Blanchard, in turn, sent a detachment of men to canvas the debris field. He also authorized public relations officer Haut to make a statement about the find. Haut's press release read:

> The many rumors regarding the flying discs became a reality yesterday when the intelligence office of the 509th Bomb Group of the Eighth Air Force, Roswell Army Air Field, was fortunate enough to gain possession of a disc through the cooperation of one of the local ranchers and the Sheriff's office of Chavez County.
>
> The flying object landed on a ranch near Roswell sometime last week. Not having phone facilities, the rancher stored the disc until such time as he was able to contact the Sheriff's office, who in turn notified Major Jesse A. Marcel of the 509th Bomb Group Intelligence office. Action was immediately taken and the disc was picked up at the rancher's home. It was inspected at the Roswell Army Air Field and subsequently loaned by Major Marcel to higher headquarters.[2]

But once the wreckage was "loaned" to higher headquarters— specifically, it was flown to the Eighth Air Force headquarters in Fort Worth, Texas— the debunking of the flying disc story quickly began. According to Berlitz and Moore, the wreckage was flown to the Air Technical Intelligence Center at Wright Field in Ohio. But the story the military released to the public stated that Brigadier General Roger Ramey, the commander of the Eighth Air Force, personally examined the wreckage in Texas and declared it to be nothing more than the tattered remains of a tinfoil and balsa wood weather balloon. Jesse Marcel was ordered to pose with some wrinkled flaps of tinfoil during a press conference. As Marcel explained in 1978 when he came forward to UFO researchers Stanton Friedman and Leonard Stringfield, the press conference was a sham. The weather balloon fragments he was given were not the same objects he collected from Brazel's ranch.

The Roswell case remained relegated to the fringes of UFOlogy until Berlitz and Moore came along. In fact, the only other places where a mention of the crash and retrieval story turns up are a couple of poorly regarded UFO books entitled *Behind the Flying Saucers* (1950) by Frank Scully and *Flying Saucers: Serious Business* (1966) by Frank Edwards. The publication of Berlitz and Moore's book proved to be perfectly timed, appearing just as the public appetite was ready for the UFO enigma to become more complex, disturbing, and conspiratorial than ever before.

The Roswell Incident, however, was not without controversy, even among UFO researchers. The book, its critics charge, gives an inaccurate timeline of some of the events and its claims are backed up by very few direct eyewitnesses. Rather than a rigorous examination of first-person testimony and public records, *The Roswell Incident*'s detractors argue, the book offers a collection of wild hearsay. These second- and third-hand accounts Berlitz and Moore then use for fantastic speculation and to jump to a lot of unwarranted conclusions.[3]

Moreover, the critics claim, *The Roswell Incident* is a quick and sloppy addition to Berlitz and Moore's cottage industry of speculation about the paranormal. The book looks more like a rush to fill a publishing quota, rather than a rigorous examination of what could amount to — if ever proven beyond a shadow of a doubt — the most amazing story in human history. In fact, a look at the previous work by the *Roswell Incident* scribes will turn up a list specializing in strange hypothesizing. Berlitz himself is the more prolific of the two writers, having penned four other speculative works by himself, and then co-authored *The Philadelphia Experiment: Project Invisibility* with Moore in 1979. Starting in 1969, Moore had written four books about Atlantis and the Bermuda Triangle. Then, from 1981 until 1995, he wrote six more paranormal books, ranging in topics from Atlantis to Noah's Ark, the coming doomsday at the turn of the millennium, a supposed Bermuda Triangle–like mystery spot in the Pacific Ocean, and a compendium of various unexplained phenomena.

While Berlitz has been the busier writer, his co-author is more controversial. Moore had attained infamy in the UFO community through his involvement in an alleged disinformation campaign that might have led to the temporary mental unraveling of businessman and UFO investigator Paul Bennewitz. A one-time Ph.D. candidate in physics, Bennewitz had devoted a great deal of his energies and resources to convincing the world that aliens were actively manipulating people and interfering with governmental and military affairs. After studying the cattle mutilation phenomenon and witnessing the hypnotic regression sessions of UFO-experiencer Myrna Hansen, Bennewitz had become convinced that an extensive network of alien bases was hidden throughout the world and, especially, under the southwest desert in the vicinity of military installations like New Mexico's Kirtland Air Force Base and the Manzano Nuclear Weapons Storage Facility. The cattle mutilation, Bennewitz came to believe, was but a part of the greater alien abduction plot, all an attempt by extraterrestrials to experiment on and extract genetic materials from humans. This secret enterprise, in turn, was but a part of an alien control and colonization plot. This plot was carried out either through a secret deal between the otherworldly creatures and the U.S. government, or by the aliens using mind control techniques to render the leaders of the world and the heads of the armed forces incapable of resisting the alien infiltration. This sort of over-the-top hypothesizing had led the UFO group Aerial Phenomena Research Organization (APRO) to conclude that Bennewitz was paranoid and mentally unstable. Once Bennewitz contacted Air Force Sergeant Richard C. Doty in 1980, detailing his invasion theories, Moore got involved in the strange Bennewitz affair for the rest of the decade. As Moore explained in a highly controversial speech given to the 1989 convention of the Mutual UFO Network (MUFON), he had also been a government operative and part of a secret disinformation campaign designed to discredit UFO researchers. According to Moore's story, he and Doty were primarily responsible for feeding Bennewitz false stories of alien invasions and mind control. Realizing that Bennewitz was both mentally unsound *and* potentially influential in the UFO community, Moore and Doty were given the task of driving Bennewitz over the edge and into a complete nervous breakdown. Bennewitz was, in fact, hospitalized in a New Mexico mental health facility on three different occasions after suffering bouts of intense, delusional paranoia. At the MUFON convention, Moore wrapped up his story by claiming that his involvement with the Bennewitz disinformation project was something akin to being a double agent. Even while working for the military, Moore explained, he was committed to exposing the truth about the alien origin of UFOs and the government's lies about the subject. The only way he could do this, however, was by appearing to aid in the disinformation while, at the same time, using his insider status to dig for the hidden truth. As expected, Moore's speech caused a firestorm at the MUFON convention and throughout the entire UFO community.[4]

For those given only to harsh, unyielding skepticism, Moore and, no doubt, Berlitz are hucksters and charlatans, doing their best to make as much money off their books as possible by spinning outlandish tales of government conspiracies. How much credence can one give to someone like Moore once he claims to have been a part of a plot to drive Bennewitz insane? In light of that story, his claims of being an undercover whistle-blower for the UFO movement sound absurd and utterly unbelievable. That is, of course, if any part of his story about driving Bennewitz to a mental breakdown is true to begin with.

Jacques Vallée examined *The Roswell Incident*, Berlitz and Moore's work and backgrounds, as well as the entire Bennewitz affair. As he explains in his book *Revelations: Alien Contact and Human Deception*, the only government conspiracy that might be afoot is the attempt to discredit serious UFO researchers and carry on a complex belief-system-manipulation experiment by furnishing the more gullible sectors of the UFO community with absurd disinformation. Vallée does not believe in the Roswell crash or most of the abduction claims, instead arguing that the retrieved saucer stories and hidden alien base yarns are all fabrications disseminated by government intelligence operatives. People like Bennewitz, Vallée hypothesizes, are conduits for the disinformation. Therefore, he speculates, Moore might indeed have been passing stories of underground alien bases and extraterrestrial mind control on to Bennewitz, but Moore is no conscientious whistle-blower. People like Moore, Vallée argues, might be a part of an ongoing psychological experiment, working on molding and manipulating the beliefs and modern mythologies of the world.

Vallée further points out that Berlitz himself had at one point been an Army intelligence officer. Lies and manipulation might have been his stock in trade as well. At the least, Vallée concludes, such disinformation campaigns serve to discredit serious UFO researchers and drive other scientists away from the field. However, he adds, it is not beyond reason to speculate that the disinformation campaign could have much more dangerous and far-reaching motivations. What if these alien base and Roswell stories are but a part of an attempt to mold a brand new belief system in the world, if not a brand new religion? Vallée points to the phenomenon of the post-contactee UFO cults cropping up in both the U.S. and in Europe. As discussed in Chapter 3, the beliefs of most of these cultic organizations are remarkably similar to those of fundamentalist religious groups. But more importantly, Vallée writes, the cults have shaped complex moral and ethical cannons—all based on the social systems of the alien races they're in contact with—that are extremely rigid, repressive and fascistic. Pointing to European UFO cults like the UMMO movement in Spain, Vallée implores his readers and serious UFO researchers to take a look at the supposedly superior social structures these cults are striving to emulate. What the discerning investigator will find, Vallée warns, are social systems "that will make Victorian England look like a hotbed of permissiveness."[5] Vallée argues that perhaps the truth of these mysterious revelations about alien activities is the existence of conspiracies to convince ever-larger segments of human cultures to embrace totalitarianism.

Controversy dogged both Berlitz and Moore throughout the decade. Aside from *The Roswell Incident*, their second best-known book was 1979's *The Philadelphia Experiment: Project Invisibility*. By now largely dismissed even by the most committed conspiracy and supernatural buffs as nothing more than a shoddy, uncritical repeat of a lingering and completely unsubstantiated urban myth, it recounts the allegations surrounding a 1943 Navy experiment that supposedly involved — depending on the theory — invisibility, time travel, teleportation or interdimensional travel.

As Berlitz and Moore document in their book, the details of the experiment were first alleged in 1955 when Morris K. Jessup, a one-time graduate student of astronomy at the University of Michigan and UFO buff, was contacted by Carlos Miguel Allende. Jessup had just published the book *The Case for the UFO*, in which he hypothesized about the origins of flying saucers and their propulsion systems possibly functioning by the manipulation of electromagnetic fields. Allende sent the author a pair of letters where he claimed to have witnessed a top secret Navy experiment in the Philadelphia naval yards. This experiment, Allende claimed, was designed to turn the destroyer escort *USS Eldridge* invisible — and succeeded. But, according to Allende's letters, not only did the experiment turn the ship invisible, but it might have also killed some sailors, fused others' bodies with the ship's bulkhead, teleported the ship to New York and back, teleported it to another dimension where it encountered aliens, or perhaps teleported it through time. In a brief series of correspondences, the mysterious Allende had also identified himself as "Carl Allen."

Although Jessup had eventually dismissed the letters as the ravings of an unstable individual, or a hoaxer of some sort, he was contacted in 1957 by the Office of Naval Research about a strange item they had been mailed. A package sent to the ONR contained a densely annotated copy of Jessup's book. Apparently someone had sent the Navy *The Case for the UFO*, filled up with a series of notes commenting on the propulsion system hypotheses, on the origins of flying saucers, and on the nature of the aliens piloting the craft, as well as references to the Philadelphia Experiment. Upon examining the notes, Jessup confirmed at least part of the handwriting as belonging to Allende-Allen. A limited edition of the annotated book was published soon after; rumors circulated that this new version was heavily read by Navy personnel. As Jacques Vallée discusses in *Revelations*, the annotated limited edition of the book became a much sought-after item among UFO believers. Apparently, a great number of these UFO buffs had wanted to believe that the Allende-Allen notes were really the words of a true insider who was privy to secret military information about UFOs and extraordinary new technology, rather than the scrawlings of a clever — if not demented — con artist. Jessup tried to capitalize on this, writing more books about UFOs. Unfortunately, none of them were successful and Citadel Press eventually dropped him. At the same time, his wife left him. His downward spiral had him struggling through bouts of depression. On April 20, 1959, he committed suicide in Florida's Dade County Park by attaching a hose to his car's exhaust pipe and asphyxiating himself. Naturally, his death remains a point of speculation and contention for conspiracy theorists.

Berlitz and Moore's critics argue that when writing *The Philadelphia Experiment*, they made no attempt to critically analyze the Allende allegations. The two writers instead took the outlandish claims of a shady individual no one had ever met and used them as their primary source in endorsing the conspiracy theory of a secret government project that turned an entire ship invisible.

Nevertheless, as weak and disreputable as *The Philadelphia Experiment* might be, its allegations did reverberate through popular culture. In 1984, New World Pictures released a film very loosely based on the book. The film spawned a direct-to-video sequel in 1993. The *USS Eldridge* legend was also the basis for James F. David's 2000 science fiction novel *Ship of the Damned*.

In December 1984, Moore became embroiled in yet another controversy that would lead to some of *the* most bruising fights between UFO believers and skeptics—as well as fights within the UFO community itself. An anonymous package was mailed to Los Angeles television producer Jaime Shandera, containing a roll of undeveloped film and what appeared to be a cover letter originally written to President-Elect Eisenhower. The letter, dated 1952, talked about top secret information relating to a UFO crash in Roswell. The information on the film itself turned out to be pictures of eight pages of official-looking documents. Soon thereafter, another sensational document came to light, this time purportedly found by UFO researcher Stanton Friedman in the National Archives: a July 14, 1954, memo written by Eisenhower's Special Assistant for National Security, Robert Cutler, and sent to Air Force Chief of Staff Nathan Twining. The memo talked about the scheduling of a special meeting for that July 16 between the president and an organization know as MJ-12. MJ-12 was an abbreviation for Majestic 12, a group that appeared to be a special research team established by President Truman and tasked with studying the UFO phenomenon, as well as the wreckage of the Roswell craft and several dead *and* surviving aliens. For some UFO proponents, this information appeared to be the holy grail itself: tangible governmental documentation that there indeed had been an alien crash in Roswell and that the highest branches of the government studied the materials.[6]

UFO skeptics were quick to pounce on this supposedly invaluable information. They quickly pointed out that the Majestic 12 memo was rife with formatting errors, making it impossible to have originated in 1954 and written by the government offices the UFOlogists claimed. For example, the document did not contain a top secret register number and was not written on official government letterhead. The letter did, however, bear the anachronistic label of "Top Secret Restricted Information." As the critics of the memo pointed out, such a designation only came into use under the Nixon administration. Furthermore, more documentation from 1954 proved that Cutler was in Europe and North Africa at the times the Majestic 12 memo and the meeting with the president were supposed to have taken place. The Majestic 12 document, skeptics quickly declared, was a transparent fraud. The accusing fingers were pointing at Moore. Other skeptics claimed that Shandera was most likely part of the plot himself. Accused of masterminding the fraud was Stanton Friedman, who had subsequently spent a great deal of research money granted by the Fund for UFO Research to try and prove the document authentic. Friedman, who to this day often appears in UFO-related documentaries and at most major UFO conventions, declared that he believes that the documents are the real thing.[7]

Unfortunately for die-hard "Roswell crash believers," many of the most reputable UFO researchers, including the ones with the impressive scientific credentials, also turned against the Majestic 12 documents. Timothy Good, the author of several best-selling investigations of the U.S. and British governments' handling of the UFO phenomenon, presented the MJ-12 memo in his 1988 book *Above Top Secret*, allowing for the possibility that it "might" be accurate, but declared it most likely a hoax in his follow-up work, *Alien Contact: Top Secret UFO Files Revealed* (1993). Vallée also vehemently denounced the entire Majestic 12 affair as a hoax. He added that the whole episode was no doubt yet another extension of the government's belief-system-manipulation program. The fact that Moore was yet again at the epicenter of the entire controversy, Vallée argued, damaged the story's credibility even more. He hypothesized that the entire MJ-12 incident was probably yet another Moore-Doty covert manipulation project.

The mainstream of UFOlogy now regards the Majestic 12 episode along the lines of

Vallée's disinformation theory. Even believers in the Roswell alien crash argue that the MJ-12 affair was yet another move by the government to discredit all efforts at investigating and authenticating the event. The Majestic papers, they elaborate, were intentionally made to look as sloppy and fake as possible, bait for the skeptics and a tool to discredit *all* investigators who claimed that the Roswell crash had taken place.

No matter where the truth lies, crashed alien saucers and government conspiracies to cover up the truth would remain concepts that would burrow well into the fabric of the conspiracy culture and popular entertainment.

Dealing with the Devil

One of the strangest phenomena of fear in the 1980s did not have quite the staying power of UFOs in the cultural imagination, yet it turned out to be shockingly destructive. The ritual child abuse hysteria, spanning much of the 1980s and into the '90s, left a string of shattered families and ruined professional reputations in its wake. Prompted by allegations of ritualistic child abuse in day care centers, an opportunistic collection of therapists, prosecutors, police officials and religious fundamentalists led a crusade to expose a worldwide Satanic conspiracy. Since nearly all of this conspiracy theory had been thoroughly discredited by the end of the 1990s, the Satanic abuse phenomenon still leaves some cultural historians shaking their heads and contemplating how a moral panic last seen in colonial Massachusetts could rear its head again in modern-day America.

The catalyst is widely held to be the 1980 book *Michelle Remembers*. Written by Canadian psychiatrist Lawrence Pazder and his patient Michelle Smith, it purports to document Pazder's recovery of Smith's repressed memories of years of childhood sexual abuse and ritualistic torture. According to the book, Pazder began treating Smith for depression following a miscarriage. During their sessions, Smith insisted that she felt there were deeply traumatic incidents in her past that she should have been telling her therapist, yet she was unable to recall them. Pazder's answer was a series of hypnotic regression session, eventually eliciting stories of lurid, grotesque abuse Smith had been forced to endure since she was five years old.

According to Smith's recollections, her family was part of the Victoria, British Columbia, chapter of the Church of Satan, an organization that supposedly spanned the globe and included thousands of members in an intricate network of crime, pornography, and child abuse. Smith claimed that under Pazder's guidance she was able to recall years of abuse, where she would be repeatedly forced by her family to take part in everything from sex orgies to torture sessions, murder, and cannibalism. She claimed to have been imprisoned in dungeons for days, made to take part in Satanic rituals, witnessed ritualistic murders, forced to drink blood, and smeared with the blood of murdered infants and adults.

The sensationalistic claims propelled *Michelle Remembers* to bestseller success and elevated Pazder to the position of a renowned expert on the Satanic conspiracy and ritual abuse. As historians of the Satanic abuse panic recall, this new role as the leading authority on an insidious new threat was something Pazder relished. He was ready to give his services to combat the worldwide Satanic threat and, in turn, there were also plenty of people ready to build similar lucrative careers out of keeping a fear of this diabolical conspiracy alive.[8] The formula for a true moral panic was established. As it would turn out, however, this panic wound up wrecking families, taking away people's livelihoods, and imprisoning innocent people for years.

Once *Michelle Remembers* charged that Satanic cults were targeting children in a massive, far-reaching conspiracy, people claiming to have been devil-worship victims were ready to come forth and tell more astounding stories of abuse. The most dramatic allegations came in 1983 when Judy Johnson, a woman who had been diagnosed as a paranoid schizophrenic, told Manhattan Beach, California, police that her son had been sexually molested by both her estranged husband as well as the staff of the local McMartin preschool. It became the longest (six years) and most expensive criminal case in California history. Virginia McMartin, her daughter, Peggy McMartin Buckey, and grandson Ray Buckey were charged with molesting 360 children. Stemming from Johnson's original suspicion that her son had been abused, the prosecution presented a case alleging that the McMartin day care center staff led regular sessions of brutal Satanic orgies with the children in their care. But there was no physical evidence that any Satanic activity went on at the McMartin facilities or that any of the children had been abused in any way. The charges against the McMartins were dismissed.[9]

In 1986, Judy Johnson died from chronic alcoholism. To critical observers of the trial and the entire Satanic abuse issue, how the case could have gone so far when it was founded on so little (the fantastic accusations of a mentally ill alcoholic) remains the most astounding aspect of the entire debacle. Johnson, after all, had also claimed that her son told her that he had seen Ray Buckey levitating and flying around in the air during the Satanic rites. Mental health experts reviewing the examinations of the children who had attended the McMartin school had also unanimously agreed that the tactics used to elicit the stories of abuse were examples of the grossest violations of impartial interviewing techniques. The small handful of child psychologists and the prosecutors building the case used the most coercive techniques possible to elicit testimonies they were determined to find. Nevertheless, soon after the McMartin case hit the headlines in 1983, at least a hundred other accusations of Satanic abuse were leveled against day care providers across the country. Accusations against parents abusing their own children in the sort of Satanic network Lawrence Pazder and Michelle Smith wrote about followed. Arrests and trials followed soon after that. Then, to cap a full-blown Satanic hysteria, theories of a global conspiracy of Satanic secret societies took off.[10]

Since every particular era inspires its own unique conspiracy theory, the '80s set the perfect stage for the Satanic hysteria. Laws for mandatory child abuse reports had been passed by the late 1970s. Everyone from healthcare providers to educators was required to contact the police if they suspected that a child was a victim of physical or sexual abuse.[11] After a period of rising crime rates that spanned from the 1960s through the '70s, the culture had been galvanized into taking serious action to "get tough on crime." Children had to be protected at all cost, so when children said they were victims of abuse, law enforcement and the courts had to listen and take immediate action. But from a well-intentioned effort to combat child-predators, the foundation had been laid for a whole new witch hunt atmosphere. Furthermore, as history had shown numerous times before, from the literal witch hunts of colonial Salem to the Red Scare of the 1940s and '50s, the zealous and the ambitious could always make lucrative careers and amass fame and power by routing out as many "witches" as possible.

Just as Lawrence Pazder was making a name for himself and turning a tidy profit lecturing about the dangers of the "Satanic underground"—and finding love with his patient,

Michelle Smith, whom he married — prosecutors were likewise realizing that they could fashion successful legal and political careers by jailing all the child-abusing Satanists. Together with a small handful of social workers and psychologists, prosecutors embarked on intense interviewing sessions with children whenever the vaguest allegation of abuse surfaced. Many involved hypnotic regressions and attempts to recover repressed memories, just as in the *Michelle Remembers* case. Unfortunately, many of these efforts were made by people with little or no proper training in hypnotherapy. But, more importantly, all of these coalitions of prosecutors and therapists *wanted* to find evidence of ritualistic Satanic activity. Finding and jailing a Satanist was the biggest prize in any child abuse prosecution. Every prosecutor who managed to do so, every police officer who arrested these perpetrators, and every social worker or psychologist who was able to coerce a Satanic abuse story from a child instantly became a media celebrity. Most of these people were offered hefty speaking and consulting fees to travel the country and attend conventions and training seminars and share tips on exposing the Satanic conspiracy.[12]

Once the Satanic panic subsided after the collapse of the McMartin prosecution, and more level-headed mental health professionals reviewed the records, the real outrages appeared to be the wholesale abuse of the tools and techniques of mental health therapy, compounded by investigative and prosecutorial misconduct. Essentially, small children had been subjected to coercive interview sessions by people who used everything from leading questions to threats, browbeating, bullying, and intimidation to make sure the children told only one acceptable story: that they had been victims of Satanic abuse.[13]

Historians of the ritual abuse panic also make a point of trying to identify a greater cultural and political context that set the stage for this modern-day witch hunt. This context was a strengthening movement of fundamentalist, politically active evangelical Christianity looking to expose the hand of Satan in a rapidly changing, sometimes radically liberalizing society.

Motivated as a reaction to the counterculture of the late 1960s and the increasingly licentious excesses of the so-called "me decade" of the '70s, the activist fundamentalist Christians saw themselves on a mission to save an ever-more morally bankrupt, disintegrating American society.[14] The fundamentalists were originally appalled by the counterculture's rejection of traditional values and authority figures, including Christian churches and their dogma. This rebellious youth culture's embrace of drugs, criticism of the traditional family structure, and open sexuality repelled those who still wanted to cling to the strict authoritarian social values of old-line conservative Christianity. Even the mainstream off-shoots of all the counterculture challenges to traditional values, like the women's lib and gay rights movements, were being interpreted as but an "attack on families."

The response to what the Christian fundamentalists saw as a new, threatening morality was the argument that a lot of America's social problems could be tied to the rebellious permissiveness of this new era. Throughout the 1960s and into the '70s, in fact, urban crime rates had started climbing. A lot of the violent crime could be tied to the drug trade. Drugs, in turn, were a representation of the dark side of the hippie movement's romanticized use of narcotics as "mind-expanding" tools to achieve enlightenment and moral superiority. The drugs of the counterculture, according to the fundamentalist argument, had been the conduit for a society, morality- and peace-destroying menace like violent crime to weaken America. Furthermore, the fundamentalist Christians pointed to the rapidly rising divorce rate, tying it to feminism and its "assault" on traditional family values. By the 1980s, the term "latch key kids" had entered the cultural lexicon as a very dubious, guilt-inducing reference to unsupervised, neglected children left to their own devices all day long while their self-centered parents (especially mothers) were busy pursuing their careers. But perhaps the biggest boon to conservative Christians trying to scare a wayward, rebellious America straight was the emergence of a frightening new type of cultural icon.

Murderers like the Boston Strangler, Richard Speck, the Zodiac Killer, Charles Manson and his brainwashed, cult-like "family," John Wayne Gacy, the Hillside Stranglers, Ted Bundy, and the Son of Sam shocked America in the '60s and '70s with appalling, unimaginably sadistic killings. But what was more shocking about most of these criminals—or at least those who were eventually caught, unlike the Zodiac Killer whose identity is still unknown—was their apparent banality, their *averageness*. The serial killer was so frightening because he could be (and most often was) the mild-mannered man next door. Of these murderous predators, the first true superstar was Charles Manson, and almost immediately the conservative impulse was to tie him to the values of the counterculture.

In fact, for social and religious conservatives looking to tie the corruption of modern America to the 1960s counterculture movement, there was perhaps no better gift than Manson. To this day, documentaries about his gang's murderous rampages still call him "the man who killed the '60s" and speak of how Americans looked at the counterculture and saw madness.[15] Manson, a manipulative sociopath, had indeed been able to shrewdly speak the language of the hippies and the radicals. He told his followers to question the social constructs of reality and reject all rules and values but the ones the individual made for himself. Manson's disciples—groups of troubled, disenfranchised, and highly impressionable teenagers—allowed him to redefine their values and reality into one where Manson was a messianic prophet and where morality meant the overthrow of a corrupt system through the slayings of nine innocent people. Once Manson's madness was exposed during his trial and that of four of his followers for the killings of the actress Sharon Tate, three of her friends, and the killings of Rosemary and Leno LaBianca, the "family's" depraved value system was instantly interpreted as being emblematic of the entire counterculture movement. As far as many Americans were concerned — especially those who were the most conservative, the most traditional, and the most religious—they really were looking at an accurate representation of hippies and drop-outs and flower children and, indeed, they were seeing pure evil.

But more signs of a Satanic presence in crime, as well as all aspects of American culture, soon started disturbing more and more of those people who were evangelically inclined, or just paranoid. During his 1977 arrest for the murders of six people and the attempted murders of seven others, New York's Son of Sam killer, David Berkowitz, claimed he did not act alone but was a part of a Satanic cult. In the 1980s, California's "Night Stalker" Richard Ramirez, convicted for thirteen murders, five attempted murders, and eleven sexual assaults, claimed to be a Devil worshipper as well. Such twisted, vicious killers, fundamentalists would argue, were just a natural creation of a society that had not only rejected its traditional Christian values, but whose popular culture embraced Satanic and occult messages every day. Moreover, these killers were just the beginning in what would surely be an immense, diabolical wave of occult criminals terrorizing modern America.

Conservative Christian critics of the mass media started making a mission out of identifying Satanic symbolism and lyrics in hard rock and heavy metal music. They pointed to bands like Black Sabbath and AC/DC that displayed the most obvious Satanic imagery in their concerts, on their album art works, and their song lyrics. The fundamentalists zealously examined the LP and audiotape recordings of popular rock and metal albums for signs of "backmasking," or the recording of subversive or Satanic lyrics that could only be heard when the LP or tape was played backward. These hidden lyrics were supposed to have been brainwashing impressionable kids into pledging their allegiance to Satan and embarking upon lives of drug abuse and crime. Ironically enough, backmasking accusations turned out to help some rockers rather than hurt them. Being accused of sneaking Satanic lyrics onto an album helped enhance a performer's outlaw and rebel image. Some bands back-masked Satanic lyrics on purpose and advertised it as their act of defiance against the music critics. However, other than the most zealous backward-lyric hunters, no one has ever proven that any of the hidden Satanic lyrics ever existed on any of the accused records and tapes. Many of the most successful rock musicians and bands of all time were accused of backmasking, including The Beatles, Pink Floyd, AC/DC, Led Zeppelin, Electric Light Orchestra, Queen, Styx, Judas Priest, The Rolling Stones, The Eagles, and Jefferson Starship. The consensus among psychologists and cognitive researchers is that even if messages are backmasked into music, there is no proof that the brain can ever understand them on either a conscious or subconscious level, much less be influenced in any way by them.[16]

Popular culture itself inadvertently aiding the cause of the fundamentalist Satan-fighting Christian right could be seen in a popular line of Devil and possession-themed horror films that were extremely popular in the 1970s. Starting with director William Friedkin's 1973 horror masterpiece *The Exorcist*, many horror films of the decade dealt with demonic possession and the minions of Satan threatening innocent children and teenagers. In the *Omen* series (1976, 1978, 1981) a cherubic-faced child was actually the Antichrist, groomed to climb to positions of power in the American business and political arenas and take over the world. Although the success of both *The Exorcist* and *The Omen* spawned a long line of imitation films, the most interesting film in this trend is actually its initiator. While it was one of the most explicit and shocking horror films of its time, *The Exorcist* is also perhaps one of the most conservative horror films ever made. It was based on a novel by screenwriter William Peter Blatty, who never made a secret of the fact that he intended his book to be a call to renewed faith by Christians in a time when traditional values were being mocked and abandoned. In the course of the story, a young girl's possession by a demon can only be fought by a skeptical priest who is able to rediscover his own lapsed faith.

The sway of the message of evangelical, fundamentalist Christianity, in fact, had grown strong enough by the mid–1970s that it was growing into a powerful social movement standing in vocal opposition to the counterculture liberalism. Evangelical Christian ministers had seen their following swell in numbers until they could pack massive sports stadiums for special sermons in what would be the forerunners of the 1990s and 2000s "mega-churches." The predominant message of all the evangelists was a warning that America was heading for a downfall because of its abandonment of traditional values and morality. By the latter half of the decade, this message began wielding political power. The call for a renewal of traditional values had turned into a call for the election of leaders who would use the power of the law and the government to promote old-fashioned values. In 1976, even a liberal Democrat like Jimmy Carter declared that he was a proud born-again Christian. One of his platforms was a promise to help re-establish traditional values and mores in both the government and the greater American culture.

But the strongest supporter of the evangelical movement proved to be Ronald Reagan. Through a promise to support conservative Christian platforms like the opposition to abortion and the support for school prayer, Reagan's election to the White House in 1980 cemented a connection between the Republican party and fundamentalist Christianity that would last into the 21st century. In fact, it was in the Reagan era and under the charismatic leadership of evangelists like Pat Robertson and Jerry Falwell that the Christian fundamentalist right had declared its new mission as firm and aggressive political activism. The agenda for conservative Christians, Robertson and Falwell made no effort to hide, was to influence legislation and ensure that the country would be governed according to strict Christian values.[17]

Soon after the publication of *Michelle Remembers*, the newly empowered Christian right had yet another ideal mission. For over a decade they had been warning that Satanic forces were lurking in America, and now they had a chance to prove it and to fight the Devil for all the country to see. In fact, the hand of Christian evangelical conservative movement was everywhere in the Satanic abuse panic. The various seminars to educate communities, parents, therapists, and law enforcement professionals about the Devil's conspiracy were, in large part, funded by evangelical churches and activists. (They did not advertise this fact, and most of the seminars made a point of declaring that they were completely secular affairs and run as educational efforts to help expose a secret crime wave.[18])

Critical historical analyses of the ritual abuse hysteria have shown that the phenomenon played out as a series of attacks on everything the Christian far right wing wanted to punish in society. For one, the focus on daycare centers, analysts argue, is a thinly veiled attack on feminism and working mothers. As the 1980s had seen popular media like TV talk shows and news magazine programs running discussions with a generation of working women contending with feelings of guilt over not being homemakers and stay-at-home moms, the horrific accusations of Satanic child abuse in daycare centers helped rub salt in the psychic wounds of such women. The insinuation is loud and clear, critics contend: The conservative right was implying that thousands of children could have been spared brutal, perverse torture if their mothers had been responsible enough and stayed home the way women were supposed to.[19]

For other historians, the way the accusations against Ray Buckey were presented and then covered in the media — along with accusations against other male daycare workers— had the disagreeable whiff of homophobia. The McMartin prosecution and its zealous child psychologist advisors, the Children's Institute International, went to great lengths to insinuate that Buckey *had* to have been guilty of child molestation because he was somehow "abnormal" for working in a daycare center in the first place. The Southern California press covering the McMartin case liked to focus on the fact that Buckey always looked very much like a prototypical "geek" or an introverted "nerd." People interviewed by the press liked to expound on theories that "real" men did not work in daycare centers.[20] The implications of homosexuality were loud and clear. During that period, however, the fundamentalist right-wing and organizations like Jerry Falwell's "Moral Majority" vehemently argued that most homosexuals were also pedophiles and child predators. In 1977, for example, when militant anti-gay activist Anita Bryant crusaded to repeal a Florida law protecting homosexuals from discrimination, she called her efforts the "Save Our Children" campaign.[21] As Falwell himself had once remarked on the issue of gay rights in America, "They are brute beasts ... part of a vile and Satanic system that will be utterly annihilated, and there will be a celebration in Heaven."[22]

Still others put the Satanic hysteria in the context of religious intolerance and bigotry against non-traditional spiritualities. This, too, is an issue that traces its roots back to the counterculture days of the 1960s. When hippies had moved to distance themselves from all things "establishment" and traditional, many of them began dabbling in everything from Eastern religions and mysticism to variations of ancient pagan nature worship, animism, and occultism. Eventually, an amalgamation of beliefs focusing on cosmology, astrology, a belief in UFOs, human potential enhancement, esotericism, environmentalism, and very individual-oriented spiritual practices like meditation and healing through herbs and the supposed power of crystals came to be known as the "New Age" movement. In part, even the name of the movement is a derivation of the counterculture concept of the dawning of the "New Age of Aquarius." The Christian far-right-wing's reaction to New Age beliefs had also been swift and negative. They charged that New Age spirituality was nothing more than Satanism in disguise. With the quickly spreading popularity of New Age beliefs in the '70s and '80s, Christian fundamentalists again had reason to believe that what was really spreading was a vast Satanic underground. With the New Age focusing on self-actualization, increased potentials, relaxation and "mind expansion," the movement took root among people in the entertainment industry and highly ambitious, upwardly mobile professionals, with the phenomenon essentially writing a new script for a belief in a vast Satanic conspiracy. The wealthy and the powerful, the entertainers and musicians— who had already been suspect in the eyes of right-wing fundamentalists for their embrace of the counterculture's drug use, sexual liberation, and liberal politics— had virtually sold their souls to the Devil for their earthly wealth and power, this script read. These elites, in turn, were now about to corrupt the world, destroy Christian traditions, brainwash the young and the vulnerable through subversive rock music and sexually explicit TV shows and movies, and worship Satan in rites of grotesque child abuse.[23]

At the height of the hysteria, believers of the Satanic abuse theory attempted to prove that this was not only an American problem but a worldwide plague. What historians of the panic now contend is that something akin to a self-fulfilling prophecy began to take place in several countries once American experts— or, more accurately, abuse theory proponents like the staff of Children's Institute International — embarked on an international tour to "help" police agencies and therapists spot Satanic activity. In effect, what happened was that the vague indicators of Satanic abuse, the coercive and manipulative interviewing techniques, had been exported. As a result, authorities in Canada, England, New Zealand, Australia, the Netherlands, and Scandinavia all embarked on similar, McMartin-esque prosecutions of alleged daycare center Satanists. To the true believers, however, this was all evidence of the existence of wealthy secret societies of Satanists operating a global conspiracy of crime, child abuse, and human sacrifices.[24]

In the United States, however, not only did the McMartin case eventually implode, with no prosecutions resulting from the long and expensive trials, but much of the Satanic conspiracy theory had been dealt serious blows by law enforcement authorities and investigative journalists finding no credible physical evidence to support it. With the theory proponents making such ghastly allegations as Satanic cults kidnapping people and forcing them into prostitution, birthing children solely for sacrificial murders, and killing kidnapped people in snuff films, the FBI had also taken an interest. The kidnapping and imprisonment charges, after all, would have been federal crimes. But, the Bureau turned up no proof. "Satanic crime" in America, the FBI and most police agencies concurred, was no more extensive than local, isolated incidents of disaffected, alienated — most often drug-addicted and alcoholic — teenagers vandalizing buildings with Satanic graffiti or abusing some animals. The consensus was that people already given to antisocial and destructive behavior might adapt the trappings of Satanism in their demented efforts at acting out and getting attention.[25]

Furthermore, the eventual debunking of much of *Michelle Remembers* helped discredit a lot of the Satanic network allegations by severely damaging the very work upon which the moral panic was founded. Michelle Smith, for example, claimed that sometimes her parents would keep her locked away for days in various Satanic ceremonial lairs for marathon sessions of debauchery and torture. Investigators took a look at the attendance records kept at her elementary school and found documentation suggesting that she had been in school during the periods of her alleged imprisonment. Moreover, Smith's claims of having taken part in numerous Satanic rituals in the local cemetery also strained credibility for most of the people of Victoria. In her recollections, she claimed that each ceremony was attended by a crowd of local Devil worshippers. Victoria residents argued that the cemetery was closely bordered by neighborhoods and houses. Investigators examining the layout of the area also concurred that it would have been impossible to hold the sort of ceremonies Smith described in such a location without it being noticed. No trace evidence of Satanic activity turned up in any of the other locales Smith identified as cultic ceremonial sites either. One of Smith's most outlandish claims was that many members of the cult pledged their loyalty to the Devil by cutting off one of their own middle fingers. But, in fact, no one had ever found a single Victoria resident with a missing middle finger, and no one in town could ever recall having met anyone with a sign of such mutilation.[26]

Nevertheless, to this day, conspiracy theories claiming the existence of these massive, well-organized Satanic networks persist. According to the "either you're with us or against us" logic of the most zealous conspiracists, the lack of evidence is in itself a sign of the existence of a conspiracy. In this case, the argument goes that the Satanists are so well-organized and connected into such powerful networks of government and business power brokers that they can completely hide all evidence of their activities. In the Smith case, for example, they would argue that the Victoria Satanic cell can easily create false school attendance records for Michelle Smith because "their reach extends everywhere." Moreover, the Satanic reach, according to conspiracy theorists, also extends into the FBI itself, helping hide evidence of the nationwide (and worldwide!) network.

The ironic postscript to the *Michelle Remembers* case, however, was the fact that Smith and Pazder were threatened with a lawsuit by very real "Satanists." Since the book identified the "Church of Satan" as Smith's abusers and the perpetrators of human sacrifices, the management of San Francisco's actual Church of Satan promised to bring a civil suit against Pazder and Smith, their leader claiming that he was libeled by *Michelle Remembers*.

The Church of Satan in San Francisco was founded in 1966 by Anton Sandor LaVey, a former carnival barker and police photographer. In reality more of a counterculture joke than an organization with any sort of spiritual orientation, the "Church" steeped itself in Satanic symbolism and paraphernalia, and its flamboyant leader liked to give shocking interviews extolling the greatness of Satan and invoking the blessings of Hell. As far as most historians are concerned, however, the Church of Satan, in the epicenter of the counterculture movement, was just another attempt at shocking the sensibilities of mainstream America. When drugs, draft card-burning, and free love were not quite shocking enough, a huckster like LaVey figured out that he could still startle the "establishment" and get media attention by putting on black robes with a horned hood and praising Satan. Those who observed the ceremonies and "black masses" of the Church all concurred that the place was nothing more than a glorified sex club dressed up in Halloween attire and the rhetoric of social constructionism. LaVey's "philosophy," published in his *Satanic Bible*, was a series of exhortations for people to reject all belief systems, to create their own values, to be self-centered, and to live for nothing but the pleasures of the moment. None of the Church's members, however, had ever been suspected of cannibalism, human sacrifice, or any of the gruesome crimes reported in *Michelle Remembers*.[27]

Soon after the threat of legal action, Pazder withdrew his claim that Michelle Smith's tormentors were members of the Church of Satan or that LaVey had any connection to her "abuse."

The legacy of the Satanic ritual abuse panic has been summed up in the most disturbing and poignant terms by child welfare advocates and the majority of the mental health community. Because of a manufactured moral panic by a small handful of opportunists and zealots, perhaps hundreds of instances of real abuse went uninvestigated and unpunished. For example, they argue that while people like Pazder, his fundamentalist right-wing supporters, the police, and the media looking for sensational headlines were chasing nonexistent Satanic cults, the plight of children suffering from incest — the most common type of child sexual abuse — were largely ignored. Many children who recalled experiences of real abuse yet wouldn't tell stories of Satanic ceremonies had likewise been ignored by the witch hunters who were on the lookout for the more lucrative, career-making, and headline-grabbing stories of human sacrifices, black masses, and cannibalism.[28]

The Secret Policy

By the 1980s, conspiracy theorists looking for evidence of massive-scale government and financial corruption thought they found it in the secretive workings of various policy organizations. While the search for aliens and murderous cults attracted more headlines, the most radical kin to the JFK assassination buffs, the theorists looking for villains spawned by capitalism and the military-industrial complex, sought to uncover evil and manipulative deeds among the country's economic and legislative elites. The main targets of many theorists became organizations like the Council on Foreign Relations, the Trilateral Commission, and the powerful banks and corporations that funded and staffed these policy centers.

Although founded in 1921, the Council on Foreign Relations attracted zealous scrutiny after Ronald Reagan disparaged the organization during the 1980 presidential election, then turned around and chose George H.W. Bush, a CFR member, as his vice presidential running mate. According to those ever on the lookout for the hidden hands of secretive cabals influencing the government, the Council on Foreign Relations is one of the power centers of the conspiratorial elite, running both the U.S. government *and* guiding all major world events.[29]

The CFR traces its roots to a study and strategy group of President Woodrow Wilson's advisors and some one hundred prominent political, business, and intellectual figures meeting in 1917.[30] Calling itself "The Inquiry," the group discussed what the role of the United States needed to be in the world that was to take shape in the aftermath of World War I. In 1919, while attending the Paris Peace Conference, Wilson and several Inquiry members met with British conference delegates and conceived of a joint U.S.-British Institute of International Affairs. The Institute was to have two major branches, one in the United States and one in England. The U.S. branch, headquartered in New York, was formally called the Council on Foreign Relations. Throughout the decades and to the present day, the CFR remained a collection of business and intellectual elites functioning as a think tank and research center, analyzing world events and presenting policy suggestions that the United States government should consider adopting. In its most benign form — and according to the CFR's own public mission statement — the group is but a meeting of the sharpest minds in the country to analyze the state of world affairs, recognize problems, and suggest courses of action that would most benefit the U.S. and help ensure world peace and stability. The CFR also claims to be a training ground for future international affairs experts since according to its membership rules, new members must be between the ages of 30 and 36 at the time of induction.

The Council, claiming to be but an analysis, study, and advisory organization with no political biases, has also always been strictly bipartisan. Not only have conservatives and liberals been CFR members, but some of the most staunchly right-wing and committed left-wing members of the cultural elite have claimed membership. For example, one of the organizers of the original "Inquiry" group, Colonel Edward Mandell House, an advisor to Wilson, had at one point described himself as a Marxist socialist. Over the years, such conservatives as Allen Dulles, George P. Schultz, George H.W. Bush, Fred Thompson, Dick Cheney and John McCain have been members, along with liberals Adlai Stevenson, Dianne Feinstein, George Soros, Donna Shalala, and Katrina Vanden Heuvel, editor and part owner of the left-wing magazine *Nation*.

The group's diverse political and ideological makeup, one might guess, could make it safe from accusations of conspiracy. What kind of a major, far-reaching and nefarious plot could such ideological opponents like Dick Cheney and George Soros possibly collude on secretly? But, according to paranoid psychology, the diversity of the CFR is what makes it all the more dangerous.

Conspiracy theorists claim that the Council on Foreign Relations has been working for decades to create a single world government. This single government (controlled, of course, by CFR members) would exert its power over the nations of the world through a global banking system and ever-widening networks of the free-trade alliances. The ultimate power of this new governing body would lie in its control of currency, credit, debt, and trade, in effect making obsolete the concept of national sovereignty. People like Wilson, House, and the original Inquiry members had argued that the only way to avoid future world wars was through the establishment of international organizations where all countries would have an equal say in the conflicts and controversies of the day — and the entire organization would have the power to band together to condemn or militarily oppose any single belligerent and warlike member nation, but conspiracy theorists and their sympathizers saw such supranational bodies as the ultimate elite world rulers. When Wilson proposed the League of Nations at the Paris Peace Conference, the United States itself never entered it. The U.S. Senate, fearing that the League was about to become the usurper of national sovereignty, failed to ratify the covenant. Later, the foundation of the United Nations was again pointed to by conspiracists as yet a newer, more powerful version of an emerging one-world government.

Furthermore, the CFR always had something for both the left-wing and the right-wing conspiracy-believers to fear. The large number of bankers and industrialists making up the rank and file of CFR members had always troubled the left-wing, who fear the spread of world capitalism. In fact, corporate members that help bankroll the CFR include American Express, AIG, Bank of America, Boeing, BP, IBM, Halliburton, Chevron, Citigroup, Shell, De Beers, Deutsche Bank, ExxonMobil, MasterCard, Lockheed Martin, ABC News, Merck, Merrill Lynch, and Morgan Stanley. Troubling conspiracy theorists even more — and inspiring uber-theories of decades- and centuries-long world-controlling plots by international bankers — is the fact that members of the Rockefeller, Morgan, and Rothschild banking and industrial dynasties have all been members and supporters of the CFR. These theorists, in turn, claim that the banking and industrial interests of the world have been working at least since the nineteenth century, and then through the twentieth by way of the CFR, to manipulate the world's economies and to create cycles of prosperity, recession, and depression. Through the resulting global unrest and turmoil created by cycles of boom and bust, according to the conspiracy theory, the hidden elites of the world have always been able to instigate unrest, revolutions, and wars. These wars could then be used by bankers and weapons manufacturers to continue reaping profits and influencing world governments.

Right-wingers, on the other hand, have long been opposed to the internationalist nature of the group, fearing the end of national sovereignty. The undermining of sovereignty, they claimed, was the first step toward global totalitarian socialism and communism. As counterintuitive as it might sound, according to the ultra right-wing John Birch Society (one of the most vehement critics of the CFR), the United Nations, and all supranational organizations, the world's banking elites are conspiring to create one planet-ruling mega-organization that would institute global communism. This point of view admonishes against the naïve belief that communism would abolish class systems. A classless society, they charge, is a Marxist fantasy well suited for fuzzy-headed intellectuals and scruffy graduate students tucked away on their campuses and libraries, far from the real world and out of touch. The ultimate goal of the one-world government, and the reason bankers and industrialists support it, is the establishment of their own world hegemony, a new system where various industries would have global monopolies and no fear of competition. The new world, according to this point of view, would be a draconian dictatorship of the wealthy elite. Even in all of the world's communist systems, the right-wing conspiracy theorists point out (not incorrectly), the heads of the party have all lived lives of lavish material excess to rival the lifestyles of the most conspicuously consuming capitalist billionaires. Like George Orwell wrote, all are equal, but some are more equal than others. But the conservative conspiracists also argue that a number of wealthy industry heads of the Western capitalist nations in the early 20th century enthusiastically sang the praises of socialism and Marxism, and hoped to see the success of Lenin's experiment in Russia. Among the capitalist friends of the far left were banker Jacob Schiff, attorney and CFR member Elihu Root, and Sir Alfred Milner, England's high commissioner in Africa. These men had, in fact, contributed money to Leon Trotsky and the organization of the Russian Revolution. Milner had also become a principal trustee of the estate of Cecil Rhodes, who, in turn, had been the founder of the DeBeers diamond mining empire and a major architect of British foreign policy think tanks called "Round Tables" and the Royal Institute of International Affairs. The RII neatly connects back into the establishment of the American Council on Foreign Relations. Rhodes himself, according to conspiracy theorists, was not hostile to the ideas of Marxism. Conspiracy theorist Jim Marrs, tying even more secret societies to the "vast network," writes that the Round Table concept comes from the Freemasons and the Illuminati.

Ultimately, the most paranoid of conspiracy theorists argue that concepts like right-wing, left-wing, capitalist, fascist, or communist are all archaic and outmoded when it comes to the emergence of a new global totalitarian state by way of the machinations of secretive policy groups. Whether the CFR and the RII members call themselves liberal or conservative, whether it's a George H.W. Bush or a Jimmy Carter or a Bill Clinton in power, these people are all members of the country's — the *world's*— ruling elite. These are people who are after power and wealth; who want to control world affairs and popular opinion;

who want to make sure they keep ruling. Taking this thinking to its logical conclusion, a conspiracy theorist would argue that the very liberal-conservative, Democrat-Republican spectrum in American politics is but a careful ruse, a sham created to fool people into thinking that a diverse organization like the CFR could not possibly be pulling off the world's biggest conspiracies.

According to conspiratorial thinking, the proof that the CFR is implementing all of their plans lies in the fact that most opinions and positions the group makes public through its various books and in the pages of its magazine, *Foreign Affairs*, soon become government policy in the U.S. This theory argues that there is a ruling elite at the head of the CFR, a secretive group of the most powerful industrialists and bankers that makes decisions about American domestic and foreign policy with only an eye toward keeping their hold on power. Then the various academic and intellectual members of the group (experts and policy wonks) go to work manufacturing data, studies, and policy recommendations that U.S. Senators, representatives, and even presidents dutifully implement.

Counter-arguments against both left-wing and right-wing theorists, however, have often pointed out that the CFR — or its offshoot organization, the Trilateral Commission, a group created in the 1970s to study and analyze issues facing the United States, Western Europe, and Japan — is hardly as secretive as conspiracy theorists charge. Moreover, CFR defenders argue that Wilson's original vision for a more closely interconnected body of nations trying to defuse global tensions is hardly a sign of evil intent. Quite to the contrary, the argument would present. But, moreover, minutes of both CFR and Trilateral Commission meetings have been made public, policy positions and recommendations of the group are also always publicly disseminated, and anyone is free to subscribe to *Foreign Affairs*. On the CFR website, one can download podcasts of select CFR meetings.

Furthermore, CFR historians have pointed out that Council members do *not* march in lock step when it comes to various controversial issues of the day. For example, numerous CFR members were loudly and publicly at odds over the Vietnam War as well as the invasion of Iraq.

The fact that CFR members have the ears of legislators and presidents, counter-conspiracy arguments charge, is also hardly evidence that the Council is some sort of sinister puppetmaster undermining democracy. Members of the CFR, after all, are the top minds in their fields. The very reason they are recruited into the organization is because they are the best at what they do. It only makes logical sense that politicians and policymakers would seek out and listen to their advice.

Nonetheless, the activities of the CFR are sometimes insular and secretive enough that one can hardly be surprised that conspiracy theories persist. Since the group does admit that there are numerous meetings where the minutes are *not* made public and secretive discussions of issues take place, adequately cynical minds will want to know what is kept hidden and to what end. Making public only *some* of the work the group does creates an impression that disinformation campaigns are afoot. According to conspiracy theories, the public minutes and the podcasts on the CFR webpage are but a smoke screen while the real machinations for global enslavement go on behind the scenes. In the same vein, even the Council's recruitment and membership-admission practices smack of elitism. One cannot merely apply for membership. A prospective Council member must be recruited by one CFR member, and then the recommendation must be supported by three more CFR members. For those believers in a power elite's careful propagation of its own agendas, policies, and values, this sort of selective membership policy reaffirms their suspicions.

Overall, from the largely apolitical world of the UFO conspiracies to the right-wing fears of a Satanic underground and conservatives and liberals equally fearing the shadowy intentions of bankers, policymakers, and the wealthy cultural elites, the major conspiracy movements of the 1980s signaled an era where fear and distrust reigned across the political spectrum. As the following chapter will document, conspiracy theory-oriented films spoke to the paranoia of left-wingers and right-wingers, and even — if not *especially* — to those who claimed no political affiliation. Conspiracy films of the 1980s dealt with more supernatural and alien plots than the genre had done before, while the worlds of cops, politicians, government operatives, businessmen, and military strategists were more corrupt than ever.

CHAPTER 5

Aliens, Rugged Individualists, and Incompetent Conspirators
Conspiracy Films of the 1980s

The turbulence of the 1960s and '70s gave birth to modern American conspiracy culture; a decade later, Hollywood found itself in the powerful grip of full-blown paranoia. The Kennedy assassination, the bureaucratic lies, bungling and cover-ups of the Vietnam War and the Watergate scandal taught Americans to question everything, and in the 1980s, mainstream action films, thrillers and science fiction were completely taken over by the conspiratorial mindset. But mainstream, popular entertainment has always been a cautious, conservative enterprise. Filmmakers are generally more comfortable reflecting the Zeitgeist than shaping it. A handful of films like *The Parallax View* (1974), *Chinatown* (1974), *Three Days of the Condor* (1975) and *Close Encounters of the Third Kind* (1977) established some of the early archetypes of the genre, but in the next decade, conspiracies were truly everywhere.

Conspiracism in the 1980s is not without paradox, however. November of 1980, after all, was the beginning of the "Reagan Revolution," with voters reacting to a call for renewed optimism, patriotism and, most importantly, faith in the system. As far as popular tastes in entertainment went, the blockbuster successes of a number of unabashedly uplifting films throughout the Carter era had already been hinting that people wanted a change. The ironic nihilism of the old counterculture wave of the late '60s and early '70s filmmaking had run out of steam as early as 1976, when Sylvester Stallone's punchy Cinderella story *Rocky* beat out the conspiracy theory film *All the President's Men* for an Oscar. The following four years' worth of feel-good hits like *Star Wars* (1977), *Saturday Night Fever* (1977), and *Superman* (1978) were signs that change was in the air.

As it turned out, however, conspiratorial thinking had not turned into an anachronism during the conservative revolution. As a matter of fact, Reaganism brought its own unique spin to conspiracy theory. If anything, conservative conspiracy theories proved another grim point. In modern America, no one trusted anyone else, and *everyone*, from conservative Republican to liberal Democrat, felt like there was some big, faceless, amoral power structure allied against them. Reagan's brand of cinematic, cowboy conservatism, what his supporters like to call "rugged individual" conservatism, had its own built-in conspiratorial program. Social ills, according to this program, are caused by the system, the bureaucracy, office-bound policy wonks and crooked insiders who stifle the freedoms, creativity and opportunities of the individual. This "big government" is, most importantly, overloaded with paternalistic liberals who like to tell others how to live. They don't trust the individual to make his or her own choices in life; they like to burden everyone with intrusive, overbearing, micro-managing laws and regulations. "Big government" became coded as the new face of society's main face of evil. "Big government" functioned for its own welfare alone and did not see to the needs of the individual. Big government bureaucracies, according to this perspective, strive only to stay alive, to stay funded, to keep from solving the social ills they have been created to solve, lest the bureaucracy become obsolete and its armies of paper pushers find themselves out of jobs.

An indictment of the system like this could be seen in films as early as 1971, in *Dirty Harry*. While the film was directed by liberal Don Siegel and starred libertarian Clint Eastwood, it immediately sparked controversy. Its take-no-prisoners approach to law enforcement didn't jibe well with the left-wing counterculture. In *Dirty Harry*, criminals are loathsome, vile sociopaths who kill without a conscience. They are a world away from the Warren Beatty school of *Bonnie and Clyde* (1967) and its rehabilitation of real-life sociopaths as metaphors for youth unrest. Even film critic Roger Ebert, an Eastwood fan, labeled *Dirty Harry* "fascist." Although *Dirty Harry*'s liberal detractors would usually focus their hatred of the film on its violence or concern over its muted messages tacitly endorsing vigilantism, its true offense was is its suggestion that the system, the "hegemony" is, in fact, liberal. *Dirty Harry* declares that the system is ineffective, corrupt, and dangerous, but the fault lies with the left. The conspiracy here is a conspiracy of incompetence and cover-up. Everything from concerns over the protests of special interest groups, the rights of criminals, liberal judges who don't punish severely enough, and radical intellectuals who want to open the prisons and release all the convicts add up to a society that has devolved into a dangerous, degenerate madhouse. Justifying the failure of the system, covering up the culpability of the career social theorists and bureaucrats that are sinking America, is the true face of the conspiracy.

This conservative conspiratorial bent, in fact, can be seen in the 1980s' most successful, loudest, most aggressive hyper-kinetic action films. Heroes in the *Rambo* series (1983, 1985, 1988), the first two *Die Hard* films (1988, 1990), and the first two *Lethal Weapon* films (1987, 1989) not only win spectacular victories against criminals, foreign aggressors and terrorists, but they must fight just as hard against crooked, duplicitous and traitorous government agencies that plot, scheme and conspire to cover up their own incompetence and failures.

Cinematically, this approach can easily be crafted to look apolitical and attract the largest possible spectrum of audience sensibilities. David Denby remarked on the 1980s action films in *New York* magazine, arguing that

> they make contact with a stratum of pessimism that runs very deep in this country — a sort of lumpen despair that goes beyond, or beneath politics. In these movies, America is a failure, a disgrace — a country run on the basis of expediency and profit, a country that has betrayed its ideals. The attack is directed not merely at liberals or "permissiveness" but at something more fundamental — the modern bureaucratic state and capitalism itself.[1]

A conservative conspiracy theory warning of bureaucratic incompetence is merely a natural continuation of the theme that brought the Reagan administration into power. The tipping point in the 1980 election was the Iranian hostage crisis and the general public impression that a weak, indecisive Jimmy Carter was incapable of dealing with aggressive foreign enemies. The Iranian situation, the conservative argument claimed, was but the culmination of a recent history of weak-willed liberal political theory. Liberal indecisiveness and appeasement of enemies shaped a faulty Vietnam doctrine that didn't let the military win the war, and this same weakness was letting communism spread across the world.

Ironically, by the end of Reagan's tenure in office, his own administration would be tainted by conspiracy and scandal as well. The Iran-Contra affair was a real-life conspiracy that was as layered and colorful as any military action film with a handful of larger-than-life figures like Oliver North at its epicenter, along with networks of Central American mercenaries and Middle Eastern arms dealers conspiring to subvert laws and lie to Congress.

Many films of the 1980s also honed the archetypal characters, themes and plot structures of the science fictional conspiracies. UFOs, time travel, artificial intelligence and other such world-altering — and world-threatening — technologies were usually intertwined with oily, double-talking government, business and military bureaucracies. The optimism of the decade, it turns out, could never completely dispel the previous twenty years' worth of disillusionment. The most hyperbolic and fantastic conspiracy films of the '80s were well in line with one of the bedrock implications of paranoid psychology: enlightenment, transcendence, miracles that could set the world free are real, but someone is keeping it all hidden for his own gain.

Retrieve and Hide

Although Steven Spielberg's *Close Encounters of the Third Kind* laid part of the foundation for the melding of UFO contact with the fear of a government cover-up, 1980 provided a much more modest film dramatization of what would turn into one of the canonical beliefs in the UFO mythos. *Hangar 18*, starring Robert Vaughn, Darren McGavin and Gary Collins, is the first film to involve the retrieval of a crashed alien spaceship.

The timing of the film is quite fortuitous, premiering the same year Charles Berlitz and William Moore published their book *The Roswell Incident*, although the book and the movie are not connected. Crashed UFO stories are actually quite old. The first supposed incident of a crashed UFO took place in Aurora, Texas, on April 17, 1897. Townspeople were said to have retrieved dead humanoids from the wreckage and buried them in the local cemetery. Alien saucer crashes have been rumored to have occurred in Ubatuba, Brazil, in either 1933 or 1934; Spitzbergen, Norway, in 1947; Aztec, New Mexico, in 1948; Death Valley, California, in 1949; Argentina in 1950; Brady, Montana, in 1953; Kingman, Arizona, in 1953; Mattydale, New York, in 1954; Frdynia, Poland, in 1959; New Paltz, New York, in 1960; Chili, New Mexico, 1974; and Padcaya, Bolivia, in 1978.[2]

Although it is largely believed by those who only have a passing, superficial acquaintance with UFOlogy that "Hangar 18" is the fabled storage space at Wright Patterson Air Force Base where the wreckage of the Roswell UFO was secreted in 1947, the term "Hangar 18" actually originates from the alleged Aztec, New Mexico, crash of 1948.[3]

The film *Hangar 18* is an amalgamation of the basics of all crashed UFO legends. In these stories, a freak accident aboard the alien craft, or a run-in with an Earthly natural disaster like a lightning storm, forces a spaceship to ground in a smoldering heap of mangled and scattered wreckage. Alien bodies, either dead or severely injured, lie among the debris. Locals stumble upon the accident site, but so does the government. Using strong-arm tactics or bribery, military goons or nondescript "men in black" swiftly move in to silence all the witnesses. Nevertheless, a lone believer, or a team of believers, is willing to risk everything to penetrate the veil of secrecy and bring the truth to the people.

In *Hangar 18*, the UFO crash is caused by a close encounter with a satellite deployed from the space shuttle. The satellite accidentally strikes an alien craft hovering nearby, monitoring the activities. The collision kills one shuttle crew member and brings the alien ship down in the Texas desert. To complicate matters, there is a tight presidential election season under way and the incumbent president's shifty chief of staff, Gordon Cain (Robert Vaughn), decides the UFO story could sway the election in favor of the challenger. The Air Force, as a result, takes over the retrieval of the alien craft and the space shuttle's two remaining crew members, Steve Bancroft (Gary Collins) and Lew Price (James Hampton), are accused of incompetence and causing their crewmate's death. Hoping to clear their names and prove what really happened, Bancroft and Price set out to find the crashed alien ship and expose the conspiracy.

Although following the archetypal UFO conspiracy plot and enacting the thematic undertones rather faithfully, *Hangar 18* suffers from various holes in its logic. Mainly, the reasons for orchestrating the cover-up don't make much sense. Rather than hoping to back-engineer the alien technology for military use, to monopolize or suppress a new source of free energy or avoid general panic, the conspirators merely want to keep the event from tipping the scales in an election. Gordon Cain's fears of the UFO–election connection also strain logic. He reminds his co-conspirators that the president had once ridiculed the other candidate about UFOs. The challenger, at one time, had told the press that he saw what he believed to have been a UFO. So if the president used this incident as an opportunity to take a jab at his opponent's fitness for office, a crashed UFO in Hangar 18 would now destroy his reelection chances. The reasoning here is obviously quite weak. One could assume that perhaps the other candidate mistook something ordinary for a flying saucer; perhaps he might have been fantasy-prone or psychotic and the president's questioning his fitness for office *at the time* might have been entirely legitimate. The existence of a very real alien ship, plus two dead aliens inside, in the here and now would make the previous ridicule a moot point.

Nevertheless, Cain's fear over the compromised election launches the film into the typical mid-point high-speed chase sequence. While a team of scientists studies the space-craft in Hangar 18, Bancroft and Price set out to find the truth. Close on their heels is a cadre of suit- and sunglasses-wearing hitmen deployed by Cain. Along the way to Hangar 18, Cain's thugs kill Price, but Bancroft manages to evade them and sneak onto the Texas airbase where Hangar 18 sits. There he confronts Harry Forbes (Darren McGavin), his former NASA mission controller who now works on the UFO study team. The earnest Forbes swears he had nothing to do with the cover-up and even takes Bancroft inside the flying saucer. But just as the study team's computer expert reveals that he decoded part of the alien language and discovered a series of records in the craft's data banks that hint at plans for a future wave of alien landings, a plane loaded with explosives crashes into the hangar, obliterating everything. As it happens, Cain's backup plan for salvaging the election was the destruction of the UFO and everyone involved in the conspiracy.

The ending was given a more hopeful revision when broadcast on television, however. The final shot of the UFO standing amidst the flaming wreckage of Hangar 18 had a voice-over narration approximating a late-breaking news broadcast. The voice-over announced a plane crash on a Texas air base, but a small group survived inside what is rumored to be an alien spaceship.

Although the election as a motivator for the conspiracy is the weakest element of the plot, it does have its roots in an interesting incident in UFO lore. In 1969, while the governor of Georgia, Jimmy Carter saw a UFO and even filled out a sighting report form for the private investigation group, Mutual UFO Network. During the 1976 presidential election, he admitted to this and promised that "if I become president, I'll make every piece of information this country has about UFOs available to the public and the scientists." He never did.[4]

Reagan never ridiculed Carter's UFO encounter, although Reagan is frequently referenced in UFO conspiracy theories. For one, he admitted that in 1974, while the governor of California, he and a plane full of staff and a pilot watched a UFO temporarily trailing their flight. He also gave a speech to the United Nations in 1987 where he said, "In our obsession with antagonisms of the moment, we often forget how much unites all the members of humanity. Perhaps we need some outside, universal threat to make us recognize this common bond. I occasionally think, how quickly our differences worldwide would vanish if we were facing an alien threat from outside this world. And yet, I ask is not an alien force *already* among us?"[5] Although this is very obviously a hypothetical statement, UFO believers often quote it as Reagan's none-too-subtle hint at the Big Secret. In fact, most UFO conspiracy accounts quote only the last two sentences, removing the context. But rumor has also persisted that during a 1983 screening of *E.T.: The Extra-Terrestrial* at the White House by Steven Spielberg, Reagan remarked that "there are probably only six people in this room who know how true this is."[6]

Although hurt by its plot holes and shoestring budget, *Hangar 18* took an earnest approach to its subject matter *and* served as the decade's first in a series of films where contact with the paranormal is thwarted by bureaucracy. The story's implications, much along the lines of conspiracy theory traditions, are effectively chilling. World- and perception-altering truths are humankind's to discover, were it not for the pettiness and greed of the elites and the political power brokers. The crashed UFO's data banks, in this case, reveal that a race of ancient aliens had visited the Earth and conducted genetic experiments on prehistoric man. The UFOnauts, looking very much human, but for their bald heads and several slight internal anomalies, are part of an alien and human hybrid race. Further records aboard the ship suggest that the aliens had also been actively aiding and manipulating the development of human history. Finally, the Hangar 18 research team discovers that the aliens are not only on their way back, but they had already designated various landing areas all across the planet. However, these spectacular findings are almost all but wiped out by a plot to win an election.

The second cinematic take on the crashed alien technology mythos was actually comical, in the form of 1984's *Repo Man*. Now considered a cult classic, the film involves a group of seedy East Los Angeles car repossessors trying to find the car of a rogue scientist with an alien engine in the trunk. In a departure from the driven, frantic archetype of the conspiracy film hero, *Repo Man*'s protagonist, Otto Maddox (Emilio Estevez), wanders through most of the film in an oblivious haze. In fact, he does not really ever influence any of the action around him, but finds himself bounced from incident to incident like a human pinball paddled around by the unseen forces of cosmic fate or the influence of the invisible conspiracy. Even a fast pronunciation of his full name makes it sound almost like "automatic," connoting a lack of conscious control. But while *Repo Man* does not faithfully follow the action of the typical conspiracy film, it is true to its *spirit*. The individual, after all, can never really act freely. We can never really influence our world and destiny. The individual is always at the mercy of some bigger, invisible manipulative force that delights in abusing and exploiting him.

Not surprisingly, the *Repo Man* production team includes executive producer Michael Nesmith (a former member of the 1960s *faux* TV rock band The Monkees), who was the co-writer of 1982's *Time Rider*, about a dirt bike racer (Fred Ward) who stumbles onto a secret time travel experiment. In that similar droll, ironic film, the biker gets time-warped into the nineteenth century western frontier, but he doesn't realize what has happened to him. Much like Otto, dazed and confused by the world of oddball repo men, the Ward character wanders through much of the film believing he has merely stumbled onto a lot of desert eccentrics.

The reasons for the appearance of a number of similar science fictional, paranormal-themed conspiracy films throughout the decade can be attributed to several causes. For one, as previously discussed, conspiracy theories always have the evolutionary pattern of a growing snowball. Conspiracist claims always need to grow. They need to top themselves and lay claim to ever more epic levels of criminality and audacity. If Americans can believe that one president was assassinated by not one lone nutcase with a rifle but a far-reaching network of virtually every branch of the government, the military, big business, the CIA, the FBI, foreign spies, the Russians, the Cuban government, Cuban expatriates, and the Chicago mob, then they can believe that every other nationally prominent individual's murder is likewise more that meets the eye. If the John F. Kennedy assassination was something much bigger than just Lee Harvey Oswald, then so was the killing of Robert F. Kennedy, or that of Martin Luther King, or Malcolm X, or John Lennon. If shadowy forces can easily kill those who stand in the way of their agendas, they can certainly suppress world-altering clean-fuel technologies for the sake of corporate profits. They would also just as easily kill, intimidate, cover up and hide anything and anyone related to alien contact in order to maintain the status quo. Much the same way, while audiences have grown to love a good conspiracy in the movies, the scope of the activity in the films needed to get larger.

By the 1980s, special effects technology had also revitalized the science fiction genre. In the wake of the groundbreaking effects techniques of *Star Wars*, *Superman* and *Close Encounters of the Third Kind*, the appetites of audiences had been whetted for the fantastic and otherworldly. These special effects extravaganzas are often looked upon with a jaundiced eye by critics, leery of the "blockbuster movement" that supposedly killed off the age of the edgy, counterculture moviemaking of the so-called "sex, drugs and rock 'n' roll" movement of the late '60s and early '70s[7]; but upon closer inspection, one can actually see the gee-whiz, super hi-tech era of '80s fantasy films often leavened by a cynical conspiracy theory subplot.

A prime example of what could be called a lingering "conspiracy effect" is the intrusion of a suspicious, conspiracy-fearing, decidedly modern attitude into a film that is *supposed* to evoke all things quaint, "old Hollywood" and innocent. Steven Spielberg and George Lucas' first Indiana Jones film, *Raiders of the Lost Ark* (1981), was conceived and, more or less, executed as an homage to the 1930s Saturday morning serials. The film is a throwback to all that Hollywood adventure films used to be long before Vietnam. The hero (Harrison Ford) is a self-assured, ultra-virile specimen of all–American manhood. All the women around him love him, and the enemies he doesn't hesitate to fight are loathsome, sadistic, goose-stepping, mindless Nazis who deserve to be wiped out. Indy joins the fight against the country's enemies when the government calls and asks him to devote his academic expertise and research skills to the war effort. He is, however, a follower of the cause only up to a point. He agrees that the Nazis must be stopped from finding the Ark of the Covenant, but he no longer trusts the wisdom of the government once the Ark has been found. He angrily parts company with the Washington bureaucrats when they refuse to listen to his warning about the dangers inside it. He does not accept the government as a collection of infallible, selfless public servants with a passion for freedom, democracy and Our Way of Life. "Fools! Bureaucratic fools," Indy fumes as he marches down the steps of the Capitol in the last scene. No good will come of the government holding onto a relic of such power, and if something catastrophic does happen, Indiana Jones and we both know that they will obfuscate, lie, conspire and cover-up to save their reputations.

An interesting take on the paranoid bureaucratic instinct surfaced in another 1981 film dealing with a manifestation from the spiritual realm. Although it hardly became a landmark of haunted house horror films, *The Entity* introduced the idea of an organized, bureaucratic effort to hide the truth of hauntings and demonic activity. The film is a rather thoughtful entry into the ever more lucrative horror genre of the late '70s and early '80s that had been gathering more and more momentum with the smash hit successes of *Halloween* (1978), *The Amityville Horror* (1979), *Friday the 13th* (1980), and *Poltergeist* (1982). *The Entity*, however, briefly considers the impulse to conspire and distort the truth by the academic elites. A couple of skeptical psychologists agree to take part in a "scientific" investigation of a woman's repeated assaults by a supposedly demonic force. By the end of the film, the evidence of the haunting is quite real. It is so real, in fact, that the demons destroy all the sensors and recording equipment used to try and produce some sort of tangible proof of their presence. All the members of the investigative party have seen and felt the demons, but there is still nothing tangible they can show the rest of the world to prove their story. What would go a long way toward granting paranormal investigation scientific legitimacy, however, would be the two eminent psychologists coming forward and at least saying that they, too, saw the ghostly activities, that they are willing to put their names and reputations on the line to validate the existence of something beyond the physical world. They quietly refuse, however. To admit to what they have seen would be too damaging to their scientific rationality. The film suggests that the men would even go as far as willfully suppressing the evidence had the demons not destroyed it themselves.

Even the quintessential 1980s children's fantasy, the mega-blockbuster *E.T.* (1982), tells its story of alien contact with the added edge of threatening government agents and scientists. Interestingly enough, in this film even the smallest kids know right away that if they happen upon a sweet-natured, gnome-like little alien in their tool shed, they should hide it immediately and even keep their mother from knowing the truth. The fear of conspiracies had so permeated the culture that even children seem to know instinctively that men in dark suits from the government and scientists— adults and agents of authority, simply— cannot be trusted. These agents of a threatening system will never act on behalf of peaceful contact with a benevolent space visitor. Paranoia over national security and the cold, rational quest for scientific knowledge fuel these conspiracies, and the men behind it are hard, murderous, implacable and utterly without humanity.

E.T. broadens the boundaries and archetypes of the alien-supernatural contact conspiracy film in a way that can be seen as a direct repudiation of the 1950s alien invader formula. In the old alien contact films, children or teens who might have been the first ones to stumble upon the alien presence knew enough to seek out the authorities. In the 1958 version of *The Blob*, Steve McQueen and his girlfriend know what to do: convince the "grownups" that an invader is about to threaten America. In the '50s, filmmakers knew that teenagers were the primary target audiences for these films, thus their heroes were clever, observant and resourceful teens who needed to work doubly hard to get their wrong-headed and oblivious elders up to speed. But ultimately, these kids still functioned as the best examples of patriotic young Americans. They were vigilant for foreign threats, for invasion, for subversion where their parents (and "the system") might have let their guard slip. They helped spur the authorities to take up arms and fight the threatening outsider.

The kids of the 1980s, despite the optimistic Reagan revolution, knew better. Despite the ongoing Cold War, the *E.T.* era teens and preteens can tell an angelic alien from a bloodthirsty communist invader. Aliens, fantastic creatures and people endowed with superpowers are symbolic of innocence and idealism in a series of films about vicious conspirators attempting to hide the presence of something otherworldly. Such fantastic beings finding instant kinship with children is only natural. The government agents, the bureaucrats, the paranoid military brass and the cold-blooded scientific establishment are emblematic of an adult world that is handing their offspring a damaged, defiled legacy — a world plagued by hatred, war, crime and environmental devastation.

In *Firestarter* (1984), based on the Stephen King novel, the child and the supernatural being are one and the same as an evil cabal of government conspirators try to hunt down a ten-year-old girl with pyrokinetic abilities. A product of government experimentation on her parents in college (reminiscent of the MK ULTRA LSD experiments conducted by the CIA on college campuses), little Charlie McGee (Drew Barrymore, who played Gertie, the youngest of the conspiracy-evading children in *E.T.*) can set blazing fires with her mind whenever she gets angry. Naturally, a slimy collection of paranoid military conspirators want to use her as a human weapon.

In *D.A.R.Y.L.* (1985) the fantastic other is a robot endowed with artificial intelligence within the form of a small, innocent-looking boy (Barret Oliver). In the best classic science fiction tradition, D.A.R.Y.L.'s artificial intelligence programming crosses the line between robot and human, becoming self-aware and longing to *be* human. A government conspiracy, of course, soon wants to take control of D.A.R.Y.L. and destroy him.

Small kids and fantastic creatures would also bond and fight conspiratorial authority figures in *Watchers* (1988) where a boy (Corey Haim) and a genetically engineered, supersmart golden retriever flee government assassins and another genetically engineered monster. In *Flight of the Navigator* (1986), a boy (David Scott Freeman), time-warped into the future by a UFO, defies a group of wrong-headed scientists with the aid of a robot named Max.

Director John Carpenter's second attempt at alien contact during the decade was 1984's *Starman*, where a Christ-like alien being is hunted by government agents. Here, a ball of alien light takes the shape of a woman's (Karen Allen) dead husband (Jeff Bridges) and learns that despite the evil, aggression and paranoia humans are capable of, they can also be loving and idealistic. The woman had been told she can't have children, and yet the alien impregnates her in a straw-filled cattle car, none too subtly reminiscent of the Christian nativity.

The irony of the commercial and critical success of *Starman* (Bridges was nominated for an Oscar) was that Carpenter's first alien effort, a remake of Howard Hawks' *The Thing from Another World* (1951), was a failure at the time and he usually blamed its lack of success on *E.T.* Carpenter's 1982 *The Thing* has shockingly brutal scenes of violence as all but two of the main characters are dismembered and mutilated from within in a variety of bloodspattering ways by the alien organism that infects them. For example, one particularly creative scene has a character's head ripping off, falling to the ground, sprouting large spider-like legs, and scampering away in a trail of bloody gore. While *The Thing* does not deal with a conspiracy, it is unrelentingly claustrophobic and paranoid. Although conventional wisdom would have predicted its success, counting on it working on a metaphorical level as a representation of the heightened state of paranoia over war and invasion during the Reagan Cold War years, Carpenter himself has repeatedly said that he believes that *E.T.* suddenly changed what audiences were expecting of aliens. Aliens needed to be cute, sweet, and child-friendly after *E.T.* became the highest grossing film in history.

By the latter half of the decade, however, alien conspiracies moved beyond the cuteness of the post–*E.T.* cycle. A notable film in the ongoing repudiation of the alien contact film's roots in '50s anti-communist and invader paranoia was the 1988 remake of *The Blob*. On the surface, the plot structure of the new *Blob* is similar to the old, except this time the adults are either more clueless than in the original or more evil. The kids who discover the Blob, in turn, are much more rebellious. Outfitted in a leather jacket, sporting long hair and enamored of his noisy motorcycle, the hero of the new *Blob* is Brian Flagg, the local kid from the wrong side of the tracks. Played by Kevin Dillon who, along with his older brother Matt specialized in a number of tough guy punk roles in his early career, Brian does not trust authorities for a moment, whether they are the local cops who like to hassle him on a regular basis, or the sinister government agents who show up too soon after a mysterious object from space deposits the Blob in the backyard of the Average All-American Town. His instincts, of course, are correct because this Blob is not an alien but a biological weapon created by the military.

The edgiest alien conspiracy of this decade, however, came from yet another John Carpenter take on visitors from beyond. *They Live* (1988) not only brings back evil aliens, but this time they are a metaphor for Reagan-era yuppies and the success ethic of the decade. Considered by its cult fan base to be one of the most subversive films ever turned out by a major Hollywood studio (Universal), *They Live* is a science fiction action-adventure version of basic Frankfurt School critical theory. The film takes its primary shot at the media itself, where TV signals, advertising and films are embedded with subliminal signals ordering the "sleeping masses" to "consume," "don't think," "obey authority," "marry and reproduce," or "buy." Even dollar bills are imbedded with subliminal messages reading "this is your God." The aliens are in charge and they run a vast right wing conspiracy to hide their presence. The invaders are a group intergalactic "Free Enterprisers," imperialists who have taken over without anyone noticing. They have planted themselves as the wealthy upper classes controlling the economy so their tiny minority can prosper while the rest are sinking into squalor. Running industry, the aliens pour pollution and greenhouse gasses into the atmosphere to slowly change the Earth environment into that of their home world. The only hope for change comes when a group of researchers, led by a scientist with a balding pate and a large bushy beard, more than slightly resembling Karl Marx himself, stumble onto the alien signal disguising the subliminal messages from the conscious mind. Then, after a homeless drifter (WWE pro wrestler "Rowdy" Roddy Piper) gets a-hold of special sunglasses created by the scientist-led resistance to see the alien messages, he goes about launching a series of blitzkrieg-like "terrorist" strikes against the aliens, trying to find and destroy the source of the subliminal signals.

Sinister conspiracies in the films of the 1980s would not only hide aliens, but various revolutionary technologies as well. In 1983's *Brainstorm*, conspirators are attempting to hijack technology for glimpsing into another person's thoughts and feelings. In *Dreamscape* (1984), a mind-reading experiment is almost taken over by a fanatical covert operative hoping to use it to manipulate the president during nuclear treaty negotiations with the Russians.

Despite moviegoers' interest in the hyperbolic, otherworldly, and horrific in the 1980s, the one major conspiracy theory generating sensational headlines that decade, the Satanic cult hysteria, did not receive a great deal of attention from Hollywood. Although Satan-themed films like *The Exorcist* and the *Omen* series were major hits and trend-setters in the '70s, by the time a real Satanic fear was making the news, Hollywood appeared to have lost interest in the Devil.

The most noteworthy Devil worship films of the decade were *Angel Heart* (1987) and *The Believers* (1987). In a much more fanciful setting than these two films, *Indiana Jones and the Temple of Doom* (1984) involved a plot about a demon-worshipping Indian cult that abducts children and conducts gruesome human sacrifices. But not even *Angel Heart* and *The Believers* were made in the true spirit of the Satanic underground conspiracy theories.

Angel Heart, set in the 1940s, played out like a classic *film noir* private detective story, with only the final moments taking a turn into the horror genre, revealing that devil worship and Satanic manifestations were the true motivating forces of the plot. In fact, as the film completely veers into horror, revealing that Mickey Rourke's amnesiac gumshoe not only made a deal with the Devil, but that the true, supernatural Satan exists and has been pursuing him since, the film becomes so fantastic that all connections are broken with the world of the 1980s and its fundamentalist paranoias.

The Believers, while set in the 1980s, also does not treat the Satanic conspiracy quite faithfully. Martin Sheen's psychiatrist character is menaced by a Haitian Santeria cult, not worshippers of the Judeo-Christian Satan. In fact, *The Believers* managed to generate a minor controversy in its treatment of Santeria. Several practitioners criticized it for implying that a legitimate Afro-Caribbean religion was a cult of evil that condones human sacrifices.

The reason for Hollywood's reluctance to deal with the Satanic abuse panic might have had to do with the underlying sordidness of the topic. Most conspiracy films are, ultimately, proverbial "popcorn" entertainment. Even stories about assassins and political corruption are meant to be exciting and *fun*. They are about heroes and villains, chases, shootouts and intrigue. They are stories where good guys and the truth, in some form, triumph over evil and corruption. The sexual abuse of children is just too gruesome a topic for "popcorn" entertainment.

Although one could also make the argument that the Satanic hysteria of the '80s simply melded into the subtle subtext of so many horror films of that decade. Eighties horror cinema, after all, saw a surprisingly inordinate number of dead, mutilated, and terrorized teenagers. Films like the *Nightmare on Elm Street, Friday the 13th* and *Halloween* series defined mainstream horror in the 1980s. Indestructible demonic killers Freddy, Jason, and Michael Myers ran up a massive teenage body count in these films, all the while parents and authority figures were conspicuously inept and incapable of protecting children when these villains went on the rampage. But even this connection to the Satanic hysteria is a bit tenuous. All three of these franchises — the "dead teenager films," as they were called by critics — really started before the Satanic conspiracy phenomenon. Their true progenitors, in fact, might have been such 1970s horror films as *The Last House on the Left* (1972), *The Texas Chain Saw Massacre* (1974), and *The Hills Have Eyes* (1977). Those films, horror historians and film scholars often argue, were really rooted in the Zeitgeist of the Vietnam and Watergate eras.

Fantasy and science fiction films mixed with conspiracy theories would keep reappearing throughout the decade, but not always in the format of a cover-up and suppression storyline. Several would cross over into the business conspiracies. But the second major theory of the decade would turn up in military action/adventure films and they would be rooted in the unresolved turmoil of the Vietnam era.

Assassinations and Abandonment

The most notable turn Hollywood took in the 1980s was the confrontation of the Vietnam experience and the culture's complex stew of feelings about the conflict. While America's involvement in Southeast Asia went through a turbulent spectrum of support, to a rising counterculture protest movement and a deep generational division, and finally to the mainstream's turning against the war, Hollywood avoided dealing with the issue as long as it could. By the late '70s, the dramatic films *Apocalypse Now* (1979) and *Coming Home* (1978) had addressed the effects of the war on the soldiers in the field and the nation at home. Even television joined in by 1980, when the private eye adventure series *Magnum, P.I.* became the first to foreground its heroes' status as Vietnam veterans. In the 1980s, popular genre films also incorporated Vietnam into their plots, but they were often as mixed and conflicted in their sentiments about the war, the politics behind it, and its execution as the rest of the country. The fact that the war had also been badly mismanaged made these stories perfect for the conspiratorial mindset.

One sinister phenomenon of the '60s Vietnam era that, strangely enough, quickly faded from theaters was the political assassination. The earliest conspiracy theory films like *The Manchurian Candidate*, *The Parallax View*, *Three Days of the Condor* and *Winter Kills* (1979) all found their inspiration in assassinations. By the 1980s, this aspect of conspiracy theories had lost its appeal. Vietnam-themed and supernatural conspiracies would quickly come into vogue, but several exceptions do stand out.

The strongest conspiracy-assassination film of this era is Brian DePalma's 1981 thriller *Blow Out*. In a very loose remake of Michelangelo Antonioni's 1966 art-house film *Blow Up*, Jack Terry (John Travolta) is a sound engineer for horror movies who accidentally records the sounds of a political assassination.

It is slyly reminiscent of the Ted Kennedy Chappaquiddick car crash scandal: After a sniper shoots out a tire on the car of a Senator with presidential aspirations, the car plunges into a lake, killing the Senator and almost killing the woman with whom he was having an extramarital liaison. Listening to the recording of the event, Jack starts noticing that the timing of the bangs and noises of the crash don't sound right. Before the crash, there is a gunshot, his trained ear notices. Unfortunately, Jack is the only one who believes that a murder has been committed. To the police, it looks like a cut-and-dry accident case. As far as the cops and a special investigative commission is concerned, Jack is just another "conspiracy nut" piecing together puzzles and signs no one else can see or hear. As is usually the case in the genre, Jack's insistent meddling eventually attracts the attention of the actual conspiracy and its deranged, uncontrollable hitman (John Lithgow).

Much like *The Parallax View*, *Blow Out* keeps the details of the conspiracy off screen. Like its main character, the audience does not know what is going on, who is killing whom or for what reason. We only know that something is amiss. The film delivers its chills through the suggestion that there are power brokers in this country who operate outside of the law, manipulating national events through layers of pawns and dupes. They are so powerful and have so many resources at their disposal as to always be invisible and above prosecution.

A much more kinetic assassination-conspiracy-action thriller came from director John Badham in 1983's *Blue Thunder*. It combines the lingering effects of Vietnam on veterans, conspiracy theorist paranoia about political assassinations, and hi-tech, explosive special effects and military machinery. Blue Thunder is an experimental military helicopter adapted for police crowd control, to be used as an anti-terrorist tool during the 1984 Olympics in Los Angeles. The machine is virtually unstoppable, outfitted with a Gatling gun, an armor-plated shell and surveillance microphones. It has a "whisper mode" that lets it hover almost soundlessly.

Recruited to test and fly the ultra-lethal machine is Frank Murphy (Roy Scheider), a Vietnam veteran who might suffer occasional debilitating flashbacks to the war, but is still the best helicopter pilot in the LAPD. Murphy, as is the case with Vietnam vet action heroes who would become a major archetype of the genre in the '80s, is also cynical and suspicious of authority. His war service taught him to question superiors, orders, and the "official version" of events. He is the only one to start asking the kinds of questions none of the police brass, enamored of Blue Thunder's technology, do. Isn't the arming of police helicopters supposed to be illegal? Can't this much technology easily be abused? The Blue Thunder program is headed by an old acquaintance from Vietnam, the sinister Col. Cochrane (Malcolm McDowell). In Vietnam, Cochrane, a sadist, used to specialize in interrogation. He would get information out of suspected Viet Cong sympathizers by dropping their comrades to their deaths from a helicopter.

Murphy eventually takes Blue Thunder on an unauthorized flight and uses its whisper mode and surveillance microphones to spy on Cochrane and his group, uncovering a massive conspiracy. The group is apparently part of a crypto-fascist military organization with designs on increasing police powers across the country and slowly curtailing civil liberties. Blue Thunder will be but the first piece of hi-tech weaponry in their arsenal. The helicopter does have its liberal and libertarian critics, though. Therefore, the conspirators decide that the best way to silence them is to kill the most outspoken critics of Blue Thunder, making it look like a random street crime. The critic's death becomes an argument for the need for a weapon like the super helicopter.

Once his insubordination is discovered, Murphy steals Blue Thunder, leading to an explosive showdown with fighter jets, heat-seeking missiles and, eventually, a helicopter-to-helicopter duel with Cochrane in the skies over Los Angeles.

Interestingly enough, *Blue Thunder* had a greater influence on television than on theatrical films. Although it was preceded by one year by the TV show *Knight Rider*, *Blue Thunder* helped further inspire a number of 1980s super-vehicle shows. In fact, the film was adapted into a short-lived ABC series and quickly imitated by CBS with its own super helicopter show, *Airwolf*. This was followed by *Street Hawk*, about an ultra hi-tech motorcycle, and *The Highwayman*, about a super truck that can turn invisible and transform into a helicopter. This was a peculiar trend because theatrical films would have had bigger budgets to lavish on the types of stunts and special effects a super-vehicle needed to look good. Furthermore, while conspiracy films thrived on the big screen, on television their anti-authoritarian edge was quickly blunted.

In the TV version of *Blue Thunder*, the pilot—renamed Frank Chaney (James Farentino)—does not have to steal the helicopter and pursue a one-man justice mission because there is no conspiracy here. Neither the police nor the military have any sinister designs for the helicopter. Television might have attempted to keep the controllers of the super-vehicles somewhat edgy, but this edge went only as far as presenting overgrown adolescent cool guys who liked to push their vehicles too hard, who listened to their music too loud or bedded a different sexy co-star every week. Teenage boys were the primary fan base for these shows.

The one exception, actually, might have been *Airwolf.* The premise involved embittered Vietnam vet Stringfellow Hawke (Jan Michael Vincent) who steals a military super-helicopter and tries to force the government to give some satisfactory account of what happened to his brother St. John, who disappeared during the Vietnam War. In return for the government promising to look for St. John, Hawke agrees to use Airwolf on a series of missions fighting various terrorists, spy rings, and criminals. In a number of episodes, interesting dramatic tension is maintained as the government agents Hawke is blackmailing would just as soon kill him as work with him to fight the country's enemies.

To understand why television did not jump on the conspiracy bandwagon gathering so much momentum in 1980s cinema, one must understand the nature of the medium. TV is the most cautious of all major mass media. As TV industry researchers Horace Newcomb and Robert Alley explain in their book *The Producer's Medium,* TV is the easiest technology to turn to every day for news and entertainment and, therefore, it's the one medium audiences want to be safe and familiar. Television, for example, will never promote any radical, society-altering viewpoints, especially in escapist entertainment. Even after radical, status quo-challenging ideas have entered the mainstream, TV will take its time dealing with them. A TV set, in effect, is something that lets an entire world intrude into people's most intimate spaces. The TV brings outsiders into our living rooms and bedrooms. These are places where people do not like being challenged too aggressively, where they might not like being told that the system they hold dear is an exploitive sham. Furthermore, since TV is not subsidized by tickets bought at a box office but by advertising, those advertisers would be loathe to pay for programming that might unduly antagonize viewers and prospective consumers. If it took film almost an entire decade to fully embrace the edgy cynicism of conspiracy theories, TV would take two decades. The conspiracy watershed would only begin on television in 1993 with the premiere of *The X-Files.*

One notable departure in 1980s TV was the NBC miniseries *V* (1983) and its sequel *V: The Final Battle* (1985). They both dealt with media conspiracies in a peripheral way. These miniseries are science fiction, however, almost as if NBC was more comfortable cloaking the stories' political statements in the hyperbole of aliens and *Star Wars*–like laser battles.

Produced by Kenneth Johnson, the creative force behind SF series like *The Bionic Woman* and *The Incredible Hulk,* *V* tried to examine individual reactions to the rise of totalitarian regimes, told in the guise of an alien invasion story. The two *V* miniseries involve the sudden appearance of an alien fleet of 50 three mile-wide mother ships over the world's major cities. The aliens emerging from the craft look perfectly human and they offer a fantastic deal to the people of the world. Their planet, their leader (Richard Herd) explains, is on the brink of environmental disaster and they need chemicals that can only be found on Earth. If the Earthlings cooperate, the aliens—calling themselves Visitors—promise to endow them with all the secrets of their advanced technology. In an effectively menacing scene near the beginning of the film, a shrewd yuppie — no doubt pondering the money-making potential in all the fantastic alien technology — sees the deal as an obvious "offer we can't refuse." His more level-headed and skeptical scientist girlfriend replies, "Can you imagine what would happen if we did?" Antagonizing aliens who can build city-sized interstellar mother ships might not be a prudent move. In the beginning of the film, however, none of the characters have yet noticed that the Visitors' insignia looks suspiciously like a Nazi swastika.

The apparently benevolent Visitors quickly begin to insinuate themselves into every facet of Earth's cultures. They become the friends, co-workers, even lovers of Earthlings. Every small kid soon wants to play with Visitor action figures and every teenager wants to join the Visitor Youth Corps.

The warm relations between Earth people and the Visitors become strained when the aliens announce the existence of a vast network of scientists plotting to destroy several mother ships and take control of the otherworldly technology. The only option, the aliens argue, is to ask the governments of the Earth to allow the imposition of a "temporary" Visitor martial law, only until the scientist conspiracy has been routed out.

Skeptical news cameraman Mike Donovan (Marc Singer) is disturbed by the Visitor stranglehold over American society. Seemingly overnight, civil liberties are suspended, police powers are increased and critics of the Visitors mysteriously disappear. Especially frightening is the way his fellow newscasters, including his girlfriend Kristine Walsh (Jenny Sullivan), abandon their journalistic objectivity and become obedient mouthpieces for the Visitors. Going along with the Visitor party line has become lucrative for everyone in the media. Those who cooperate are promoted and quickly become stars. Kristine, the most enthusiastic supporter of the Visitor policies, becomes the main spokesperson for the aliens in the U.S.

Donovan sneaks aboard the Los Angeles mother ship and uncovers the grisly truth: The aliens are not on Earth for chemicals. Their home planet's real environmental calamity is a severe water and food shortage. They have come here to siphon water into the mother ships' enormous holding tanks. The most shocking truth, however, is the Visitors' true physical nature. They are not human at all, but reptilians disguised in flawlessly realistic masks and flesh-like bodysuits. Aside from the water tanks of the mother ships, special containers hold thousands of abducted humans, packed away to be processed for food.

Although conspiracy theories had not yet become fashionable on 1980s TV, the original *V* miniseries, about the "unmasking" of the alien plot, and its sequel *V: The Final Battle*, about resistance movements waging urban guerrilla warfare against the Visitors, were remarkably successful. To a certain extent, the films were glaringly heavy-handed in their message. However, at the same time, there was some subtle commentary on the nature of conspiracies driven by greed and complacency. While TV producers might not yet have felt that audiences were ready for cynical conspiracies coming out of their prime time entertainment shows, *V* was palatable because of its obvious parallels to World War II and the Nazi rise to power. No one, after all, can really court controversy by casting Nazis as their villains. In fact, in hindsight, a flaw of these films lies in how *obviously* Nazi-like the Visitors are. The alien insignias resembling swastikas are especially damaging to the first of the miniseries because they tip off viewers too early. The monstrous nature of the Visitors, revealed in the second hour of the first installment of the miniseries, is supposed to be a shock. Too much of the shock effect, however, is taken away by the revelation of the swastika-style symbol a mere 15 minutes into the film. Characters who wear a symbol reminiscent of Nazis can only be up to no good.

The heavy-handedness of *V*'s visual symbolism, however, is offset by some remarkably deft and disturbing implications about human nature, moral weakness and the thirst for power. According to Kenneth Johnson's commentary on the DVD of the first miniseries, he was mainly interested in the human drama of what happens when people are suddenly confronted by a totalitarian political movement. His main inspiration, he says, was the 1935 Sinclair Lewis novel *It Can't Happen Here*. (The story, though, is also strongly reminiscent of the *Twilight Zone* episode "To Serve Man.") If the U.S. were to face a fascist insurgency, Johnson asks, how would various people react? Who would be the ones to resist? Who would be the opportunists and the collaborators? Who would try and turn a blind eye to what was happening? *V*'s answer is often disturbing: It claims that no one can know for sure. In fact, through the course of the film, some of the lowliest characters find the strength to become heroes, while others turn on their friends, even families, when there is something to be gained by allying with the seductive Visitors.

When dealing with the media's culpability in the Visitor takeover, Johnson offers a unique vision of a conspiracy of greed, ambition and basic intellectual and moral laziness. The media in *V* wind up *inadvertently* conspiring with the aliens, not so much out of calculated malice but avarice. Reporters like Kristine Walsh sell out because they let ambition and the thirst for stardom and power cloud their objectivity, critical thinking skills and the kind of skepticism that should be the stock in trade of every good reporter. As Johnson's story seeks to find conspirators in modern America, he doesn't merely present the stereotypical "men in black," the "shadowy government operatives," and "wealthy cabals," but he shows his audience something much more frightening. Given the right circumstances and the right kinds of promises of wealth, fame, power, and easy solutions to our everyday problems, we might all conspire with evil.

In an interesting postscript to *V*, the two miniseries, as well as the (inferior) short-lived 1985 weekly TV series they inspired, have found a very active cult fan base. There are a number of Internet fan sites where devotees continue to discuss their social significance. In the aftermath of the Iraq invasion, an anti–Bush, anti-war faction of science fiction fans have even adopted *V* as a metaphor for today's political environment. They claim that the uncritical media coverage of the Bush administration's rush to war and the ongoing Iraqi occupation mirror the world *V* warned about over twenty years ago.

Interestingly, the kind of conspiracy of complacency charge Johnson levels at the media in *V* is in line with most critical analyses of mainstream commercial news organizations in times of war and crisis. What conspiring goes on between the government and the press to deceive the public in times of trouble, this view argues, is not so much a conscious collusion to enact some fanciful master plan, but rather the simple phenomenon of timid, opportunistic reporters acquiescing to power. In return for access to the highest levels of the government, reporters all too often betray their roles as objective watchdogs of the powerful and influential. Interviews with presidents, the heads of the military, and various legislative power brokers make careers, earn ratings, and sell newspapers. Criticism and objectivity, on the other hand, can result in accusations of being unpatriotic, or worse. A disturbingly large segment of the American public often resents media that choose to focus only on the negative and not the positive, happy-time events that make for more pleasant viewing on the evening news.

Aside from television staying away from conspiracy theory entertainment for the most part, it is also remarkable that assassination plots did not have greater drawing power in 1980s cinema, even as Reagan was nearly felled by an assassin's bullet on March 30, 1981. What could have accounted for this was the fact that no major conspiracy theory lingers about the shooting. It was only in the late 1990s that several secret society conspiracy theorists revisited it and became ever more vocal about connections between John Hinckley, Jr., and the Bush family. In the '80s, the assassination attempt seemed to be a clear-cut case of things being exactly what they appeared: a deranged celebrity-stalker trying to impress Jodie Foster took a shot at the president.

Another possible reason for a lack of conspiratorial interest, one can hypothesize, could be Reagan's politics. Previous assassinations, like the JFK and RFK killings, as well as the murder of Martin Luther King, Jr., and Malcolm X, claimed figures on the political left. Thus, most of the major assassination conspiracy theories have been liberal territory. In all the previous cases, the theorists argue, business interests, military interests and various reactionary right-wingers, opposed to the sweeping social reforms each of these men worked for, ordered the killings. Simply, the right-wing carried out conspiracy killings, they were not *getting* assassinated. Similarly, the fact that Gerald Ford was almost killed *twice* in the space of less than three weeks by deranged leftists—first, by Lynette "Squeaky" Fromme, a former Manson "Family" member, then by self-described leftist radical Sara Jane Moore — also has not inspired any major conspiracy theories.

John Lennon's 1980 shooting murder by Mark David Chapman, on the other hand, has led to several theories and a number of books that keep turning up as a refutation of the official version of the crime. Since at one point Lennon had been under surveillance by the FBI for his radical political activities, conspiracy theories have fingered both the Bureau and the CIA as the masterminds behind the killing. Nevertheless, assassinations no longer held any major cache in 1980s conspiracy cinema.

One of the most provocative and cinematically lucrative conspiracy theories of the 1980s, however, involved soldiers missing in action during the Vietnam War. Since hundreds of U.S. servicemen had been prisoners of war during the conflict, many wondered if any of the 2000-plus soldiers missing and presumed killed in action might actually have been left behind alive. Were any of these men still wasting away in captivity somewhere, willfully forgotten by the U.S. government?

A number of the conspiracy theorists who said "yes" had, at one time, pointed an angry finger at the Carter administration, accusing them of knowing for a fact that Americans were still alive in Vietnam but concealing the evidence. The renewed patriotism and machismo of the Reagan era created a atmosphere in which this theory could flourish.

The first film to confront the theory was the 1983 action thriller *Uncommon Valor*. Probably the earthiest, most realistic of the back-to-Vietnam films, it involves former Marine Colonel Cal Rhodes (Gene Hackman) receiving intelligence that there might be POWs still alive in Vietnam. Since the government won't back him, Rhodes assembles a group of veterans who fought alongside him in the war and they secretly plan to return to the jungles of Vietnam. The mission, it turns out, is more than just bringing home American soldiers for Rhodes. It's personal. His own son is missing in action.

The success of *Uncommon Valor* launched a new subgenre of action films in the early to mid–80s, a successful conservative amalgamation of patriotism and conspiracy theory. Their stories were tailor-made for the Reagan era "rugged individual" conservatism. The crisis in these films is a true conspiracy of incompetence. Inept bureaucrats and civilians had botched the war effort because their policies wouldn't let the soldiers use proper tactics on the ground to win a guerrilla war against the North Vietnamese. Later, they conspired to cover up their mistakes. The biggest of these mistakes was the abandonment of the captive soldiers for the sake of a quick end to the war and the placating of radical protesters and flag burners who wouldn't fight for their country. A hero for a crisis like this is a rugged loner, or team of loners, who take things into their own hands and strike out on their own to bring the captives home.

Even though a majority of the public had eventually turned against the war by the early 1970s, a decade later there was still a sizable audience for this conspiracy-oriented action film. While many had come to believe that the war should not have been started in the first place, the fact that America had been beaten and humiliated left a psychic scar on the nation. Plus, the possibility that Americans might have been abandoned in captivity is an offense transcending politics. The formula for the success of these films was perfect.

After the realistic start to the back-to-Vietnam saga with *Uncommon Valor*, the films took a very quick turn into hyperbole with Chuck Norris' entry into the fray. His *Missing in Action* (1984) not only depicts a metaphorical refighting of the war, but now it is waged by a rampaging, larger-than-life one-man army. Whereas Gene Hackman takes a team into a Vietnamese prison camp to free American captives, Norris takes on hordes of Vietnamese troops single-handedly.

The apotheosis of the POW–rescuing action hero of the 1980s, however, came in Sylvester Stallone's *Rambo: First Blood Part II* (1985). The year's second highest grossing film, its plot efficiently combines ultra-violent action with the conspiratorial view of the Vietnam War and the ongoing effort to cover up the abandonment of POWs. It begins with ex–Green Beret war hero John Rambo (Stallone) being retrieved from prison and recruited for the top-secret mission. He had been doing time after his rampage in the first Rambo film, *First Blood*, that inadvertently set up the antiwar left's culpability in the conspiracy plot of the second film. *First Blood* involves an unstable, embittered Rambo wandering the Pacific Northwest as a drifter until he gets harassed by a redneck sheriff (Brian Dennehy) and his sadistic, thuggish chief deputy (Jack Starrett). Escaping and leading the police department, along with an enormous detachment of National Guardsmen, on a destructive chase, Rambo nearly destroys a town in a fury of repressed rage over his mistreatment by American society, namely antiwar protesters who spat on him and called him a baby-killer. In the second film, however, Rambo gets a chance to confront the source of his demons in the jungles of Vietnam.

Except the mission, just like the war, is a sham. Rambo's hands are tied by the bureaucracy from the get-go. He is only allowed to take pictures of a suspected prison camp. Under no circumstances is he to engage the enemy. When he disobeys orders and tries to bring out one of the POWs—in effect to win the war by proxy—the conspiracy kicks in and things go haywire.

The mission is a lie and Rambo had been set up to fail. It was all designed as a public relations hoax. Government bureaucrats were hoping to quell the demands of family members and Congressional investigators to know the fates of thousands of MIAs. Now Rambo was supposed to have found an empty prison camp and taken pictures that would silence the critics and families once and for all. Had he taken pictures of any prisoners, they would have been destroyed (and Rambo killed, we presume). When he attempts to return with a live POW, however, he is abandoned and left to fend for himself.

Of course, he is more than able to do this, enduring sadistic torture and decimating a small army of Vietnamese and Russians in the process. Liberating the entire camp of American POWs, he flies back to the mission's home base in Thailand to exact vengeance on the covert operations traitors and conspirators who betrayed him and all of America's fighting men. In the final scene, he destroys the massive bank of computers and hi-tech gadgetry monitoring the operation — the corrupt war machine, in effect — and goes after the head of the operation himself. Holding the chief conspirator (Charles Napier) by the throat, he growls, "You know there are more men out there. Find them. Or I'll find you."

Rambo II's position in the pantheon of right wing conspiracy cinema, however, should be qualified with a few details about its production history, the various versions of its screenplay, and plot details that are often ignored. Looking at the film closely, it becomes obvious that Roger Ebert rendered the most accurate verdict on its politics when he wrote, "*Rambo* is neither left wing nor right wing, but comes from that paranoid wing of American politics that believes the military was not allowed to win the war."[8] Casting the film solidly into the conservative camp, however, was a comment from Ronald Reagan when he made a joke during an interview about his favorite films, saying that "last night I saw *Rambo* and boy, the next time we have a hostage crisis, I know who to call."[9] Soon after, someone made and successfully marketed a bumper sticker—which Reagan was quite fond of—reading "Rambo Is a Republican."[10]

Ironically, David Morrell's *First Blood* was conceived as an anti-war novel and Rambo was the representative of disenfranchised, radicalized young leftists. As Morrell explained to Susan Faludi for her book *Stiffed: The Betrayal of the American Man*, Rambo was not merely a spokesman for the left, but the angriest, most aggressive leftists. He stood for militants like the Weather Underground. Rambo had answered his country's call to war and now he turned on that same country for what it put him through in Vietnam. The novel's Rambo wanted to destroy America.

For this very reason, the book's adaptation to film was a very long and troubled process. Almost immediately after reaching the bestseller lists in 1973, it interested Hollywood. Yet *First Blood*'s angry storyline and its bitter, homicidal anti-hero made filmmakers and stars nervous. The fact is that for a film to show a profit, it needs a lot more ticket-buyers than a book needs readers to place it on a bestseller list. Hollywood studio films must be more mainstream than books to succeed. To find such a mainstream success, a film must have a likable lead character (or so Hollywood conventional wisdom argues). Furthermore, stars usually don't like playing unsympathetic characters. Although stars Michael Douglas, Steve McQueen and Clint Eastwood had been temporarily attached to *First Blood*, they all eventually bailed because they felt Rambo was too edgy, too dangerous to be filmable. Sylvester Stallone felt differently.[11]

Reading *First Blood*, Stallone believed that Morrell's Rambo was essentially Rocky, but with a military background. Rambo could be acceptable to audiences, he believed, if they see him very clearly as an underdog, an innocent man wrongly persecuted. After all, by 1982 Stallone had made three phenomenally successful *Rocky* films, each one a variation on the same underdog theme. As long as audiences could see Rambo as a victim, a good man pushed too far, a hero fighting for his life against unjust oppression, they would be willing to sympathize with him and cheer for him. In Stallone's version of the *First Blood* script, Rambo is not an America-hating radical but a downtrodden drifter, minding his own business until he is harassed and brutalized by redneck cops. He does not hate all of American society, only the war protesters who called him a baby-killer and didn't honor his service to his country.[12]

When it came to the sequel, Stallone had free rein with the character and the story. Unencumbered by anyone else's source material, he got on the popular back-to-Vietnam bandwagon. But even in *Rambo II*, bumper sticker and Reagan's fandom notwithstanding, the Rambo character is truly more of an outsider than a champion of right-wing foreign policy. In the tradition of classic American Westerns and action-adventure films, he is a reluctant fighter, hesitant to take up arms until absolutely necessary. Rambo fights for the abandoned veterans, not politics or ideology. More importantly, the government in this film is even more clearly vilified than in *First Blood*. As a number of critics have pointed out, it is actually strange that Reagan should become such a fan of *Rambo II* as the film draws a connection between the corrupt bureaucrats running the phony rescue operation and Reagan's own administration. The villainous, incompetent conspirators of the film are never identified as the liberal government bureaucracy right-wing conspiracy theorists rail against. Quite to the contrary, the chief of the corrupt mission is clearly shown displaying a picture of Reagan on the wall of his office.

If anything, *Rambo II* can be seen as a very sly open text, designed to be palatable no matter which way a viewer's politics might lean. On the one hand, the film never actually supports the Vietnam War. Rambo's closest ally and surrogate father figure, Col. Sam Trautman, even angrily denounces both the rescue mission and the war itself. Rambo is also angry at his country for getting into the war. But, on the other hand, he is driven by an abiding patriotic love for America and he doesn't hesitate to mete out brutal punishment to the Russian and Vietnamese communists the conservative right loves to hate. Ultimately, its view of a conspiracy carried out by ineffective, incompetent bureaucrats to cover up their failures is in sync with the conservative "rugged individual," anti-big-government atmosphere of the Reagan era to still let it stand as an accurate representative of the 1980s Zeitgeist.

Following in *Rambo II*'s wake, returning to Vietnam and exposing the governmental cover-ups and lies had become a Hollywood boon for about three years. Chuck Norris would do it two more times in the films *Missing in Action 2: The Beginning* (1985) and *Braddock: Missing in Action 3* (1998). Many direct-to-video B-movies imitated the formula. On television, most action and detective shows with Vietnam veteran heroes had at least one episode about a return to Southeast Asia to free the abandoned POWs. Lee Majors went back to Vietnam in *The Fall Guy*, Tom Selleck went back in *Magnum, P.I.*, Jan Michael Vincent and Ernest Borgnine went back in *Airwolf*, and the entire A-Team went back as well.

Ends and Means

The ironic turn in the 1980s conspiracy cycle was the Iran-Contra scandal. This time, the Reagan administration itself appeared to be in the middle of a deep web of corruption and illegality. More ironically still, it all seemed to mirror so much of what went on on the movie screens reflecting conspiratorial action films.

Another major paradox of the conservative relationship with conspiracy theories is that a political movement that had always held itself as a champion of law and order could so readily endorse entertainment that showed as much disdain for rules and laws as any radical, far-left counterculture film could. On the one hand, conservatives would show contempt for the glorification of murderous thugs like Bonnie and Clyde, but on the other, a right-leaning film like *Dirty Harry* would end with Harry Callahan throwing away his badge in disgust and rejecting the justice system. By the action Renaissance of the 1980s, heroes would only be in top form if they bent rules, disobeyed superiors, or realized that they, too, just like Dirty Harry, had to sever their ties to the system to set things right. The system, according to this formula, was so hopelessly broken that only through vigilantism could any measure of justice be effected. As action film scholar Susan Jeffords has pointed out, according to Reaganist conservatism, an identification of traitorous, disloyal, and unpatriotic laws justified the abandonment of the supposed conservative ideal of "law and order."[13]

It appeared that the same mindset was at work in real life during the Iran-Contra scandal. By interpreting Congress' prohibition against aid to the Nicaraguan Contra rebels as being unpatriotic, conspirators in the Reagan administration justified their illegality. In the latter half of that decade, several notable films seemed to have been echoing the scandal.

Mixing the elements of science fiction and corrupt business conspiracy theories, 1987's *RoboCop* presents a conspiracy among the executives of a megacorporation unfolding much like Reagan's defenders claimed Iran-Contra unfolded: corrupt underlings scheming and breaking the rules behind the back of the organization's boss, a benevolent, yet clueless, old father figure. In a dystopian future of decaying cities, rampant crime, failing industries and an ever-widening chasm between rich and poor, an enormous conglomerate, Omni Consumer Products, is about to privatize all the public services of Detroit before tearing it down and rebuilding it as the shiny, upscale Delta City. But first crime has to be reduced, and the company institutes the RoboCop option from among various competing plans for robotic law enforcement. Crime, however, provides profits as well, and as a company executive (Ronny Cox) turns to murder to remove a rival, he strikes a deal with the city's major drug lord (Kurtwood Smith) to carry out the hit. He promises the criminal unlimited employment and profit in the very near future. The construction of Delta City will bring in thousands of workers whose needs for drugs, gambling, prostitution, and various illegal activities will all have to be accommodated.

The obliviousness of the company head — referred to only as the "Old Man" — is an uncanny reflection of the growing public perception of Reagan during the unfolding Iran-Contra scandal. If indeed Reagan was as ignorant of the rampant corruption in his administration as he and his defenders claimed, he had become the very embodiment of the conspiracy of incompetence theory. In *RoboCop*, too, ruthless corruption and criminality are unfolding under the nose of a leader who is little more than a doddering old fool.

It must be emphasized, however, that *RoboCop*'s appearance at the time of the Iran-Contra affair is more of an odd bit of coincidental timing rather than filmmakers commenting specifically on the Reagan administration's problems. Screenwriters Edward Neumeier and Michael Miner had been attempting to sell their script for several years before it got in the hands of Dutch director Paul Verhoeven, who was still working on establishing himself in Hollywood. Supposedly, even Verhoeven wanted to reject the script, but his wife read it and loved its biting satire. As Neumeier and Verhoeven discuss on the film's DVD commentary track, the primary targets of *RoboCop*'s social statements are the economic trends they saw contributing to urban decay and violence in the '80s. With so many of the film's key action scenes set in abandoned, decrepit warehouses and factories, *RoboCop* argues that the failures of the American steel, auto and production industries left big cities spiraling into decay, unemployment and rampant crime. With cities going bankrupt, there is also an ever-widening gulf between the working urban poor, the blue collar service providers on the bottom of the socioeconomic ladder, and the ultra-wealthy upper classes getting richer from stock market speculation and corruption. As Neumeier and Verhoeven admit, the film's statements come from a general left-wing social critique, but they're not focusing specifically on any one event for their satire. *RoboCop*'s plot of corporate corruption unfolding in front of a clueless, Reaganesque CEO nevertheless provides an uncannily familiar, if not intentional, reflection of the Iran-Contra conspiracy.

In 1988, Warner Brothers attempted to groom Steven Seagal, the former martial arts instructor of super-agent and Creative Artists Agency boss Michael Ovitz, as the next major action star to rival Sylvester Stallone and Arnold Schwarzenegger. Seagal's debut came in

Above the Law, an angry indictment of those who feel they can break laws out of a fervent belief in their own moral superiority and contempt for rules and regulations they happen not to like. Seizing on the various conspiracy theories accusing the CIA, the Nicaraguan Contras, and the Reagan administration's various right-wing allies in Central America of drug trafficking, the film involves Chicago cop (and deadly Aikido expert) Nico Toscani (Seagal) discovering that a local drug ring is being protected by intelligence agents from Washington. Toscani is ex–CIA himself, having been an idealistic college kid recruited into the agency during Vietnam. During his tour of duty, his voice-over narration in the beginning of the film explains, his eyes "were opened to a whole new world"— one of rampant, unchecked corruption within the intelligence community, with the agency either full of or doing business with killers, assassins and drug runners every bit as evil and depraved as all the forces of darkness American foreign policy supposedly committed itself to fighting. As the film's plot unfolds, Nico's case, of course, is merely the tip of the iceberg in a massive conspiracy where CIA agents are flooding America's streets with drugs and using the profits to fund their illegal anti-communist missions in Central America.

The film derives its title from a speech by Richard Nixon about getting tough with radicals, criminals, drug addicts and anarchists during the most chaotic days of the counterculture movement. A clip from a Nixon speech begins the film: "Nobody is above the law and nobody is below the law, and we *will* enforce the law." The irony, of course, is that just as the "law and order" Nixon turned out to be one of the biggest criminals of the 1970s, so too the Reagan era's super-patriots and self-appointed defenders of the American way — by any means necessary —could turn into a gang of unchecked, dangerous criminals. The film is wrapped up by a voice-over from Nico Toscani as he begins a statement to a reporter doing a story on the CIA drug scandal: "Whenever you have people who can't be held accountable, who don't answer to Congress, the courts or the press, you will always have those who are above the law."

The story of *Above the Law* is perhaps one of the most colorful in '80s action film history. Seagal gets screen credit for the original concept on which the screenplay by director Andrew Davis and Steven Pressfield is based. Seagal and the Warner Brothers publicity machine seemed fond of claiming that parts of the film were based on Seagal's own life. Seagal repeatedly insinuated that while living in Japan and training in Aikido during the '70s, he was recruited into the CIA and served as a counter-terrorism expert.

When reporters attempted to dig into Seagal's past, none of the CIA claims could be substantiated. One infamous incident involved a 1991 *GQ* article by Alan Richman. Like a number of entertainment journalists, he wrote that Seagal's claims were little more than mythmaking, backed quite enthusiastically by Warner Brothers in an attempt to build the mystique of their new action star. Whereas established action heroes like Stallone, Schwarzenegger, Chuck Norris, and Mel Gibson merely *played* tough guys and killers, Seagal and Warner Brothers were trying to claim that he was the real thing.

Where Richman's story took a decidedly bizarre turn was his follow-up claim, soon after *GQ* published the piece, that Seagal was so outraged by the article that he threatened his life. As Richard Corliss wrote in *Time* in 1993, Seagal enjoys boasting that he has mob connections and the power to kill people who cross him. "Steven likes to hang out with the underworld of espionage," Corliss quotes J.F. Lawton, the writer of Seagal's biggest hit, *Under Siege* (1992), "and maybe also crime." In the same story, Andrew Davis says that the actor "likes to be on the cutting edge of the unsaid truths about 'how the world works.' He enjoys that kind of stuff…. He tries to live it." According to Richman, Seagal threatened to have him killed over the *GQ* article and hired private investigators and "underworld figures" to try and frame him in a homosexual liaison.[14]

Wherever the truth may lie in Seagal's past, his story for *Above the Law* does make for a very good film and it's founded on a conspiracy theory that has been around since the 1970s. Investigative journalists have often claimed, with very sketchy proof, that certain CIA operations have been funded by illegal drug money. Then, during investigations of Oliver North and company's funneling of money to the Nicaraguan Contras, some asserted that certain Contra factions were making extra money in the cocaine trade.[15] The CIA–cocaine conspiracy theory eventually snowballed into the claim that crack cocaine was a U.S. intelligence plot to destabilize minority communities.

Greed Is Not Good

Conspiracies by corrupt business interests were also a recurring concern of filmmakers in the era of Wall Street greed and materialistic yuppies. Conspiracy believers, after all, had started arguing with greater force than ever before that all of the country's most crucial domestic and foreign policies were written by the wealthy, secretive power brokers funding organizations like the Council of Foreign Relations and the Trilateral Commission. As evidenced even in science fiction thrillers like *They Live* and *RoboCop*, corporate evildoers were often present in each of the permutations of conspiracy theory cinema.

In fact, especially when dealing with science fiction, the conspiracy film seemed to be predicting a post–Cold War, post-communist future even before the fall of the Berlin Wall. In films like *Aliens* and *The Running Man* (1987), for example, corporate capitalism rules the world at last, and it even rules other worlds as well. However, these films warn, unchecked profiteering, the corporate impulse to plot to acquire more wealth, can be as threatening as any stifling, controlling "big government."

In *Aliens*, for example, writer-director James Cameron puts an even greater accent on a corporate conspiracy than the first film did. A closer look at the company the heroine of the first *Alien* film works for, 1980s sensibilities argue, can only uncover corruption, fraud and a murderous conspiracy. Once the existence of the parasitic aliens is discovered by the evil Weyland/Yutani Corporation, its board of directors hatches a plan to sacrifice a platoon of Marines to bring the aliens to Earth and use them in bio-weapons research.

In the dystopian future of *The Running Man*, defense, law enforcement, the criminal justice, and prison systems are all run by giant corporations. Punishment, in fact, is meted out by an entertainment giant that frames all critics of the status quo for crimes they did not commit and executes them in televised duels to the death.

The decade began by presenting a version of the 1970s suppressed energy source conspiracy theory in *The Formula* (1980). A synthetic oil formula has existed since World War II, when it was developed by the Nazis, but now the oil companies are willing to commit murder to keep it a secret.

Even in action films and suspense thrillers where a far-reaching conspiracy was not the primary plot concern, the rich, businessmen, and corporate titans could regularly be expected to get unmasked as the perpetrators of crimes. The dark side of any society that encourages unfettered acquisition and greed, these films suggest, is one where many will soon race to amass fortunes by any means necessary.

Conspiracies Everlasting

Although the culture seemed to have taken a shift to the right in the 1980s, the cynicism and distrust underlying the concept of conspiracy theories would not go away. If the theory of film genre argues that an art form of limited conventions addresses a limited range of social concerns, then conspiracy films must obviously let us confront our fears of losing power to immense, invisible cultural elites that manipulate us like puppets, whether we are conservatives or liberals, whether our favorite political party has won an election or not.

CHAPTER 6

Millennial Fears

Conspiracy Theories of the 1990s

In the 1990s, speculation about alien influences on history remained a major preoccupation of conspiracy theorists. Large segments of the UFO community sought proof that the American government — if not world governments — had been actively and successfully doing research on recovered alien technology. Others believed that secret contact had already been made with extraterrestrials and that the alien abduction phenomenon was unfolding with the knowledge and active participation of the American government. Also in this decade, segments of the Christian fundamentalist and evangelical communities expounded on their own unique interpretation of how conspiracies were shaping the world.

By the 1990s, belief in conspiracy theories had become a multigenerational phenomenon. Many people who were not born at the time of the Kennedy assassination and did not even have a clear recollection of Watergate were giving credence to claims of hidden histories, criminal cabals, and the idea that gross corruption was the true driving engine of the world. The late 1980s and early '90s saw the maturation of "Generation X," people born, roughly, between 1961 and 1981. This generation, according to cultural historians, didn't reject their parents' values the way many Baby Boomers had rebelled against the cultural conservatism of their elders, but they felt betrayed by a previous generation that had made promises they did not deliver on. For some analysts, Generation X's fondness for conspiracy theories was linked to this cultural identity. As clinical psychologist Katherine Ramsland discussed Generation X's fascination with vampires and conspiracy-oriented vampire role-playing games in the 1990s with a group of social researchers for her book *Piercing the Darkness*, a common motif among this generation's concerns was a lack of order, predictability, and stability. As she writes:

> The psychological and physical trauma of growing up amidst a breakdown of political leadership, a disturbing dissolution of family structures, a chaotic education with no clear objectives has taken its toll. What results is a fractured self. And just as GenX grew up and entered the job market, the U.S. shifted from being the world's largest creditor to the world's largest debtor nation. The concern for financial stability is reflected in the growing belief that the best has passed; only drudgery and decay are to come.[1]

For many Generation X-ers, the media's unrealistic and idealized portrayals of a normal life had likewise contributed to a feeling of malaise and fearful dissatisfaction. As Ramsland writes, quoting one researcher studying the vampire subculture:

> [O]ne grows up watching *The Brady Bunch* and gets a certain perspective of what family life should be, despite the fact that the majority of younger adults were latchkey kids whose families were in shambles. Thus, many are cautious about marriage and family, and have given up on the TV dream. Another assumption is a lack of trust in leaders coupled with the disappearance of heroes.[2]

Celebrated and controversial literary works of the '90s examined this theme of disillusionment with media- and popular culture-driven expectations young people either could not live up to or felt unfulfilled by. Bret Easton Ellis' *American Psycho* (1991), set in the 1980s, revolved around the hollow and depraved fantasy life of Patrick Bateman, a yuppie who can create no identity for himself aside from what high-end luxury items he constantly acquires. He is a product of a deadening society where the mass media instruct their audiences that they can have a sense of self through the products they buy. The only unique identity Ellis' protagonist can create for himself is one where he fantasizes of gruesome torture and murders. Chuck Palahniuk's *Fight Club* (1996) covers a lot of the same territory with a story about a young mid-level executive who grows disenchanted with a world of vapid, one-dimensional materialism. Much like Ellis' Bateman, he rebels through destruction. His way out of a meaningless life is to organize bare-knuckle fight tournaments where similarly disenfranchised and aimless young men vent their rage at existence.

In her non-fiction book about post–Cold War masculinity, Susan Faludi likewise identifies this same sentiment among young men in the 1990s. A generation has emerged, she argues, that feels like it had been let down by the promises of its fathers.[3]

Then, as Ramsland finds a connection between Generation X frustration and vampire fandom, she argues that many people of this generation see their own parents as vampires. They have been so obsessed with pursuing their own pleasures that they left nothing for their children. Or they left little else but a world of problems, diminishing expectations, finances, and options.

This attitude, in turn, can be quite receptive to the conspiratorial mindset. Conspiracism also insists on bringing order to the chaos by finding cause-and-effect chains. Who created this world, conspiracy theorists ask, and how are they gaining from it?

Thus, it is not a coincidence that the most popular vampire role-playing game of the 1990s revolved around conspiracies by hidden clans of the undead to control human history. Introduced in 1991 by White Wolf Game Studio, *Vampire: The Masquerade* allowed its players to assume the roles of vampires living in a hidden network throughout the world. These vampires were descendants of the Biblical killer Cain, cursed to become a vampire for his act of fratricide. A subsequent society of vampires created by Cain, called "the Kindred," at one point lived on the periphery of human society. But after the Holy Inquisition set out to exterminate all vampires, the Kindred went into hiding, working hard at convincing the rest of history that vampires were nothing more than myth. Today, all of the world's major cities have hidden populations of the Kindred lurking among mortals, secretly manipulating and influencing human affairs.[4]

But Generation X was raised on conspiracy theories and watched films like *E.T.* and *Raiders of the Lost Ark*, where it was a given that organizations of power could not be trusted. They were really receptive to conspiratorial claims, even the most fantastic ones.

Dreamlands

If UFO conspiracy theories did not push the boundaries of belief hard enough, by the 1990s some conspiracy theorists argued that the role of the intelligence community and the military in the UFO phenomenon was much more extensive than suspected before. The '90s offered speculation about a direct relationship between the U.S. government and extraterrestrials. The focus of several UFOlogists was no longer the question of where the aliens might have come from. They were already *here*, conspiracy theorists argued, and the real powers pulling the strings of all the conspiracies were creatures that were not even human.

The idea that there were functioning alien spacecraft, or spacecraft built on Earth but using alien technology, is actually the next logical step that all UFO conspiracy theories lead to. If one believes that an extraterrestrial flying saucer crashed in Roswell, then it would make sense that the government and scientists would attempt to study it and understand how it works. Whether they were called Majestic 12 or any other name, there had to have been some kind of a secret group tasked with managing the research project. Then, since conspiracy theories never like to stay static, it is only inevitable that someone would, at some point, claim that the U.S. government successfully back-engineered and reproduced an actual UFO. It also just happens that the military has a top-secret facility for advanced aircraft research and testing, as well as the back-engineering of foreign aircraft and weapons technology.

Since the beginning of the Cold War, many of the military's cutting-edge technology- and weapons-development programs had been run out of the Nellis Air Force Range and Nuclear Test Site in Nevada, ninety miles northwest of Las Vegas. Starting in 1951, the government began conducting atomic bomb tests there. The development and test-flying of *the* most highly classified military aircraft had also always taken place at Nellis. The U-2 spy plane, as well as the A-12 and SR-71 Blackbirds and the stealth fighters and bombers, had been built at Nellis. As of the 1990s, rumors and speculation have been circulating within aviation enthusiast communities about the development of a hypersonic aircraft named the Aurora.

The most secretive and controversial area of the Nellis test site encompasses the Groom Lake and Papoose Lake testing ranges. The government's most sensitive "black budget" research projects— or projects Congress allocates defense dollars to without ever being told about the nature of the research —are managed here. This ultra-high security area, off limits even to most of the Nellis personnel, has become part of popular culture lore by the names Area 51 or "Dreamland." It contains various research facilities, as well as some of the longest runways in the country. Rumors have long suggested that there are massive underground facilities beneath the Papoose Mountain range. Aside from designing top-secret military aircraft, Area 51 has also been home to the military's facilities for evaluating and reproducing foreign military technology. At the height of the Cold War, captured Soviet-bloc aircraft and weapons systems have been brought to Nellis for study.[5] Much of this work is done with the support of "The Alien Technology Center," just outside of Las Vegas. According to the government, the "alien" in the title of this center refers to the technology of foreign governments. Conspiracy theorists, however, take the moniker much more literally.[6]

In the '90s, the most heated topic among conspiratorially inclined UFO enthusiasts was the question of whether or not the U.S. government was reverse-engineering alien spacecraft in Area 51. Since the 1980s, eyewitnesses claimed to have seen strange lights and unusual aircraft flying in the general vicinity of Nellis Air Force Base. These craft, some of which were supposed to have looked suspiciously saucer-shaped, were said to have maneuvered in ways that should have been aerodynamically impossible. The mystery flying machines were said to have been able to accelerate to speeds in excess of any aircraft built on Earth, decelerate suddenly, perform impossible turns and sudden stops, and, according to some eyewitnesses, just disappear into thin air. If these machines resemble all the classic characteristics of UFOs, conspiracists argue, the explanation must be that the mystery craft of Area 51 are either built using extraterrestrial technology, or they are actual alien spaceships the U.S. government had somehow obtained.[7]

For some, the reverse-engineering of alien flying saucers is just the logical extension of the Roswell crash conspiracy theories (or the conspiracy theories regarding all the numerous other purported crashes in the U.S. and around the world). Wright-Patterson Army Air Base in 1947, they say, was merely the original repository of the Roswell wreckage. But Nellis and Area 51 are the research and testing facilities where government scientists went to work studying and reproducing the otherworldly craft.

Just as in the case of the Roswell UFO crash allegations, claims about the alien technology in the U.S. government's possession actually have a spotty and convoluted history stretching back several decades. These claims, however, have largely hovered on the fringes of UFOlogy. Investigators with solid scientific credentials have largely avoided the issue since it was always entangled in allegations of deep conspiracies that were largely impossible to investigate or prove. But by the '90s, much of the UFO enthusiast community had grown tired of the cautious conservatism of professional scientists. As Jacques Vallée lamented in his book *Revelations*, by the beginning of the '90s, the agendas of even the largest UFO conventions had come to be dominated by speculations about conspiracies, hidden alien bases, and back-engineered flying saucers. The study of sightings and physical traces of alleged UFOs was no longer exciting enough. What used to be fringe speculation and anti-authoritarian paranoia had come to take over the UFOlogical mainstream.

Claims of the U.S. government's possession of and experimentation on alien technology surfaced as early as 1972. As Timothy Good details in his book *Alien Contact: Top Secret UFO Files Revealed,* independent filmmakers Robert Emenegger and Allan Sandler claim to have been approached by Air Force officers suggesting that the two produce a documentary on the UFO phenomenon and the government's involvement in extraterrestrial research. According to Emenegger and Sandler, they were invited to the Pentagon and shown photos of alien spacecraft and dead aliens. The alien corpses, according to the filmmakers, did not come from the 1947 Roswell crash, but a second crash that took place in the New Mexico wilderness in 1949. Making their tale even more astonishing, Emenegger and Sandler claimed their military contacts revealed that one of the aliens from the 1949 crash had actually survived and lived in a Los Alamos "safe house" until its death in 1952. As if these charges were not explosive enough, the two filmmakers also described how they were invited to Norton Air Force Base in San Bernardino, California, in 1973 for even more stunning revelations by military operatives ready to tell all of the shocking truth to the public. At Norton, they were told that aliens had initiated contact with the U.S. government in 1964 when one of their spacecraft landed at Holloman Air Force Base in Alamogordo, New Mexico. Emenegger and Sandler said that they were shown film footage of the landing and the emergence of three small humanoid aliens. The creatures were supposed to have conversed with the heads of the air base via translation devices. Right after the arrival, the aliens and the base commanders allegedly retired to private quarters for an extensive series of discussions about what would later become a long-running extraterrestrial-human project of cooperation and technology exchange. For their documentary project, which was going to be titled *UFOs: It Has Begun*, Emenegger and Sandler were promised clips of this landing footage. The government, they were told, was ready to go public with all the conclusions its Project Blue Book and various other UFO investigation efforts reached.

Unfortunately, just before Emenegger and Sandler could actually start working on their film, the government suddenly withdrew support. The two claim that they were told the release of the UFO information was "politically inappropriate" in light of the growing Watergate scandal.[8] Although they did produce *UFOs: It Has Begun*— a documentary still available on DVD — the project had to rely on a "reenactment" of the "real" Holloman landing. This lack of government support, not to mention verifiable footage of an actual alien spacecraft and extraterrestrial creatures, blunts the force of the film. To skeptics, Emenegger and Sandler's story might as well be a clever PR stunt.

Further hurting Emenegger and Sandler's credibility, even Timothy Good — a staunch supporter of the extraterrestrial nature of UFOs— reveals various inconsistencies in the two filmmakers' story in *Alien Contact.* For example, they have given different dates for the alleged UFO landing at Holloman. At one point they claimed the landing took place in 1964; then in an interview with Good, Emenegger said the incident happened in 1971. Emenegger had also insisted at one point that his Norton Air Force Base contacts allowed him to borrow and take home the Holloman film. Later, though, he reversed his position, denying the loan ever took place.

While the skeptic would quickly dismiss the entire Emenegger-Sandler affair as an obvious hoax, those who believe in a much different conspiracy are not so quick to write them off. For UFO investigators Jacques Vallée and Timothy Good, the incident suggests a disinformation campaign. All that the incident accomplished, this point of view insists, is to tarnish the reputations of all who believe in the UFO phenomenon. The bait and switch tactic by the Air Force managed to make Emenegger and Sandler — and all UFOlogists— look like charlatans.

Emenegger and Sandler are not the only ones to claim that government agents had offered them access to UFO information for a documentary, only to renege at the last moment. According to Linda Moulton Howe, while doing research in 1983 for an HBO documentary on animal mutilations, she was promised classified UFO information as well as the Holloman landing footage. As Howe details in her book *Alien Harvest*, Sergeant Richard C. Doty at Kirtland Air Force promised her unprecedented access to military UFO files and a full governmental endorsement of her work. Howe writes that she was shown scores of documents about various UFO research projects, including briefing documents written for President Jimmy Carter about what the military had learned about alien visitors. According to these documents, Howe claims, the government has been studying how alien manipulation of ancient primate DNA steered human evolution; that the government has been regularly communicating with aliens on Earth; that various Air Force bases have been the headquarters of UFO reverse-engineering projects; and that the very evolution of human social and religious structures had been secretly directed by aliens. One of the documents, Howe writes, discussed how the roots of Christianity originate in an alien-human hybridization project. Two thousand years ago, this document said, the aliens had created a being to teach humans about peace, love, and non-violence. However, just as in the case of Emenegger and Sandler, Howe claims that ultimately Doty and his superiors refused to further cooperate with her documentary. Doty, Howe writes, told her that that the government could not admit to its knowledge of the extraterrestrial nature of UFOs for "political reasons." Doty himself would later deny ever having shown Howe any secret documents or promising her official cooperation. Thus, just like Emenegger and Sandler, Howe's credibility and her entire documentary project were severely compromised. In fact, Howe was apparently hurt by the situation much more than Emenegger and Sandler because HBO cancelled the entire animal mutilation film project once it heard that she could not produce the Holloman footage.

Howe's claims are difficult to assess. The documentary, according to Howe's version of the events at least, was something HBO had green-lit, only to back out when government cooperation was denied. However, the Holloman footage and the military's endorsement were not part of the original condition for HBO to approve of the project. Howe's story of Doty's promises and the explosive revelations in the briefing documents only hurt her. It is not easy to claim that she had concocted the story in an attempt to get a film made. On the other hand, however, Howe did write a book about the experience, and it's become one of the major pieces of reference literature on animal mutilations. She has become a famous figure in the UFO community, a fixture at conferences, and regularly interviewed on television documentaries about aliens, UFOs, and animal mutilations. Can it be said that, despite losing one documentary, she had been able to strengthen her career and reputation in the UFO movement just as that movement embraced ever-more complicated and over-the-top conspiracy theories? For those who believe that the real conspiracy is a massive disinformation project, Doty's connection to Howe is suspect. Doty had also been accused of manipulating and deceiving Paul Bennewitz. Doty's deception of Howe and the derailment of her documentary might have been yet another government attempt to hurt UFO researchers by painting them as fantasy-prone con artists.

As the 1990s arrived, UFOlogy made speculation about alien bases, hidden government bases housing alien spacecraft, abductions, and secret alien-government liaisons their top order of business. Much of this theorizing would be inspired by the revelations of two men who made complex and startling accusations about the extraterrestrial presence on Earth.

In 1988, John Lear began lecturing at UFO conventions about the startling secrets he had learned from his own government contacts. Far from the stereotype of scientifically illiterate fanatics desperate to believe in any claims of supernatural phenomena, Lear was a captain for a charter airline company. The son of William P. Lear, an aeronautical engineer and founder of Lear Jet, John also held various aviation records and had an extensive background flying for the government, including the CIA, in and out of various trouble spots around the world. As Jacques Vallée writes, "John Lear might be mistaken and misinformed … but he is not lying and he is certainly not an armchair traveler. His exploits are real. Presumably, his contacts are real, too."[9]

According to Lear, his contacts told him of a joint U.S. government-extraterrestrial research project inside a massive alien-controlled subterranean city beneath Area 51. It traced its roots to the years spanning from 1969 to 1971, when the government forged a deal with alien visitors. The specifics of the deal, Lear believes, involved an exchange of alien technology for human guinea pigs. The aliens needed to abduct and experiment on humans and they needed the government to help them keep their mission secret. In return for intimidating eyewitnesses and suppressing the truth of the alien presence on Earth, the aliens were willing to share their advanced technologies with the U.S. government. Aside from the secret base, Lear also claims that there is a similar alien research facility under the New Mexico town of Dulce, where human UFO abductees are regularly killed in gruesome experiments.

The problem that skeptics have with claims of enormous plots that would require hundreds, if not thousands, of conspirators to pull off, is the idea that no reliable and verifiable inside information ever leaks out of these conspiracies. Since the early days of UFOlogy presented insiders like J. Allen Hynek, Edward Ruppelt, and Donald Keyhoe who publicly accused the government of not being entirely forthcoming, conspiracies as massive as what Emenegger, Sandler, Howe, and Lear were alleging should have provided at least a few reliable whistle-blowers who could have furnished some tangible proof. Lear's anonymous sources who refused to go on the record with their identities and information just do not qualify. Such was the case, however, until late 1989, when an enigmatic man visited Las Vegas reporter George Knapp of KLAS-TV and claimed to have worked inside Area 51.

Robert Scott "Bob" Lazar quickly became the superstar of the UFO community, and much of the back-engineered-UFO-conspiracy paradigm in popular culture incorporated his claims. Arguably, Lazar is as important to the UFO conspiracy mythology as Berlitz and Moore had been with their book *The Roswell Incident.* As David Darlington writes,

> [W]ithin the world of UFOlogy, meeting Bob Lazar is tantamount to meeting Bob Dylan, Lazar is similarly a reclusive superstar and a legend in his own time; if not exactly the voice of a generation, he has nonetheless had a defining impact on popular consciousness, and finding himself (also like the fabled singer-songwriter) overexposed to onrushing masses with whom he had no desire to associate, he subsequently retreated from public view, assuming a notorious role as an enigma.[10]

As Lazar told his story to Knapp, in 1988 he had been hired by the Edgerton, Germeshausen, and Grier company (EGG) to fill a position in one of their test facilities at Nellis Air Force Base. EGG had a longstanding relationship with the U.S. government, managing top-secret research projects for NASA, the Department of Energy, and the Department of Defense. According to Lazar, who claims to have worked at the Los Alamos National Laboratory on high-energy particle beam acceleration research for the Reagan administration's Strategic Defense Initiative projects, he got the interview with EGG after he was recommended by famed Manhattan Project atomic weapons pioneer, Edward Teller. Lazar's job, he claims, involved the testing of several different designs of flying saucers. Lazar explained that he had seen at least nine functioning UFOs at Area 51; then he accidentally happened upon a group of scientists congregating around a live extraterrestrial. As Lazar described it, the creature looked exactly like the small, spindly, gray-skinned, large-headed aliens of popular lore. The propulsion systems of the UFOs, he said, utilized an antimatter reactor. This was a device he was required to try and dismantle, yet a task he felt was dangerous and something he and his colleagues were ill-equipped for. They were given shockingly inadequate and substandard electrical equipment to work with, Lazar said, with the entire enterprise striking him as a somewhat amateurish trial-and-error attempt at tinkering with a device no one really understood. Furthermore, reminiscent of Linda Moulton Howe, Lazar said that he was given access to files on the scope of the government's overall knowledge of extraterrestrial activities on Earth and the extent of the creatures' involvement in human history and development. Lazar, too, said these files explained how the Earth's religions were really a result of early man's contact with aliens and that the aliens very specifically molded and manipulated humankind's spiritual beliefs.[11]

Lazar said that his experience at Area 51 soured very fast. A major problem for him, he explained, was the draconian security system. Everyone was constantly monitored and, Lazar claimed, bullied and intimidated by the private security forces employed by Nellis. Aside from what he called a "buddy system," where each employee was required to work closely with a partner, close friendships and acquaintances were forbidden. This, Lazar said, was an attempt at making sure that all the work and all the people stayed strictly segmented and compartmentalized where no one could ever get a true sense of the big picture. Area 51 supervisors also took an interest in their employees' private lives, and Lazar's bosses were not happy to find out that his marriage was deteriorating. He claims that this marked him as a poor security risk. Then, when he invited a group of friends for a desert get-together to look at the lights of aircraft test flights, his security clearance was entirely revoked. Shortly after leaving Area 51, Lazar contacted Knapp.[12]

Since Lazar's story seemed to confirm everything conspiracy enthusiasts had already believed, they quickly made him into the sort of UFO-community rock star David Darlington describes. He was sought out by authors, TV and documentary producers, and conference organizers. His tales cemented conspiracism as the driving issue of UFOlogy for the 1990s. Nonetheless, Lazar's critics, even within circles of UFO enthusiasts, quickly pointed out some glaring red flags. It appeared as if Bob Lazar was not the man he said he was. At first, the Los Alamos National Lab denied that he ever worked there. Later, once Lazar produced a W-2 tax form that said he had been employed by the Department of Naval Intelligence, Los Alamos admitted that they *had* at one point employed him. However, spokesmen for Los Alamos appended their information, claiming Lazar had only worked on non-sensitive projects. Nellis Air Force Base had likewise denied ever employing Lazar.[13]

On the issue of how he had initially gotten his position at Area 51, the facts are equally muddled. When Edward Teller was approached by journalists for a verification of Lazar's story, his response was confusing: "Look, I don't know Bob Lazar. All this sounds fine. I probably met him. I might have said to somebody that I met him and I liked him, after I met him, and if I liked him. But I don't remember him.... I mean, you are trying to force questions on me that I simply won't answer."[14] Then in 1990, Lazar was arrested and pled guilty to one count of pandering. He received three years probation and the judge's recommendation that he get psychological counseling. For Lazar's supporters, the case, however, was little more than an unfortunate misunderstanding that UFO debunkers liked to blow out of proportion. They argued that Lazar's "connection" to a brothel—in one of three Nevada counties where prostitution is still illegal — was little more than the installation of some computers and electrical equipment for a friend.[15]

Those who do not dismiss Lazar as a fraud usually claim that he could be either a willing or unwilling disinformation agent for the government. For this perspective, Lazar is something akin to the Majestic-12 documents. He could be a disreputable vessel for factual information. Perhaps Lazar was duped into working for Area 51 for a short while, then manipulated into going public with his allegations, only to have his past and credentials erased by government operatives and to be made to look like an unbalanced, lying fool. Adding credence to this point of view were some statements by Lazar himself. In his interviews with Knapp, he readily admitted that he had always wondered whether or not the alien he saw at Area 51 was but an elaborate hoax. There was so much deception going on at Nellis, he said, that he could not be entirely sure how much of what he did and saw pertained to legitimate research. For believers in the disinformation hypothesis, the "dupe" explanation makes perfect sense. They can point out that Lazar's claims of what he had been shown at Nellis contain glaring contradictions. For example, if all the work on the UFO projects was so compartmentalized, why would his employers bother to show him files on other top secret projects like the aliens' religion-manipulation activities? That was information an engineer would not need to know. For the more cynical school of the "disinformation" hypothesis, Lazar could just as well have been a willing participant in a grand conspiracy to discredit the UFO movement. Jacques Vallée wrote in *Revelations* that, after interviewing Lazar, he came to the conclusion that his story sounded much like "pure theater."[16]

But the fixation was here to stay in the UFO community. Most of the speculative books and documentaries produced in the 1990s dealt, to some extent, with the scope of the alien presence on Earth and the extent of the extraterrestrial influence on human society, rather than the old speculations of whether or not unidentified flying objects were some other-worldly craft. As David Darlington maintained in his book *Area 51*, and Phil Patton in *Dreamland: Travels Inside the Secret World of Roswell and Area 51* (1999), subcultures almost as colorful and obsessive as the contactees of the '50s had built up around the Area 51 mythology. Roswell embraced its UFO–linked past, making museums, crash-site tours, and alien-themed souvenir shops lucrative local ventures. In public lands around Nellis Air Force Base, hundreds of UFO enthusiasts congregated year-round, looking for signs of unusual flying craft. In 1996, just preceding the release of 20th Century-Fox's big-budget alien invasion film *Independence Day*, Nevada renamed Route 375 the "Extraterrestrial Highway."

In 1997, Pocket Books released what it billed as "a landmark exposé firmly grounded in fact": retired Army Colonel Philip J. Corso's book *The Day After Roswell*. In his memoirs of working for the Army's Foreign Technology Desk, Corso claimed to have been present at the recovery of the Roswell UFO, to have seen the removal of the wreckage from Mac Brazel's ranch, and the beginning of a decades-long cover-up and disinformation campaign. Whereas Lazar always left his allegations in the realm of ambiguity and conjecture, Corso unequivocally claims that the government recovered an alien spacecraft and that the Pentagon has been "seeding" the civilian technology-development sector with data gleaned from its wreckage. According to Corso (and his co-author, William J. Birnes, the publisher of *UFO* magazine[17]), microchips, fiber optics, and lasers were developed thanks to the objects found inside the spacecraft. But if these allegations were not far enough over the top, Corso claims that the Cold War era had repeatedly come to the brink of an all-out war between the Earth and an extraterrestrial invasion force. Corso writes that the aliens were bent on an invasion, but because the U.S. government got its hands on the Roswell craft and did such a fast job of unraveling its technology and applying it to military uses, the aliens kept their distance. The reason the military was given so much control over the space program, Corso reveals, was because Washington knew that every space shot, not to mention a lunar expedition, was an intrusion into the territory of the hostile aliens. Ronald Reagan's Strategic Defense Initiative, Corso adds, was actually more of an effort to shield the entire planet from an extraterrestrial invasion, not just from the nuclear missiles of the Soviet Union. The end of the Cold War, according to Corso, was a realization by both Reagan and Soviet General Secretary Mikhail Gorbachev that advanced technology needed to protect all of humanity from the alien threat.

Since Corso's book is filled with outlandish and unsupported claims and logical holes, he did not exactly become the next Bob Lazar his publishers hoped he would. In fact, a rather embarrassing blow was soon dealt to Corso's credibility: South Carolina Senator Strom Thurmond had agreed to write an introduction with the understanding that the book would be a straightforward and down-to-earth memoir of Corso's career in the Army and the Pentagon. He wrote an endorsement of the book without having read Corso's manu-script. Once he saw that he had put his name behind a story of flying saucers and a Cold War against aliens, he withdrew his support and demanded that the foreword be excluded from subsequent editions.[18]

As for the specific inaccuracies, the biggest issues were presented in a History Channel episode of the *UFO Files* series. Essentially, physicists and engineers rebutting Corso's arguments claim, technologies like the laser, the microchip, and fiber optics had all been at least in a theoretical phase of development before 1947. There is nothing to indicate that such technologies could not have been achieved without the sudden introduction of otherworldly help. Moreover, Corso's explanation for why the alien ship crashed in the first place sounds patently unbelievable for those with any rudimentary knowledge of radar equipment and basic flight instrumentation. Corso's book, in fact, repeats a theory advanced by John Lear about the crash. For Lear's outspoken critics, like Jacques Vallée, the crash theory sounded like the weakest part of Lear's entire argument. Lear's, and in turn Corso's, accounting for the crash argues that the Roswell Army Air Base's radars interfered with the flight controls of the UFO, making it lose control and plummet to the ground. As Vallée writes:

> The idea that our primitive radars of 1949 would have repeatedly knocked alien spacecraft out of the sky was utterly ridiculous. Our own aircraft carry a device lovingly known in the electronic warfare trade as a DERFUM (for "digital radio frequency modulator"), which is a little bigger than a shoe box and has the capability to learn instantly all the characteristics of the electromagnetic sources that are operating in its vicinity, to respond to them and even to provide false information if necessary in a matter of seconds. It is hard to believe that visiting spacecraft ... would not have similar, or superior, capabilities.[19]

Although *The Day After Roswell* was a bestseller, Corso did not achieve the sort of long-term stature Lazar did. Only the most die-hard (and profoundly uncritical) alien visitation buffs still give credence to any of his claims. The mainstream of UFOlogy has largely written him off as either a disinformation operative working to discredit the field, or a simple opportunist spinning a fictional yarn to cash in on the Roswell craze.

But in the 1990s, alien-base enthusiasts were ready to look for more of the sinister headquarters of otherworldly and dictatorial regimes putting their designs for the enslavement of humanity into action. Perhaps the most colorful conspiracy theory about one such base identified Denver International Airport as one of the biggest centers, if not *the* central location, for a grand cabal dedicated to eradicating freedom and democracy from the world forever.

When Denver International opened for business in 1995, for most locals it was yet another example of a complex public works project running amok. The airport was two years behind schedule and a staggering three billion dollars over budget. The local media reported wasteful spending, bureaucratic mistakes, design flaws, malfunctioning equipment, and even disputes with local Native American groups claiming that the airport was disrupting sacred grounds. While not many of these problems are unique to Denver International (save, perhaps, for the sacred ground issue), various quirks in the complex's design and decorations have attracted the attentions of conspiracy theorists. As of this writing, scores of conspiracy-oriented blogs and webpages and a number of YouTube videos are devoted to exposing the "truth" about Denver International. Depending on which theory one subscribes to, the airport is the gateway to a massive underground base where the heads of government will be evacuated in case of a national emergency; an alien-run research facility; a landing port for UFOs; the headquarters of the Illuminati, the Freemasons, and their Satanic minions; or one enormous concentration camp where dissenters will be incarcerated once the conspiratorial elites take over the world and institute a global fascist ruling order.

The roots of these theories can be traced either to several news stories of flawed access tunnels, or the striking designs of three large murals by painter Leo Tanguma — pictures meant to call for global peace and multiculturalism.

According to the airport commission managing the construction, a number of service tunnels had been compromised by irreparable design and construction flaws. As a result, the construction crews were ordered to bury the tunnels and start from scratch. For conspiracists, the order to "bury" the tunnels sounds suspect. The real truth, they say, is that the tunnels make up the enormous underground complex that will serve the nefarious purposes of the elites.[20]

Once the complex was eventually finished — but not without more design and engineering snafus — Tanguma's murals were accused of being "morbid," "creepy," "fascistic," "apocalyptic," and "Satanic." Situated across three large panels, the artwork attempts to trace how humanity will move past militarism, oppression, genocide, and war to embrace global disarmament, peace, environmental consciousness, and conservationism. Although upon first glance the mural might appear to be a visual shorthand for standard, politically correct calls for global good will, conspiracy theorists built their grisly fears of concentration camps and global fascism on the mural depicting the world Tanguma is imploring humanity to *reject*. The centerpiece of the painting contains an enormous depiction of a soldier with a sword and a machine gun spearing the dove of peace and massacring women and children. There are also images of dead children in coffins, people being marched into what might be a concentration camp, and forests being laid to waste by massive conflagrations. Upon taking a close look at the burning forest images after September 11, 2001, some conspiracy theorists claimed that one can see what look suspiciously like the burning Twin Towers. Furthermore, since a number other works of art throughout the airport incorporated various Native American cosmological images, the conspiratorially inclined have charged that the complex is "filled" with "occult" symbolism. The fact that Denver Masonic lodges contributed money to the airport and donated a keystone to the complex, conspiracists say, proves that the fingerprints of a global conspiracy are all over the airport.[21]

For any skeptic, these theories indicate a lack of common sense. It is hard to name any large-scale construction project that was not plagued by mistakes, setbacks, cost overruns, and mechanical failures. They are not a sign of a conspiracy at work. Moreover, the people who claim there are passages beneath the airport offer no evidence. And if a genocidal cabal had indeed built the airport as a part of its global agenda for enslavement, the last thing it would do is put up murals hinting at their diabolical plans.

Nonetheless, for the most suspicious of conspiracy theorists, there are mysteries still surrounding the nature and "true" purpose of Denver International. With a name like New World Airport Commission, conspiracy theorists argue, something is darkly, dangerously amiss. The phrase "New World," after all, is the root of 1990s conspiracy theorists' greatest fears: the New World Order.

"New World Order" found its sinister cache after President George H.W. Bush used it in a speech announcing the start of Operation Desert Storm in 1991. Bush's speech, conspiracists maintain, was a none-too-subtle manifesto for the "global elites," the non-democratic ruling order comprised of the "international bankers," the Illuminati, the Freemasons, and the "bloodlines" of centuries-old aristocratic dynasties to use whatever military force is required to keep their hold on power and maintain their "interests." To this day, "New World Order" remains shorthand for all the dangerous schemes the elites are attempting to put into effect. The headquarters of the dictatorial heads of the New World Order, a number of conspiracists claim, will be Denver International Airport.

A rarely appreciated retort to the fears of President Bush's New World Order is an argument similar to the debunking of Ronald Reagan's alien invasion speech. Most conspiracy theorists actually take the "new world order" phrase out of context. When one listens to the full speech, it is obvious that Bush is not talking about global elites; the New World Order he speaks of is a hypothetical, ideal new "order" to the world, a post–Cold War planet ruled by international laws, so that warlike nation will ever be able to unilaterally wage war on anyone. In essence, the Bush speech is a strong pro–United Nations speech. As Bush said:

> This is a historic moment. We have in this past year made great progress in ending the long era of conflict and cold war. We have before us the opportunity to forge for ourselves and for future generations a new world order — a world where the rule of law, not the law of the jungle, governs the conduct of nations. When we are successful — and we will be — we have a real chance at this new world order, an order in which a credible United Nations can use its peacekeeping role to fulfill the promise and vision of the U.N.'s founders.[22]

Fighting the Forces of Evil

The 1990s was also a time when the phrase "culture wars" became a part of the national lexicon. Liberals and conservatives fought a war of values throughout the decade, or, more specifically, a war over the way values and morals stood to be defined in the spotlight of the national mass media. An aggressive conservative faction was given a voice in the '90s by the popular and influential talk-radio phenomenon and its new superstars Rush Limbaugh and Sean Hannity. Aside from championing traditional conservative platforms (limited government, small taxes, and a strong national defense), talk radio gave voice to the religious factions of the political right-wing, to social conservatives who believed America's morality was in a steady decline. The so-called "moral majority," followers of evangelical Christian activists like Jerry Falwell and Pat Robertson, who had fought the values of the counter-culture in the late '60s and '70s and warned against Satanism in the 1980s, argued that the nation's dominant value system was fast degenerating into licentiousness, excess, and god-lessness. Social conservatives were determined to fight a cultural atmosphere that was becoming, in their estimation, increasingly secular, hostile to religion (particularly Christianity), more tolerant of homosexuality and non-traditional family structures than ever before, and overwhelmed by media messages of violence and hedonistic sexuality. These cultural and religious conservatives quickly made the forty-second president of the United States the emblem of everything they saw wrong with the values of the nation: Bill Clinton, the first Baby Boomer in the Oval Office, was a man constantly dogged by accusations of extramarital sexual escapades. In fact, whereas past presidents were embroiled in scandals like the Watergate burglary and the guns-for-hostages scheme of Iran-Contra, Clinton's tenure was tainted by his affair with intern Monica Lewinsky. While only the first years of the decade were marred by a deep recession, with the economy recovering quickly and rebounding into a long stretch of prosperity, for the religious right the decade was a moral disaster.

Social conservatism — and very specifically evangelical, fundamentalist Christian conservatism — also found tremendous success in publishing and in independent film production in the 1990s. Aside from issue-oriented didacticism, these media put their resources behind producing fictional entertainment as well. It was entertainment, writers, publishers, and film producers argued, that conservative Christian audiences could not get from the mainstream media. Going even further, some of the more pugnacious members of the Christian media claimed that they produced fiction and non-fiction entertainment that the mainstream "liberal" media was actively hostile to and worked hard to suppress. This line of reasoning itself, of course, had a strong conspiratorial program built in. In fact, fundamentalist Christians brought unique conspiracy theories to issues like the UFO phenomenon and the future of all life on Earth.

One can argue that conservative Christian UFO conspiracy theories are a natural reaction to some of the subtle — and some not-so-subtle — anti-religious implications of all the speculation surrounding the role extraterrestrials played in ancient history. From ancient astronaut theorists like Erich von Däniken, who argued that the beings whom ancient civilizations worshipped as gods were actually alien visitors, to the abduction proponents who claimed that early man was a product of extraterrestrial genetic experimentation on apes, the gauntlet, some Christians felt, had been thrown down for people of faith. A large segment of the UFO community, it seemed, was on a mission to negate religion and spirituality. The claims of the supposed hidden files about alien genetic experimentation (shown to Linda Moulton Howe and Bob Lazar) suggested that religion is nothing more than a primitive misconception. If God was nothing but an astronaut, Christianity — and most other religions, for that matter — was nothing but a fantasy. Christian conservatives, so ready and willing to fight the culture wars of the 1990s, had their own retort to what they saw as yet another assault on their faith: The UFO phenomenon, they said, was Satanic.

The fundamentalist Christian approach to UFOs is an attempt at reconciling the phenomenon with the literal interpretation of passages in the Bible. To some, it might seem an odd approach to counter a movement they see as hostile by acknowledging the existence of that movement's paranormal beliefs. Rather than getting on the skeptical bandwagon, the fundamentalists accept the objective reality of UFOs. The flying disks and aliens, they argue, are truly a supernatural manifestation, but a manifestation of evil.

UFO occupants, according to the fundamentalist Christian interpretation, are demonic in origin.[23] The entire phenomenon, this point of view argues, is what the Bible speaks of when warning about false prophets. Disturbed by the sort of messianic role a number of abductees and abduction researchers have placed the aliens in, the fundamentalists counter that the false prophets of the Bible appear to behave exactly — and have the same effect on people — as modern-day UFO occupants do. The Biblical false prophets, fundamentalists warn, will preach a gospel opposing Jesus, will appear to perform miracles, and they will tempt believers to reject Christ. False prophets will promise to create a Utopia on Earth, to solve all of mankind's problems, to give them unending pleasure and wealth, while in reality leading them into the service of Satan and eternal damnation. Listening to the interpretations of the most optimistic of UFO abductees and researchers, fundamentalists are troubled when they hear stories of "aliens" promising to save the environment, put an end to war, and to deliver wondrous technologies that will create a heaven on Earth. This orthodox Christian point of view is both frightened by and vindicated by secular, psychological approaches at debunking alien contact, particularly when the debunkers claim that the UFO phenomenon is but an emerging, technological-age religion. A new religion that comes to replace old belief systems, specifically replace a dominant Christian hegemony, will be, in the eyes of evangelicals, a Satanic threat and the fulfillment of Biblical prophecy.

Other books on the UFO phenomenon, written from the fundamentalist Christian perspective and published with regularity well into the 2000s, claim that the so-called extraterrestrials are misinterpretations of the "Nephilim" of the Old Testament rather than false prophets. Mentioned in the books of Genesis and Numbers, these creatures have been seen through a broad range of interpretations, from "giants" and "fallen angels" to "demons," and even human descendants of the most righteous followers of God. The general consensus about the translations of the ancient descriptions of the Nephilim is that they are the offspring of the "sons of God" and the beautiful daughters of men. These hybrids of humans and otherworldly beings, depending on whichever translation one chooses to believe, were "giants," or fearsome, or supernaturally endowed beings. In the fundamentalist Christian UFOlogical perspective, the Nephilim are the evil offspring of rebellious fallen angels that seduced humans and created unholy offspring. These creatures, fundamentalists warn, are now deceiving humankind in the guise of aliens. The true conspiracy, according to this interpretation, is the effort to convince the world to embrace the "aliens" and look to them as the potential saviors of mankind. UFO enthusiasts and researchers who forward the positive image of these creatures are doing Satan's work, brainwashing the world into welcoming a diabolical takeover.

But according to another major Christian conspiratorial school of thought, the forces of Satan are not merely operating in the form of small, gray, black-eyed UFOnauts. The evil counterpart of Jesus Christ walks the Earth today, some fundamentalists believe, and he looks quite human and attractive, and he will one day be able to seduce all but the most righteous Christians. This figure is none other than Satan's ultimate tool, the Antichrist. The Antichrist, however, turned out to be one of the most lucrative boons for the Christian media in the 1990s, a marketing phenomenon that has been yielding profits for writers and independent filmmakers well into the twenty-first century.

The evangelical Christian community's use of the Antichrist in conspiracy theories derives a lot of its main ideas from Hal Lindsey and Carole Carlson's *The Late, Great Planet Earth*. Just as Lindsey and Carlson argued in their speculative nonfiction book, a growing number of fundamentalist Christians in the 1990s believed that the Antichrist was living on Earth and quietly manipulating world events in such a way as to push the most powerful and the must unstable nations toward the brink of apocalypse. The son of Satan in essence, he would in the last moment emerge as an international figure and a savior, apparently the only person in the world with the ability to forge a new era of peace. This Antichrist figure, fundamentalists speculate, would be a skilled manipulator of the media, a superb communicator and a man of magnetic, captivating charisma. Once he emerges onto the world stage, he will be able to unite some of the bitterest historical enemies in peaceful alliances. He will, most likely, emerge from either the worlds of finance or the media, or perhaps he will be an up-and-coming politician who is suddenly embraced by all and catapulted into positions of immense power and influence. Global stability and peace will follow — probably within the United Nations, fundamentalists hypothesize — but it will be a brief period of very deceptive peace. Three and a half years into his reign, the Antichrist will break the peace treaties he forged, declare himself the only living god, and force the entire world to worship him. Those who do not will be persecuted, hunted down, and exterminated in the worst mass murders history has ever seen. The world will be plunged into war and chaos until Jesus Christ returns to rescue all those who have accepted him and been "born again" as fundamentalist believers in the literal truth of the Bible. All others, along with the Antichrist, will be defeated and cast into Hell for all eternity.

The true conspiracy among the power brokers of the world, believers in the Antichrist argue, is the conspiracy to engineer this demonic figure's rise to power. Those who are willing to trade their souls for power on Earth are in league with the Antichrist and they are ready to use the global reach of the mass media and the resources of financial institutions to make sure that this evil being will soon be able to assume his role as the ruler of the world.

No one has been more successful in popularizing the concept than authors Tim LaHaye and Jerry B. Jenkins in their *Left Behind* novels. First published in 1995 by Christian publisher Tyndale House, *Left Behind: A Novel of the Earth's Last Days* became a blockbuster success. Over the next decade, it spawned an industry that included twelve sequels, a prequel trilogy, a spin-off series of young adult novels, graphic novels, and video games. In 2000, the first book in the series was adapted into a film starring teen idol turned born-again evangelical activist Kirk Cameron (*Growing Pains*). Each book was a high-ranking *New York Times* bestseller, with all the books selling, to date, some sixty-five million copies around the world. In an examination of the cultural impact of evangelical Christians, *Time* magazine named LaHaye one of the most influential evangelicals in America today.[24]

The *Left Behind* series comprises an ongoing story arc novelizing a fundamentalist eschatological interpretation of the Bible's book of Revelation, written in the style of action-adventure and conspiracy thrillers. The series begins with a global "premillennialist" Rapture event where the coming of the end of the world, wars between the forces of God and Satan, and final judgment are preceded by the removal of all born-again Christians to Heaven. Everyone who has been "left behind," those who are evil as well as the ones who are just simply not Christian or not devout enough in their faith, take sides in the coming battle between Heaven and Hell. The sinners are quickly seduced by the Antichrist, who has taken leadership of the United Nations and moved to eradicate all national sovereignties and unite the entire planet under his absolute rule. Those who did not believe, or allowed their Christian faith to lapse, realize that they must accept Jesus as their savior. The series is a long, complex adventure story about the "tribulation" (the war between the Antichrist and the newly born-again). In the conclusion of the story arc, Jesus returns to Earth, gathering followers, rewarding them for their faith, and eradicating the Antichrist and his minions.

As popular as the *Left Behind* books were, they were just as divisive and controversial. They were quickly assailed for the ideas and social agendas of one of their writers, along with denouncing the Biblical interpretation espoused by the saga.

Tim LaHaye was an evangelical minister and far-right-wing political activist. LaHaye dictated the creative direction and themes of the books while Jenkins did the actual writing. For the series' critics, the story was but a medium for LaHaye's radical, exclusionary theology and political agendas. LaHaye, after all, had written in his 1973 book *Revelation Illustrated and Made Plain* that having no religion was preferable to Catholicism and that Pope Paul VI was the priest of Satan, if not the Antichrist himself. Once the media had unearthed that statement in 1988, when LaHaye was serving as the co-chairman of Jack Kemp's presidential campaign, he was pressured into resigning. His 1978 book *The Unhappy Gays* was also denounced for its scalding homophobia and suggestions that the application of "Biblical law" to punish homosexuality was much more merciful than the acceptance of a lifestyle that condemns gays to what LaHaye deems an existence of misery and suffering. Biblical law, however, prescribed execution for homosexual behavior.[25]

Liberal columnist Michelle Goldberg had a point of view that a number of Christian theologians concurred with: The *Left Behind* books are a powerful revenge fantasy for evangelicals. In these books, the fundamentalist interpretation of the Bible is proven true, and all who have not accepted it are condemned to suffer, at best, years of tribulation and war, and, at worst, eternal damnation. The books are fundamentalists' dreams of telling their critics "I told you so." The ultra-conservative Christians who had been mocked and derided by a lax, lapsed Christian community, by the liberal, secular world, get the last laugh in these books. They are raptured to eternal happiness in Heaven while all of their critics are left behind to suffer or die on Earth.[26]

The world of conspiracy theories in the 1990s can ultimately be described as a very sharp turn into the territories of hyperbole and high strangeness. Aliens and the Antichrist became more of an obsession for the suspicious-minded than ever before. Forgoing such mundane concerns as assassinations, political corruption, or the POWs of decades-old wars, the theorists of the '90s fixated on the questions of life in the cosmos, gods, demons, and the very future of mankind here on Earth. The truth about all these questions, of course, was hidden by secret fraternities and diabolical pacts with beings from other realms.

CHAPTER 7

Extreme Possibilities
Conspiracy Films of the 1990s

Conspiracy theory entertainment in the 1990s went mainstream in a much bigger way than ever before. Conspiracy storylines continued to proliferate not only in theatrical films, but on television as well. Chris Carter's *The X-Files* was one of the most influential TV phenomena of the decade, and the concept of conspiracies spread to every major entertainment genre. From science fiction to action films, horror films, cop thrillers, spy thrillers, and even comedies, conspiracy theories became mainstream hip.

Conspiracy-themed action films at the start of the decade had still been expressing a great deal of the liberal outrage over the Iran-Contra era corruption in the Reagan administration. Or, one might hypothesize, the criminality that zealous super-patriots were capable of, as seen during the Iran-Contra debacle, had given a liberal slant to a genre that had been leaning hard right since *Dirty Harry* in the 1970s and a genre whose conservatism appeared to have been cast in stone by the *Rambo*, *Lethal Weapon*, and *Die Hard* school of 1980s action cinema. But in the post–Reagan years, the abuse of power and the subversion of laws in the name of "national security" and "patriotism" had become the new fear in action films. In fact, for a while, it looked as if Steven Seagal's *Above the Law* might have been turning into the new template film for conspiracy-oriented action thrillers.

Nearly identical in its conspiracy plot to *Above the Law*, *The Last of the Finest* (1990) starred Brian Dennehy, who had played Rambo's nemesis in *First Blood*. The film involves a squad of narcotics cops taking down a warehouse full of drug smugglers. As had often been the case in tough, maverick-cop action films, Dennehy's team can sometimes act on their instincts and not follow police protocol to the letter. But their sense of justice is much more finely honed than the details of the police rule book. In their warehouse sting, however, the group did not notify all the proper authorities in their LAPD chain of command, choosing instead to raid the drug lair without proper backup. After each member of the group is fired, Dennehy begins suspecting that the bureaucratic outrage might be rooted in corruption. Investigating the matter, the group stumbles onto an *Above the Law*–type drug-money-for-illegal-anticommunist-covert-operations conspiracy. In fact, the Dennehy character realizes that his immediate superior (Henry Darrow) is one of the conspirators. Dennehy's captain, a Cuban expatriate, justifies the drug-running as a necessary evil in combating the much bigger threat of Latin American communism.

The most surprising liberal turn in the action genre in 1990, however, came in *Die Hard 2: Die Harder*, also tying the South American drug trade to corrupt U.S. covert operations missions. The *Die Hard 2* villains are an uncannily loyal group of former Special Forces commandos outraged at the way the brutal dictator of Val Verde, General Ramon

Esparanza (Franco Nero)—a man they had trained—is being treated by Washington. The right-wing Esparanza had been considered a valuable U.S. ally in combating South American communism, but, it seems, only until Washington decided that the drug trade had become a more dangerous national security threat than communism. In a radical change of policy, the American government chose to indict Esparanza for his drug trafficking, helped his opposition remove him from power, and shipped him to Washington to stand trial.

This expository backstory of the two key villains—Esperanza and the stiff, blustery, Oliver North–esque Col. Stuart (William Sadler)—is inspired in no small measure by the Bush administration's indictment and jailing of Panamanian dictator Manuel Noriega. Noriega had ties to the United States going as far back as the 1950s and had learned intelligence and counterintelligence tactics at the School of Americas at Fort Gulick, in the former Panama Canal Zone, in 1967. From the early 1970s and throughout the 1980s, Noriega had also been a CIA asset in Panama, although investigations of his regime would later claim that he had always been a "double agent," deftly playing all sides against each other in Latin American politics. For example, Noriega was believed to have been aiding Fidel Castro in Cuba while pledging his anticommunism to the U.S.; had sold weapons to the Nicaraguan Sandinista government while funneling American money to the Contra rebels attempting to overthrow the communist Sandinista regime; and refused Oliver North's requests for direct military aid to the Contras. In the meantime, he also had a close partnership with Colombia's Medellín drug cartel and had enriched his own regime through drug smuggling.[1] To conspiracy theorists, the United States' troubled history with Noriega was much more than a mere series of bad decisions and the "accidental" creation of a drug-producing strongman dictator. According to conspiratorial thinking, Noriega was a problem Washington knowingly created in order to later mount a costly invasion of Panama. Costly invasions, conspiracy theorists argue, are gifts to the weapons manufacturers and bankers who profit from them.

In *Die Hard 2*, the conspiracy plot is even more intricate. In a midpoint plot twist, it is revealed that Col. Stuart had established and maintained his own secret network of ultra right-wing operatives within the Special Forces. Once Washington had gone soft and turned on its own dictator allies in Latin America, Stuart and his conspirators went into action and planned a takeover of Dulles International Airport in Washington D.C. in an attempt to free Esperanza.

Keeping the Cold War Alive

Die Hard 2 and its concern with anticommunist zealots and what becomes of them in the waning days of the Cold War also had roots in an overall worry that was specific to writers and filmmakers at the time, more so than believers in real conspiracies. As soon as East-West relations began improving in the late '80s, culminating in the 1989 dismantling of the Berlin Wall and the obvious end of the Soviet Union as a world superpower, artists—from spy novelists to action-adventure filmmakers—had run out of an easy and convenient source of villains. The late '80s, in fact, had seen both adventure books and films scrambling for new threats to world peace, security, and freedom. A number of action films quickly shifted to drug dealers and terrorists. In 1989, the James Bond film *Licence to Kill* replaced its usual rogues' gallery of megalomaniacs bent on world domination (stand-in villains for communism and the Soviet bloc) with a South American drug kingpin (Robert Davi) out to monopolize the global cocaine trade. Other storytellers imagined a different kind of post–Cold War conspiracy theory. This theory, however, had no parallel in the real world.

If major players in the worlds of espionage, the armed forces, and the military industrial complex had too much invested in a status quo where the East and West are perpetually locked in confrontation, this conspiracy theory asked what would happen to such men if the Cold War was suddenly over. In the imaginations of authors and screenwriters, such ruthless and retrograde characters might conspire to keep the Cold War alive.

The most successful of the "reignition of the Cold War" conspiracy films made it to the screens in the summer of 1989: *The Package* involved a plot to kill the Soviet General Secretary during his visit to Chicago. With the Soviet leader dead, communist hard-liners would have taken his place and the era of Glasnost and nonconfrontational U.S.-Soviet relations would have been over. More than a bit prescient about the type of obstacles Soviet reformers like General Secretary Mikhail Gorbachev and President Boris Yeltsin were about to face in real life,* *The Package* spread its accusations of villainy around. In the course of the film, Army Master Sergeant Johnny Gallagher (Gene Hackman) stumbles onto a stunning collusion between American generals and their Soviet counterparts in a plot to stop Glasnost and peace. The ongoing nuclear standoff between the East and the West, according to the leader of the American conspirators (John Heard), was the only thing preventing full-scale wars. In the details of the assassination, the film also borrowed liberally from the John F. Kennedy conspiracy lore: The conspirators of *The Package* work with a seasoned sharpshooter (Tommy Lee Jones) who will fire the killing round into the Soviet leader, all the while setting up a Lee Harvey Oswald–like patsy to take the fall for the crime.

Although convoluted and fanciful, the film's verisimilitude is aided by director Andrew Davis' gritty visual style. The action sequences are meticulously realistic, with Davis and his stunt coordinators avoiding the over-the-top, one-man-against many action sequences of the *Die Hard* and *Rambo* action films of the 1980s. Furthermore, characters, especially hero Hackman and villain Jones, look and act perfectly lifelike. There are no superheroes and super-villains. Moreover, using his large stock company of Chicago-based character actors in supporting roles, Davis manages to make the film feel like it is populated by individuals who might have stepped from the real worlds of political corruption and working stiffs plodding through the bureaucracies of police work and military intelligence.

The plot of paranoid conspirators stuck in the past, unable to let go of the Cold War, turned into an oft-used device in a number of television thrillers in the late '80s and early '90s, including episodes of the *MacGyver* series and a movie-of-the-week revival of *The Six Million Dollar Man*. Many straight-to-video spy and action thrillers likewise worked with the same plot, and spy novels were also greatly fond of this conspiracy.

In 1991, the second most visible adaptation of this particular conspiracy theory came by way of *Star Trek VI: The Undiscovered Country*. It deals with the end of a centuries-long conflict and state of cold war between the democratic United Federation of Planets and the militaristic, dictatorial Klingon Empire. After a Chernobyl-like disaster in space, where an explosion at a primitive, unsafe mining operation nearly destroys the Klingon home planet, a peace-making Klingon leader (a sort of alien Gorbachev) calls for an end to hostilities. While the starship *Enterprise* is called on to escort a Klingon delegation to a peace conference on Earth, Captain James T. Kirk (William Shatner)—contending with his own hatred of the

*In August of 1991, an attempted coup by communist hard-liners nearly toppled Gorbachev and, according to historians, greatly damaged his power in the U.S.S.R., letting Yeltsin emerge as the major force in Soviet restructuring and the dismantling of the communist system.

Klingons and skepticism over peace — realizes that a murder aboard his ship is a part of a conspiracy of Klingon and Federation hard-liners trying to derail the peace proceedings.

While this type of conspiracy theory about keeping the Cold War alive had, naturally, a short shelf life around the turn of the decade, a new version of it reappeared in the 1996 Geena Davis action thriller *The Long Kiss Goodnight*. Directed by *Die Hard 2* helmer Renny Harlin, using many of the same hyperbolic action, fighting, and shootout sequences as in the Bruce Willis vehicle, the film involves Davis' amnesiac housewife character discovering that she is a former government operative. When she regains her memory, Davis' ex-employers target her for assassination, fearing that she might remember a plot to kill four thousand people in a fake terrorist attack. In what conspiracy theorists have taken to calling a "false flag operation"— a term that would become an oft-used buzzword in the world of September 11 conspiracy theorists—covert operatives in *The Long Kiss Goodnight* plan to use the ersatz terrorist bombing as a means to increase government funding of their agency.

Back to the '60s!

While suspicion and conspiratorial paranoia remained in vogue at the turn of the decade, the most influential and controversial of all conspiracy-themed films of the 1990s turned the clock back to the early 1960s. In his 1991 film *JFK*, director Oliver Stone revisited the Kennedy assassination and attempted to make a film that would encapsulate all of the major conspiracy theories in one story. To the legions of critics who wound up crying foul in the wake of the movie, *JFK* did more than document the president's murder and the conspiracy theories surrounding it. They charged that it rewrote history. *JFK*, Stone's critics argued in every available medium, was little more than an alternate reality version of the 1963 assassination, a fantasy about people who never existed and incidents that never took place.

Should *JFK* be judged entirely as an art work or does its historical accuracy need to be examined? Stone, after all, had never minced his words when he said that he hoped his movie would be used as a tool for activism and inspire its viewers to demand that the government release all of its information about the Kennedy assassination. Thus, if the film's director implicitly wants his work to be more than mere entertainment, then is a film historian not justified in subjecting *JFK* to much closer scrutiny than most historical dramas? Moreover, since the film is a very *angry* piece of activist filmmaking, accusing real people of various degrees of criminality, those who evaluate it often feel like they must deal with extremely weighty ethical dilemmas.

A number of historians and reviewers chose the route of taking the film to task for its historical inaccuracies. The criticism of the content was so loud so soon after its premiere that both Stone and star Kevin Costner were pressured into admitting that extreme liberties were taken with the facts. In those moments, Stone defended *JFK* as a film artist and not as a historian or activist. The movie, he argued, has "an inner truth."[2] Costner likewise admitted that much of *JFK* could not stand up to historical scrutiny, yet, he said, the "movie as a whole has an emotional truth."[3] Columnist John Leo wrote that Stone's and Costner's arguments carry very ominous implications about the ethics of the mass media in the 1990s:

> But inner truths and emotional truths are the stuff of fiction, or used to be. What I think Stone and his actor are saying here is that it doesn't much matter whether this is literally true or not, so long as it steers the culture where we want to go. This has become an increasingly modish opinion as the line between fact and fiction grows ever more blurry.[4]

Since the film was critically praised as an excellent piece of art *and* became one of the most famous films of the decade for the controversy it generated, looking at it as both art and history is warranted. In its narrative structure, *JFK* is an example of the quintessential conspiracy theory story formula. Its characters, scenes, plot points, and resolution are a pastiche of all generic components of the conspiracy film.

The film focuses on New Orleans District Attorney Jim Garrison (Costner) in his 1969 attempt to prosecute businessman Clay Shaw (Tommy Lee Jones) for conspiring to assassinate the president. Stone's version of Garrison is a pure-hearted, idealistic, all–American patriot who does not hesitate to right wrongs. As embodied by Costner, who at that point in his career had regularly been compared to Jimmy Stewart, Gary Cooper, and Gregory Peck for his portrayals of principled characters in films like *Field of Dreams* (1989) and *Dances With Wolves* (1990), Garrison appears to be a hybrid of Jefferson Smith from *Mr. Smith Goes to Washington* and Atticus Finch in *To Kill a Mockingbird* (1962). At the opening of the film, Garrison, who had been shocked and saddened by the murder of the president, is at first intrigued by the way the events unfold in Dallas. He seems to have an instinctive notion that there's more to the story than what is told by the Dallas authorities and the police. By the time Garrison has finished reading the Warren Commission report, he is convinced that Lee Harvey Oswald (Gary Oldman) was but the tip of a violent Louisiana and Texas subculture of right-wing fanatics and their military and industrialist financiers. But the mastermind behind the conspiracy, Garrison comes to believe, is Shaw.

Following the conspiracy film story arc faithfully, Garrison is spied on and harassed by the government and attacked by the media, and he sees his professional and private life unraveling under the strain. His various colleagues quit the prosecutorial team when they can't take the pressure; even his own wife (Sissy Spacek) can't understand his dogged determination to see such a seemingly fruitless effort as the Shaw prosecution through to the end. Although Garrison's quest is occasionally aided by shadowy insiders—like a Deepthroat-esque Air Force officer (Donald Sutherland) calling himself "X"—who confirm that the conspiracy was hatched to keep the U.S. in Vietnam, Garrison ultimately loses the trial. Although he puts on a passionate closing speech, once again reminiscent of characters like Jefferson Smith and Atticus Finch, Shaw is quickly acquitted. Just like those of many other conspiracy film protagonists, Garrison's victory can only be a symbolic and moral one. He is but one of a very few idealists in a country that has either abandoned its democratic ideals or is so apathetic that it does not care enough when a vicious cabal of murderers has perpetrated the ultimate act of treason in the name of "patriotism."

JFK is perhaps the best cinematic representation of how the assassination of John F. Kennedy provided the liberal left with the perfect opportunity to rewrite the cultural script about patriotism. Just as real conspiracy theorists could cast themselves in the role of the purest patriots in the aftermath of the Kennedy murder (after years of McCarthyite paranoia accused them of disloyalty for their left-wing politics), *JFK* is structured as a dialectic between those on the left who are passionate about preserving the American system and those on the far right who are scheming to subvert it and overthrow it. The film repeatedly suggests a barely maintained balance between the cultural forces of order and chaos, patriotism and disloyalty, law and criminality, and idealism and cynicism. The traditional, all–American hero of this story, however, is the liberal Garrison. A veteran of World War II, he is the sort of patriot who did not back down when he had to defend his country on the battlefield. He is a devoted family man, the idealized cinematic representation of a cultural catchphrase that had become ever so ubiquitous in the political lexicon at the time audiences were watching this film: "family values." Garrison's entire motivation for pursuing the Shaw prosecution is driven by his family. When his angry wife demands to know why he can't give up his fight, Garrison tells her that it's all for his kids. He hopes that his fight might in some small way create a better future for them, an America where law, order, and democracy still prevail. The conspirators, however, exist as a perverse inversion of everything in Garrison's world. Whereas Garrison is the perfect family man in a glowing, Capra-esque suburban existence, his opponents cower and conspire in swamps, in back alleys, and in dark, smoke-filled rooms. In the film's most dubious piece of dialectical storytelling, Garrison's traditional family life is contrasted with Shaw's homosexuality. While Garrison exists in a world of family, children, and domesticity, Shaw's is a world where murder conspiracies are hatched amidst drug- and alcohol-fueled gay orgies. The conspirators easily turn on each other—Oswald is sacrificed and Shaw associate David Ferrie (Joe Pesci) gets killed when he becomes a liability—but Garrison is a loyal colleague and the ideal boss. In a Christ-like gesture, he warns his associates that they will be attacked and vilified if they join the team. But Garrison always stands by each of his aides and supports them, even when they buckle under pressure and quit the crusade. Simply, Garrison embodies all the wholesome, brave, faithful, and patriotic old-fashioned values the right-wing always claims to champion. But in the world of *JFK*, the right-wing has allied with evil, perversion, and fascism.

Stone's critics never denied his masterful abilities as a storyteller who could do a virtuoso job of manipulating the emotions of his audiences. The explosive controversy generated by *JFK* came from his fabrication of events and people, and his selective presentation of facts in order to manufacture a version of the Kennedy assassination and the Shaw trial that never happened.

As writers like Vincent Bugliosi and Patricia Lambert[5] argue, Stone's most egregious distortion is his presentation of Jim Garrison as an idealistic hero. The real Garrison, they write, would have been disbarred and probably prosecuted and jailed had he served in a state that did not have the sort of corrupt political culture Louisiana did. Far from being a victim of the government's harassment, Garrison and his various staff members were accused of harassing and intimidating witnesses. A lawyer for an associate of David Ferrie even made a tape-recording of Garrison attempting to bribe his client into giving favorable testimony for the prosecution. Eventually, several people from Garrison's group resigned the case in protest, telling the local press that the district attorney was on a crusade to railroad a man whom Garrison and everyone in his office knew full well to be innocent. Only four months into the Shaw prosecution, the New Orleans Metropolitan Commission reported that local citizens had made 22 criminal allegations against Garrison and his staff, including bribery, intimidation, suborning perjury, and threats of battery. The first people to denounce him were the major conspiracy theorists. Not long after he announced his case against Shaw, legions of conspiracy theorists poured into New Orleans, happy to see someone within the establishment taking their beliefs seriously. But the closer they looked at Garrison's case, the less they liked it. Even before the D.A.'s disgruntled staff did, conspiracy theorists went to the press, denouncing Garrison as a charlatan bent on destroying the life and reputation of an innocent man.

Moreover, as books like Bugliosi's *Reclaiming History*, Gerald Posner's *Case Closed*, Mark Fuhrman's *A Simple Act of Murder: November 22, 1963* (2006) and new investigative documentaries like the ABC News program *The Kennedy Assassination: Beyond Conspiracy* (2003) argued, *JFK* made much of its case for a conspiracy based on allegations that have long been debunked. For example, Oswald was not as incompetent with a rifle as Stone's film claims; he had rated as a "sharpshooter" in the Marines. He had consistently proved proficient and very fast with rifles similar to the one found in the Texas Book Depository with his fingerprints on it. Furthermore, what conspiracy theorists derisively call a "pristine" "magic bullet," the slug that tore through Kennedy's body and that of Governor John Connally, was not "pristine." Contrary to what *JFK* claims, an examination of the bullet showed it to have been fired from Oswald's rifle, to have been dented and misshapen and even to have been missing metal fragments that were found inside Connally's wounds. But an offense of the film that critics found outrageous is a scene where the impossibility of the bullet's wounding of both Kennedy and Connally is demonstrated on a chart. The placement of Connally's seat in the film's chart is not accurate. The scene, critics charge, is much more than a case of Stone's unique interpretation of the events. The scene is an example of his willful deception of the audience.

Ultimately, the success of *JFK* was assured by the controversy it generated. People lined up to see it so they could understand what the debate and outrage were about. This success at the beginning of a decade that was slightly less optimistic, less idealistic, and more cynical than the one that had passed suggested that conspiracism would stay an indelible part of American popular culture for a long time to come.

The Truth Is Out There: On Television

If *JFK* cemented paranoia and conspiracy theories into the forefront of American consciousness in the early 1990s, *The X-Files* kept them firmly in the popular imagination for nearly a decade. This television series is important to the history of conspiracy entertainment because it did more to keep the theme of distrust in high authority figures a central theme of 1990s pop culture more than any film, book, documentary, or television series. In 1998, in fact, its producers were able to accomplish a rarely heard-of feat in television history: releasing a successful theatrical film version of *The X-Files* while the program was still on the air. Even as the millennium approached, or perhaps exactly *because* of it, the fear of conspiracies sold like no other theme in mainstream entertainment.

The series originated from a rather surprising source. Television writer-producer Chris Carter, formerly a journalist for *Surfing* magazine and the writer of comedies like *B.R.A.T. Patrol, Meet the Munceys*, and *A Brand New Life*, had long been interested in writing something dark, intense, and suspenseful — a TV show that would scare audiences the way he had been scared as a kid watching *The Twilight Zone* and *Kolchak: The Night Stalker*. In its general structure, *The X-Files* most clearly resembles *Kolchak*, a show about an open-minded, yet cynical and inquisitive, reporter (Darren McGavin) stumbling onto supernatural manifestations that no one else wants to believe in. But on a deeper, thematic level, Carter had explained, he always admired the way Rod Serling was able to use the frightening and supernatural stories of *The Twilight Zone* to hold up a mirror to American society and comment on the most pressing — if not troubling — issues of the day.[6] Carter's take on the themes had an equally dogged pair of investigators looking for UFOs, mutant creatures, vampires, and werewolves, all the while operating in a culture of political corruption and governmental abuse of power.

The most obsessive fans of all supernatural-themed TV programs, however, will point out that *The X-Files* also had a 1985 forerunner called *Shadow Chasers*. Created by *V* writer-director Kenneth Johnson, the tongue-in-cheek mystery series involved an uptight, boorish anthropology professor (Trevor Eve) being forced by his department chair to investigate paranormal happenings while partnered with a free-wheeling, wisecracking tabloid reporter (Dennis Dugan). The professor was an unyielding skeptic, while the reporter had an open mind about all claims of the paranormal. *Shadow Chasers* aimed squarely for a light, comedic tone rather than dark, intense paranoia. Plus, the show always concluded with an ambiguous ending, suggesting that the mysteries may have had a rational explanation, while at the same time tossing in a hint that the supernatural might have had some part in the plot after all. Interestingly, Carter had also mentioned in several interviews that an early version of *The X-Files* concept toyed with this sort of ambiguous, double-interpretation format.

In *The X-Files*, the FBI has a special set of archives for unsolved cases that seem to have no logical, rational explanation, and may cross into the realm of the paranormal. The special X-Files division is an area where few agents want to work. One exception is Fox Mulder (David Duchovny). A brilliant, Oxford-trained psychologist whose specialty is serial killers and occult crimes, Mulder, derisively nicknamed "Spooky" by some colleagues, is also a headstrong maverick. Open-minded to what he calls "extreme possibilities," he is the one agent determined to work with the X-Files. Mulder's obsessive zeal is driven by a personal tragedy. He believes that his sister was abducted by aliens while they were children. The path to the truth behind UFOs and the abduction phenomenon, Mulder is convinced, lies within the X-Files. But not everyone within the government is happy with Mulder prying too deeply into the bizarre mysteries of this minor division of the FBI.

In the 1993 pilot episode, Mulder is ordered to carry out his investigations while partnered with special agent Dana Scully (Gillian Anderson). Originally trained as a physician, Scully is also a strict adherent to rigorous scientific investigative methods, and opposed to wild speculation about the existence of the supernatural. In the classic tradition of mismatched-partner cop and suspense thrillers, Mulder and Scully appear, at first glance, to be oil and water. Mulder, in what would become one of the show's major catchphrases, "wants to believe" when it comes to the paranormal. Scully is a skeptic and a driven debunker. Her assignment is to offer a down-to-earth scientific explanation for each of Mulder's hypotheses about alien abductions, hauntings, mutant creatures, and psychic phenomena. But the true motives for the government's need for skeptical Scully might just be a part of a bigger, hidden conspiratorial agenda. While Mulder believes that Scully truly does not know that she is being used by shadowy forces within the U.S. government, he is convinced that there is an extensive conspiracy to squash all evidence of the objective reality of paranormal manifestations, especially UFO contacts and alien abductions.

Through its nine-season run, *The X-Files* alternated its stories between stand-alone episodes and "mythology" stories. In the stand-alone episodes, Mulder and Scully investigated various crimes with an apparent touch of the paranormal. But none of these episodes was part of a larger, continuous story arc. Some of the most memorable stand-alone stories involved a mutant who killed people and ate their livers to stop his own aging, a man-sized fluke worm (spawned by Chernobyl radiation) that travels in the sewer lines, computers run by a malevolent artificial intelligence program, and a pyrochinetic assassin. Sometimes referred to by fans—*and* the show's creative staff—as the "monster of the week" episodes, these stand-alone stories wound up giving *The X-Files* a stronger connection to the *Kolchak* series that had made such an impression on a young Chris Carter.

But the most popular episodes, the stories that would catapult the program to pop-culture phenomenon status, were the recurring mysteries of UFO abductions and a vast, international conspiracy to hide them. In fact, it could be argued that the series-long UFO "mythology" storyline helped give *The X-Files* the sort of longevity *Kolchak* never enjoyed. Had *The X-Files* been a series of unconnected "monster of the week" programs, audiences would not have been able to completely suspend their disbelief for more than a season. Like Stephen King wrote of *Kolchak* in his 1981 nonfiction work on the horror genre *Danse Macabre*, someone stumbling onto a vampire or a ghost or a mutant once can be palatable for an audience. But to believe that the same man accidentally crosses paths with other-worldly creatures every single week is impossible. *Kolchak* quickly floundered in the ratings, never holding on to more than a tiny, die-hard, cult audience, and it was cancelled.

In the course of *The X-Files'* mythology arc, Mulder fought to uncover the truth behind the UFO phenomenon and figure out the reason for a worldwide network of shadowy military, espionage, and industry figures keeping it hidden. The show built one of the most fascinating relationships on television: Throughout this dogged, personal crusade, Scully would act as the rational counterpoint to Mulder's need to believe. A complex partnership between the two FBI agents developed, their oppositional points of view actually bringing out the best in each other. While Mulder's idealism and imagination helped Scully to think outside of conventions and to question authority, her rationalism helped ground Mulder and to question his own willingness to believe every whimsical conspiracy theory or monster sighting. As Mulder would tell Scully in the 1998 feature film *The X-Files: Fight the Future*, he could never really have made any headway with the vast UFO cover-up conspiracy without her. She had kept him from getting derailed and deceived because of his own blind faith.

One interesting footnote to the Mulder-Scully bond became a bone of contention for many fans: The producers' attempt to keep the two characters in a strictly platonic relationship, while at the same time maintaining a subtle undertone of sexual tension. As Chris Carter had decreed upon the creation of the pilot episode, Mulder and Scully should never become romantically involved because then the show would be forced to veer away from its mystery and conspiracy plots. In essence, he did not want to risk the show becoming a relationship melodrama. A number of shows where the male and female leads eventually acted on their attraction and "did it" had lost viewer interest in the aftermath. The most referenced example of this was the 1980s Bruce Willis-Cybill Shepherd ABC-TV comedy *Moonlighting*. As long as the unresolved sexual tension between the two main characters was allowed to smolder, the show was a ratings powerhouse. But once the Willis and Shepherd characters had sex, the mystique collapsed. Unfortunately for ABC, so did the show's ratings. So, although Carter's explanation does make sense from a genre perspective, a faction of fans often commented that sexual tension can only be realistically maintained for a very limited amount of time. If the lead characters never "do it," their relationship still changes irrevocably and they become less and less interesting for the audience. As *The X-Files'* most famous fan, Stephen King, said, after a while one begins to wonder just what is the matter with these two people. "Did aliens abduct Agent Mulder's libido?" King joked while discussing romantic TV relationships for the DVD commentary track of his own miniseries *Storm of the Century*.

Fight the Future did the most blatant teasing of the audience with the sexual undertone of the Mulder and Scully relationship. In one scene, two of them almost kiss, appearing unable to contain their feelings for each other any longer, but Scully is suddenly stung by an alien organism-infected bee. In season eight, once Carter and company knew that *The X-Files* was heading toward its end (and David Duchovny had left the show, only appearing is several cameo spots), Mulder and Scully finally became lovers and conceived a child.

In the mythology arc, Mulder and Scully would uncover a conspiracy by a worldwide cabal of financiers, scientists, and military-espionage operatives—calling themselves "The Syndicate"—that had been created to hide, in the words of Alvin Kurtzweil (Martin Landau) in the feature film, a "negotiated Armageddon." Very much in line with the Area 51 and back-engineered alien technology theories, these conspirators knew that UFOs were an advance wave in what would eventually turn into an invasion and colonization of the Earth. While the conspiracy turned a blind eye to the aliens abducting and experimenting on humans, they tried to get a-hold of as much extraterrestrial technology as possible in an attempt to find a defense against the invaders. All the while, the Syndicate had been working to determine the nature of a black, oil-like substance created by the aliens' bodies. It has powerful mind-altering properties and can put those affected by it under the aliens' control.

The X-Files becoming a cultural phenomenon is both obvious and, to a degree, surprising. In the TV history of official corruption and conspiracy theories, everything that had come before Mulder and Scully's adventures looks quaint and lightweight. *The X-Files* had often been one of TV's darkest, most paranoid, and pessimistic programs. Yet the series ran during a relatively peaceful, secure, and prosperous period of history. Spanning all of the Bill Clinton era, *The X-Files* had come along at a time when the Cold War was already in the past, the threat of nuclear confrontation seemed less and less likely, the economy had recovered from the recession that wrecked the George H.W. Bush presidency, and all of the country's recent military actions, from the invasion of Panama to the first Gulf War and the peace-keeping missions in the Balkans, were successes. The World Trade Center had been attacked by terrorists during the same year *The X-Files* premiered (1993); the perpetrators were caught and shown to be stunningly, almost comically inept. Homicidal Islamic fanatics turned up in a number of films and TV programs, but terrorism (despite the World Trade Center incident) was still a problem for the *rest* of the world. Yet, for *The X-Files* to strike such a nerve with audiences, there had to have been an undertone of anxiety, distrust, and even profound fear in the minds of most Americans.

"The world isn't safe at all," Carter often said about the sort of real world anxieties that inspired his show. "Good doesn't necessarily win. In fact, it wins a surprisingly paltry amount of time—and we often live in denial of that."[7]

According to Ted Edwards, author of *X-Files Confidential*, perhaps the greatest fears of the 1990s were really the fears of the unknown. Perhaps there were still threats that could one day become much more dangerous than anyone could imagine. While two superpowers were no longer on the brink of annihilating each other with stockpiles of nuclear weapons, how much more unstable could the world become in the near future? One Gulf War was handily won, but what about the next war? In the midst of disarmament and the destruction of some of the world's nuclear weapons, how could we be sure that a warhead wouldn't fall in the hands of a rogue dictator? And might the next gang of fanatical terrorists prove to be much more capable and deadly than the ones who blew a hole in the basement of the World Trade Center? "And Carter understands that the best way to scare people is to hit them where it already hurts," Edwards writes, "the very real fears—about crime, about money, technology, officialdom — that keeps them up at night."[8] Edwards quotes Karl Schaefer, the creator of *Strange Luck*, one of the paranormal-conspiratorial shows that cropped up in the wake of *The X-Files*:

> There are no clear-cut bad guys any more. The Soviet Union is gone, and it's a big mess. Things used to be pretty simple, and now it's a little bit like when the original [film] noir came along at the end of World

War II. Women were in the workplace, we were rebuilding Germany and Japan, and nobody knew exactly
what shape the world was going to take. Even though it was ostensibly a happy, peaceful time, there was
the undercurrent of darkness and fear beneath that. I think that's similar to the times we live in now.
There's not one big enemy to focus our energies on, so we're turning on each other.[9]

Another worry crystallizing in the minds of Americans in the early to mid–1990s was
the very technology that the *X-Files* producers credited with building the show's first-season
cult following. As producer J.P. Finn explained, "We arrived at the same time the Internet
took off. We were probably the first show to be adopted by the Internet, and that drove the
underground word of mouth."[10] Although the Internet created the forum for a diehard
group of *X-Files* fans (calling themselves "X-Philes") to coalesce into a community, online
technology itself and the ubiquity of computerized communication, tracking, and surveillance began worrying more and more people. Just like the end of the Cold War left so many
international strategists publicly scratching their heads and announcing that the 1990s would
be heading into uncharted territories on the international scene, communications specialists,
sociologists, computer engineers, and civil libertarians could likewise be heard saying that
the Internet was on its way to completely changing everything in our lives. From business
to education, communications, and social interaction, the entire world was about to be
reshaped into something radically new. Except none of these eminent thinkers and "experts"
could quite predict how. For many, one troubling fact was fast emerging; online technology
and the ubiquity of computers now had a record of absolutely everything every American
was doing every day, and all this information was available to those who had the right connections in the worlds of business and the government.

"Today the big thing," says Stuart Fischoff, professor of media psychology at California
State University, Los Angeles, "is that government, corporations, computer hackers and
everybody else can get access to your private life. Their reach is far more pervasive now
than it was back in the sixties and seventies when people who were good didn't really have
to worry. Today it doesn't matter if you're good or not. People want a big uncle to look out
for them, but they feel that all they're getting is Big Brother."[11] According to film scholar
Leo Braudy, "People are more apt to believe in conspiracies now because of the information
superhighway, because the technology seems so powerful and there are so many organizations out there that seem to be coercive and repressive. It's the all-powerful eye of God —
but it's some malevolent God who not only has his eye on the sparrow but wants to squash
the sparrow."[12]

More than ever before, there was also a growing sense of unease about a large, monolithic collusion between officialdom and ultra-powerful, immensely wealthy global corporations and a financial elite. After the demise of communism, many had hailed the end of
the Cold War as proof that capitalism was the only natural economic and political order.
For those on the far right wing of conservatism, the end of the Cold War was a sign of the
natural superiority of completely unfettered, unregulated corporate capitalism. Much of
the intrusiveness of the new interconnected, online computer technology was being developed in the name of free, rapid, global trade — so advertisers could monitor purchases to
better target ads to the individual, so companies could monitor people's online activities
to create lifestyle profiles, purchasing, and consumption profiles, so banks and credit companies could constantly rate individuals' worthiness for loans and credit. A fear began forming in the minds of many Americans, even a lot of conservatives, that Big Brother was not
just government, but that it wasn't even *primarily* government. Banks and credit companies
had gotten even better at monitoring the day-to-day lives of people than the old Soviet

Union ever could with its cadres of spies and snoops following their targets on the street and bugging telephones.

As Carter discussed on the *Fight the Future* DVD commentary track, the conspiracy theories of his show and film were mainly metaphors. Admitting a penchant towards a sort of open-minded skepticism when it comes to claims of the paranormal, Carter insisted that what audiences should take away from *The X-Files* is a symbolic statement about all the ways the lives of everyday Americans are being controlled by the unseen hands of powerful cultural institutions. *The X-Files* may not be suggesting that there literally are crashed alien space ships hidden away in secret bases, Carter argued, but that there is an immense concentration of wealth and power in the hands of a small elite that has an inordinate amount of influence. Most people are not even concerned enough with the issue to demand more transparency and accountability from the government, from corporations, from banks, and from all the lobbyists of all the big businesses and the big money that funds and controls so much of the political process. Rob Bowman, the director of *Fight the Future*, adds:

> Mulder represents the current seeker of the American dream. And he can only achieve it by finding the truth. There's something very classic and American about Mulder. If you strip away the obsession with the paranormal, he's a very ordinary person who is kicked about by a big, dark overseer that doesn't necessarily have the best interests of the people in mind. It's hard for him to handle. "I thought you were supposed to represent the people," he says to them. "Why do I find constant cover-up? I'm really confused by this." I identify with him completely, and I think the audience does as well.[13]

In fact, Leo Braudy thought that Mulder was so easy to identify with that he felt *The X-Files* was the most realistic show on television during that decade.[14]

As *The X-Files'* popularity soared and it became a mainstream hit and a barometer of the 1990s Zeitgeist, conspiracy theory entertainment proliferated in its wake on television and in films. The Fox network, the home of *The X-Files*, naturally wanted to repeat the paranoid magic in a number of new shows it quickly green-lit.

In the middle of *The X-Files'* second season, it was joined on Friday nights by *VR-5*, about a telephone company technician (Lori Singer) who tries to unravel the connection between her scientist father's (David McCallum) death and the revolutionary virtual reality technology he invented. The show, unfortunately for Fox, did not attract the same loyal fan-following. Although *VR-5* hinted at an intricate conspiracy storyline and had the same murky and film noirish look as *The X-Files,* it lacked the engaging characters that made Carter's show such a success. As the producers of *The X-Files* always claimed, the atmosphere, the mysteries, the monsters, and the conspiracy theories were only as strong as the characters who helped carry the plots. The chemistry between David Duchovny and Gillian Anderson was as enjoyable for audiences to watch as the way they investigated all the paranormal manifestations. The cold, dark, and unapproachable *VR-5*, all revolving around a main character who did most of her work alone, did not offer the same sort of connection between fans and the show. The 1995 season was *VR-5'*s first and last.

But Fox did not give up on their quest to replicate the success of *The X-Files*: The network next debuted *Strange Luck*, a show about Chance Harper (D.B. Sweeney), whose life is full of unexplainable twists. Harper was the sole survivor of an airline crash when he was only an infant. No relatives came forward to claim him and the authorities could never determine who his family was and how he wound up on the doomed airplane. Whatever stroke of luck (or otherworldly forces) saved him from the crash, continued to follow him throughout his life. In the course of the series, Harper would commit to using his "powers" to help others, all the while trying to find out who he was, how he got on the ill-fated flight as a baby, and why luck and fate go haywire around him. The likable, boyish-looking Sweeney made for an engaging main character and he was joined by a supporting cast of quirky friends. But audiences didn't care about Harper's mysterious past any more than they warmed up to the cyberspace conspiracies of *VR-5*. *Strange Luck* was also cancelled after a single season.

In the meantime, conspiracy theories spread across the broadcast spectrum on network television. In the fall of 1995, CBS premiered the dark, atmospheric supernatural series *American Gothic*. It starred the versatile Gary Cole as Lucas Buck, the sinister sheriff of a small Southern town. Played with oily, charming menace, Lucas, as suggested through a series of sly hints across a number of episodes, might have been possessed — or the very incarnation of the Devil himself. The show suggested that a long, complicated series of secrets would be revealed over time, including Lucas's true identity, his designs on the town, who his unholy allies might have been, and his intentions toward a son (Lucas Black) he sired by raping a local woman. It was also remarkable how well the series consistently infused an extremely dark, very menacing atmosphere in all its episodes. Each episode played out almost like a well-written mini-horror movie for television each week. But *American Gothic*, unfortunately, also lasted a single season.

NBC's *Dark Skies*, an interesting variation on the alien conspiracy theme, bowed in the fall of 1997. If the philosophical foundations of conspiracy entertainment are postmodernism, social constructionism and the concept of a manipulated false consciousness, as academics have claimed, *Dark Skies* was the most obvious manifestation of those concepts. Set in 1963, *Dark Skies* involved low-level Washington bureaucrat John Loengard (Eric Close) accidentally stumbling onto the government's UFO secrets. As he learns, the military had been observing alien spaceships since the Foo Fighter sightings of World War II. Then, in July of 1947, the Army was at last able to shoot one of the craft out of the sky above Mac Brazel's ranch outside Roswell. According to *Dark Skies* the UFO conspiracy was really behind most of the major cultural turning points of the latter half of the twentieth century. Nothing that we thought we knew about history was really true. For example, the Kennedy assassination was really carried out because JFK learned of the Roswell crash and was thinking of going public with the information. The Beatles' 1964 appearance on *The Ed Sullivan Show* is also about to be tampered with by aliens, trying to hijack the television signal and corrupting it with a mind-control wave that would brainwash all viewers. Loengard, going on the run from both government agents and alien-controlled human drones, also gets help from a pre–Doors Jim Morrison in his attempt to expose an alien organism-farming operation inside a chemical plant, learns that Francis Gary Powers' U2 spy plane was brought down by a UFO over Russia, and that the Gulf of Tonkien incident was instigated by aliens from an underwater base. *Dark Skies* had impressively high TV production values and tempered its paranoid tone with a very sly, tongue-in-cheek sense of humor — could *every* single major pop cultural and historical turning point since the early '60s really have an extraterrestrial double meaning? But quickly dwindling ratings after a strong premiere claimed this show as well. NBC did not renew the series.

The fledgling UPN and TNT networks also joined the conspiracy theory craze with *Nowhere Man* and *Lazarus Man*, respectively, premiering in 1995. *Nowhere Man*'s very chilling premise revolved around a photojournalist, Thomas Veil (Bruce Greenwood), whose identity was erased from every single computer, database, government office, and bank record shortly after he took some pictures of an execution in a war-torn Third World country. Week after week, Veil was on a quest to unravel who it was that stole his entire life, for what reason, and what the pictures had to do with it all. In a decade where the dark side of the Internet started manifesting itself in the new crime of identity theft, the sudden erasure of a man's identity carried a much more chilling verisimilitude than the more hyperbolic conspiracy theories about aliens. Moreover, as the series unfolded, Veil grew to believe that some sort of far-right-wing paramilitary organization might have been at the center of the execution he photographed and the conspiracy that erased his life. In the aftermath of the 1994 Oklahoma City bombing and the mainstream media's newly focused attention on right-wing extremists and domestic terror groups, the show deftly played off of more key headline-making fears Americans were feeling in the 1990s. *Nowhere Man*, in fact, earned roundly positive reviews from most critics and attracted a devoted cult audience.

In *Lazarus Man*, perennial TV leading man Robert Urich (*Vegas, Spenser: For Hire*) played a character who lost his memory after receiving a head wound in connection with his role in a conspiracy behind the Abraham Lincoln assassination. In the course of the show, the Urich character, calling himself "Lazarus," tried to piece together his past and uncover the part he played in the murder of the president. But, just like all of the conspiracy shows aside from *The X-Files*, *Lazarus Man* disappeared from the airwaves within a season.

But not all the other conspiracy series flamed out after a strong premiere. One of the more successful series came from Chris Carter himself. Premiering in 1996, *Millennium* combined the concepts of serial-killer profiling, conspiracies, and end-of-the-world prophecies. While the show lasted three seasons, it never quite got to *The X-Files'* level of iconic success. The problem could have been the show's heady brew of disparate concepts and an end result that made the series feel almost schizophrenically uneven.

Starring Lance Henriksen, a character actor with a strong science fiction fan following from his roles in *The Terminator* and *Aliens*, the show revolved around retired FBI profiler Frank Black, who used his skills as an occasional consultant to police organizations on particularly difficult serial slayings. Black is doing more and more work for the mysterious Millennium Group, an organization of former FBI agents that likewise consults on such cases. As the show progressed through its three seasons, Black started noticing a disturbing link between many of the serial murders, one that often appeared to be either occult-related or sometimes clearly paranormal. The Millennium Group begins hinting to Frank that the link might be nothing less than a harbinger of apocalyptic events to come by the year 2000.

During the series' run, there were several changes of the show's production teams. As conceived and helmed through its first season by Carter, *Millennium* was more along the line of a realistic serial-killer procedural thriller like *The Silence of the Lambs* than a supernatural horror story or science fiction. In fact, most critics remarked that the show was almost exactly like NBC's new series *Profiler*, also premiering in 1996 and focusing on a single mother (Ally Walker) trying to balance her home life with the demands of her grisly job as an FBI criminal profiler. By the second season of the show, Carter had stepped aside to devote more of his time to *The X-Files* and the development of *Fight the Future*. In his absence, former *X-Files* producers Glenn Morgan and James Wong took over *Millennium*, putting the accent more on the supernatural and a more explicit suggestion that all the serial slayings were being controlled by a single demonic entity. When Morgan and Wong opted to leave the show after that second season to pursue feature film projects, Carter asserted more control over *Millennium* again and toned the supernatural elements down. Perhaps because of these radical shifts, a consistent fan base could never build around the program.

Another successful conspiracy-themed TV show—running a season longer than *Millennium*—premiered on NBC in the fall of 1996. *The Pretender* was the story of Jarod (Michael T. Weiss), a genius who had been kidnapped from his family as an infant and raised in the hidden laboratories of a group called The Centre. The Centre had hoped to use Jarod's incredible intellect to aid its own shadowy, illegal agendas. Jarod, however, escapes and goes on a cross-country journey, attempting to find his birth parents and to figure out The Centre's secret plans. While on the run, Jarod also uses his preternaturally high IQ and skills in assuming different identities to help people in trouble.

While conspiracy theories became the holy grail that TV programmers were pursuing in the wake of *The X-Files*, theatrical films continued getting more and more paranoid. On the big screen, however, conspiracies seemed to thrive with much greater consistency than on television. Conspiracy theory films of the 1990s turned out to be some of the biggest blockbusters of the decade. These film projects attracted some of the biggest stars in the film industry.

Shortly after *The X-Files* established itself as a first-season cult favorite, the HBO cable channel produced its own alien spacecraft film. Starring Kyle McLachlan and Martin Sheen, *Roswell* was a faithful adaptation of Kevin D. Randall and Donald R. Schmitt's book *UFO Crash at Roswell.* Told in a series of flashbacks, the story focuses on an elderly Jesse Marcell (McLachlan) recounting his experiences at Roswell after years of silence. When he is approached by a mysterious figure calling himself "Townsend" (Sheen) interested in the rumors about a strange aircraft crash in 1947, Marcell remembers being pulled into the center of a recovery operation that collected strange, tinfoil-like scraps of metallic wreckage from Mac Brazel's ranch. Marcell's superiors refuse to give him any straight information about the wreckage and he is ever more frustrated by and slowly disillusioned with the way the military and the government he took an oath to serve is lying to the public. Once Marcell's story is revealed to Townsend, the stranger, who had implied that he might be able to help get the story out and convince the world of what happened, turns on Marcell and intimates that he might be a government agent himself. Townsend's supportive probings and questions suddenly appear to be a spy's gauging of how much Marcell knows. Eventually the shifty Townsend departs, glad to know that Marcell has no "smoking gun" evidence that could threaten the government's secrets.

Roswell is as creepy as the best *X-Files* episodes can be when they insinuate that not only are people in positions of power holding dark secrets, but the agencies and organizations Americans think they can trust would kill anyone when it comes to the protection of those secrets. Trust in power, in institutions, in ideals, is a passé notion, founded on lies and deceit that had duped generations of Americans into supporting a system that harbors an elite class of thieves, liars, and killers.

A film like *Roswell* is successful, ultimately, because it presents its grandiose conspiracy theories and accusations of far-reaching conspiracies with complete seriousness. As David Lavery, Angela Hague, and Marla Cartwright wrote in their study of the subtext of *The X-Files*, entertainment like this lingers in the proverbial neighborhood of postmodernism, yet the film is in no way self-conscious, self-mocking, or ironic. A good conspiracy film gets its power from its committed, indignant demand that people of power stay accountable and tell Americans the truth about everything that is going on.

This sort of earnestness could be seen in a pair of alien abduction-themed films that successfully premiered before *The X-Files*, suggesting that the 1990s were going to be very good to the alien conspiracy genre. One was a miniseries made for television, the other a theatrical feature. But the film on television was far more paranoid than the film made for the big screen.

The CBS miniseries *Intruders* (1992) endeavored to take a hard-hitting look at UFO abductions and made charges of government conspiracies and a cover-up of the phenomenon. In turn, Paramount's theatrical film *Fire in the Sky* focused on controversial real-life abduction claims by Arizona logger Travis Walton. Both films presented their tales very seriously, but they are problematic to UFO buffs. *Intruders*, for example, is based on the book by Budd Hopkins and involves a skeptical psychiatrist (Richard Crenna) becoming convinced that the abduction phenomenon is real. Yet the miniseries' second episode veers very quickly and very thoroughly away from Hopkins' source material. The TV movie inserts a conspiracy subplot into the driven Crenna's search. In a major second-episode plot point, the film charges that the government knows all about the abductions, but since there is nothing they can do to stop them, they choose to cover it up. In fact, the end of the film even weaves in a few strands from the crashed flying saucer and back-engineered UFO conspiracy theories. Once government agents realize that the dogged Crenna character could be of use to them in their effort to understand the aliens, they offer to reveal all of their secrets—including extraterrestrial technology hidden in top secret military installations—as long as he supports the efforts at secrecy and publicly denies the reality of UFOs. Crenna refuses to go along with the deception, even though the alternative is professional derision and public mockery. Since leading abduction researchers like Hopkins and David Jacobs have never endorsed any of these conspiracy theories, abduction buffs have criticized the film for tainting what could have been a compelling and accurate account of the research behind the phenomenon with cheap, predictable Hollywood conspiracy potboiler tricks.

Fire in the Sky, on the other hand, includes no conspiracies, yet in its own way it is just as flawed when it comes to the reenactment of the Travis Walton incident. This film stays fairly close to the series of events alleged in Walton's book, depicting a rowdy, reckless Walton (D.B. Sweeney) and his logging crew approaching a hovering UFO. After a beam of light knocks Walton unconscious, the rest of his crew, including his best friend Mike Rogers (Robert Patrick), panic and abandon him under the alien craft. As a result, Walton disappears for several days, bringing overwhelming international media attention down on their home town of Snowflake. Massive search efforts scouring the forest wilderness for any sign of the missing logger begin. Rogers and the rest of the crew face increasing hostility from their neighbors, some of whom accuse the men of killing Walton, while skeptics claim the group concocted a hoax to get out of a logging contract. Walton turns up several days later, naked, filthy, and disoriented inside a gas station in the middle of the night, unable to immediately recall what had happened to him. While the real Mike Rogers and his crew faced the same unpleasant dilemma in 1975, those who read the book were unsatisfied with the film's presentation of the time Walton spent inside the UFO. The film made the recollection of the encounter with the alien UFOnauts even more convincing than Walton did. As Roger Ebert opined in his review, the scenes inside the UFO were extremely satisfying to see because the inner recesses of the craft looked truly *alien*. This movie managed to present an alien spaceship that did not look like it was designed by Hollywood set decorators doing yet another variation of the shiny halls and bulkheads seen in *Star Trek* or *Star Wars*. In fact, the design of the ship made it look like the bowels of some enormous, otherworldly beast. The entire ship looked organic, dank, slimy and hellish. But Walton's description of the UFO *did* sound *Star Trek*–like and he wrote about lengthy discussions he had with the aliens. The film version of the abduction event included a brutal series of experiments done on Walton, with drills and needles getting inserted into his eyes, nose, and mouth, and a milky liquid nearly drowning him as it pours down his nostrils and throat. The aliens of the film behave the way the aliens do in the most convincing of real-life abduction reports. They appear to be little more than dispassionate researchers examining a lower form of animal life. The real Walton, however, claims to have met not only the small, gray, large-headed creatures, but also tall, handsome, blonde human aliens (who sound too much like the Space Brothers of the old Contactee movement). The Walton incident still has the UFO and abduction research community split. A number of staunch believers accuse Walton of being a charlatan and a fraud, while others say they believe his story. The film strikes some viewers as an effort to revise, correct, and make believable a hoax perpetrated by an unsophisticated liar who had used some of the most disreputable figures in UFO history and a lot of films and TV shows as inspirations.

A Part of Americana

By the middle of the decade the conspiracy theory juggernaut was rolling through theaters with greater force than ever before. Although alien-themed and fantastic conspiracies would keep dominating this form of entertainment, some films managed to strike an even more sensitive nerve by setting their conspiracies in the real and recognizable worlds of big business and government.

One of these films was Sandra Bullock's 1995 thriller *The Net*. Finding its paranoia in the brand new world of online technology, *The Net* warns about the sort of control and terror people could theoretically fall victim to when computers run every part of their lives. Angela Bennett (Bullock) becomes suspicious of a software company that is doing unprecedented business installing new security software in computer systems around the world in the wake of costly and crippling hacking and virus outbreaks. Subsequently she finds that the records of her existence have vanished from all computer databases. Afterward, assassins move in to try and kill a woman who now "no longer exists." *The Net* manages to frighten its audiences by reminding them how many times they are forced to keep updating their computers, to keep installing newer and newer security and antivirus programs to feel safe. What would happen, the film asks, in true conspiracy theory fashion, if all those hacker attacks and computer virus outbreaks were created deliberately by companies that then turn around and sell software to fix the problems? Moreover, *The Net* warns, what if all those programs are really hidden surveillance mechanisms that can wipe out the entire life of any person who starts asking too many questions?

Interestingly enough, *The Net*'s frightening scenario was never referenced by anyone during the 1999 Y2K computer hysteria. Just like in *The Net*, millions of computers around the world were updated with new programs (or replaced altogether), because many believed that a dire, apocalyptic threat was at hand. (The aftermath of the turn of the Millennium proved the entire event to be little more than unfounded paranoia.)

The summer film season of 1996 turned out to be a major multimillion-dollar-boon to conspiracy theory entertainment, as the very concept of conspiracy theories seemed to undergo a profound shift. Two of the top money-makers of that summer were *Independence Day* and *The Rock*. These films represented the most "establishment" of all Hollywood films, but they made charges of vast, dark conspiracy theories with a sort of flip, off-handed casualness.

Independence Day was essentially an old-fashioned space invader adventure story infused with a breakneck-paced plot, a lot of self-referential humor, the cheeky, likable charm of star Will Smith, and top-of-the-line special effects. But its most important feature was that it was essentially a pastiche, or what postmodern film theorists would claim is a deconstruction of genre conventions and a humorous revelation of how such conventions are unrealistic, random constructs. To the more jaundiced science fiction fans, the film was not so much "postmodern deconstruction" but a grand, noisy, anarchic monument to unoriginal, formulaic filmmaking. In essence, just about every scene, plot point, character, and theme seemed to have been lifted from other films. The opening, with enormous UFOs appearing over all the major cities of the world, could just as well have been a remake of *V.* Once the aliens prove to be hostile, cocky American fighter pilot Steven Hiller (Smith) is presented as little more than a reincarnation of Tom Cruise from *Top Gun.* A shell-shocked UFO abductee (Randy Quaid), captured aliens, and a secret base under Area 51 were all archetypes that had been presented by *The X-Files.* Even a dogfight between an alien attack craft and Hiller's jet fighter, careening through a tight, jagged canyon, looks like a reimagining of the end of *Star Wars.* Finally, in case the audience did not quite get that *Independence Day* was but a series of homages to other films, a computer aboard a commandeered alien fighter, used by Hiller and nerdy scientist David Levinson (Jeff Goldblum) to plant an electronic virus aboard the aliens' command ship, sounds exactly like HALL-9000 from *2001: A Space Odyssey.*

Independence Day, however, turned out to be the top money-earner of 1996, proving that conspiracy theories had become an essential part of mainstream entertainment and a central concept of modern Americana. In *Independence Day*, the idea of the grand government conspiracy had been reduced to the film's biggest joke. In one scene, the president of the United States (Bill Pullman), a ragtag remnant of his cabinet and a handful of refugees are aboard Air Force One, escaping the global Armageddon and helplessly watching one major city getting erased after another by the aliens' energy rays. The president wonders what chance we have when nothing on Earth has the power to stand up to the assault. A quick retort comes from Levinson's cranky old father (Judd Hirsch), who knows full well that the U.S. government can rely on the alien technology hidden away in Area 51. The old man, of course, is right. The government's biggest, most shocking, most far-reaching and vast conspiracy had become the stuff of everyday popular culture.

In the hyperkinnetic action film *The Rock*, Alcatraz Island has been taken over and a group of tourists imprisoned by renegade Special Forces operative General Francis X. Hummel (Ed Harris). Hummel is outraged that the families of secret "black ops" commandos who had died in the line of duty had never been given a full accounting and financial support promised by the government. He now demands full disclosure by the government and that the families of the dead soldiers be given the support they are due. To accent his point, the angry general and his men have set up missile-launching platforms on the island, outfitted with VX nerve gas and aimed at San Francisco. The only way the situation might be defused is by getting an assault team onto the island to take on and kill the renegades. Unfortunately, Hummel had been so thorough in securing "The Rock" that an invasion seems impossible. The one hope for success is one of the U.S. government's deepest and dirtiest secrets. For over thirty years, the government had kept John Mason (Sean Connery), a British spy, locked away in prison, his identity erased, his death reported to the English government. In 1963, Mason had managed to stumble onto some of the U.S. government's most embarrassing secrets, all of which he recorded on microfilm and kept hidden away. He was imprisoned on Alcatraz, but promptly escaped. Since his recapture, the U.S. has kept him in prison, in maximum security confinement. In 1996, though, since he is the only living person who could bypass Hummel's defenses on Alcatraz, Mason is offered a deal: If he helps get a Navy SEAL assault force onto Alcatraz island, the government will release him. Now, teamed with the SEALs and a nebbishy chemist (Nicolas Cage), Mason embarks on his mission, only vaguely suspecting that the same people who kept him locked away for over three decades will never let him leave Alcatraz alive. And, sure enough, the director of the FBI (John Spencer) already has a plan to make sure that Mason gets killed before the mission is over. Although much of the plot could have been wrapped up in the very straight, very serious tones of an intense action thriller, the film is only thrust into the area of burlesque when the nature of the secrets Mason has stolen is revealed. Mason, essentially, found confirmation of the most iconic conspiracy theories: His microfilm reveals who *really* killed John F. Kennedy (and it's *not* Lee Harvey Oswald, but the film never names the actual killer) and what happened to the aliens that landed in Roswell.

Also released in the summer of 1996, the Keanu Reeves action thriller *Chain Reaction* was helmed by Andrew Davis in his favorite location, the streets of Chicago. While tuning his guitar in the laboratory of scientist friend Dr. Alistair Barkley (Nicholas Rudall), machinist Eddie Kasalivich (Reeves) accidentally stumbles onto the missing piece of the puzzle to creating cold fusion. This creates an explosion that wipes out several city blocks—but Eddie is able to outrun it on his motorcycle. He now finds himself on the run from sinister suit-and sunglass-wearing assassins. Shadowy government and business interests, it seems, have major stakes in keeping the source of clean, inexpensive energy hidden. The stakes, apparently, are high enough that they are willing to kill anyone who might try and make the technology public knowledge, including the kindly, idealistic Dr. Barkley.

The final revelation of who the conspirators are and why they are trying to keep cold fusion a secret is quite interesting and thought-provoking. The major problem of *Chain Reaction* is that the truth behind the conspiracy takes up less than about five minutes of the film's running time just before the end credits roll. Once Eddie finds himself face to face with the menacing Paul Shannon (Morgan Freeman), a government operative trying to keep the lid on the cold fusion discovery, the agent explains that the sudden release of this revolutionary new knowledge could topple an already precarious world order. If the need for oil was suddenly eliminated overnight and all the oil companies and their attendant industries went out of business, Shannon explains, global economic panic, mass unemployment, catastrophic depressions, and worldwide chaos, disorder, and wars would follow. The world in its present state, Shannon claims, could not survive radical, overnight upheaval. This argument, essentially, is at the crux of all the hidden and suppressed technology conspiracy theories. Although there are plenty of economists who would disagree with this dire scenario, the examination of the issue could have made for an interesting and engaging film. The fact that the script at least presents some of the conspiratorial viewpoint seems to suggest that the filmmakers might have given the issue some thought. Unfortunately, *Chain Reaction* appears to have been cast in the mold of too many 1990s summer blockbusters; its primary agenda was visual spectacle and not cerebral debate and analysis. Although competently staged and executed, the film is little more than a series of chases, shootouts, fights, and last-moment escapes.

But as the end of the decade was approaching, the overabundance of conspiracy theories would be dramatized by fewer and fewer dark, paranoid thrillers and more light-hearted capers, comedies, and parodies pointing out how predictable and formulaic conspiracy theory films really were. One of the biggest hits of 1997 was the UFO conspiracy farce *Men in Black*, once again starring Will Smith — anointing him as the box office king of the Fourth of July movie weekend and inspiring him to boast that the holiday was now known in Hollywood as the "Big Willie Weekend." The film did not put the conspiracy theorists at the center of the narrative, but the conspirators themselves. It was the first time the sinister topic of the Men in Black phenomenon was examined in a major film. (*The X-Files* had an MIB-oriented episode in its second season, one of the show's rare early self-parody episodes, titled "Jose Chung's from Outer Space.")

The real themes of the Will Smith film were multiculturalism, integration, and the problematic issues around immigration. The Men in Black of the film are hi-tech versions of Immigration and Naturalization agents, working for a secret organization that monitors and regulates extraterrestrial settlement on Earth. Aliens who come to Earth are usually granted asylum, as long as they are not hostile and don't bring any interstellar conflicts along that might threaten the world. The immigrant aliens, in turn, are given human disguises to wear and allowed to blend in with the rest of humanity. One of the film's best sight gags involves a large viewer screen that monitors the Earth's most famous alien immigrants. Among them are Senator Newt Gingrich, motivational speaker Anthony Robins, designer Isaac Mizrahi, and Sylvester Stallone. Lampooning both conspiracy theorists and the skeptical debunkers of the UFO phenomenon, one of the film's ongoing jokes dealt with the Men in Black constantly needing to cover up their activities and using patently absurd-sounding explanations like weather balloons, swamp gas, and misidentified lights from star formations as the cover stories for violent and destructive encounters with some of the aliens and extraterrestrial spacecraft.

Keeping the comedy much more subtle and matched with very intense, dark paranoia and brutal violence, Mel Gibson's *Conspiracy Theory* distills much of the conspiracy theory formula into the tale of the lowliest outsider stumbling onto the biggest secrets through sheer luck and his own dogged determination to find "the truth." Jerry Fletcher (Gibson) is a slightly unbalanced New York City cab driver obsessed with conspiracy theories and harboring a crush on Alice Sutton (Julia Roberts). Outside of his job, he is a withdrawn recluse with no interests other than his obsessive-compulsive fixation on looking for conspiratorial connections between all of the world's events—from the biggest headlines and major public figures to seemingly random and mundane everyday occurrences. One of Jerry's theories actually proves true and he is suddenly targeted for assassination by the usual cadre of men in dark suits who rappel seemingly out of the sky in the middle of crowded city streets, and icy, sociopathic government scientists ready to torture him to death if necessary. As Jerry races to both escape and fight a conspiracy out to assassinate the president, getting Alice embroiled in the plot along the way, he not only unravels the details of who the conspirators are and how they're planning to pull off their nefarious plot, but he learns the details of his own forgotten past. Again, just like in the fantasy world of the most driven conspiracy theorist, Jerry proves to be not an unbalanced outsider who can't function in society, but a heroic victim of the government's mind control experiments.

While proving successful at the box office — aided in main part by Gibson and Roberts' star power and chemistry —*Conspiracy Theory* received an indifferent reception from most critics. But most of that criticism seemed to miss the movie's bigger social and entertainment context. For the most part, critics complained about the film's humor and by-the-numbers action sequences. While they might have had a point about the action, most of which was expensive and well-choreographed but perfunctory, the humor provided the sort of well-honed edge that could serve to critique the very culture and concepts of conspiracism it was enacting so faithfully. Much like *Independence Day, Conspiracy Theory* was wondering about how much of the secret, far-reaching, evil plots one could really believe in at a time when suspicion, paranoia and distrust were all a fabric of mainstream Americana. The film's best joke is Jerry ruminating on the Oliver Stone-George Bush connection. When Alice is puzzled by this, Jerry explains that far from being a crusader for the truth, Stone must be a part of the grand conspiracy himself, otherwise "the system" would not allow him to get away with making the films he has been making. Indeed, the purest retort one could raise to the various JFK assassination theories— and most big business and government conspiracies— is to point out that the evil cabal controlling everything, including the mass media, would have just killed or derailed the careers of every Oliver Stone and every author, documentary filmmaker, and publisher before conspiracy theories turned into a multibillion dollar industry.

A more straight-faced thriller, 1998's *Enemy of the State* once again sounded alarms about the dark side of the rapidly advancing state of Internet technology and the sort of Orwellian misuse it can be put to by unscrupulous government agencies. Once again starring Will Smith, and joined by Gene Hackman in a role that could just as well have been a reprise of his Harry Caul from *The Conversation, Enemy of the State* concerned itself with the National Security Agency developing ultra-advanced cyberspace and surveillance technologies that allows them to monitor every American's whereabouts, phone calls, computer records, etc. When Smith's character, an unsuspecting labor lawyer, is slipped a computer disc with damaging evidence against the NSA by a whistleblower targeted for assassination, Smith, too, finds his entire life wrecked by phony computer data incriminating him in everything from racketeering to extramarital affairs. Once Smith's life is turned upside down and he has lost everything, teams of black-clad assassins move in and try to kill him.

But the most interesting dramatization of the *spirit* of 1990s conspiracy theories came from director Peter Weir and writer Andrew Nicol in their 1998 film, *The Truman Show.* Starring Jim Carrey in one of his first subdued, less comedic roles, the film's outlandish plot is a parable for a modern America where even the most average man's seemingly mundane life is constantly manipulated by unimaginably big, bureaucratic forces forever outside of his control and comprehension. *The Truman Show* presents the hyperbolic life of Truman Burbank (Carrey), the first person to have been adopted at birth by a television production company. Since infancy, every moment of Truman's life has been recorded by television cameras and broadcast to the world as *The Truman Show.* It quickly became the most successful TV show in history; its producers were soon wealthy enough to build an entire town where they continuously tape their show, all encased in a dome so gigantic it can be easily seen from space. Inside this dome, the show's producer, the omnipotent Cristoff (Ed Harris), controls and manipulates everything in Truman's life, all for the sake of "real" and captivating television drama. From the sun and the moon in the sky, the tides of a fake ocean, the rain, the wind and the temperatures, everything is a simulation of a real world. In turn, from Truman's parents to his friends, even his wife, all the people he interacts with are actors. But after a mishap with one of the dome's ceiling lights, it slowly starts to dawn on Truman that everything he has been brought up to take for granted as being real has been deceitfully programmed into him for someone else's trivial amusement.

The Truman Show is a fascinating film because it proves to be more eerily prophetic with each passing year. Usually film critics and analysts praise it for its prescience about reality television (especially the advent of such surveillance-oriented programs as *Big Brother*) and academics are excited by its dramatization of the tenets of postmodernism and social constructionism. (Writer Andrew Nicol conceived the film and wrote his first draft of the script in the early 1990s, nearly a decade before shows like *Survivor, Big Brother*, and their plethora of imitators.) But at its core, putting Truman in the center of the story, the film is speaking about the same fears that fuel conspiracism. The real fear of the conspiracy theorist is the fear that he is but a puppet of forces beyond his comprehension. The protagonist one identifies with in *The Truman Show* has been deprived of his free will. Nothing that Truman Burbank experiences, from friendship to love, the joys and the frustrations of his life, all his emotions essentially, is really his own. He is but a lab rat who responds to someone else's stimuli every moment of his life. Conspiracy theories, taken to their extreme, ultimately imply this. No part of the reality we think we experience, conspiracy theorists argue, is truly "real." Everything we know, everything we've read, all the values we've been brought up with are lies, are the stimuli fed into a lab rat by a remote, all-powerful, all-knowing cabal.

Taking this postmodern tenet of *The Truman Show* one step further, the writing and directing team of brothers Larry and Andy Wachowski crafted their seminal 1990s action-science fiction epic *The Matrix* into an even more frightening and literal dramatization of the conspiratorial mindset. In *The Matrix*, the control of the individual is taking place at the most basic cellular level inside the brain. People are batteries in a giant global network of supercomputers, their bodies creating the energy the machines need to exist. In turn, humans are fed dreams and fantasies as their minds are wired into the system.

Just like *The Truman Show, The Matrix* has gotten some of the most fervent academic analysis of all popular films released in the last two decades. Shortly after its release, and then upon the release of its two sequels, major commercial publishing houses devoted considerable money and marketing resources to publishing the sort of dissection of the films usually to be found in academic books and scholarly journals. *The Matrix*, it seemed, inspired the sort of philosophical reflection in the mainstream moviegoer that few Hollywood films had. And many of its analysts came from backgrounds as diverse as postmodernist and social constructionist studies, psychological analysis, political science, and religious studies. Depending on the intellectual school of thought, it appeared as if everyone could see the concerns of their own discipline and dogma reflected in *The Matrix*. The Wachowskis, it seemed, had created the most perfect open text of a film. *The Matrix* appeared to be the biggest cinematic Rorschach test ever made. Or, perhaps, the film put its finger on the one universal concern everyone in the modern world has: the concern over deception by hidden, exploitive forces beyond our control.

Like all conspiracy theorists, the protagonist of *The Matrix* seems to instinctively know that there is something wrong with the world. Rank-and-file computer programmer Thomas Anderson (Keanu Reeves) feels like there is a much more complex and dangerous world just around the proverbial corner. He feels like the life he is leading is pointless, and that someone might be actively trying to keep him from finding out what the problem is. Caught in a stultifying state of ennui, he believes that the way out is being hidden from him by a force of some repressive, conspiratorial evil. The only way he can feel a measure of power is by living the secret life of a clandestine hacker, in effect trying to break through barriers and defy all rules that seem to have been erected for no other reason but to control and limit individuals. Then, as any conspiracy theorist can only dream, Anderson gets sudden confirmation that everything he has suspected and believed about a grand, exploitive lie manipulating the world is true — and *then* some!

Anderson is contacted by a pair called Morpheus (Laurence Fishburne) and Trinity (Carrie-Anne Moss) who claim that the world he thinks he lives in is nothing but an illusion. In the early twenty-first century, the duo explain, a network of artificial intelligence computers called the Matrix took over the world, enslaving mankind. In a last-ditch effort, the besieged humans launched an all-out nuclear attack on the computers, but it was ultimately useless. The resulting thick cloud cover of the ensuing nuclear winter, however, blocked the sun from the Matrix's solar power cells. But the computers and their robotic armies retaliated by capturing most of the remaining humans and plugging them into energy pods, using the heat and energy generated by their bodies to provide power for the Matrix. Future generations of humans were then bred to be new bio cells for the machines, growing up inside the pods. While existing as living batteries, however, all humans plugged into the Matrix were implanted with a virtual reality-like set of endless dreams of a world that looks roughly like the year 1999. No human inside this Matrix has any memory of the war against the machines or suspects that the life they are living is an artificially constructed dream. However, as is the case with Anderson, there are a few exceptions.

Morpheus and Trinity explain to Anderson — now calling him by his hacker "handle," Neo — that a small, ragtag band of war survivors dedicated itself to breaking as many of the humans out of the Matrix as they could. Morpheus and Trinity had, at one point, been inside the bio-cell pods themselves. While most people inside the Matrix never question its reality, there are always a few, like Neo before his liberation, who have an instinctive feeling that the world they are told is the real and natural way of existence is somehow all an exploitive sham. But, it turns out, Neo's doubts about reality were so strong as to mark him as the prophesized "The One," a messianic figure destined to become the ultimate agent of salvation. Neo takes his first step into a new world, a *real* world, by accepting from Morpheus an awakening drug that breaks the Matrix's hold on him and rouses him from his bio-cell pod. While the world Neo wakes up to is a post-apocalyptic wasteland, he and his fellow rebels can reenter the Matrix and try to break as many others out of its web of implanted illusions as possible, to build an army of self-aware humans that will fight the machine overlords.

The blockbuster success of *The Matrix*, and all the attendant books and merchandise devoted to ruminations on the nature of reality, was remarkable because it helped put the accent yet again on the issue of why is it that in the late twentieth century so many Americans are so captivated by these questions of truth and reality. Certainly, *The Matrix* is remarkably multi-layered and it touches upon a wide plethora of turn-of-the-millennium anxieties, not just conspiracism. The rapidly evolving state of technology is certainly a part of *The Matrix*'s horror story: The dark side of intelligent machines and the development of artificial intelligence is the source of humanity's enslavement. Mankind's downfall, we are told by Morpheus' tutorial after Neo has taken the red pill, is brought about by an over-reliance on technology, on intelligent machines deciding that humans are but a superfluous contaminant on the face of the Earth, and the total destruction wreaked by nuclear weapons. But, then again, these are the same fears that have inspired science fiction for decades. But the very specific terror in *The Matrix* is deception. These machines enslave without their victims knowing that they have been enslaved. They make enslavement seem normal and the natural order of things. Much like the television- and advertising-induced blindness by control-messages embedded all around the characters of John Carpenter's *They Live*, coercion and control are happening in every aspect of every human being's life, yet people cannot recognize the bars of their jail cells or the faces of their jailers. As Morpheus tells Neo, the Matrix is there "when you watch TV. It is there when you go to work. It is there when you go to church. It is there when you pay your taxes." *The Matrix* warns that an ever more complex and controlling modern society is also complex enough to be run by a manipulative, exploitive elite who do not care about the welfare, safety, rights, and liberties of the individual. But these were the same warnings of *The X-Files'* Fox Mulder, and these are still the warnings of every paranoid, cynical conspiracy theorist.

The Matrix was seen by most audiences as such a thoughtful, knowing, hip, and edgy piece of science fiction that it almost threatened to overshadow the other major, iconic science fiction epic of the summer of 1999. Two months after *The Matrix* came out, the first in George Lucas' second *Star Wars* trilogy, *The Phantom Menace*, premiered after nearly six months of overpowering — and perhaps unprecedented — media hype. Yet after *The Matrix*, *Star Wars* suddenly felt a step behind. *Star Wars* was your father's science fiction. It felt quaint and somehow irrelevant after *The Matrix* appeared to speak so directly to the most amorphous, most disquieting anxieties of the times. As media studies professor and film analyst Read Mercer Schuchardt writes, *The Matrix* might be nothing less than "a new testament for a new millennium, a religious parable of the second coming of mankind's messiah in an age that needs salvation as desperately as any ever has."[15] But as conspiratorial entertainment would continue into the second millennium at full speed, eventually even the fantasy innocence and escapism of *Star Wars* would turn into something suspicious, cynical, and conspiratorial with the arrival of the second and third entries into that film franchise.

CHAPTER 8

Retro and False-Flag Conspiracies
Conspiracy Theories of the 2000s

The 2000s, culturally, began on the morning of September 11, 2001. Ultimately, the first decade of the 2000s offered the most fascinating glimpse of the relationship between mainstream American sensibilities and conspiracism ever. The terrorist attacks on New York and Washington, D.C. at first appeared to have killed the culture of conspiracy for most Americans. Cynicism and irony in the aftermath of 9/11 were no longer appropriate. But by the middle of the decade, all that would change.

The opening of the new millennium had already seen somewhat of a dearth in original, fresh conspiracy theorizing, as far as the cultural mainstream was concerned. The Internet was certainly full of thousands of webpages and chat lines committed to endless pontifications about hidden cabals controlling all of history and discussions of how daily world events constantly betrayed clues about "something much bigger" going on. But as far as popular culture was concerned, no new theory was catching on. Roswell, UFOs, Area 51 and alien abductions appeared to have been beaten to death by *The X-Files*, documentaries, books, cartoons, made-for-TV movies, and even a "tween" soap opera (the UPN network's *Roswell* show). Furthermore, the fact that the turn of the millennium had come and gone with no major world-altering events betrayed a sign of conspiracy fatigue in American audiences. Even the supposedly catastrophic Y2K computer glitch that so many alarmists claimed would send the world back to the Stone Age had proven a bust. The world was running along on its mundane course like always. The most dramatic news stories of 2000 came near the end of the year and they involved the bizarre spectacle of the Florida ballot recounts in the presidential election. Days, then weeks dragged on and no one could tell whether George W. Bush or Al Gore was the new president of the United States. "Hanging chads" and "dimpled chads" became the newest cultural catchphrases, not "The New World Order" and not "conspiracy."

After the morning of September 11, 2001, however, conspiracy theorizing not only looked to be dated and unoriginal, but suddenly felt uncomfortable. To some it felt outright unpatriotic. In the collective consciousness, the attacks on New York and Washington were attacks on American culture and values. The terrorists had destroyed symbols of American business and enterprise when they brought down the Twin Towers. They seemed to strike at and damage American power and military strength when they blew a hole in the Pentagon. Americans responded by being more conspicuous in their display of patriotism than perhaps ever before in history. Flags were displayed on cars, windows, and streets, and there appeared to be no type of clothing in any store that could not be bought in a stars and stripes version.

Moreover, the newest cultural icons were the "insiders." After the deaths of the policemen and the firefighters in the World Trade Center and the government workers in the Pentagon, unquestioning, dutiful public servants had become the new American heroes. After the invasion of Afghanistan to hunt down Osama bin Laden and topple al-Qaeda's Taliban supporters, special operations soldiers like the Navy SEALS and the Army's Green Berets joined the firemen and the police officers as the country's most admired figures. America applauded the sacrifice of men and women who left lives and families behind to join the military and do their part to fight the war on terror. They mourned a patriot like football player Pat Tillman, who left behind a multimillion dollar professional football career and a beautiful young wife to fight and eventually die in Afghanistan. They anointed Army Private Jessica Lynch as the newest "America's Sweetheart" when she was rescued from the clutches of the Iraqi Army by a Green Beret assault force. And Americans rallied around their leaders and celebrated them like politicians hadn't been celebrated in decades. New York mayor Rudolph Giuliani, who had kept his cool so well during the September 11 attacks, was christened "America's Mayor." President George W. Bush's support and approval ratings shot to historic highs.

Conspiracy theory entertainment did not fit into this new cultural landscape. Conspiracy theorists had, since the 1960s, pointed their accusations of villainy at the leaders of the country. They had derided and feared public servants, the agents and enforcers of the "system," as strong-arm villains of the evil masterminds who enslaved and exploited Americans from within the corridors of power. The attacks of 9/11 seemed to shatter this conspiratorial template. Evil, this attack from al-Qaeda seemed to prove, really *was* coming from the outside. The threats to Americans' lives and liberties were not men in dark suits flying black helicopters and communing with aliens in Area 51. The very real threats were foreign fanatics who wanted to remake the world in some twisted, Stone Age vision of religious fundamentalism.

X-Files writer-producer Frank Spotnitz often explained that he believed the show owed its demise to September 11. He would look at the *New York Times Magazine* two weeks after the attacks and see a list called "Things that are in and out after 9/11"; *The X-Files* was now on the "out" list. This, unfortunately for Spotnitz and Chris Carter, was just as the show seemed to find its footing once more after a period of eroding ratings. In the wake of David Duchovny's gradual withdrawal from the series, *The X-Files* had seen its ratings steadily declining, only to show a rebound in its 2000–01 season. But *The X-Files'* new direction with new star Robert Patrick still involved its trademark tone of suspicion, dread, and mistrust of officialdom and government abuse of power. When the flags appeared all over the country post–9/11, no one wanted to see the U.S. government as villains and conspirators. The byproduct of September 11 was a newly simplified worldview. For the first time in a long time, Americans had a clear, uncomplicated view of who the villains and who the heroes were. The enemy was the outsider, Osama bin Laden and his al-Qaeda fanatics, and the heroes were America's leaders and soldiers. "In the months and years since then," Spotnitz said, "I've come to believe that was a big part of what happened in season nine. Things in *The X-Files* didn't feel fun any more in that post–9/11 atmosphere."[1]

Within a few years, of course, all this would change. Super-patriotism went into decline as America found itself fighting two wars and having very serious second thoughts about at least one of them. In the meantime, conspiracy theorizing changed in a profound way. It would shift to a new focus on ancient cabals and generations-old secret societies that were above the political concerns of early 2000s America. The villains of the new conspiracy movement were alleged to have been powerful enough to manipulate our perceptions of reality itself for much of history. The conspiracism of the new millennium had entered the true age of postmodernism.

The Codes

What would shape up to be a true, two-sided battle of conspiracy theorizing in mainstream popular culture found its most successful voice in the 2000 novel *Angels and Demons*. Written by Dan Brown, a former musician and author of one nominally successful previous thriller, *Digital Fortress* (1998), *Angels and Demons* could be seen as a secular answer to the Biblical and spiritual conspiracy theory movement fictionalized by Tim LaHaye and Jerry B. Jenkins in the mid–1990s. Whereas Jenkins and LaHaye's *Left Behind* books told of a conspiracy to destroy the Christian faith and usher in the age of the Antichrist, Brown wrote about the Catholic Church's history of often brutal suppression of all challenges to its political and social power.

Angels and Demons is thick with nefarious plots set in the distant past as well as plots in present-day Rome. Brown couches his fictional plot of a phony attack on the Vatican in a history of the Catholic Church's very real battles against enlightenment science and rationality. The story has Harvard "symbologist" Robert Langdon called in to try and find a hidden meaning behind the word "Illuminati" branded onto the dead body of physicist Leonardo Vetra of the Swiss CERN research laboratories. Before Langdon can get any sort of a lead, the murderer's much larger scheme appears to be announced to the Vatican. Aside from killing Vetra, the perpetrator stole from CERN a canister of antimatter, a single gram of which has the destructive power of the atom bomb dropped on Hiroshima. What the killer intends to blow up is all of Vatican City. But it just happens that Vatican City is crowded by thousands of visitors and world media as the church is in the midst of electing a new pope. Unbeknownst to anyone outside the Vatican, a group of cardinals on the short list for the papacy has also been kidnapped. According to a statement by Vetra's killer, his goal is the destruction of the entire Catholic Church. The killer also claims to be a member of the Illuminati and he is committed to exacting vengeance on the Church for its historic persecution of the secret organization's rationalist thinkers. Frantically racing to uncover hidden clues and codes in sculptures, ancient manuscripts, and the very architecture of Rome itself, Langdon and Vetra's adopted daughter, Vittoria, try to find hints to the Illuminati's secret hiding places and the location of the antimatter.

The most interesting aspect of *Angels and Demons* is the fact that it can almost be read as an anti-conspiracy thriller, if anything. The story revolves around the murder of Vetra and several cardinals, but its climactic plot twist reveals that the Illuminati have not, in fact, resurfaced in twenty-first century Rome. The attempt to blow up the Vatican is also a sham, perpetrated by one Carlo Ventresca, the late pope's "camerlango" (personal assistant). Ventresca, it is revealed, is a traditionalist zealot, having been dismayed that the pope had gone too far in liberalizing the Church, especially reaching out to the scientific community and looking for a compatible link between faith and reason. Not only did Ventresca murder the pope in retaliation, but devised a scheme where the world would believe that the church, that all of Christianity itself, was under attack by a homicidal secret society of atheistic fanatics. The plot to blow up the Vatican, according to Ventresca's calculation, would also be averted in the last moment when he would appear to find the antimatter canister, flee in a helicopter, and save all of Vatican City. The heroism of the Church and a man of faith would appear to triumph over the evil and destructiveness of science. In turn, Ventresca would count on the papal conclave immediately electing him the new pope. The new pope would then go about undoing all his predecessor's compromises to science and rationalism.

The most interesting aspect of the plot is the way it tantalizes its audiences with the idea that so many of the world's most visible cultural artifacts hide clues to conspiracies. While some of them lie between the lines of texts of ancient manuscripts, most are hidden in plain sight in paintings, sculptures, and architecture, ready to reveal a hidden history if one is clever enough to decipher the hidden meanings and metaphors. The conspiracies of *Angels and Demons* are something like a classical world's version of *The Matrix*; the visible world of Rome is really but a façade, for just beneath the statues and art works lies a secret battle between the forces of religion and the forces of enlightenment rationalism. This ancient battle shaped the modern world, yet few people alive today can truly appreciate this.

But in the conspiratorial view of Brown's thriller, the villains are the traditionalists of the Catholic Church. They fight to suppress scientific reason, technological progress and knowledge of the natural world in order to maintain their hold on social and political influence. But this is just a continuation of what a powerful Church has always done, *Angels and Demons* accuses. Ventresca's plot to blame the Illuminati for the attempt to destroy the Vatican might have been entirely fraudulent, but at one point the church did persecute and attempt to wipe out the very real Illuminati. The church zealously plotted and conspired to root out and destroy all who attempted to use empirical scientific methods to challenge Christian dogma. A challenge of church dogmas, after all, led to a challenge of the church's political authority and the tight rein it held on European governments. In turn, the book claims, rationalists had long attempted to challenge church authority, in spirit at the very least. Architects and artists would plant hidden, subversive codes in their work; they would paint religious pictures, carve statues of Biblical figures, and build monuments to the church, yet imbed symbols and double meanings in all this work, espousing scientific tenets, formulae, and anti-religious statements.

Although *Angels and Demons* sold well, it was not the book to catapult Brown to the A-list, household-name status of celebrity author. But he became one of the most successful and influential authors of all time with the 2003 sequel *The Da Vinci Code*.

Repeating much of the plot structure of *Angels and Demons*, *The Da Vinci Code* has Robert Langdon thrust into yet another mystery when Jacques Saunière, the curator of Paris' Louvre museum, is found murdered, his body posed in an imitation of Leonardo's Vetruvian Man, with code symbols painted in blood on his naked body. This time Langdon teams up with the dead man's estranged granddaughter, the Paris police department's cryptography specialist, Sophie Neveu. Just as in *Angels and Demons*, the plot turns into a frantic race against the clock, this time with Langdon and Sophie having to elude both the police — who believe Langdon is Saunière's murderer — and a killer named Silas, a fanatic in the employ of the rogue cardinal Aringarosa of the Catholic Church's ultra-conservative Opus Dei order.

What the pair discover is that Saunière was a member of the Priory of Sion secret society, a centuries-old organization tasked with keeping secret the true nature of the fabled Holy Grail. Saunière and his group were hiding proof that Jesus and Mary Magdalene had been husband and wife and that Mary was pregnant at the time of the crucifixion. Mary's womb, according to the Priory, was metaphorically referred to as the "chalice" and the "grail cup" that carried Jesus' blood line. After the crucifixion, Mary fled Jerusalem and resettled in Gaul. There she gave birth to Jesus' daughter Sarah, whose descendants would form the Merovingian royal dynasty. Sophie's family was a part of the bloodline, making her a direct descendant of Jesus. This is all part of an alternate theory of the history of Christianity that had already been presented by other scholars, something Langdon is familiar with. He and Sophie discover that Saunière was killed by forces that want to get their hands on the actual, irrefutable proof of the truth behind the theories. Langdon and Sophie figure out that Silas and Aringarosa want the evidence to be able to destroy it. However, in the book's final plot twist, Langdon and Sophie realize that Langdon's mentor, Sir Leigh Teabing, one of the world's foremost Grail experts, has been manipulating Silas, ordering him to kill Saunière and to track down the Grail evidence. While Silas and Aringarosa want to forever destroy this evidence, Teabing wants to reveal the secrets to the world and damage the Catholic Church.

The runaway success of *The Da Vinci Code* could be attributed to various cultural trends in the early 2000s. Like *Angels and Demons*, it revolved around intricate, layered conspiracies that were safe for mainstream consumption in the post September 11 world. Brown was lucky that he chose to base *Angels and Demons* in the world of ancient secret-society conspiracy theories and the political machinations of the Vatican rather than in a world of corrupt American government operatives. Both books have the requisite anti-authoritarianism of most conspiracy theories, condemning fanatical, conservative religiosity, yet the stories are also put at a safe enough distance from American society and governmental institutions as to not be too unsettling for audiences that were still mourning the 9/11 dead and flying their flags.

On the other hand, the fascination with conspiracies that run to the very core of Christianity can be seen as yet another progression of conspiracism toward the furthest reaches of hyperbole. Conspiracy theorists had originally feared threats from outside the country, then sought to uncover political assassins and treachery *within* the highest corridors of governmental and financial power, and eventually wound up looking for otherworldly beings and crashed alien flying saucers. Looking for corrupt plots within the most powerful church in the world is yet another step in the endless quest for that elusive "something much bigger," a more powerful cabal of powerbrokers they can accuse of wrongdoing.

The secret society conspiracy theories that had come into vogue in the 1980s had found an audience among mainstream Americans in the 2000s. Popular culture in the new millennium was ready for conspiracy theories about esoteric cults and nefarious plots in the world of religion and spirituality. Just like the most zealous of conspiracy theorists, mainstream Americans wanted to graduate to higher, more complex, and more intricate conspiracies. These audiences had been able to accept the Area 51 and Roswell conspiracies. Their minds were open to Fox Mulder's extreme possibilities when it came to extraterrestrials. Now they were ready and eager for stories that questioned the politics behind religion, that accused churches of using faith as a control and manipulation tool against the masses. In *The Da Vinci Code*, after all, the most radical passages were not merely the ruminations about whether or not it is conceivable that Jesus and Mary Magdalene might have been lovers. Audiences had already dealt with that controversy in 1988 upon the release of Martin Scorsese's film *The Last Temptation of Christ*. *The Da Vinci Code*'s angriest accusations against the church were based on actual, documented historical facts. The book accuses the Catholic Church of manipulating the interpretations of the Bible for its own political and financial gain in order to establish the Vatican as the sole political power broker in the world, and to establish an exploitive patriarchal social order that denies women power and autonomy over their own lives.

A great deal of 2000s conspiracy theorizing stayed focused on the past as much as it tried to find signs of secretive, underhanded behavior in the present. In fact, the gestalt of a lot of conspiracy theory arguments had become the claim that the roots of modern conspiracies are, for the most part, rooted in the ancient past. The origins of world religions, especially Christianity, religious orders like Opus Dei, and various Christian splinter groups like the Cathars, the Gnostics, and the Rosicrucians were pored over by conspiracy theorists in hope of uncovering hidden truths about the chaotic state of the modern world. The Freemasons and the Illuminati were scrutinized and accused of controlling American and world governments in their centuries-old master plan for world domination. Even collegiate fraternal orders, like Yale University's exclusive Skull and Bones organization, were accused of being training grounds for a future generation of world-controlling power elite.

The impact of ancient secret society conspiracy theories on popular culture, particularly on publishing, was almost immediate in the wake of the *Da Vinci Code* phenomenon. Well-read protagonists stumbling onto complex hidden codes and intricate strings of clues that unraveled centuries-old secrets started crowding the bookshelves. This comprised both fiction and nonfiction publishing.

For example, in 2003, right after *Da Vinci*'s debut, Steve Berry saw his first novel, *The Amber Room*, turn into a hit and launch him on a successful career. Conspiracies involving lost heirs to Russia's Romanov dynasty and the Vatican's hidden secrets concerning the 1917 Fatima revelation made up the plots of Berry's action yarns. In 2005, Gregg Loomis launched a series of books involving government operative Lang Reilly getting embroiled in secret society mysteries and secret codes—most often in famous art works—revealing the hidden truth about major historical events. In 2006, former investment banker and screenwriter Raymond Khoury published *The Last Templar*, about an embittered archaeologist racing against the Vatican to unearth ancient manuscripts that prove Jesus Christ's divinity was nothing more than a hoax perpetrated by the early Church.

Even before Dan Brown and his imitators plumbed the depths of history for conspiracies, Jim Marrs' 2000 "underground" bestseller *Rule by Secrecy* extended the historical chicanery by secret society conspirators all the way to the time of ancient Egyptians. Marrs, who had moved from journalism to books in the late 1980s with *Crossfire*, one of the reference works for Oliver Stone during the making of *JFK*, had never been one to keep his distance from hyperbole. His second conspiracy book, 1992's *The Stargate Project*, attempted to shed light on the military's secret research project involving psychics and remote viewing. In 1998, he published *Alien Agenda*, a survey of the most colorful and controversial issues in UFOlogy. Everything from ancient astronauts—first popularized in the 1960s by Swiss speculative writer Erich von Däniken—to alien abductions, Roswell, extraterrestrial artifacts on the moon, cattle mutilations, Area 51, and underground alien bases are all given equal credence by Marrs. But whereas in *Alien Agenda* he briefly ties the UFO phenomenon to the clandestine activities of the CIA and policy organizations like the Council on Foreign Relations and the Trilateral Commission, in *Rule by Secrecy, everything* is tied together. According to *Rule*, secretive government agencies, cabals of corporate power brokers, and cliquish policy wonks are the modern incarnations of age-old secret societies like the Masons and the Illuminati who, in turn, are the descendants of even older orders like the Knights Templar. The Templars then are just a part of various organizations that had gotten a glimpse of older esoteric secrets. These secrets, Marrs argues, are information about the intervention of ancient alien visitors in the affairs of primitive man. From conducting genetics experiments to breed modern humans from the stock of prehistoric hominids, to the building of the pyramids and inspiring mysticism and religions, the human race is the complete creation of aliens. Throughout history, secret societies have kept this information hidden in hopes of one day profiting from the miraculously advanced alien technologies.

The Da Vinci Code even helped revive and take mainstream a secret society conspiracy theory that had already been expounded upon in the 1960s, '70s and '80s. In the 1970s, British actor and screenwriter Henry Lincoln produced a series of BBC documentaries about a spectacular "treasure" that might have been found in a small church in the French town of Rennes-le-Château by a priest named Bérenger Saunière. Lincoln based the documentaries on the 1969 book *Le Trésor Maudit de Rennes-le-Château*, by Gerard de Sede and his uncredited co-author, Pierre Plantard. The de Sede–Plantard book argued that what Saunière found was a pair of parchment scrolls claiming that King Dagobert, the descendant of a woman who had been impregnated by a fisherman, had a treasure trove hidden on the premises. According to de Sede and Plantard, the real treasure was the information about the king's sacred bloodline. The "fisherman," *Le Trésor* hypothesized, was a veiled reference to Jesus Christ. In his documentaries, Lincoln claimed to have attempted to disprove the theory that Jesus could have fathered a child with Mary Magdalene — a daughter whose descendants would be the founders of a royal family — but could not do it. As dubious as the logic of not being able to prove the negative might have been, Lincoln's documentaries proved to be successful. In fact, Lincoln found it wise to further parlay their theme into publishing.[2]

Lincoln teamed with novelist Richard Leigh and New Zealand photojournalist Michael Baigent and in 1982 published the speculative nonfiction work *The Holy Blood and the Holy Grail* (later retitled *Holy Blood, Holy Grail*). With the book turning into a controversial bestseller, the trio wrote the follow-up *The Masonic Legacy* (1987). The theses of these books, as Dan Brown would later fictionalize them, was that Jesus and Mary Magdalene had indeed produced a child; that four hundred years later her descendants would form the Merovingian royal family; and that the secret of their ancestry and ongoing bloodline is protected by the secret order of the Priory of Sion, which, in turn had created the Knights Templar as their military and financial branch. Throughout the centuries, according to Lincoln, Leigh, and Baigent, the Priory would add such illustrious figures to its membership rolls as Leonardo Da Vinci, Sir Isaac Newton, Victor Hugo, and Jean Cocteau. In fact, Brown's titular "Da Vinci" "code" is a series of clues in Leonardo's artwork hinting at Jesus' ongoing bloodline and the attempts at keeping it hidden until the world is ready for the truth.

The blockbuster success of *The Da Vinci Code* proved that, as Laura Miller of the *New York Times* wrote, the proverbial rising tide can lift all boats as Lincoln, Baigent, and Leigh's books suddenly returned to the bestseller lists.[3] But this was not without a great deal of controversy for all parties involved. As soon as Lincoln and his coauthors had written *Holy Blood, Holy Grail* in 1982, their book's research methodology and conclusions had been savagely criticized by historians and the media. Upon the work's revival, the same criticism was back. This time, however, it was also leveled at Brown, who adapted *Holy Blood*'s theories wholesale and publicly defended them as being incontrovertible historical facts.

The main problem was that their holy bloodlines theories were based on a series of proven hoaxes. For example, *Le Trésor Maudit de Rennes-le-Château* had long ago been demonstrated to have been based on a pair of forgeries. The parchments the priest Saunière was supposed to have found were dismissed as obvious forgeries well before Lincoln even read the book. His critics charged that he should have known better than to base his documentaries and Grail-speculation cottage industry on flim flam. Moreover, co-author Plantard had been unmasked as, at best, a political fanatic and, at worst, a con man. He had originally fabricated a series of documents purporting to be evidence of the existence of a modern-day Priory of Sion. The *Le Trésor Maudit* parchments were just more examples of his unscrupulous handiwork.[4] Although there really existed a Middle Ages order called the Priory of Sion, there is no evidence to suggest they had anything to do with the Holy Grail or Jesus' bloodline, much less that the order was still active in the twentieth century. Plantard's motive for his hoax has most often been attributed to politics. He had been a member of the conservative, nationalist political movement French National Renewal, whose chief platform was a call for the restoration of the descendants of the Merovingian royal family to a position of power in France. Tying a new royal family to Jesus Christ's bloodline, Plantard and his political allies apparently surmised, could only aid their cause.[5]

As far as Brown was concerned, though, his readers were looking for a good thriller and didn't seem to mind the same criticism from historians. Although a veritable anti–*Da Vinci Code* publishing and TV-special industry sprang up in the wake of his book, with everyone from historians to conservative Christians deriding his work, Brown could always retreat behind the fact that he was, ultimately, telling a fictional story about fictional character Robert Langdon on a globe-trotting caper with assassins and conspiratorial intrigue. His readers either didn't care about the fact that *The Da Vinci Code* was founded on the Priory of Sion hoax, or they might have been satisfied with the *spirit* and *intent* of the book. Brown fans could simply have been happy with a book championing secular humanism and standing as a counterpoint to the burgeoning evangelical entertainment industry and its exclusionary horror stories where all but a few fundamentalist Christians escaped the Rapture and the torments of the Antichrist.

But the final twist in the saga of Brown's connection to *Holy Blood, Holy Grail* came in 2005.[6] Baigent and Leigh, without Lincoln's participation, brought a lawsuit against Brown's publisher, Random House, contending that *The Da Vinci Code*'s liberal use of the bloodline theories from *Holy Blood* constituted a copyright infringement. They pointed out that the entire central thesis of *The Da Vinci Code* was adapted directly from their book, with Brown going as far as naming his villain after Leigh and Baigent. The Leigh Teabing character's name was an obvious anagram of the last names of *Holy Blood*'s authors. Furthermore, they claimed that the infirm Teabing character was also an imitation of an ailing Henry Lincoln.

Baigent and Leigh eventually lost their suit, the court deciding that their arguments for how a fictional book basing its plot on nonfiction work constituted copyright infringement were vague and poorly articulated. In fact, in the pages of *The Da Vinci Code*, Brown acknowledges Lincoln, Baigent, and Leigh's work in a way that is somewhat akin to an academic researcher using references to bolster his or her arguments. The Robert Langdon character makes a very specific reference to *Holy Blood, Holy Grail* in a scene where he talks to Sophie Nuveu about the Christian world's hostile reaction to the idea that Jesus and Mary Magdalene might have been husband and wife. Almost immediately after losing their lawsuit, Baigent and Leigh appealed the decision. That, too, was unsuccessful.

Baigent and Leigh remained active and successful in the aftermath of the court battle. Writing both together as well as separately, they continued expounding on theories that stood to "shatter" the world's understanding of all of history, religion and spirituality. In

2005 they published *The Elixir and the Stone: The Tradition of Magic and Alchemy*, investigating the history of occult beliefs and mystery religions and examining their role in the late twentieth and early twenty-first century revival of interest in alternate spiritualities. In 2006, Michael Baigent returned to the theme of the hidden truths behind Jesus' life and crucifixion with *The Jesus Papers: Exposing the Greatest Cover-Up in History*. Here he reiterates the points of *Holy Blood, Holy Grail* and argues an entirely new conspiracy theory: Not only were Jesus and Mary Magdalene man and wife, but Jesus did not even die on the cross. Then, in 2009, Baigent took on the contentious issue of fundamentalist religions and apocalypticism in *Racing Toward Armageddon: The Three Great Religions and the Plot to End the World*. Just as the fairly self-descriptive title suggests, there is a conspiracy among fundamentalist zealots of the three major religions to instigate a Middle East crisis that will lead to a global war and an establishment of world theocracies.

The entry of all this arcana into conspiracy theorizing took on its strangest form when the supernatural had become one of the strongest components of paranoid "truth" seeking. The first decade of the new millennium saw conspiracism seeking to find the ancient roots of modern covert plots, plus a strong interest in prophecy and the supernatural. This orientation toward the mystical, it must be noted, is somewhat different from even the high strangeness of UFOlogy and claims of alien contact. Most UFO believers and alien-conspiracy theorists would contend that extraterrestrials are not supernatural beings, gods, spirits, demons, or any such manifestations of the spiritual realm. Many UFO magazines might be found carrying an overabundance of advertising for such New Age products as crystals, Ouija boards, and divination objects, along with books on alternative spiritualities, reincarnation, and ghosts; but the more academic members of the UFO research communities have been openly disdainful of the rise of occultic movements and their association with the extraterrestrial research field.

The prominence of occultic belief systems and claims of prophecies in the 2000s was foreshadowed in the first couple of hours immediately after the 9/11 attacks. *Literally*, within hours of the planes crashing into the Twin Towers and the Pentagon, e-mails purporting to be a 1654 Nostradamus prophecy began circulating on the Internet:

> In the City of God there will be a great thunder. Two brothers torn apart by chaos, while the fortress endures, the great leader will succumb. The third big war will begin when the big city is burning.[7]

The passage was quickly proven a hoax. It was pointed out that Nostradamus, the fabled seer whose barely penetrable quatrains of predictions had been pored over for decades, had actually died in 1566. Furthermore, even those Nostradamus experts who had long entertained the idea that the French prognosticator might actually have been able to glimpse the future pointed out that the e-mail message was a bastardization of a very real quatrain. The actual Nostradamus passage reads:

> The sky will burn at forty five degrees latitude,
> Fire approaches the great new city
> Immediately a huge, scattered flame leaps up
> When they want to have verification from the Normans.[8]

The reference to the "two brothers" of the hoax had obviously been inserted by the perpetrators to make clearer allusions to the Twin Towers. But even this altering of the original material, which in itself is extremely nebulous, is not as dramatic as some of the subsequent e-mail hoaxes tying Nostradamus' quatrains to the September 11 attacks. Perhaps the most blatant corruption of the Nostradamus source material is the hoax reading:

Two steel birds will fall from the sky on the Metropolis. The sky will burn at forty-five degrees latitude. Fire approaches the great new city.

Immediately a huge, scattered flame leaps up. Within months, rivers will flow with blood. The undead will roam the earth for little time.

The forty-five degree latitude line, also a part of the original Nostradamus quatrain, was interpreted as a very specific reference to New York City, which is situated between forty and forty five degrees. In fact, the reference to forty-five degrees in the authentic quatrain had long intrigued Nostradamus buffs and inspired them to speculate about a possible calamity befalling New York City. Since skeptics usually charge that prophecies are generally worthless because their believers always tout their accuracy *after* something has happened, the forty-five degree line of the quatrain and the Nostradamus community's tying of it to New York as early as the 1980s is impressive.[9] But, again, the rest of the original quatrain is so jumbled and incoherent that one could truly use it for any interpretation at all. The hoaxers, of course, made the effort to remove a great deal of the ambiguity. The "two steel birds" passage is the most obvious of these alterations. The "huge, scattered flame leaps up" passage brings to mind the flames and cloud of debris of the Towers' destruction. "Within months, rivers will flow with blood" is a fairly obvious reference to the invasion of Afghanistan.

But Nostradamus and his prophecies enjoyed a revival of interest in the 2000s. Scores of new books analyzing his life and work were published throughout the decade. Documentaries, many of them airing on the History Channel, pored over his writings, searching for clues about whether the prophet might actually have predicted the violent world events after the turn of the millennium. In 2009, the History Channel even went one step beyond its frequent specials about apocalyptic prophecies and devoted an entire weekly series called *The Nostradamus Effect* to end-time predictions. The premise of the show is the investigation of whether the tumultuous world events of the 2000s might have been predicted by seers like Nostradamus, Edgar Cayce, the Chinese I-Ching divination techniques, the Tibetan Book of the Dead, the Oracle of Delphi, and various others throughout history. If reasonable signs seem to suggest that more than one of these ancient seers appeared to have foretold the problems of the modern world, the show asks if one may give the doomsday prophecies some credence because of this sort of future-casting triangulation method.

An audacious pair of books claimed that ancient prophecies could be verified by the modern scientific method. In journalist Michael Drosnin's books *The Bible Code* (1997), *The Bible Code II: The Countdown* (2002), and *The Bible Code III: The Quest* (2006), the arguments were made that information about modern world events could be found encoded in the Bible. Incredibly, Drosnin's work was based on the statistical research of mathematician Eliyahu Rips of the Hebrew University of Jerusalem. While the history of the Bible code claims reaches back to the 1990s and Drosnin's first book was published in 1997, well timed to coincide with millennial fears, the impact of the work was truly felt in the general atmosphere of post–September 11 conspiracy- and apocalypse-theorizing. In 2003 and 2004, the History Channel produced documentaries based on the first two books.

The claims of a "Bible code" first received worldwide attention in 1994 when Eliyahu Rips and religious scholars Doron Witztum and Alexander Rotenberg published a paper on their remarkable statistical find in the peer-reviewed scholarly journal *Statistical Science*. Rips had heard of Slovakian Rabbi Michael Ben Weissmandel using a statistical technique called the Equidistant Letter Sequence (ELS) to look for hidden messages about the lives of famous rabbis in the Torah, or the Old Testament of the Bible. According to the writings of the late Weissmandel's students, the rabbi had been able to find accurate personal information like birth dates, birth locations, and places where these rabbis had lived their lives. The ELS method involved the isolation of letters at equal given distances apart in the Hebrew text of the Torah. These letters were then analyzed to see whether they formed any sort of understandable anagrams. To Weissmandel's—and later Rips'—astonishment, words emerged from these letters. Oftentimes, the words were but the parts of entire phrases and sentences. According to Rips and his co-authors, it would have been impossible for these sentences to appear in the Biblical text by pure statistical chance. When Rips, Witztum, and Rotenberg were able to replicate Weissmandel's findings, they published their work in *Statistical Science*, where their paper was labeled a "challenging puzzle." The implication of the label was that although the work Rips and his partners had done was methodologically sound and the journal's reviewers could find no fault whatsoever with their calculations and conclusions, the journal invited other mathematicians to examine, further replicate, and try and explain what *really* could account for the mysterious phrases encoded within the Torah. What followed were years of challenges to the Rips work and more and more colorful controversy.

Essentially, the Rips work was replicated a number of times, with some researchers supporting the assertions of the Bible code and others bitterly refuting it and going as far as accusing Rips, Witztum, and Rotenberg of perpetrating an elaborate hoax. Perhaps the most outspoken critic of Rips and the code was Australian mathematician Brendan McKay.[10] Along with Israeli mathematicians Dror Bar-Natan and Gil Kalai and Israeli psychologist Maya Bar-Hillel, McKay charged that Rips and his team manipulated the ELS process to produce words and phrases they were expecting to find. Using the Rips paper's methodology, McKay claimed, one could find the same phrases in William Shakespeare's plays as well as on the pages of *Moby Dick*. On the other hand, Rips' defenders included game theorist Robert Aumann, the winner of the 2005 Nobel Prize for Economics. In his *highly* qualified defense of Rips, Aumann wrote, "Though the basic thesis of the research seems wildly improbable, for many years I thought that an ironclad case had been made for the codes; I did not see how 'cheating' could have been possible. Then came the work of the 'opponents'.... Though this work did not convince me that the data had been manipulated, it did convince me that it could have been; that manipulation was technically possible."[11] Ultimately, though, Aumann declared that although he could find no evidence of a hoax, he feels that the existence of a genuine code is improbable.

While Rips' assertions remain in dispute to this day—and no doubt will remain so indefinitely—Michael Drosnin's *Bible Code* books were bestsellers around the world. But what generated even more controversy for the Drosnin books were their claims that the hidden information in the Bible went way beyond a few facts concerning the lives of famous rabbis. Drosnin claimed that major world events, wars and assassinations taking place as late as the twentieth and twenty-first centuries, could all be found encoded in the pages of the Bible. In fact, Drosnin argued, if read correctly, the Bible code contained the secrets of mankind's imminent destruction in a nuclear holocaust in the early twenty-first century.

Conspiracy theorists tracing secret societies to the ancient times, along the lines of Jim Marrs' work, have tended to argue that the ultimate secrets the elite conspirators have long sought to keep hidden were of a mystical and supernatural nature. There are paths, these lines of argument have presented, to a higher consciousness, to God, to alternate realities and dimensions, to aliens, that are attainable for humans. This secret knowledge, in turn, has been kept hidden by occult groups. Adepts at mysticism and their close-knit circles of allies and descendants have, according to the meta-conspiracy theories, guarded their secrets throughout the ages. This elite has used this knowledge to secure positions of economic and political privilege. The reasons for their secrecy, according to various conspiratorial schools of thought, have ranged from the sinister to the paternalistic. Some conspiracy theorists argue that the reason is pure greed and a lust for exploitive privilege. Those in positions of power, the argument states, do not like sharing that power with the world. The more paternalistic argument says that perhaps all the adepts at accessing the ancient spiritual-magical-alien sources of power are afraid of what such power can do to the world in the "wrong hands."

A refutation of this idea of hidden supernatural knowledge has come from an interesting, although not surprising, source through a work of fiction. In his third Robert Langdon book, *The Lost Symbol* (2009), Dan Brown built his plot around a psychotic killer attempting to find ancient sources of otherworldly knowledge and power he believes the Freemason hid somewhere in Washington, D.C. Holding a friend of Langdon's hostage, the madman forces the symbologist to decode clues that might lead to the Masons' "ultimate secret." As it turns out in the end, all that was hidden by the Freemasons, committed rationalists and believers of the power, rights, and dignity of the individual, was a statement that the ultimate power is the power of the mind of a person who has devoted himself to constant self-improvement and enlightenment. In a way, much like the first Langdon novel, *The Lost Symbol* is really more of an *anti*-conspiracy book. There is no ancient hidden power, the book declares. In a way, such an anti-conspiratorial statement is ironic, since Brown and his hero, Langdon, have become synonymous with conspiracy entertainment. But, again, this is not surprising. The Langdon character has always been presented as a man of rationality and logic. Although he is not anti-religious and not an atheist, the two preceding books had him declare that he is not a religious man either and he is not capable of having faith in claims he cannot investigate and cannot prove to be true.

The Reptilians

Perhaps the most prolific of the supernatural meta-conspiracy theorists has been former British sportscaster David Icke. In his seven books (to date) bridging alien-contact hypotheses and New Age–occult mysticism, Icke has also presented some of the most bizarre and controversial theories in the annals of paranoid literature.

The crux of Icke's worldview, first committed to paper in his 1999 book *The Biggest Secret*, is that reptilian aliens from the Draco constellation have been controlling human affairs since time immemorial. The reptilians are adept enough at camouflage techniques as to be able to conceal their true physical natures from the world they are manipulating. As a matter of fact, Icke claims, the reptilians have been very directly controlling Earthly activities by assuming human form and situating themselves in the highest positions of power. Essentially, Icke accuses virtually every head of state in the world and most financial and political power brokers of being alien lizards in disguise. The alien agenda, in Icke's estimation, is to maintain an ever-increasingly fascistic stranglehold on human affairs, and to constantly foment disorders, wars, and all manner of chaos that keeps people in fear, beholden to authoritarian leaders, and ignorant of consciousness-altering, mystical, and spiritual alternatives.

Icke has expounded on this thesis in his books *The Biggest Secret: The Book That Will Change the World* (1999), *Children of the Matrix* (2001), *Alice in Wonderland and the World Trade Center Disaster* (2002), *Tales from the Time Loop* (2003), *And the Truth Shall Set You Free* (2004), *Infinite Love Is the Only Truth: Everything Else Is Illusion* (2005), and *The David Icke Guide to the Global Conspiracy (And How to End It)* (2007). In each, Icke references the most current world events—crises most often — as examples of the otherworldly creatures exerting more and more control over the unsuspecting human race. From the September 11 attacks to the invasions of Afghanistan, Iraq, and the most controversial provisions of American anti-terror initiatives like the Patriot Act, all the events have, in Icke's reckoning, been milestones in the reptilians' ongoing efforts to eradicate individual liberties and democracy.

Perhaps rather than looking for ways in which his ideas have permeated popular culture, one might opt to examine how some of the most successful themes in science fiction-oriented entertainment seem to have shaped Icke's ideas. From his reptilian aliens to the invisible methods of social and political manipulation, Icke's writings seem to be an amalgamation of *V*, *They Live*, and *The Matrix*. In fact, Icke appears to have felt such kinship with the core ideas of *The Matrix* films that he adopted the "matrix" concept into the title of his second book on reptilian manipulation. Just like in the Wachowski brothers' film, Icke expounds on the idea of the false consciousness that has been implanted in people's minds by an unseen, inhuman enemy. People are slaves and prisoners, his book argues, yet the victims of the "global fascist state," just like the characters of *The Matrix*, are unable to recognize their jailers, and they believe that their existence is the only normal, natural, and thoroughly free way of life. The enslavement, Icke argues, is perpetuated by the everyday rules, social structures, and channels of communication — the "matrix" of all human social structures— that have been created by the reptilian overlords.

This sort of melodramatic goulash of ideas, culled together from popular culture, social constructionist and postmodernist philosophy, and a great deal of New Age mysticism, had served to both make Icke one of the most successful conspiracy theorists in the world, as well as one of the most controversial figures even among conspiracist circles.

Although he was not the only conspiracist to have a degree of pan-political appeal, Icke was certainly the only figure of the fringe paranoid community to attract a committed core of fans among the militia and survivalist right-wing faction of the conspiracy community, as well as fans among the New Age–oriented left-wingers who are perpetually seeking to uncover the corporate-big business-international-financier cabals of world-controlling elites. Icke has made appearances and given rousing speeches at conventions where "patriot militia" members gather to denounce gun control laws, and also spun some of the most sordid and byzantinze theories about policy organizations like the Council on Foreign Relations and international banks being the seats of all global evil, disorder, wars, and intergalactic reptilian manipulation. Simply, whether it is the big government bureaucracy and the rise of the one-world government that frightens one, or the power of mega-corporations and the wealthy power elite, Icke has always been able to deftly speak the language of conspiracy believers. But it was very specifically the farthest fringes of the right-leaning conspiracy community that have given Icke more trouble than closed-minded skeptics who had long ridiculed him for his outlandish ideas.[12]

In 1999, Icke was nearly barred from entering Canada to give a speech in Vancouver. Upon the petitioning of the Canadian Jewish Congress, immigration authorities detained Icke at the airport and searched through the literature he had brought along, trying to determine whether or not his writings were a collection of anti–Semitic screeds.[13] Icke had a strained relationship with Jews going as far back as 1994 and the publication of his New Age empowerment book *The Robot's Rebellion*. In that work, he endorsed a notorious 1903 Russian hoax: a book entitled *The Protocols of the Elders of Zion*. Icke argued that although many things were inaccurate in *The Protocols*, it did attempt to shed light on a very real global conspiracy by a malevolent "elite." Unfortunately for Icke's image, *The Protocols* was not only thoroughly discredited by 1920, thanks to *The Times of London*, but it was also one of the most virulent examples of anti–Semitic agitprop in the twentieth century. *The Protocols*, essentially, purports to identify a worldwide cabal of powerful Jewish bankers and industrialists questing to undermine and control all countries and economies, subjugating and exploiting everything and everyone, all for the profit of the Jews. Many of the twentieth century's most rabid and discriminatory anti–Semitic belief systems and policies—including the Nazi party's anti–Semitism — drew their inspiration from *The Protocols* and used it to justify their persecution of the Jews. Icke, however, had long continued to insist that although he was not an anti–Semite himself and did not believe that there existed a world-wide Jewish conspiracy, he *did* believe that a small collection of wealthy elites exists and is secretly running the world. Flirting with controversy even further, in his 1995 book, *And the Truth Shall Set You Free*, Icke wrote:

> I strongly believe that a small Jewish clique which has contempt for the mass of Jewish people worked with non–Jews to create the First World War, the Russian Revolution, and the Second World War. This Jewish/non–Jewish Elite used the First World War to secure to the Balfour Declaration and the principle of the Jewish State of Israel in Palestine (for which, given the genetic history of most Jewish people, there is absolutely no justification on historical grounds or any other). They then dominated the Versailles Peace Conference and created the circumstances which made the Second World War inevitable.[14]

The book argues that the claims of the number of Jewish deaths during the Holocaust are unreliable and the very details of the Nazi extermination of the Jews have been manipulated by the "clique." This, for Icke's critics, smacks of anti–Semitic Holocaust denial. Moreover, Icke has never made an attempt to denounce or distance himself from any fringe groups that showed an interest in his work, even when the extremists were publicly avowed fascists and Neo Nazis. In 1995, he gave a talk in Glastonbury, England, where the affair was vig-orously promoted by the Neo Nazi group Combat 18. When Icke was criticized for giving the talk and not making it clear that he did not endorse the Neo Nazi agenda, his reply was a convoluted, yet classic, conspiratorial explanation. He claimed that Combat 18 was a front for the Anti-Defamation League and the Israeli intelligence agency, the Mossad, both of whom were a part of the global conspiracy. The conspiracy, in turn, would create disrep-utable fronts like Combat 18 and damn with praise anyone who got too close to the truth. "What better way to discredit an investigator," Icke asked, "than to have a far right group like Combat 18 to praise them?"[15]

Even Icke's flirtations with the racist ultra-right did not seem to tarnish his reputation. He is perhaps the highest earning and most visible conspiracy theorist in the first decade of the twenty-first century. Each of his books has been an international bestseller, he runs a webpage that sees 600,000 hits in the average week, and he has hosted sold-out speaking events around the world. His success has been attributed to the fact that his messages are at once clearly articulated, yet vague and polysemic enough that virtually any philosophical or ideological movement can graft them onto their own beliefs. Those who believe in literal alien visitations and extraterrestrial interference with Earthly affairs can find a kindred spirit in Icke's books. Those with an apocalyptic bent, awaiting a final confrontation between good and evil, can likewise find their beliefs reflected in Icke's work. Syracuse University professor Michael Barkun termed Icke's work "improvisational millennialism," fitting in well among the ideas of various end-times scenarists who have gained power and followers in the years leading up to the year 2000 and past the events of September 11.[16] Even those whose fears are more down to earth, worrying about the advance of a mere global totalitarian state, perpetrated by very human, flesh-and-blood dictators and a corporate-military-intelligence cabal of evildoers, can ally with Icke, despite all the hyperbole and alien shape-shifters in his books. In the eyes of these more pragmatic of conspiracy believers, Icke is merely writing in allegories, his reptilian aliens little more than symbols of an increasingly repressive global elite. Icke's work, to this school of followers, is but a clever, critical, post-modern interrogation of belief systems. According to this interpretation, Icke's books serve up outrageous stories that are impossible to believe for "rational" audiences in an attempt to make them question where all their rational belief systems are coming. Icke, his supporters claim, forces his reader to question all of the world's systems of authority and the extent to which these organs have defined reality for the masses. In fact, just a quick perusal of the user comments for Icke's books on any online bookseller's webpage will turn up a trend in most of the reviews posted by his ardent fans. Most of Icke's acolytes are not making arguments defending the literal truth of the shape-shifting reptiles, but they praise the author for making one question reality. The praise for Icke usually reads to the effect that "Icke makes you think," or "He makes you question what you've been told to believe in."

Icke is shrewd enough never to endorse or reject any one interpretation of his words. Whenever he holds a lecture or gives an interview — many of them available for examination on his website (www.davidicke.com) or on YouTube — he appears to be dead serious about his claims, even when speaking about the alien reptilians. When interviewed for History Channel documentaries about secret societies and conspiracies, there is never a hint of irony in his words or delivery. He appears to be simply speaking his mind and expounding on his dearly held theories and philosophies. For his supporters, of course, he is either a true believer in "the hidden truth," or a clever, postmodern critical thinker forcing his audiences to re-examine their beliefs. For the more cynically inclined, Icke is a wily showman who somehow figured out how to get immensely rich from selling the exact same message to audiences holding diametrically opposed beliefs.

The David Icke phenomenon of the early 2000s can also be seen as a sign of how strong the conspiracist impulse is in American society, and how tenuous the post–September 11 super-patriotism movement had been. The attacks of September 11 may have killed *The X-Files*, but America was hardly on its way back to the 1950s and an unquestioning, flag-waving faith in the system and authorities. September 11 may have shown America under attack from a foreign enemy, it might have rallied the country behind its soldiers, behind a charismatic mayor, and the president of the United States, but the country was still not willing to give its leaders unlimited blind trust. It would take a massive and costly misstep from Washington for the era of divisive politics, suspicion, and conspiracy theories to be back in full force. That misstep turned out to be the invasion of Iraq.[17]

Inside Job?

According to historians, and especially the critics of the George W. Bush administration, the post–September 11 surge in patriotism quickly spilled over to the legislative arena as well, manifesting itself as a fear of dissent, disagreement, and debate over the White House's anti-terror policies. While opinion polls showed overwhelming approvals of Bush's handling of the attacks and his call to hunt down and eradicate the terrorists anywhere in the world, many in Washington quickly feared that any disagreement and opposition to his policy plans might be interpreted as being "soft" on terrorism, if not unpatriotic. Bush, after all, had declared in a speech to Congress that the world either stood behind the United States or behind the terrorists. With opinion polls solidly approving of this statement, it became a political liability to deconstruct and analyze — or publicly challenge — the more disturbing and politically opportunistic aspects of a statement like that. Americans appeared to have spoken and they seemed to concur that even disagreements with the Bush administration's specifics on how best to deal with the terrorist threat were tantamount to treason, to "standing with" the terrorists.

The first result of this political atmosphere was an overwhelming Congressional support for the invasion of Afghanistan to rout out Osama bin Laden's al-Qaeda terrorists and remove the Taliban government sheltering them. Since the American military was able to overthrow the Afghan government with relative ease, Washington's support for Bush's more far-reaching military plans for the Middle East held. For one, the president argued that the ultimate weapon against terror in the region would be the democratization of as many Arab countries as possible. Freedom, he said, would ultimately provide Arabs a quality of life and governmental systems that would not support extremism and terrorism. It was the role of the American government and the war on terror to bring democracy to as much of the Middle East as possible. Furthermore, Bush argued that the overthrow of the Taliban's direct supporters could not stop in Afghanistan. Anyone aiding, abetting, and arming Osama bin Laden and his followers needed to be toppled. After Afghanistan, the White House argued, Iraq was the next major link to al-Qaeda. Bin Laden's operatives, the Bush administration claimed, had been active in Iraq as well. Iraq, said the administration, had vast stockpiles of chemical and bacteriological "weapons of mass destruction." These were the weapons the world had seen the country's brutal dictator, Saddam Hussein, use against his Kurdish population after the Gulf War. These same weapons, the administration warned, could easily fall in the hands of al-Qaeda. Furthermore, Bush argued in his 2003 State of the Union address, the White House had intelligence suggesting that Iraq was trying to acquire uranium from Nigeria for the development of an atomic weapons program. The next terrorist attacks, the administration warned ominously, could happen under a radioactive mushroom cloud. When the president pushed for an invasion of Iraq because a United Nations weapons inspection delegation could not fully verify that the Hussein regime had no WMDs, Congress again gave him what he asked for. On March 20, 2003, the United States and a coalition of allies invaded Iraq.

The war in Iraq, however, would deteriorate into a costly and protracted occupation, fraught with mistakes and a mounting casualty count that eventually turned American public opinion against the campaign. The emerging details of all the miscalculations, in fact, would be so extensive and the reactions of the public so angry that a perfect climate for conspiracy theorizing would be fostered within a few very short years of the invasion. To inspire the most anger and distrust in Americans, the very reason for invading Iraq had soon turned out to be a mistake. The WMDs the Bush administration used to sell the war did not exist. Moreover, with each passing year, the very accuracy of the intelligence the White House used to justify the war proved more and more insubstantial and the Bush administration's handling of it more and more dishonest. The WMD argument, it appeared, had been based on the unverified claims of a very few and highly disreputable Iraqi inform-ants. The claims of Iraq's attempts to acquire nuclear materials had also been incorrect, and the Central Intelligence Agency, it turned out, knew about it. Leading to one of the major and highly embarrassing scandals of the Bush presidency, CIA agent Valerie Plame's identity had been leaked to the press in 2003 — in effect ending her career as an opera-tive — after her husband, Joseph Wilson, wrote an op-ed article for the *New York Times* arguing that Bush's State of the Union address claims of the Nigerian uranium purchase were incorrect and willfully dishonest. There was, Wilson wrote, no sound, incontrovertible CIA evidence of the purchase attempt. Wrecking Plame's career, Bush critics charged, was punishment from a vindictive administration that could brook no criticism or questioning of its policies.[18]

In the eyes of critics of the Iraq war, the Bush administration was bent on going to war at all costs and they lied about and manipulated thin and inconclusive intelligence information to justify the invasion. To many, this amounted to evidence of a White House mired in shady conspiracies. Perhaps, conspiracy theorists then argued, as they usually do, the public information was but the tip of a much bigger iceberg. If the WMD claims were lies, then might the administration not have manipulated and manufactured the entire cul-tural atmosphere that allowed it to get into two majors wars so easily? The circumstantial link between Iraq, Afghanistan, and the attacks of September 11 had been established for conspiracy theorists. They could now see an administration that wanted to invade oil-rich Middle Eastern countries, that wanted industries profiting from weapons manufacturing, and wanted to increase police and domestic intelligence powers in an atmosphere of height-ened paranoia and super-patriotism. To accomplish all this, a new conspiracy theory move-ment would argue, the Bush administration needed a spectacular attack on America, the kind that had not taken place since Pearl Harbor. In the crisis and panic atmosphere fol-lowing 9/11, Americans needed to trust their leaders and, in turn, they were ready to give those leaders anything they asked for.

In an uncanny parallel to the birth of the John F. Kennedy assassination conspiracy theories, the first books alleging that the September 11 attacks were not what they appeared to be showed up in Europe. In 2002, French journalist and left-wing political activist Thierry Meyssan published the books *9/11: The Big Lie* (*L'Effroyable Imposture*) and *Le Pentagate*, arguing that the U.S. government was entirely behind the September 11 attacks. In the two books he laid out an argument for why the American government would perpetrate the attacks and how the Pentagon was not hit by a plane but by either a missile or a truck bomb. According to Meyssan, the attacks were but the first step in what would turn into a military regime taking over the U.S. government. The military-industrial complex, supported by the Bush administration, Meyssan argues, needed to create an emergency that would allow the complete overthrow of civil liberties and help usher in the new military dictatorship. Most of the enemies of the U.S., Meyssan further argues, are also little more than fake threats created by the government to give reasons for military spending and foreign involvement.

Even Osama bin Laden, the books claim, is an agent in the employ of the CIA. The reason the Twin Towers were chosen for the most devastating attack, according to Meyssan, was because one of them had a secret CIA office that needed to be shut down and all evidence of its existence erased.

Reactions to Meyssan's book in Europe included swift and scathing criticism, as well as blockbuster success. Most mainstream publications in France and England denounced the book, essentially arguing that it was full of unsubstantiated fantasies. Meyssan could offer no proof for any of his allegations of a far-reaching military junta organizing and executing the September 11 attacks, other than testimony from a handful of unnamed "insider" sources. For example, he claims that airline pilots told him that terrorists with the sort of limited flight training the 9/11 hijackers were supposed to have had could not possibly have guided the planes into the World Trade Center and the Pentagon. Yet none of these sources, Meyssan claims, were willing to go on the record and reveal their identities. Similarly, he claims that radio hobbyists in the New York City area were able to pick up the signatures of navigational beacons in the Twin Towers remotely controlling and guiding the airplanes to their impact points. But, once again, Meyssan is not making any of these recordings available for examination and he is not revealing the identities of any of the hobbyists. In response, even left-leaning magazines and newspapers in Europe, ones typically given to critical coverage of the U.S. and Washington's policies, have denounced his books. The French magazine *Liberation* ran its critique of the books under the headline "The Big Swindle."[19]

Despite the criticism, or perhaps because of it, both of Meyssan's books rocketed to international bestseller status. In France, the books sold out, sometimes within hours of their placement. Meyssan set new sales records throughout the country, eventually selling more books in the single first month of publication than any other book ever marketed in that country. Some, especially American media watchers and cultural analysts, have credited the appeal of his books to a strain of anti–Americanism running through a number of European countries in the 1990s and 2000s. As Bush moved to invade Afghanistan and called for an invasion of Iraq, the anti–American animosity was the strongest in France. Perhaps the support for Meyssan's books was a symptom of this anti–American anger. Or, perhaps, as other — French — media analysts have hypothesized, the interest in Meyssan's conspiracy theory might have stemmed from their sheer, over-the-top audaciousness. Perhaps the interest in the book was something akin to staring at a grisly accident.[20]

In the years since the September 11 attacks, Meyssan has continued to be active in conspiracy theorizing. His Voltairenet webpage (www.voltairenet.org) espouses left-wing, anti–American and often anti–Vatican conspiracy theories. Meyssan often "investigates" and criticizes the Catholic Church; in the *Da Vinci Code* tradition, he focuses on the church's Opus Dei order, accusing it of spearheading an advance of worldwide fascistic social policies. He also regularly attempts to expose major world leaders and figures of influence as being covert CIA agents. For example, he has accused French president Nikolas Sarkozy of being on the CIA payroll and the puppet of a hidden American takeover of France. In early 2010, he called for investigations and attempts to verify Venezuelan president Hugo Chavez's accusations that the January 12 earthquake in Haiti was a result of a secret U.S. seismic weapons test.

Similar September 11 conspiracy theory books, blogs, and webpages quickly followed in Europe, before catching on in the U.S. In Germany, Andreas von Bulow, a former parliament member of the left-wing Social Democratic Party, published the book *The CIA and September 11* (2003), and journalist Gerhard Wisnewski wrote *Operation 9/11* (2003). Both books accused the U.S. government of masterminding and perpetrating the attacks on the WTC and the Pentagon. Similarly, Mathias Broeckers, another German reporter, devoted a blog (www.broeckers.com) to discussing how the official Washington accounting for September 11 was a lie.

In the U.S., the first conspiratorial responses to 9/11 took place on the Internet, and many of them came in the most dubious form. They claimed that the attacks were most likely masterminded by a joint U.S. intelligence and Israeli partnership, and staged to demonize the Arab world and pave the way for the invasion of Arab countries like Iraq and Iran. These pages quickly began spreading rumors that no Jews died in the attacks; they claimed that Jews in both New York and Washington received warnings to stay home from work that day.[21]

By September 2002, the first rallies decrying the U.S. government's assertion that the September 11 attacks were committed by al-Qaeda were held in San Francisco and Oakland, and organized by the leftist All People's Coalition. The group's mantra — displayed prominently on dozens of placards and banners—was that "Bush Did It." Its contentions were that either the U.S. government had advance knowledge of an al-Qaeda plan to launch the attacks and chose to let it unfold, or the government itself had planned and orchestrated the attacks.

As of this writing, the American 9/11 conspiracy movement has produced arguments for its position that can easily rival all the volumes of Kennedy conspiracy allegations forwarded over the past five decades. A simple Internet search for "September 11 conspiracies" will yield somewhere in the neighborhood of 7,850,000 hits. By the time this book will be read, that number is sure to have climbed much higher. Discussing all of them is far beyond the scope of this book, but it is worth taking a very brief look at some of the leading figures and organizations in this movement, as well as some of their lynchpin arguments.

One of the most outspoken and prolific September 11 conspiracy theorists is David Ray Griffin, a professor of theology and religion at Claremont School of Theology. By 2004, Griffin had written the first of his six books on the issue, *The New Pearl Harbor: Disturbing Questions About the Bush Administration and 9/11.* As conspiracy theorists generally underpin their beliefs with a lengthy analysis of who is benefiting from some catastrophe or alleged crime, Griffin focuses on the political gains the Bush administration stood to make from a manufactured crisis. The motivation behind the 9/11 conspiracy, Griffin argues, is Middle Eastern oil. The invasions of Afghanistan and Iraq for oil had always been the primary goal of the Bush White House and it masterminded a fake terrorist attack on New York City and Washington, D.C. to be able to have "terrorism" as a pretext for going to war.

Very much like the Kennedy conspiracy canon argues that the assassination of the president was actually a *two*-stage conspiracy — one to carry out the murder and the second stage to cover it up through the fraudulent investigation of the Warren Commission — Griffin and his followers also believe that the National Commission on Terrorist Attacks Upon the United States (commonly referred to as the 9/11 Commission) helped cover up the conspiracy. In *The 9/11 Commission Report: Omissions and Distortions*, published in 2005, Griffin accuses the Congressional investigative body of picking and choosing facts about the attacks that place the blame on Osama bin Laden and al-Qaeda, while omitting and refusing to address questions that hint at a conspiracy.

After the publication of his third book, *Christian Faith and the Truth Behind 9/11: A Call for Reflection and Action* (2006), Griffith's own publisher issued a statement of critical skepticism over his conspiratorial arguments. The company, almost in effect disowning Griffin and his ideas, declared that its editorial board "believes the conspiracy theory is spurious and based on questionable research."[22]

Nonetheless, Griffin and his supporters are undaunted by the criticism. When *Popular Mechanics* magazine published a book debunking some the key arguments of the conspiracy movement (*Debunking 9/11 Myths: Why Conspiracy Theories Can't Stand Up to the Facts*), Griffin immediately responded with his own book, *Debunking 9/11 Debunking.*

Not far behind Griffin, perhaps the most vocal figure in the September 11 conspiracy community is the radio talk show host Alex Jones. Broadcasting from Austin, Texas, Jones, in the typically bombastic fashion of loud radio personalities, regularly decries the "takeover" of America by the forces of "darkness" and "evil," and the advance of the global fascist state in the form of the New World Order, all orchestrated by organizations like the Council on Foreign Relations, the Trilateral Commission, and the international bankers. Aside from his nationally syndicated show, Jones also runs two conspiracy theory websites, Prison-Planet.com and Infowars.com.

Jones also brings a degree of political complexity to 9/11 conspiracism because he is one of the relatively few figures in the movement who is not of the liberal left. Often calling himself a "libertarian" and "aggressive constitutionalist," Jones had a brief attempt at a political career in 2002 as a Republican when he ran for the office of Texas state representative from the 48th district. Furthermore, since the election of Barack Obama to the presidency, Jones has been just as scathingly critical of the Democrat as he had been of George W. Bush. Obama, in Jones' estimation, is yet another agent of the New World Order. Obama's expansion of government regulatory powers by way of health insurance legislation, corporate bailouts, and Wall Street regulatory reforms is an ongoing part of the creeping takeover of the country and the world by the emerging global fascist state.

Jones' politics and theories about global cabals are not necessarily incompatible in the annals of conspiracism. As *New Republic* journalist Michelle Goldberg writes, Jones represents "an old strain of American conservatism — isolationist, anti–Wall Street, paranoid about elite conspiracies— that last flowered during the John Birch Society's heyday."[23] If anything, Jones is close in spirit to the populist movement of the 1880s and '90s, fighting the perceived exploitation of the "little guys" (working people) by both business and government. Furthermore, for many who believe that modern conspiracies are part of millennia-old cover-ups, political divisions are irrelevant. Conspirators can easily call themselves Democrat or Republican, right or left, this uber-paranoid school of thought claims. Politics are but a smoke screen to hide the truth about the all-controlling elites.

Jones was also entrepreneurial enough to parlay his conspiracy theories into a multimedia industry beyond his radio show and webpages. He has authored one book on the subject, *9/11: Descent Into Tyranny*, and produced 26 documentaries about September 11, the New World Order, and various conspiracy topics about the coming transformation of the world into a Satanic-fascist slave camp.

Equally committed to the idea of a government-orchestrated "false flag" attack on September 11 is former Brigham Young University physics professor Steven E. Jones (no relation to Alex Jones). Although not as prominent as the talk show host, Jones still carries a great deal of gravitas within the conspiracy theory community because of his academic credentials. His chief position in the conspiracy movement has been as a proponent of the idea that the Twin Towers could not have collapsed the way they did as a result of the planes striking them. However, the National Institute of Standards and Technology released the results of their investigation into what exactly caused the two skyscrapers to collapse, citing the damage done by the impacting planes and the fire from the burning jet fuel weakening the metal columns inside the building.[24] Jones has vociferously disputed this conclusion, arguing instead that the buildings had been brought down by hidden explosives. He maintains that the jet fuel fires could not have weakened the buildings' structure enough to cause total structural failure and collapse. Moreover, Jones argues that he had been able to test metal wreckage from the Trade Center rubble and he found traces of chemicals on the pieces that seem to indicate a thermite burn. Thermite, an incendiary chemical that burns at extremely high temperatures, might have been able to melt the metal structure in a way the crashing and exploding airplanes could not have. If the columns had been treated with thermite, then one has definitive proof of a conspiracy.[25]

What tarnishes Jones' academic reputation in the eyes of conspiracy critics is the fact that he never presented or published his studies in any peer-reviewed scholarly forum or journal. He simply made his allegations public and gave his support to the conspiracy move-ment — a group that is prone to accept his theories with little critical analysis. Brigham Young University, in fact, put him on leave in 2006 after he started disseminating his paper "Why Indeed Did the World Trade Center Building Completely Collapse" on the Internet.[26] Jones' theories, BYU charged, were "speculative and accusatory," and not based on rigorous analysis guided by the strict methodology of the scientific process.[27] His suspension helped raise his profile and level of respect within the conspiracy theory movement. Punitive action by the university, Jones' supporters contend, merely confirms the fact that he is "getting close to the truth" and that BYU is a puppet of the "establishment."

A similar case almost unfolded at the University of Wisconsin, where Kevin Barrett, a lecturer on Islam, African literature, and foreign languages, had been threatened by Wis-consin state legislators. Sixty-one legislators sponsored a petition to have him fired. Citing a commitment to the academic freedom of its faculty, the university refused to dismiss Bar-rett. But just as in Jones' case, the attempted attack on Barrett's career gave him a martyr status in the eyes of the conspiracy theory movement.[28]

The 9/11 conspiracy theory community is largely represented by various organizations of believers advancing an "alternate version of the events." But these groups often subscribe to the ideas that are strongly opposed to each other, leaving the movement highly fractious and given to bitter infighting.

Perhaps the largest and most active of these factions is the group that became the de facto namesake for the entire 9/11 conspiracy theory movement, 9/11 Truth. They refer to themselves as "truthers." The 9/11 cover-up conspiracy, they claim, involves the Bush White House, the Pentagon and most of the branches of the military (especially the Air Force), New York authorities reaching all the way to Mayor Giuliani's administration, the National Institute of Standards and Technology, and the members of the 9/11 Commission. The truthers claim that the collapse of the Twin Towers could not have been caused by the impacting planes, but by a controlled demolition of clandestinely placed explosives inside the buildings. They point to the collapse of Trade Tower Seven as an example of their hidden explosives theory. No plane struck Tower Seven, yet it collapsed. This, they argue, makes no sense. They also claim that the Arab terrorists supposedly flying the hijacked airliners were, according to whichever faction of the truth movement is telling the tale, either aided in their suicide mission by American intelligence, were patsies with false names standing in for real terrorists still alive and well in Saudi Arabia, or did not exist at all. The "no ter-rorist" claim of the latter theory argues that remote control devices were used to comman-deer the airplanes and fly them into the Twin Towers and into the Pentagon. The Pentagon crash is also not what it appears to be. The damage seen in much of the news footage, the truthers argue, does not look "right." The crash of United Flight 93 in Stoneycreek Town-ship, near Shanksville, Pennsylvania, they claim, was not a result of a passenger revolt but, most likely, a shootdown of the plane by a missile-loaded government aircraft in the form of an innocuous-looking small passenger jet. Various factions of the truthers, though, claim that the wreckage found in Shanksville was not that of Flight 93. This theory forwards the idea that the United passenger jet was somehow diverted to Cleveland where government operatives secreted away all the passengers, making them disappear forever. Furthermore, truthers, to some extent, all believe that the Air Force and the North American Air Defense Command were complicit in the attacks by ensuring that no fighter jets would try and intercept any of the hijacked planes.[29]

The organization Scholars for 9/11 Truth, founded by Steven Jones and James H. Fetzer, claimed to be an investigative organization well-grounded in very rigorous investigative methodologies. Perhaps realizing how quickly the conspiracy movement was spiraling into the realms of wild hyperbole, Jones and Fetzer created their group and added the word "scholars" to its title to counter the sort of over-the-top lunatic image conspiracy theorists were inspiring in the popular imagination. Jones' academic credentials in the hard sciences, for the group's supporters at least, helped give it a rational-thinking patina of respectability. Fetzer is a former philosophy professor. Nevertheless, it wasn't long before radically different philosophies about conspiracy theorizing led to a schism among Scholars for 9/11 Truth members. While Jones steadfastly pushed for investigating only those conspiracy theories that sounded plausible upon first glance, Fetzer believed that their group should be a prover-bial "big tent" for theorists, where all claims and all suspicions were heard, given credence, and investigated. For Fetzer and his faction, no conspiracy theory was off the table; all ideas should be seriously considered and their proponents given equal respect. Some of what Fet-zer endorsed as being plausible included the idea that the towers were destroyed by a space-based directed-energy weapon, a small nuclear bomb, and weather-control energy weapons. He also vigorously argued that there is ample evidence to believe that the towers were not even struck by airplanes but missiles cloaked by holographic projections.[30]

Fetzer's openness to every fringe 9/11 conspiracy theory, however, split the Scholars group by December of 2006. Jones, along with a majority of the organization's membership, founded Scholars for 9/11 Truth and Justice, a new group which, they strongly maintained, would adhere to the strictest scientific methodologies and not give forum to theories that can not be substantiated by solid empirical evidence. The central platform of Scholars for 9/11 Truth and Justice remains the argument that the towers had to have been brought down by explosives planted inside the buildings.[31]

A similar organization, Architects and Engineers for 9/11 Truth, was founded by San Francisco architect Richard Gage in 2006. Gage and his supporters also argue that the col-lapse of the towers was too fast to have been caused by a structural weakening from the crashing planes; large quantities of explosives and incendiary materials would have been required to weaken its support columns. They also point to the video footage of the col-lapsing towers and focus on windows blowing outwards and plumes of dust and debris shooting out the buildings as the floors start pancaking. Such plumes, they claim, are proof of explosive charges being set off inside the buildings. Gage is also one of the strongest pro-ponents of the hidden thermite theory. Just like Steven Jones, he claims that the towers' metal skeletons had been treated with thermite in order to further weaken the entire building and, along with the explosive charges, led to a complete structural failure. Gage and Archi-tects have been vigorously and widely disseminating photos of the rubble, pointing to some of the standing columns that appear to have black, flowing blobs of some strange material all over them. Those blobs, they claim, are the hardened remnants of the thermite. Fur-thermore, those pictures have served to expose yet another method of sabotage: Some of the free-standing columns in the wreckage pile appear to have been severed in perfectly straight, angular lines. It is impossible for a metal beam, they claim, to have been broken in such perfect, straight lines. What is more likely to have happened, they say, is that certain columns must have been secretly cut to help further weaken the entire building. Only a combination of the impacting airplanes, the jet fuel fire, the thermite, explosive charges, and pre-cut support beams could have brought the towers down as fast as they fell, the Architects group claims. In turn, such a complicated demolition effort is a clear sign of a massive conspiracy.[32]

Once again reminiscent of the John F. Kennedy assassination conspiracy theories, other skeptics turned their accusatory fingers on the government's primary investigative commission. Much like David Ray Griffin and his book *The 9/11 Commission Report: Omissions and Distortions*, some groups have focused solely on the government's probe of 9/11. If there was one massive military-intelligence plot to stage the attacks, the 9/11 Commission report, the theorists argue, is a second conspiracy to cover up the first conspiracy. Organizations like 9/11 Citizens Watch and the Hispanic Victims Group have accused the Commission of not being open to the questions and suggestions of 9/11 survivors and the families of victims. The groups charge that the Commission has cherry-picked certain aspects, select events, and a small handful of witnesses to the attacks to examine. Critics of the Commission Report claim that other people who could give accounts that contradict the al-Qaeda terrorist and collapse-by-jet-fuel-fire conclusions have been ignored or aggressively intimidated and silenced by the government.

While the 9/11 conspiracy community is very large and growing, it is nevertheless a fractious coalition of individuals. While they might all share a hostile skepticism, there are so many camps of such radically different alternate explanations that these factions often fight each other as viciously as they fight to uncover the allegedly hidden truths behind the attacks.

For example, conspiracy theorists who believe that all is not as might appear in the case of the Flight 93 crash have so far broken into two hostile camps. One school of thought argues that the airliner was simply shot down by a mysterious white jet. The reason behind the shoot-down, they hypothesize, is because the passengers who fought back against the hijackers and attempted to retake the plane might have been successful and might have suddenly uncovered the hand of a government conspiracy behind the entire hijacking. An opposing camp of conspiracy theorists, as stated before, believes that the wreckage near Shanksville is not that of Flight 93; the real airplane, they claim, was hidden away somewhere in Ohio. To date, the rivalry between these two factions has gotten so vitriolic that they are both dedicating voluminous webpages and blogs to accusing the other side of having either been infiltrated by government agents or acting as willing tools for the 9/11 conspirators. Both accuse the other of being so absurd as to be a part of a disinformation campaign designed to discredit the truth movement.

Similarly, people like James Fetzer and the believers of some of the more exotic conspiracy theories, like the space-based energy weapon, have been banned from appearing at a number of conspiracy rallies. Other fringe theorists have received death threats from several of the more aggressive mainstream truthers.[33]

In turn, notable liberal critics of the Bush administration and its anti-terror and Iraq policies have loudly condemned the entire truth movement as unwittingly playing into the hands of conservatives. *Rolling Stone* writer Matt Taibi and far-left-wing scholar Noam Chomsky have argued that all the outlandish, contradictory, and unverifiable claims made by the truth movement appear to have given pro–Bush conservatives a reason to ridicule *all* of their critics. Taibi leveled his harshest criticism at the producers of *Loose Change 9/11:*

An American Coup, one of the most well-known 9/11 conspiracy documentaries. Much like Vincent Bugliosi argued in his debunking of the Kennedy assassination theories, Chomsky argued that the Bush administration would have had so much to lose if their conspiracy failed that it is simply inconceivable that they would take such a risk and put such an incredibly complicated plot into motion. Thus, just as most anti-conspiracists generally argue, Chomsky has said that a plot as complicated as a 9/11 conspiracy would have had to involve so many people that it would have been impossible to keep secret.

The infamous *Loose Change* documentary first appeared on the Internet in 2005 and underwent several revisions and re-edits over the subsequent two years. For many 9/11 conspiracy converts, *Loose Change* is usually their first exposure to the main ideas of the truth movement.[34] Conceived in 2002 as a screenplay for a fictional movie about a September 11 conspiracy, the documentary was written and edited by aspiring filmmaker Dylan Avery. He was aided in the project by Korey Rowe, a childhood friend and Afghanistan veteran, syndicated talk show host Jason Bermas, and future television producer Matthew Brown. In Avery's original vision of a 9/11 project, he was going to write and attempt to market a thriller screenplay about a government plot behind the terrorist attacks. In that iteration of the project, no pretenses were made to reality. As Avery has admitted several times, with the passage of time he came to realize that it made perfect logical sense that a government conspiracy must have been behind the real 9/11 attacks. As he began to edit news footage and narrate the documentary with Rowe on his home computer, the project turned into the "real" documentary millions of people had downloaded for free from YouTube since 2005. The documentary was such a success that Avery and his partners immediately re-edited it and released a second version, *Loose Change: Second Edition*. In 2006 he released yet another version, titled *Loose Change: Second Edition Recut*, and in 2007 they released *Loose Change: Final Cut*. The first two *Loose Change* pictures were so phenomenally successful online that *Recut* and *Final Cut* were distributed on DVD by Microcinema International. The last two editions were narrated by Daniel Sunjata, an actor on the FX television series *Fired Up* and ardent September 11 conspiracy theory buff. *Two and a Half Men* star Charlie Sheen is reported to have been such an enthusiastic supporter that he campaigned to have a major studio buy the rights to the documentary, remake it, and release it theatrically. Sheen also wanted to narrate the theatrical version.[35]

Loose Change remains one of the most controversial pieces of work in all the independently produced 9/11 conspiracy-theory media. Its origins in fiction make it suspect for all but the most die-hard of conspiracy believers. Moreover, every version of the documentary has been attacked for containing easily verifiable factual errors. Matt Taibi wrote, "Every time those *Loose Change* dickwads opens his mouth, a Republican somewhere picks up five votes."[36]

Those doubting the allegations of the 9/11 truth movement regularly argue that conspiracy theorists base their positions on factual and scientific inaccuracies—either out of malice, but most likely because of their ignorance of science and the realities of political bureaucracies—and their own psychological needs for a new conspiracy in an age of turmoil, war, and uncertainty. As MIT engineer Thomas W. Eager remarked about the scientific proof of a conspiracy behind the WTC destruction, the theorists' major flaw is that their "research" usually has an expectancy bias. This means that they want to believe so badly that they usually engage in a sort of reverse scientific process. They start out wanting to find a conspiracy and go about picking and choosing data that support their hypothesis while ignoring all the evidence to the contrary.[37] For example, conspiracy theories usually argue that jet fuel fire could not have melted the WTC's steel support structure. The amount of fuel inside an airplane could not burn long enough and hot enough, conspiracy believers charge, to melt such massive objects. Thus, this line of argument concludes, thermite and/or hidden explosives must have been used. The counterargument points out that the National Institute of Standards and Technology studies never claimed that the support structures were melted. The melting argument of the conspiracy theorists is but a misrepresentation of the government's and the scientific establishment's conclusions. The burning jet fuel, according to the NIST studies, might not have been hot enough to *melt* steel columns, but it was hot enough to *weaken* them. This weakening of the steel, coupled with the holes torn in the buildings by the airplanes, meant that the towers were bound to collapse under the weight of the floors above the impact points.

Moreover, conspiracy critics point out, the alleged evidence of detonating explosives during the collapse is nothing more than a misunderstanding of the physics of an imploding building. The collapse of one floor on top of the other acted like a giant accordion being squeezed shut. The air inside the towers had to be squeezed somewhere as an ever-increasing tonnage of concrete and steel was rushing downward. That air was forced outward, conspiracy critics charge, thus creating the bursts of dust plumes shooting out the windows.

The very logic of planting explosives and thermite inside the buildings has also been suspect for conspiracy critics. The basic counterargument to the conspiracists has pointed out that one would need an immense amount of explosives and thousands of feet of electrical wiring to prepare the two towers for the sort of controlled demolition alleged by conspiracy believers. Secretly installing all those explosives and their detonation equipment would have taken weeks, if not months. With both towers housing the offices of numerous multinational companies whose offices are virtually open around the clock (not to mention maintained by large numbers of building staff), getting so much demolition equipment in there on the sly would have been inconceivably difficult.

But should the explosives have been successfully rigged all over the two towers, one might also ask what the point was in hijacking the airliners and crashing them into the buildings. Why would the conspirators risk detection and failure by further complicating their plans? If they already had the means to destroy the World Trade Center by way of hidden explosives, why not just blow up the buildings and blame it on al-Qaeda? As scholars of the psychological power of terror usually point out, the real effect of any terror attack is not merely in the lives taken and property destroyed. A terrorist attack's true power lies in the lingering, long-term fear and insecurity it instills in a population. Thus, it is arguable that if a vast right-wing conspiracy wanted to frighten a country so badly as to make its citizens unquestioningly back any Bush military policy, would it not have been more effective to suggest that terrorists have so easily infiltrated the U.S. as to be able to plant explosives in two of the country's biggest and busiest skyscrapers? Terrorists have been able to hijack planes for decades. But to infiltrate and destroy the World Trade Center would have taken true criminal geniuses. Then again, if Bush and his conspirators would have really wanted to frighten the country about a global network of super criminals that had to be brought down by any military means necessary *and* these conspirators had the ability to secretly rig the towers with explosives, it would have been much simpler and much more effective to blow up the buildings and blame it on Osama bin Laden than to set up the airplane ruse.

The flip side of such an argument could also ask why the conspirators would need to even rig the Twin Towers to collapse at all. Just hijacking the two airliners, murdering several hundred passengers and a handful of WTC workers at the points of impact would have created the same psychological effect of vulnerability and terror in Americans. By setting up a big, complicated operation like the rigging of the towers with explosives merely created unnecessary complications, expense, and an increased chance of failure for the conspirators. It is possibly safe to assume that the nationwide air of horror, mourning, and subsequent rebound of ultra-patriotism and unconditional support for the invasions of Afghanistan and Iraq would have come about even without the towers collapsing.

This line of reasoning is equally applicable to the Pentagon attacks. Hijacking an airplane, then blowing a hole in the Pentagon with a missile, then strewing the area around the building with airplane-like wreckage sounds unnecessarily complicated. Conspirators could just as well have fired several shoulder-launched missiles, or planted hidden explosives inside the Pentagon, then blamed it all on al-Qaeda infiltrators living in the U.S. The terror, shock, and outrage could have been created without the added complication of having to steal a plane full of people, then making sure the plane gets away undetected, then having to (presumably) execute its passengers and flight crew and destroy the plane in secret.

For conspiracy debunkers, there is also no clearer example of Thomas W. Eager's reverse scientific method than the thermite argument. Steven Jones based his claims for the use of thermite on his analysis of WTC area dust and some debris. In that dust, Jones said, he and other investigators found traces of thermite. In fact, what Jones and others have found were traces of sulfur, which could also have been produced from the burning of all the WTC computers and other plastic items. Therefore, conspiracy theory debunkers argue, not one shred of evidence exists that would reasonably suggest that there was anything anomalous in the wreckage or that thermite was used. Moreover, the explanation for all the angled cuts on the remaining metal beams in the wreckage is also a simple one: The pictures that people like Jones and his supporters usually use to argue their points are pictures of beams rescue workers had started cutting apart in the recovery work.

Conspiracy debunkers have also pointed to historical evidence of catastrophic structural failures in high rise buildings to show that another lynchpin argument in the conspiracist cannon is also patently false. Conspiracy theorists staunchly maintain that the sort of structural failure witnessed in the collapse of the towers, where the floors of the building pancaked on top of each other as a result of fire-damaged steel support columns, had never occurred before outside of controlled demolitions. Only when demolition companies brought down buildings with the use of strategically placed explosives could buildings be seen imploding as perfectly as the towers did, the conspiracist argument states. But, in fact, similar support structure failures following a fire have been documented as leading to imploding buildings in Chicago in 1967, in Brackenridge, Pennsylvania, in 1991, and in Singapore in 1997.

As for the case of Flight 93, even conspiracy theorists have not endorsed one standard alternate theory of what happened to the airliner. Ironically, each of the conspiratorial scenarios about its fate has been attacked as lies and absurdities by other conspiracy theorists. The one constant in most of the alternate accounts of the events, though, seems to be the idea that the phone calls made from the doomed plane were somehow faked. For conspiracy skeptics, though, this allegation is the most outlandish of all. They point out that it is hard to imagine that family members could not realize that the person on the other end of the line was not their loved one. For many who are wary of the 9/11 truthers, the allegations of the faked phone calls are the most offensive of the conspiracy movement.

As controversial and emotionally charged as the September 11 conspiracy theories might be, their appearance and proliferation should not be surprising. As the country's support for the Bush administration's wars in the Middle East waned, it was perhaps inevitable that conspiracy theories would emerge out of September 11. The attacks of that day prompted unprecedented displays of patriotism and they inspired a country to give a political blank check to the president. Everyone, Democrat and Republican alike, fully supported a president who had been elected by less than half the popular vote in 2000 and they were willing to fully trust his judgment when he asked to invade two countries within a span of two years. When those wars did not turn out as the country had hoped, conspiracy theorizing was certain to be a part of the backlash.

Perhaps the 9/11 conspiracy theories also found fertile ground in the American imagination because the time was simply right for them. Those given to paranoid speculation were ready for a new political conspiracy theory. By the early 2000s, most conspiracy theorists were of a generation that had not even been born when John F. Kennedy was shot. They were ready for a new national tragedy to probe for "inconsistencies," "mysteries," and "unanswered questions." Perhaps September 11 provided the opportunity to pore over a plausible conspiracy, something more immediate and relatively realistic than alien abductions, UFO bases, and ancient Vatican secrets.

But because the conspiracy theories persist, so do films that use them as source materials for one shocking, stunning, and mind-bending plot twist after another.

CHAPTER 9

Conspiracies Never Die
Conspiracy Films of the 2000s

If American popular culture has illustrated the way conspiracy theories need to constantly grow and mutate in their complexity — all the way into the realm of high strangeness and hyperbole — conspiracy entertainment in the new millennium proved this beyond a doubt. Once the flag-waving and the mourning of September 11 stopped, it seemed like every sector of the American public had its own pet theory about how hidden crimes and hidden cabals were ruining and enslaving the world. In the 2000s, everyone from the conservative right to the liberal left, the secular, the religious, the spiritual, the occultist, the agnostic, and the atheist all had pet conspiracy theories. The entertainment media were all ready to feed Americans' insatiable appetites for paranoid entertainment.

By early 2000, the Fox network and Chris Carter put into production a spin-off series of *The X-Files*. Although the iconic, standard-setting *X-Files* had started showing its age by 2000, it was still a lucrative enough property for Fox to try and capitalize on it by turning it into a franchise. *The X-Files*, after all, had earned as strong a presence at science fiction fan conventions as *Star Trek* and a highly lucrative merchandizing market was bringing in steady profits from a line of memorabilia devoted to the show. For the spin-off series, Carter focused on three semi-regular *X-Files* supporting characters, comic conspiracy theorists who published an underground newsletter and often came to Agent Mulder for help in particularly perplexing cases. The show would be called *The Lone Gunmen*, taking its title from the newsletter published by the three characters. When its first episode aired on March 4, 2001, it had accidentally become one of the most prophetic episodes of that decade's television. It involved a government plot to hijack an airliner and crash it into the World Trade Center. Moreover, the conspirators hatched their plot with an eye toward blaming it on terrorists and justifying the country's military buildup and overseas weapons sales.

Although *The Lone Gunmen* was cancelled by September of 2001, further evidencing the diminishing returns of *The X-Files* in particular and conspiracy entertainment in general at the turn of the millennium, the two shows' most committed fans had good memories. The uncannily prescient *Gunmen* pilot eventually brought some uncomfortable attention to Carter and his creative team.

On 9/11, said episode co-writer Frank Spotnitz, "the first thing that went through my head was, 'I hope this doesn't have anything to do with what we did, that it wasn't somehow inspired by anything we did.'"[1]

Dean Haglund played one of the three leads and is a frequent special guest at science fiction conventions. He has also talked about the way the fan communities and the various circles of conspiracy theorists were immediately fascinated by the way a television show could create a scenario around an attack on the World Trade Center just months before a real attack took place. "All the conspiracy theorists started passing around [bootleg copies of] that pilot at conventions and UFO conventions and started propelling that forward," says Haglund. "These guys are all asking questions about, 'How much did we know?' 'Who wrote the script?'—that kind of thing."[2]

Ed Martin, a columnist for *The Myers Report*, a television industry trade newsletter, was perplexed by an overall lag in mainstream entertainment journalists catching on to the fact that an airliner attack on the towers had been predicted by a short-lived TV series. "This seems to be collective amnesia of the highest order," writes Martin. "The final act of the *Gunmen* pilot, which seemingly made no impact last year, now contains some of the most deeply disturbing images ever created for an entertainment program."[3]

Once *TV Guide* wrote an article about the *Gunmen* and 9/11 parallels, however, mainstream entertainment journalism repeated the story enough times that it would follow Carter and his creative team around for several years. In fact, in pre-production press conferences before filming started on the long-delayed *X-Files* film sequel *I Want to Believe* in 2007, reporters continued raising questions. Carter and his team routinely explained that it could all be chalked up to an uncanny coincidence.

The conspiracy theory community, however, does not like uncanny coincidences. When the DVD release of the series was announced, many wondered if the pilot episode would be excluded out of sensitivity over the real tragedy. The more conspiratorially inclined argued that there was a sinister connection between the pilot episode and a government hand in the 9/11 attacks. Thoughts of a connection, however, were eventually fueled by an unlikely source.

At first, radio talk show host Alex Jones, the most vocal and visible of the 9/11 conspiracy theorists, insisted that Hollywood was being manipulated by the government to discredit conspiracy theorists. In Jones' reckoning, much of popular culture's depiction of conspiracy theorists had been shaped by government input, with the specific intention of making the theorists look disreputable and unbelievable. Television programs like *The X-Files* and *The Lone Gunmen*, Jones wrote on a prisonplanet.com posting, were "used to subconsciously manipulate people to believe that if these events did actually happen, it would be like a film, not a part of reality, therefore we should not worry too much. Anyone who would dare to say that the Government were responsible for such terrorist attacks would immediately be branded a 'lunatic conspiracy theorist, like those guys from the *X-Files.*'"[4] Although these sorts of 9/11 claims had become a standard part of the Jones repertoire, it is quite remarkable that in an interview he was able to get Dean Haglund to admit that he found the idea of a government conspiracy behind the attacks plausible.

In the interview, available on YouTube, Haglund explained that he found the charges of a NORAD and Air Force hand in the attacks the most plausible of the conspiracy canon. The events of September 11, Haglund concluded, appeared to be "pretty much staged." Fueling charges of a *Lone Gunmen* connection to the alleged conspiracy, Haglund also discussed with Jones the way the writing and production staff of both *Gunmen* and *The X-Files* would regularly plumb the conspiracy literature and conspiracy theory websites for story ideas. Then, in both the Jones interview and various other forums, Haglund made cryptic references to visits to both the *X-Files* and *Lone Gunmen* sets by FBI agents who confirmed that "some of the things" in these shows were remarkably close to what the agency was doing.

Cryptic remarks, of course, are the most potent fuel for conspiracy theorists, and Jones steadfastly continued to argue that *Gunmen* was just one of the many TV shows and movies the U.S. government would regularly manipulate to try and sway public perception about world events.

However, the more Jones tends to expound on the idea, the further he seems to go in contradicting his own thesis that the government is using popular culture as a tool to cover up a September 11 conspiracy. For example, he often writes about the Pentagon and the CIA attempting to enlist Hollywood filmmakers in helping envision terrorist attack scenarios and crafting messages in entertainment that will help improve the image of the United States abroad. None of this, however, is a secret. The Defense Department was very vocal in the aftermath of 9/11 about its hopes to use the entertainment industry in the War on Terror. The logic of funding films and television shows where the government is depicted as a collection of amoral, mass-murdering conspirators, however, is shaky, to say the least. Depicting the U.S. government as villains cannot possibly help their agenda. It is perfectly plausible — and, again, an admitted fact — that the government would want to portray itself in the best possible light after 9/11. But portraying intelligence operatives as conspirators could not, by any stretch of the imagination, be an effective or plausible part of this plan. Thus, conspiracy skeptics point out, if there had really been an evil government plan to crash planes into the World Trade Center and the Pentagon, the conspirators would most certainly not show their hand by dramatizing it in a television show. In fact, the idea that planting clues to the real conspiracy inside the storyline of a conspiracy-themed show to help fuel the ridicule of any real theorists does not make much sense either. The "geeky" and "lunatic conspiracy theorists" of both *The X-Files* and *The Lone Gunmen* are always the heroes. If these shows have the ability to shape the public consciousness, the effect would be to convince people *not* to dismiss conspiracy theorists as "crazy." If anything, these shows always teach the lesson that the eccentric conspiracy maven is almost always right. The three *Lone Gunmen* protagonists are always right in their conspiracy theories. On *The X-Files*, Mulder, the open-minded believer ready to accept most "extreme possibilities," was nearly always right and Scully, the level-headed skeptic, was usually wrong.

For most, the *Lone Gunmen* pilot episode is as Carter and his production partners claim to this day: nothing more than a case of an uncanny coincidence. Carter and company point out that they were not the first ones to come up with the idea of using an airliner as a weapon of terror. In his 1994 novel *Debt of Honor*, Tom Clancy writes about an airliner being crashed into the Capitol Building, killing the president and wiping out the members of Congress. In Dale Brown's 1994 novel *Storming Heaven*, terrorists once again use hijacked airliners to drop bombs onto major American cities. Conspiracy theorists usually argue that President George W. Bush and Vice-President Dick Cheney vehemently saying that no one could have foreseen the use of airplanes as terrorist weapons is an unbelievable claim in light of *The Lone Gunmen* and these novels; skeptics say that the heads of the government merely developed a sudden case of popular culture amnesia in order to dodge blame for shameful holes, inadequacies, and just plain incompetence in the government's anti-terror services.

In the immediate aftermath of September 11, Hollywood continued to have as conflicted a relationship with conspiracy entertainment as the rest of America, when not completely perplexed by the very near-future of the espionage and action-adventure genres. Films making headlines immediately after the attacks were the ones pulled from theaters and re-edited in response to 9/11. The most notable was Arnold Schwarzenegger's *Collateral Damage*, a thriller about a firefighter whose wife and child are killed in the terrorist bombing of a high-rise building. Slated for an October 5, 2001, release, the film was "indefinitely" pulled from distribution for the rest of 2001. It was eventually released on February 8, 2002, to unremarkable box office. The terrorist bombing scene at its beginning was heavily edited to avoid a strong similarity to the very real images of the World Trade Center destruction.

In the summer of 2002, Paramount released an adaptation of Tom Clancy's *Sum of All Fears*, dealing with terrorists destroying the Super Bowl with a nuclear bomb. Shot before September 11, the nuclear explosion sequences were also re-edited. In this politically correct adaptation, in the film, the screenwriters replaced Clancy's Arab villains with the inoffensive, all-purpose threat of European Neo Nazis. Had the Arabs stayed in the film version of the story, one can only wonder how long its release might have been delayed. Many cultural commentators, after all, had raised the question of how the entertainment industry needed to treat Arabs and depictions of the Middle East in the wake of 9/11. The time, perhaps, had come, these commentators argued, for popular culture to react to the attacks with some degree of measured and cautious introspection. In light of this particular tragedy, many of these liberal-minded critics argued that rather than bellicose, jingoistic revenge melodramas, Hollywood needed to reassess its own possible culpability for so much of the Arab world hating the United States.

However, post–9/11 movie rental statistics showed something quite interesting about the attitudes of the American moviegoing public. People renting films were interested in *precisely* the kinds of jingoistic violence that film critics had warned against. The first films to fly off video store shelves after September 11 were blood-and-testosterone action epics from the 1980s. Films like *Die Hard* and the *Rambo* series topped the rental charts. Also popular was *Delta Force*, Chuck Norris' 1986 film about American Special Forces operatives hunting down and wiping out scores of Arab terrorists.

However, just as Chris Carter had predicted, most of the entertainment industry did indeed become skittish about directly adapting any more of the tenets of the conspiracy theory community. The first two pictures to deal in concepts like "false flag" attacks and hidden government cabals working to overthrow democracy under the guise of a national security crisis came, ironically, from the most mainstream, most conservative of all film franchises in Hollywood's history.

Released on May 12, 2002, *Star Wars, Episode II: Attack of the Clones* made it clear that the true core of the prequel trilogy in George Lucas' iconic space opera was all about a massive conspiracy. Although often summed up as the story of Anakin Skywalker's moral corruption and seduction by the Dark Side of the Force, the *Star Wars* prequels put just as much emphasis (perhaps more) on an intricate plot to overthrow the democratic Galactic Republic. To achieve this, a shadowy cabal of Sith conspirators engineers a political crisis and instigates a civil war.

The origins of the *Star Wars* conspiracy plot had been established in *Episode I: The Phantom Menace*. In that 1999 movie, the weak and overtly bureaucratic Galactic Republic's trade regulations are challenged by a group of separatists called the Trade Federation. They are attempting to defy trade taxes and break away from the Republic. Such secession will threaten the peaceful status quo of the galaxy. With the aid of the Jedi, an ascetic order adept at harnessing and channeling the Force, the Republic attempts to root out the leadership of the separatists and stop their plot before they sow disorder and violence. In the course of their investigation, Jedi Knights Qui-Gon Jinn (Liam Neeson) and Obi-Wan Kenobi (Ewan McGregor) realize that the separatist menace is much more powerful and organized than imagined. Its leadership is made up of Sith Lords, the dark counterparts of the Jedi Knights. Whereas the Jedi use the Force to maintain harmony, seek enlightenment, and keep the peace, the Sith have tapped the Dark Side of the Force for raw, brute power, and its abilities to enslave and destroy. This Sith menace, Qui-Gon and Obi-Wan discover, is committed to obliterating the Republic.

In *Attack of the Clones*, the details of the separatist plot are further fleshed out, revealing the "menace" to be, in essence, a false flag operation. The separatist confederation is a phony threat created by the power-hungry Senator Palpatine (Ian McDiarmid). At the end of the previous film, Palpatine had successfully campaigned to be elected Supreme Chancellor of the Republic, replacing a weak and indecisive leader who had been ineffective in combating the challenge of the Trade Federation. Now, as the leader of the Republic, Palpatine — who is himself a Sith Lord, the powerful Darth Siduous — begins building a massive clone army to counter the separatist "threat." Then, in the final film of the prequel trilogy, 2005's *Revenge of the Sith*, the plans of the conspiracy finally come to fruition. Having started the Clone Wars against a manufactured enemy and slowly wooing temperamental new Jedi Knight Anakin Skywalker (Hayden Christensen) to his side, Palpatine manipulates the Galactic Senate into voting him sweeping new emergency powers. In effect, the vote dismantles the Republic and establishes the totalitarian Galactic Empire. Palpatine, in turn, becomes its sole dictator for life. The clone army is now a repressive force of storm troopers tasked with wiping out all opposition to Palpatine's rule.

These follow-ups to the original trilogy were generally dismissed even by the staunchest fans as flashy, ultra-hi-tech, yet ultimately inferior. But they actually touched upon the tenor of the times much more effectively than their predecessors. *Episodes II* and *III* especially reflected Americans' growing unease with government in a time of war and their suspicions over the use of national crises for political gain. As the anger over the Bush administration's WMD justification for the war in Iraq grew into charges of deliberate deception and conspiracy, *Star Wars*' plot looked ever more like a mirror of the social mood in the post–9/11 era. In fact, for some conservatives and supporters of the Iraq invasion, *Revenge of the Sith* was offensive. Particular scenes, plot points, and dialogue, they argued, could not be interpreted as being anything other than direct shots at George W. Bush and his policies.[5] Palpatine's manipulation of the Senate into granting him emergency powers, conservatives claimed, was a thinly veiled critique of the Patriot Act. In one of the film's final scenes, after Anakin turned to the Dark Side and is on the verge of attempting to kill Obi-Wan Kenobi, he declares that the Sith will not compromise their plan for total rule. "If you're not with me, then you are my enemy," he says. Many viewers, in fact, even those who did not support the Bush policies, had said that such a line can only be interpreted as a jibe at the president's address to Congress and his declaration that "either you're with us, or you're with the terrorists." Several conservative *Star Wars* fans, in turn, called for a boycott of the film. Lucas, they said, had taken what was supposed to have been a fantasy and turned it into a piece of anti–Bush agitprop. With the Trade Federation plot, they argued, Lucas had sided the *Star Wars* films with the September 11 conspiracy movement. The Sith plot to overthrow the Republic was a stand-in for the idea that the Bush administration had planned the attacks of 9/11 in order to curtail civil liberties and go to war in the Middle East.

Although the Trade Federation plot of the prequel trilogy does incorporate many of the standard tenets of traditional conspiracism, Lucas deserves credence when he argues that his films were not any sort of a deliberate political statement on Iraq or the Bush administration. A general outline for the three films, as a matter of fact, had been written in the early 1990s. The script for *Revenge of the Sith* had been written even before *Attack of the Clones* went into production in the summer of 2000. In most interviews, Lucas even claimed that he had a rough plan for an extended series of films about the Skywalker family and the fall of the Galactic Empire as early as 1973, when he started work on a first draft of the original *Star Wars* script, *Episode IV: A New Hope*. If anything, he said, some part of the politics of *Star Wars* were inspired by the Vietnam era. Darth Vader's corruption and downfall, he claimed, was in part inspired by Richard Nixon and Watergate.[6] The general idea about the corruption, weakening, and disintegration of the Republic, he added, came from a comparative historical analysis of the way democratic systems can be undermined and destroyed from within. *Star Wars*, he explained, found most of its politics in the demise of the Roman Republic, in Napoleon's machinations to become an emperor, and, most of all, in the Nazi party's takeover of Germany.

In fact, a clear-eyed observation of the iconography and plot points of both *Star Wars* trilogies will find the most obvious parallels with pre-war German history and the Nazi era. From the design of the Imperial officers' gray uniforms that resembles SS garb to naming Darth Vader's armies "storm troopers," the resemblance of the Galactic Empire to the Third Reich is unmistakable. Moreover, Palpatine's election to chancellor resembles Hitler's taking the reins of the German government from a weak and ineffective president Von Hindenburg.

If anything, *Star Wars* is ultimately the most effective piece of pop cultural open text. Like the first *Matrix*, its story is so polysemic that it can be claimed by various political, ideological, and even mystical and religious persuasions as a representation of their own values. Lucas' original inspiration for wanting to film an epic space opera had, in fact, come from his reading of comparative religion scholar Joseph Campbell's seminal study *Hero with a Thousand Faces*.[7] Furthermore, as Peter Biskind details Lucas' position within the late 1960s and '70s "film school brat" generation of moviemakers, *Star Wars* was always strictly envisioned as a children's movie that embodied clear and old-fashioned (if not explicitly conservative) moral values. "[*Star Wars*] was a conscious effort," Lucas said, "at creating new myths.... I wanted to make a kids' film that would ... introduce a kind of basic morality. Everybody's forgetting to tell the kids, 'Hey, this is right and this is wrong.'"[8] If fact, as Biskind writes, Lucas' obsession with his *Star Wars* idea and the two and a half years he spent writing, rewriting, and polishing the screenplay earned him little more than barbs and disrespect from his cohort of newly established, edgy, counterculture filmmakers. Lucas, much like writers and directors Brian DePalma, Hal Ashby, Dennis Hopper, Robert Towne, and Martin Scorsese, was supposed to have been rocking the establishment and turning classical conventions on their heads. His homage to traditional swashbuckling heroism and conservative morality didn't jibe well with the sensibilities of his hip contemporaries. Even his own wife Marcia, who had been working as an editor on Scorsese's *New York, New York* at the time Lucas was finishing *Star Wars*, reportedly told him, "*New York, New York* is a film for grown-ups, yours is just a kids' movie, and nobody's going to take it seriously."[9] Following suit, most of Lucas' friends — save for Steven Spielberg — mercilessly derided his vision for the retrograde, family-friendly space fantasy.

Cultural historians have long pegged the first three *Star Wars* films as being profoundly conservative in their themes, even their politics. *Star Wars*, they claim, was an antidote to the national trauma of Vietnam. It stood up for the idea of heroism through military adventure. Before Ronald Reagan's calls for strengthening America, and before Rambo successfully refought Vietnam, *Star Wars* delivered a tale of strong, confident adventurers triumphing on the battlefield.

So can the second *Star Wars* trilogy really be explained as Lucas' left-field turn into

9/11 Truth movement conspiracism? Most likely, the three prequels are a natural reflection of the values of their times, as much as, and perhaps even *more* so than the first three were a reflection of the '70s and the '80s. At a moment when America was looking to overcome its Vietnam era defeat, the first three films offered escapist comic book fantasy and compensatory heroics. The prequels, however, are as much a product of the Clinton era uncertainty that had inspired *The X-Files* and Area 51 conspiracism as they are of September 11. Episodes *I, II* and *III* are a reflection of a time when audiences had grown to accept that America's innocence was gone and no matter how much peace and prosperity they enjoyed, just like the citizens of the Galactic Republic, they could always fall victim to shadowy conspirators. Furthermore, the idea that national crises are really the handiwork of a power-grabbing conspiracy is not unique to the 9/11 Truth movement. Conspiracy theorists have been blaming emergencies on shadowy cabals throughout history. The attack on Pearl Harbor was supposed to have been a product of a conspiracy; Vietnam, the drug war, AIDS, and crime epidemics have likewise been blamed on conspiracies. Thus, if Lucas was attempting to dramatize the fear of the times in the 1990s and 2000s, his most logical avenue had to be a story about the biggest crisis of the day being nothing more than the machination of a secretive order of villains.

Throughout the 2000s, conspiracy-oriented entertainment alternated between the fanciful and the realistic. Filmmakers grappled with the question of how to deal with September 11, the wars in Iraq and Afghanistan, and their impact on the culture. After a stretch of peace and prosperity that allowed popular culture to become ever more whimsical with its conspiracy theorizing, how far would audiences let entertainment go when dealing with real tragedies? Since genres like horror, fantasy, and science fiction can usually handle controversial social issues by disguising their statements in metaphor and abstract symbolism, the supernatural and fantastic continued thriving throughout the decade. As the country's regard for the Bush administration and the war in Iraq soured, themes of shadowy conspiracies and governmental corruption turned up in the genre with greater frequency. The phenomenal success of the *Da Vinci Code* novel had also inspired numerous films dealing with secret society conspiracies and hidden codes that held the secrets to ancient treasures and hidden knowledge. But while fantasy and hyperbole thrived in the 2000s, realistic genres would also, eventually, confront the ever-growing level of distrust Americans felt toward politics and organizations of power.

At the start of the decade, though, the supernaturally oriented conspiracy film genre was joined by evangelical Christianity's own take on paranoid entertainment. Tim LaHaye and Jerry B. Jenkins' best-selling *Left Behind* novels got their first film adaptation from Cloud Ten Pictures, an independent Canadian production company specializing in Christian-themed entertainment. *Left Behind* (2000) came out on videotape and DVD first, then was given a theatrical release several months later.[10] Although very successful, the film attracted some of the same controversy as the novel. Eventually, the production of the series would also be impacted by contention among its creators.

Left Behind attempts a somewhat faithful adaptation of LaHaye and Jenkins' source material. The quality of the finished product, however, was hampered by two problems. The film's 96-minute running time allowed only a very superficial skimming of the book's main plot points. The threadbare budget also left the film looking like a cheap made-for-television movie.

Just like in the novel, *Left Behind* begins with natural and unnatural calamities hitting the world. First, devastating famines lead to unrest and global instability. Then, as the world seems to be inching closer to open warfare in the Middle East, millions of people inexplicably vanish. Those who are gone appear to be a random selection from all walks of life, along with infants and very young children. The accidents and panic that ensue galvanize the world to look for the fastest solution to the disorder. This solution appears to be Romanian president Nicolae Carpathia (Gordon Currie), the newly elected general secretary of the United Nations. The charismatic Carpathia has a proposal for forging a peace treaty with Israel that might rescue the Middle East from the brink of war. Part of this plan includes a new technology funded by his financial backers. A shadowy global corporate cabal had engineered Carpathia's political career, it is revealed, and it had also instigated the food shortages. But now, with the world in the grip of chaos, Carpathia announces that Dr. Chaim Rosenzweig (Colin Fox), an Israeli botanist, has made revolutionary breakthroughs in crop engineering that will yield bountiful harvests even in formerly inhospitable parts of the world. On ten tracts of land his financiers own around the world, Carpathia promises to begin harvesting all the crops the hungry masses will need to survive. Thus, virtually overnight, Carpathia has emerged as a peacemaker and the savior of the world.

But the mass disappearances have still not been explained in a satisfactory manner. A global research effort, funded by the U.N., declares that they were caused by radiation from the world's nuclear weapons programs. Most of the world believes this. Enough people, however, are still around to question this preposterous explanation.

Much of the film's narrative, just like that of the book, focuses on a handful of people who have been "left behind." They quickly discover that the answers are clearly spelled out in the Bible. The people who have vanished were all born again Christians. Those who have been born again and fully accepted Christ and the literal truth of the Bible have been worthy of being taken to Heaven. Children, born pure and not yet corrupted by the world's cynicism, secular rationalism, and lack of faith, were likewise good enough to be spirited away from the years of conflict and violence that will soon engulf the world.

Specifically, the story centers on airline pilot Rayford Steele (Brad Johnson), his daughter Chloe (Janaya Stevens), the assistant pastor of their church, Bruce Barnes (Clarence Gilyard), and reporter Buck Williams (Kirk Cameron). Steele is the first to realize the Biblical nature of the vanishings. His marriage had been badly strained because he could not accept his wife's fundamentalist, born again Christianity. He had been on the verge of having an affair with flight attendant Hattie Durham (Chelsea Noble), as the disappearances started. But by the time he got home and found his wife and young son gone, all the pieces to the puzzle start falling into place. He recalls his wife's stories of the Biblical Rapture and realizes that she was the perfect candidate to be taken. Their son, innocent and accepting of the truth of Jesus' existence, was also taken. But their teenage daughter, who had been equally disdainful of her mother's religiosity, was left behind. A distraught Bruce Barnes comes to the same conclusion about the disappearances. Although a priest, Barnes had been harboring secret doubts about the truth of the Bible. They join with Buck Williams, who wants to investigate what's going on inside the U.N., and commit themselves to helping the world cope with the chaos.

Although the world is about to be blessed with peace and prosperity under Carpathia's U.N. leadership, Steele and his friends know that the good times are the calm before the storm. If the Rapture had just taken place, it must mean that the Antichrist is rising to power. According to Biblical prophecy, the Rapture is followed by seven years of peace. The Antichrist will then declare himself god and demand unconditional worship. As Buck Williams confirms by the end of the film, Carpathia revealed himself as the Biblical Antichrist during a closed U.N. meeting. All who will not soon pledge their allegiances to him will be enslaved or wiped off the face of the Earth.

The *Left Behind* film captures the core theme of the LaHaye and Jenkins novel fairly well and, just like the novel, it became instantly successful. Filmed and distributed worldwide on a $17 million budget, it earned $34 million. Nevertheless, some controversy, mainly among fans of the novel, persists about the overall effectiveness of the film. In shortening the story from its 320-page literary source to a 96-minute feature film, much of the complex plotting of Carpathia's emergence as a world leader had to be jettisoned. Critics *and* fans have argued that the conversion of many of the story's heroes to born again Christianity comes across as superficial. Yet, at the same time, the film also suffers because the budget constraints did not allow for the special effects and stunts one expects in a dramatization of a global catastrophe. In fact, the film feels frustratingly inert, almost as if its main characters are standing on the most remote periphery of tremendous events and having little to no influence on any of those events. The major appeal of the books, after all — aside from the message intended for those who already believe in the premillennialist dogma — was that they couched their message in a fast-moving action-adventure narrative. Reviews of the books — both positive and negative — generally characterize them as a cross between fundamentalist theology and a Tom Clancy adventure novel. The film, unfortunately, has neither action nor adventure. Emphasis, however, is placed on numerous scenes of its characters discovering the "truth" of the Bible prophecies and the need for born again conversion to make it through the coming Tribulation. Nevertheless, as even the film's most sympathetic Christian critics point out, these scenes of self-discovery and conversion come across as trite and pedantic.

Left Behind and its two sequels do demonstrate, however, the adaptability of conspiracy plot archetypes to various social and religious agendas. Just like in their source material, a global conspiracy propels the plot forward. Although preordained, the rise of the Antichrist is aided by an international Satanic cabal that manipulates politics, financial systems, scientific research, and the media. Just like in most complex conspiracy theories that attempt to explain all of the major calamities of the day as interconnected parts of one far-reaching totalitarian global agenda, major crises in *Left Behind* are being manufactured by worldly organizations for Satan's benefit. Poverty and hunger are brought about by the diabolical conspirators who intend to one day curry favor by stepping forward and solving those same problems. In turn, volatile military crises are being staged by Carpathia's coconspirators, aided, both knowingly and unknowingly, by the news media. Eventually, like in the repertoire of most media monopoly critics, part of the Antichrist's final move in securing his stranglehold on the world includes taking censorious control of the media.

In 2002 and 2005, Cloud Ten Pictures produced, respectively, the sequels *Left Behind: Tribulation Force* and *Left Behind: World at War*. *Tribulation Force*, unfortunately, has more of the same shoestring-budget look as the first film. It's also plagued by the same inert storyline and direction. This is especially damaging to the film since it's about the beginning of a struggle against the overwhelming forces of the Antichrist. Moreover, the titular Tribulation Force, God's army on Earth, appears to be little more than four people going to a few clandestine meetings in a suburban church.

Creatively, *Left Behind: World at War* is a much more impressive film, boasting more action and a tighter, faster-paced storyline. Although it is only loosely based on the ending of the second novel, its plague and World War III storylines are more effective than the Rapture and rise-of-the-Antichrist scenarios of the first two films. Directed by action specialist Craig R. Baxley (*Action Jackson, I Come in Peace*, and TV's *Storm of the Century* and *Rose Red*), its focus is on the plot more than the proselytizing. The heroes' faith is an integral part of the story, but the film does not offer lengthy sermons about how scripture predicts and offers solutions to the problems of the moment. Baxley also turns out to be much more effective an actors' director than Vic Sarin and Bill Corcoran, who helmed the first two movies. Almost all of the cast of the first two films is back for this third installment, and their performances are much more naturalistic and nuanced than before. Even the requisite conversion scene, where the president is convinced by Buck Williams to accept Jesus, is much more moving than any of the spiritual-awakening moments that had come before in the franchise. It is a scene of a nearly broken man wrestling with doubt and regret, trying to atone for his previous lack of faith and wondering if his actions now could make up for his past — if he is even worthy of forgiveness at all. Since the role is played by Oscar winner Louis Gossett, Jr., Baxley's attempt at raising the scene above a perfunctory effort to preach to the *Left Behind* choir must have been made easier.

World at War set a precedent for distribution in the Christian film industry. While *Tribulation Force* went directly to video, *World at War* first premiered at a number of evangelical churches around the country on October 21, 2005. Several days later, it was made available on DVD and VHS. This sort of church premiere has since become common practice for Christian films.[11]

World at War appears to have been the last film in the *Left Behind* series. Timothy LaHaye had apparently also taken issue with the first *Left Behind*'s ultra-low budget. He sued Cloud Ten Pictures, claiming that he had been promised a more lavish adaptation of his books, a production in the ballpark of $40 million. When the film did disappointing box office, failing to become the crossover success LaHaye had envisioned, he laid the blame on its shoddy production values. Although the sequels were produced and did as well in the home entertainment market as the first film, the ongoing court battle between LaHaye and Cloud Ten put an end to further films.[12]

In 2008, however, a settlement between LaHaye and Could Ten briefly gave control over the film rights back to LaHaye — but if he did not produce his own adaptations of his books within a year, the rights would once again be back in the hands of Cloud Ten.[13]

Although aimed squarely at the Christian entertainment market, apocalyptic stories remained a staple of the Christian movie industry. Much like in the *Left Behind* franchise, conspiracy theories continued to play a strong role in the plots. Satan's emissaries in such films remained powerful global corporations, big governments pursuing secular humanist agendas, and the mass media that disparaged Christian faith and values. Cloud Ten Pictures also released the *Apocalypse* series, three films (1998, 1999, 2000) likewise dealing with Armageddon and the final battle between God and Satan. In 2006, Christian filmmaker Rich Christiano wrote and directed *Unidentified*, the first dramatization of fundamentalist theory about the evil nature of the UFO phenomenon. In this film, a devoutly Christian journalist (Jonathan Aube) and his atheist reporting partner (Josh Adamson) investigate a series of UFO sightings. The further they probe into the backgrounds of people who have had alien sightings, the more convinced they become of the demonic forces behind UFOs. By the end of the film, not only do they commit to convincing people to reject false hopes about aliens coming to save the world, but the atheist has also made a full conversion to born again Christianity.

The 2000s also saw a connection between fantasy-oriented entertainment and conspiracy theories in the burgeoning science fiction subgenre of superhero films. With the blockbuster success of *The X-Men* in 2000 and *Spider-Man* in 2002, movie theaters were overrun by comic book characters. In fact, by the latter half of the decade, the runaway success of superhero films, especially the *Spider-Man* (2002, 2004, 2007), *Batman* (2005, 2008), and *Iron Man* (2008, 2010) franchises, would prompt Marvel Enterprises to establish their own studio. The production and distribution arm of the comic giant had geared up for the film version of superheroes and superhero partnerships like *Thor, Nick Fury, Captain America*, and the *Avengers*. As of this writing, DC Comics is likewise attempting to match its successfully rebooted *Batman* franchise with a *Superman* remake, a *Green Lantern* adaptation, and a *Justice League of America* series. A number of these films would also set their stories in the cynical world of conspiracy theories.

The *X-Men* (2000, 2003, 2006, 2009) franchise had a very strong undercurrent of conspiratorial paranoia motivating its storylines. The main characters are warring factions of people inexplicably born with various superhuman abilities. Some of these mutants can fly and control the weather, and others have various telekinetic abilities or odd physical abnormalities that make them stronger, faster, or more agile than normal humans. The films, just like their source material in the Marvel comics, use these superpowers as metaphors for conditions that mark people outsiders and minorities. The *X-Men* mutants are obvious stand-ins for racial and ethnic minorities, homosexuals, or the disabled. The conflict among the mutants arises from the philosophical differences of two leader figures in the mutant community. One, Charles Xavier (Patrick Stewart), advocates peaceful, patient advocacy for equal rights. The other, Magneto (Ian McKellen), is a radical who is willing to wage war with the world and impose a new mutant ruling order unless the mutant community is accepted as equals. What puts the franchise into a very satisfying and complex moral framework is the fact that there are no easy answers. On the one hand, the mutants' spectacular, and often lethal, superpowers can pose a true threat to the world. But the films also ask, isn't the excuse of a perceived "threat" always the justification for discrimination? Even the villainous Magneto's position is quite understandable. He is a Holocaust survivor who lost his entire family because they were minorities. But, ultimately, intolerance and fear of the mutants among some factions of society is so strong that secret government plans for either the exploitation or the extermination of the mutants have been in development for decades. The scope of this conspiratorial plan is hinted at in the first *X-Men* film, then fully fleshed out in the first sequel, *X-2: X-Men United*, and the prequel, *X-Men Origins: Wolverine*. In *X-2* and *Wolverine*, the fanatical general William Stryker (played by Brian Cox in *X-2* and Danny Huston in *Wolverine*) wants to harness the powers of the mutants as secret weapons for the military. His ultimate goal, however, is to one day exterminate all of the world's mutant population. In *X-Men: Last Stand* the paranoid human machinations for mutant extermination come in the form of a cure for all mutant powers. In a fairly obvious critical answer to fundamentalist Christian conservative claims that homosexuality is a curable disease, the film argues that prejudice and hate take their most insidious forms when dressed up in the rhetoric of paternalistic "care" and "traditional values."

The two attempts at a big screen *Hulk* adaptation (2003 and 2008) focused on the superhero's relationship with the government through slightly different avenues. Art-house director Ang Lee's iteration on the Marvel Comics character foregrounds the transformation into the creature as a metaphor for besieged masculinity and Oedipal conflict. Dr. Bruce Banner's (Eric Bana) rage is primarily fueled by his destructive relationship with a psychotic father (Nick Nolte), while a subplot of government and corporate exploitation leads to a showdown between the Hulk and the U.S. military. Louis Leterier's remake-sequel hybrid,

The Incredible Hulk, uses a plot structure that is in line with the generic conspiracy theory story arc. This time, Banner's (Edward Norton) ongoing cat-and-mouse battle with the military involves the Army's quest to get its hands on the technology that had transformed him into the Hulk. Much like military antagonists usually looking for otherworldly technology to exploit for weapons programs, the villains of *The Incredible Hulk* envision future armies of gamma ray-mutated super-soldiers.

A similar military-industrial threat lurks in the background of director John Favreau's 2008 superhero hit *Iron Man*. Yet another adaptation from the Marvel Comics universe, *Iron Man* focuses on irresponsible, obnoxious playboy Tony Stark (Robert Downey, Jr.) coming to a crisis point in his life and finding the strength to become a better man. Stark's transformation, however, does not come when he is abducted by Middle Eastern terrorists and finds the way to cobble together a flying, weapon-loaded suit of armor to escape. He becomes a true hero when he recognizes that the biggest threat to peace and security are conspiratorial war profiteers within his own family business. His real heroism, the film says, is when he decides to take control of his company and get out of the weapons manufacturing business.

In this new world of comic book movies, the only things more powerful than super-heroes are not just the super-villains and their world-destroying weapons. Corporate, governmental, and military conspirators pulling the world's strings from behind the scenes are the true threats in the twenty first century.

One of the most highly anticipated film adaptations of a comic book series came in 2009, with director Zack Snyder's big-screen take on writer Alan Moore's conspiracy-oriented *Watchmen* graphic novel. Originally published by DC Comics, *Watchmen* first ran as a limited, 12-issue series in 1987. While DC was often considered more one-dimensional, traditional, and both thematically and creatively conservative than Marvel, *Watchmen* broke profound new ground in comic book art. Moore told a tale of an emotionally troubled and sometimes morally ambiguous—when not completely corrupt—collection of costumed crime fighters. *Watchmen* also presented a political allegory that was much more intricate, sometimes even radical, than what had come before in the medium.

The *Watchmen* saga unfolds in an alternate American history where costumed vigilantes calling themselves the Minutemen took to fighting street crime and corruption in the late 1930s. Hailed as national heroes, these crime fighters garnered ever-greater fame through the decades, and assumed more and more extensive roles in national defense. The Minutemen slowly rose to the role of America's protectors, a benevolent group of unelected overseers. From street vigilantes, they transformed into a completely autonomous defense force. Some of these heroes, like the sardonic, surly, and reactionary Comedian, became government operatives working in partnership with the CIA. The Comedian, in fact, is revealed as the Grassy Knoll sniper of Kennedy assassination lore. Although the Comedian's full role in the Kennedy murder is never elaborated upon, the vagueness of this information evidences the skillful storytelling techniques of so much of the *Watchmen* series. The readers don't need to know specifically how the Comedian got mixed up in the Kennedy killing. Given everything else the comics revealed about his personality, it just makes perfect sense that he would be party to such a crime. The Comedian is a thuggish zealot. As long as he's convinced his cause is just, he is willing to commit any immorality and depravity. The Comedian had also fought in the jungles of Vietnam, unleashing a flamethrower on armies of Viet Cong with sadistic glee.

In the alternate world of the *Watchmen*, in fact, Vietnam is won by the U.S., thanks mainly to the one hero who actually has superpowers. Dr. Jon Osterman, much like scores of superheroes in numerous comic books, was a decent, dedicated scientist until a freak accident: An "Intrinsic Field Subtractor" mishap gave him literally godlike abilities. As a result, he became immortal, omnipotent, and has limitless power over time, matter, and energy.

As times change in the *Watchmen* universe, however, the public perception of the superheroes changes as well. The 1996s and '70s are a time of social upheaval, challenges to authority, and traditional values as much as they were in the real America. Furthermore, despite the Minutemen's crusades, the country seems to be sinking further into a morass of crime and depravity. The new generation no longer reveres the Minutemen but fears and challenges their unchecked, quasi-fascistic powers. In fact, by 1977, the tide of public opinion has turned so far that the government outlaws all their activities. The only Minutemen still active are the Comedian, working secretly as a government operative, and the psychotic Rorschach, breaking the law and prowling the streets dispensing old-fashioned justice. Rorschach is more than slightly reminiscent of Robert DeNiro's Travis Bickle character in *Taxi Driver*: completely unhinged and volatile, and driven by a rigid moralistic zeal to save a world he sees as rotting away from corruption, compromise, and weakness. Despite Dr. Manhattan's protection, there is a Cold War in the *Watchmen* universe as well. In fact, by the 1980s, the threat of all-out nuclear confrontation between the U.S. and the U.S.S.R. looms.

Former Minuteman Adrian Veidt, formerly Ozymandias, the smartest man in the world and now a multi-billionaire entrepreneur, comes to believe that the only way the East and the West can put aside their differences would be if they faced a threat from a common enemy. To that end, he executes a plan to fake an invasion by a giant, squid-like alien creature from an alternate universe. Its attack destroys much of New York City, killing millions of people. In essence, the plot is the false flag attack concept of so many conspiracy theories.

Leaving the story well within the realm of moral ambiguity until the end, the *Watchmen* series concludes with Veidt's successful execution of his plot. He is able to launch the attack, and a handful of his former Minutemen comrades, including Dr. Manhattan, finally have no choice but to become part of his conspiracy. They realize that Veidt had, in fact, been right in his calculations. The Americans and the Soviets, along with their respective allies, unite in preparation for any further interdimensional alien attacks. There is peace throughout the globe. Telling the truth about what happened, the superheroes realize, would push the world back to the brink of confrontation. In the end, lies, conspiracy, and even the destruction of one of the biggest cities in the world might be antithetical to everything the costumed heroes stand for, but it *is* preferable to global nuclear Armageddon. Pushing the dark irony one step further, Dr. Manhattan, the most godlike and transcendent of all the Minutemen, is forced to kill to protect that conspiracy. Rorschach is the one Minuteman unwilling to go along with the deception; his moral code is as black and white as his symbolic Rorschach-test mask, so he cannot compromise even for the sake of a greater good. The only way Veidt, Dr. Manhattan, and the rest of the Minutemen will keep him from talking will be by killing him. Knowing that it is ultimately the logical thing to do, Dr. Manhattan vaporizes Rorschach.

The *Watchmen* series—later reprinted in a one-volume graphic novel format—was immediately hailed as a major achievement in comic book art. The critical consensus was that it elevated the art form to the level of serious literature with its rich, layered characterizations and its complex moral, philosophical, and political themes.

Most have argued that the significance of *Watchmen* lies in complicated characters heretofore unseen in the comic books. Its heroes are multifaceted, conflicted, and complex even beyond anything Marvel Comics ever achieved with its collection of angst-ridden, outsider superheroes. Others argued that *Watchmen*'s achievement lies in the way it was able to interrogate and subvert the traditional, one-dimensional moral order of most super-hero comics. *Watchmen* readers are not merely given troubled heroes, but asked to figure out who the heroes and who the villains really are. Perhaps, the comic suggests in the most subversive terms, there might not be clear-cut heroes at all. Some critics have claimed that *Watchmen* might not just represent a new type of superhero story, but perhaps the death blow to the superhero genre itself. The story, after all, has no supervillain at its center. The real villain is perhaps the most idealistic and clean-cut of the superheroes. At one point in the story, the Comedian even mocks Veidt for being a hopelessly old-fashioned and naïve optimist. More than anything, Veidt wants to *save* the people of the world from the self-destruction they are incapable of abandoning on their own. Alan Moore said that his readers should be forced to reevaluate their conception of heroes altogether. He wanted his story to make people skeptical of the very superhero concept. Is it ever wise to trust anyone who claims to be an all-powerful hero, one who comes to save the world and alleviate all of its problems? In terms of the 1980s political landscape in the United States and England, Moore readily admitted that *Watchmen* was intended as a criticism of Ronald Reagan and Margaret Thatcher. Moore saw those world leaders as self-appointed superheroes, as figures who claimed to be on a crusade to fight the real world's supervillains (the communist evil empire). All Reagan and Thatcher demanded from their respective people, in Moore's reck-oning, was absolute loyalty and unquestioning trust. People, Moore argues in his comic books, need to question their heroes, not give them absolute power.[14]

In relation to conspiracy-themed entertainment, both the comic book and the film versions of *Watchmen* warn of cultural currents that empower would-be conspirators. The Minutemen can be interpreted as liberal Baby Boomers' impression of America itself. At one point, on the eve of World War II, the costumed superheroes rose to the challenge and fought a righteous battle against clear-cut enemies, much as the United States itself had emerged from the Great Depression with the will to challenge Nazism. Both America and the Minutemen had at once stood on the side of justice and freedom in an uncomplicated battle against evil. The future, however, had led both the superheroes and the country astray. Some of the Minutemen had withdrawn from the life of adventurers, while others like the Comedian had become just as brutal and corrupt as the enemies they fought. Many critics of American military, espionage, and foreign policies had asserted that the Cold War prompted the U.S. to often be as corrupt and undemocratic in its zeal to fight communism as the enemy it was opposing. After all, this position claimed, were domestic spying pro-grams against radical and liberal groups, McCarthyism, and foreign assassinations not as bad as the totalitarianism the U.S. had sworn to fight? The opening montage of the *Watchmen* film shows a passage of time from the late 1930s through the '80s, set to Bob Dylan's coun-terculture song "The Times They Are A-Changin.'" What the times had changed into, according to the *Watchmen* comics and their very faithful film adaptation, is a confusing moral gray area where one could no longer distinguish hero from villain. In the modern world, even those who called themselves heroes conspired to create large-scale devastation to further their agendas. The one person who attempted to live by a clear, uncompromised moral code was a psychotic who needed to die at the hands of the most transcendent and godlike of the superheroes.

Watchmen was not the only conspiracy-themed comic book Moore saw adapted to the big screen in the 2000s. In 2001, directors Albert and Allen Hughes brought Moore's Jack the Ripper story *From Hell* to life. The ten-issue comic series, later collected in a graphic novel format like *Watchmen*, is a combination of Jack the Ripper history, conspiracy lore, and occult mysticism functioning as a metaphor that foreshadows the coming age of violence, corruption, and brutality of the twentieth century. Moore's story borrows its central plot line from a lingering conspiracy theory, advanced forcefully by Stephen Knight, about the British royal family's hand in the Ripper killings.[15] The theory argues that the real Jack the Ripper was none other than Prince Albert Victor, Duke of Clarence, who hid a double life of debauchery and mental illness. According to conspiracists, the prince had an insatiable appetite for drugs, alcohol, prostitutes, depraved sex, and psychopathic violence. One version of the theory argued that the prince had fathered a child with a prostitute, then murdered her — or had henchmen murder her — to cover it up. The rest of the Ripper killings, in turn, were really a series of assassinations of other women who knew a secret that would devastate the royal family. In Moore's comics, the story is founded on the secret love-child conspiracy theory. Prince Albert fathers a baby girl with a Whitechapel prostitute, and several friends of the mother know about it. To protect the royal family and keep the daughter of a prostitute from having a claim to the throne of England, the royal family's doctor, Sir William Gull, goes about eliminating everyone who is privy to the government-shattering secret. Gull, to add further hyperbole to the story, is a Masonic adept, in command of psychic occult powers, able to see and project his consciousness across space and time. Gull's visions, in fact, skip ever more frequently to the fast-approaching twentieth century and all its wars, large-scale slaughter, depravities, and conspiratorial control of the masses by the corrupt elite.

Publicly Moore never claimed to have put much stock in Knight's claims and the Prince Albert conspiracy theories. The theories simply gave him ideas that could be adapted into a very colorful fictional story. In fact, much of *From Hell* is an amalgamation of historical events and figures, along with broad fabrications to fit the requirements of the narrative and the metaphorical statements.

The Hughes brothers' adaptation of the comics retained the Masonic conspiracy theory, but jettisoned the psychic visions. The story structure also changed into a mystery, foregrounding police inspector Frederick Abberline (Johnny Depp) in his quest to unravel the identity of the serial killer. At the end of the film, Gull (Ian Holm) is revealed to be the Ripper and the Masonic aspect of the plot is given a brief explanation. The idea that the Ripper killings and the conspiracy foreshadow the twentieth century are briefly hinted at in the scene of Gull's final showdown with Abberline. "They will say I gave birth to the twentieth century," Gull says cryptically to Abberline. The line's meaning is left vague and open for interpretation, perhaps referring to a coming era of more headline-grabbing serial killings. The long-term implications of conspiratorial government powers are not elaborated upon to the extent that Moore does in the comics.

The most controversial adaptation of a Moore work came in 2005 when action film producer Joel Silver (the *Lethal Weapon* series, *Die Hard 1* and *2*) and the Wachowski brothers brought *V for Vendetta* to the screen. While *Star Wars, Episode III: Revenge of the Sith* courted controversy with its highly tenuous allusion to the 9/11 false flag conspiracy theories, the film version of *V for Vendetta* pulled no punches when crafting a story about a right-wing dictatorship in England taking power by manufacturing a false crisis. An obscure conservative politician (John Hurt) rises to prominence, and eventually to the head of the government as the absolute ruler of England, when he masterminds a biological attack on the country and blames it on foreign terrorists. A conservative backlash to the film was immediate, arguing that the story was an obvious allusion to the Bush administration and a validation of the 9/11 Truth movement's conspiracy theories.

Moore refused to endorse the film. Often calling himself an anarchist, Moore didn't come to the Bush administration's defense as much as he was unsatisfied with the film's failure to see his work as general rumination on the characteristics of fascist regimes and people drawn to a fascist ideology. In response to the film, he said:

> [It] has been turned into a Bush-era parable by people too timid to set a political satire in their own country.... It's a thwarted and frustrated and largely impotent American liberal fantasy of someone with American liberal values standing up against a state run by neoconservatives—which is not what the comic *V for Vendetta* was about. It was about fascism, it was about anarchy, it was about England.[16]

A notable spin on fantastic and supernatural conspiracies in the 2000s came in the form of films that took the viewer *inside* a conspiracy. In these films, much like the *X-Men* series, creatures and people with various paranormal abilities had a tenuous existence alongside the human world. Moreover, these fantastic creatures are just as factional as the mutants of the comic book universe. Some are hostile to the human world, while others struggle to protect it and peacefully coexist. Unlike *The X-Men*, however, these are stories where the supernatural entities struggle to keep their identities secret. Humans do not suspect that paranormal beings are anything more than myths, much less that secret wars are perilously close to destroying the world.

In 2003, writer-director Len Weisman debuted the first installment of his successful *Underworld* trilogy. The films follow the centuries-old secret wars between vampires and lycans (werewolves). The sexy Selene (Kate Beckinsale), one of the most skilled members of the vampire "Death Dealer" assassination squads, is tasked with exterminating lycans. Her mission is also personal, spurred by her family's death at the claws of werewolves centuries ago. (Selene had been adopted and transformed into a vampire by Viktor, one of the vampires' powerful ruling elites.) But once Selene meets and starts falling in love with Michael Corwin (Scott Speedman), a victim of a werewolf bite and the carrier of a rare genetic anomaly that allows him to become a vampire-lycan hybrid, her eyes are opened to the lies and conspiracies that have perpetrated the ongoing war.

Selene, just like all protagonists in the conspiracy genre, comes to see that the status quo she believed in and fought for was built on lies. The werewolves are not the mindless animals that vampire history claimed they were, but simply victims. The lycans had been a slave race created by vampires to protect their lairs while they slept during the day. Lycans were men forced against their will into becoming animals, subservient to the aristocratic vampires. After Viktor's daughter fell in love with Lucian (Michael Sheen), one of the original werewolves, Viktor executed her and adopted a new child as her replacement. Because a young Selene so resembled his real daughter, Viktor killed her family, letting her believe the lycans were responsible. Turning her into a vampire, Viktor had also created one of the most driven lycan-hunters among the vampire race.

The discovery of this conspiracy, just like in all conspiracy entertainment, is symbolic of a character's growth. Selene essentially steps into a larger world when she becomes a critical thinker, able to reexamine the rules, the values, the history, the very social structure of the world she had accepted at face value.

The conspiracy theme had also been well-adapted by acclaimed fantasy and horror director Guillermo del Toro's rendition of Mike Mignola's *Hell Boy* comic book series. The two *Hell Boy* movies present a unique character arc for its protagonist, a participant in a supernatural cover-up conspiracy who also comes to reevaluate his position in a society he fights so fiercely to protect.

Hell Boy is a creation of a World War II Nazi experiment in opening the doorway to an alternate dimension. Borrowing from the historically verified accounts of Hitler's fascination with occultism and the very real Thule Society of Nazi-party members who ran expeditions to track down religious artifacts around the world,[17] *Hell Boy*'s prologue witnesses an attempt to breach the barriers between Earth and an alternate universe. This alternate reality, and what can be interpreted as the possible inspiration for many religions' concept of Hell — using visuals reminiscent of H.P. Lovecraft's realm of the exiled dark gods — is home to creatures the Nazis want to harness for world domination. Since an American strike force interrupts the breach of the interdimensional doorway, only one of the otherworldly creatures makes it through. Instead of a world-destroying monster, what the Americans find is a baby demon with a fondness for candy bars. The demon, nicknamed Hell Boy by the soldiers, is adopted and raised by Dr. Trevor Broom (John Hurt), a young scientist who works as the U.S. government's advisor on occultic and supernatural matters.

Once the narrative shifts to the twenty-first century, we find an adult Hell Boy (Ron Perlman) — or one whose slow aging process suggests he is at the maturity level of an adolescent boy inside a hulking red body that's a cross between an archetypal horned demon and a bodybuilder. He is still in the care of a now old and ailing Dr. Broom. The two are members of the top secret government Bureau of Paranormal Research and Defense (BPRD). In this world, the supernatural realm is very real, but it's hidden from most humans. As in *Men in Black*, the U.S. government knows about this vast traffic of otherworldly beings and it is working hard to keep it all a secret. Some of the supernatural beings are benign, while others are threatening or at risk of falling into the hands of Earthly powers who might exploit them as weapons, much like the Nazis tried to do with Hell Boy. BPRD's job is to keep the world safe from these beings and to prevent mankind from panicking at the thought of living in the midst of these paranormal creatures.

These motives, of course, are well in line with conspiracy theories alleging UFO cover-ups. The UFO conspiracy theorists usually accuse the government of keeping a lid on the existence of aliens out of either a profit motive or the fear of panic. While the profit motive is not explicitly stated in *Hell Boy* — the heads of BPRD are never seen discussing ways of exploiting the supernatural realm for weapons or high technology — the government does work diligently at covering up the existence of paranormal manifestations. The glimpses of the paranormal in *Hell Boy*, in fact, are quite frequent. Drawing a droll parallel between sightings of Hell Boy and the real-world UFO conspiracy community, the film presents the head of the BPRD, Tom Manning (Jeffrey Tambor), as an unctuous bureaucrat who makes frequent media appearances to debunk Hell Boy conspiracy theories. His explanations for the sightings are as weak as the real UFO conspiracists claim the weather balloon and swamp-gas explanations are.

This conspiracy element, however, was not a prominent part of the comic book source material. As Guillermo del Toro explains in his DVD commentary for the film, he wanted to add that dimension because conspiratorial accusations are now so much a part of the dialogue of any discussions about the paranormal. In effect, paranoia had come to suffuse the culture so much that any contemplation of alternatives to the consensus reality are ultimately met with fears of forceful subversion and suppression by agents of the status quo.

The 2008 *Hell Boy* sequel takes a dark turn in its contemplations of the metaphysics of the conspiracy theory concept. While the first film is an understated parody of the *X-Files* and Area 51 school of government cover-up paranoia, *Hell Boy II: The Golden Army* recasts its relationship between the human world and the supernatural realm in terms of domination and subjugation. Whereas in the first film Hell Boy is often at odds with his BPRD superior because Manning is a wrong-headed, officious buffoon—*a la* the wrong-headed police captains, politicians, and judges in action-adventure films—the sequel lets Hell Boy consider Manning an agent of the repressive human ruling class. In *Hell Boy II*, the renegade Prince Nuada (Luke Goss) of the elf race wants to unleash a mechanical army upon the human world and bring it to its knees. But rather than being a one-dimensional villain driven by his lust for power, like the Thule Society Nazis of the first film, Prince Nuada harbors an understandable grudge.

Millennia ago, the film's prologue explains, there was peace and harmony between the human world and the supernatural realms. But because of man's lust to rule the world, the peace was broken. In retaliation, the king of the elves fought back with a mechanical golden army. This army dealt a powerful blow to humans, easily killing thousands of them. The elf king, however, was so dismayed by the slaughter that he deactivated the army. He forged a new era of peace by creating a magical crown that can reanimate the army. He split the crown into three pieces, giving one piece to humans and keeping two for the supernatural world. The golden army can only be turned back on if all three parts of the crown are reassembled. Part of this peace agreement also divided the world into separate sectors to be controlled by humans and the denizens of the supernatural races. Humans could have the cities while trolls, elves, and goblins were given dominion over the forests and the seas. But the king's son Nuada was angered by this magnanimity. Humans, he believes, need to be crushed and subjugated, just as they have always sought to subjugate all the denizens of the supernatural world. Nuada attempts to have his way by rebelling against his father and trying to track down the third piece of the crown to reactivate the golden army.

Hell Boy, tasked with saving the world from Nuada, finds himself facing a crisis of identity. Throughout the first film and the opening of the sequel, he had been committed to fitting into the human world as much as he could. His work as a BPRD operative had him defending humans. Then, when he is finally given an opportunity to reveal his existence to the world, he jumps at the chance, defies BPRD rules of secrecy, and appears in front of a throng of New York City news reporters. Just like an attention-hungry adolescent, he wants to be accepted as a hero and treated like a much-beloved celebrity. This, in fact, happens, but for a fleeting instant. Once a public confrontation with one of Nuada's gigantic creatures lays waste to several blocks of Manhattan, the human witnesses to the melee quickly turn on him and the other supernatural members of his team. Hell Boy and his compatriots are derided as "freaks" by an angry mob and blamed for the destruction. Suddenly, Nuada's hatred of the violent, bigoted human race starts to make some sense to Hell Boy. Much like Selene in the *Underworld* films, Hell Boy is forced to reevaluate whether he truly is working for the good guys. He does accomplish his mission to stop Nuada from plunging the world into another human-vs.-supernatural war, but walks away from BPRD at the end of the film.

One of the most iconic action heroes of the past three decades also played a part in an otherworldly conspiracy in the 2000s. In a sudden revival trend that saw sequels and adaptations of 1980s action franchises and television shows like *Rocky, Rambo, Die Hard,* and *Miami Vice,* Steven Spielberg and George Lucas premiered their long-anticipated *Indiana Jones and the Kingdom of the Crystal Skull* in 2008. Since each episode of the *Indiana Jones* film series had some element of the supernatural, the science fictional conspiracy plot was a natural fit for the latest effort.

In 1957, Indiana Jones gets caught up in the quintessential unexplained phenomenon of that decade: UFOs. Jones had been one of the scientific consultants on the government's investigation of the Roswell crash. (The giant government hangar seen in *Raiders of the Lost Ark*, the last resting place of the Ark of the Covenant, is also revealed to be in the fabled Area 51 of recovered-alien mythology.) In this film, Jones is locked into another breakneck-paced struggle against foreign enemies trying to harness an otherworldly power as a tool for global domination: A team of Soviet agents are after the Roswell alien and attempting to track down an ancient UFO hidden somewhere in the Amazon jungle.

Jones' relationship with the U.S. government is even more strained than in *Raiders of the Lost Ark*. The story, after all, is set at the height of the Cold War and the McCarthy era paranoia over communist infiltrators persists. At the beginning of the film, Jones' own loyalties to the country are questioned after he is kidnapped by the Soviets and brought along on an infiltration of Area 51. Although he had tried to foil the enemy agents, a pair of government operatives let him know that he is seriously suspected of being a communist spy. He will be closely watched from now on, the goonish pair lets him know. Furthermore, they explain, the government is not impressed by his World War II service to the country. Many communist sympathizers, after all, had also opposed Hitler.

Although Jones never questions his allegiance to the U.S. the way Selene and Hell Boy come to be alienated from their respective vampire and BPRD circles, the film is critical of the sort of ultra-patriotic paranoia that spawns conspiracies. It acknowledges the legitimate threat the Soviet Union posed in the '50s, yet it condemns the American handling of the Cold War. Irrational paranoia over a threat from outside the country spawned a threat within. The destructive secrecy that led to the conspiracy to cover up the Roswell crash could eat up the best of America. Much as McCarthyist paranoia turned on the men who helped win World War II — like suspicions of Albert Einstein's and J. Robert Oppenheimer's communist sympathies — the hysterical fears and conspiracies in the fictional world of Indiana Jones threaten one of the country's bravest heroes.

Conspiratorial allegations also form the plot of one of the biggest blockbusters of 2009. In disaster-maven Roland Emmerich's epic about the end of the world, *2012*, not only is the apocalypse approaching, but collusion among the world's governments is keeping it a secret.

This was the first major Hollywood production to exploit the 2012 craze that had been gaining momentum in publishing and documentary television since the early years of the decade. Using sensationalistic interpretations of the Mayan calendar's cycle system, various New Age and prophecy analysts have claimed that the pre–Columbian calendar had actually foretold the exact date of the end of the world. Since the Mayans' long-count calendar functions on a system of celestial cycles, the current cycle is calculated to end on December 21, 2012. According to analysts given to apocalyptic fears, the date is the exact moment doomsday is scheduled to hit. Some Mayan calendar buffs have argued that another pre–Columbian Maya text, a book that had been named the Dresden Codex after it was purchased by the Royal Library at Dresden in 1739, depicts a deluge of tidal waves destroying the Earth. The trigger for this doomsday event, they claim, will be a galactic alignment where all of the planets will supposedly line up with the center of the Milky Way galaxy. Other historians, however, have dismissed the apocalypse scenario as nothing more than misinterpretation or willful misrepresentations of Mayan history, beliefs, and the ancient culture's entire calendar system. It is true, these skeptics say, that the Mayan long-count calendar was cyclical. But, they add, when a cycle comes to an end, another one will simply begin, so there is no reason to believe that any sort of doomsday event will take place on December 21, 2012. The end of the world prophecies may be nothing more than the husckesterism of the American New Age publishing industry. In a time when ancient conspiracies fuel so many adventure thrillers on the bestseller lists, the so-called Mayan doomsday prophecy might be yet another source to tap for a market obsessed with ancient mysteries.[18] For Hollywood, the 2012 hysteria was also too good to resist.

For Roland Emmerich, who had been staging large-scale destruction in *Independence Day, Godzilla* (1997), and *The Day After Tomorrow* (2004), smashing the entire planet was merely the next logical progression. It is interesting, however, that *2012* actually downplays the Mayan calendar and prophecies. Instead, solar flare activity reverses the Earth's polarity and drastically realigns the continental plates. Computer-generated earthquakes, volcanoes, and tsunamis follow. In the beginning of the film, though, it is quickly established that scientists have warned the world's governments about the impending global catastrophe. Knowing that nothing can be done to save the majority of the Earth's people, an international conspiracy of survival is put into effect. A fleet of super-ships is built at a hidden base in the Himalayas. These modern-day Noah's Arks will carry to safety a select few, along with animals, plant seeds, and history's greatest art treasures. The would-be survivors are chosen from among the world's top scientists and intellectuals, people who are supposedly the best candidates for rebuilding civilization. Others are chosen by a random lottery selection. Eventually, however, the film's protagonist (John Cusack), a divorced, down-on-his-luck author whose literary career has stalled, stumbles onto the ugly truth about the selection process. The majority of the people on the ships are not really there because they got lucky in the secret lottery. They are the world's wealthiest people — and not necessarily the most honest, with a Russian gangster among the soon-to-be-rescued masses. The film handles this sort of class antagonism theme with very interesting subtlety and matter-of-fact understatement. The world's millionaires and billionaires were needed because their money paid for the construction of these arks. "The world is not fair," a presidential advisor (Oliver Platt) simply tells the Cusack character. In turn, the bureaucrat does not even get an angry populist retort in defense of the little guys. Logically, the world really cannot function as a perfect egalitarian democracy at the time of the apocalypse. Either some of the people, the ones most fit to live as a result of their economic and political cunning, will survive the end of the world, or the entire human race will be wiped out. It is a surprisingly cold, Darwinist stance to take by mainstream, Hollywood popcorn entertainment.

In the Real World

As the years passed and the country was able to put the September 11 terrorist attacks into historical perspective, the more realistic, political- and business-oriented thrillers began incorporating conspiracies into their plots once again.

By 2004, Tina Sinatra, who held the right to remake her father's seminal political conspiracy film *The Manchurian Candidate*, partnered with director Jonathan Demme on an updating of the film for a post–Cold War, post–September 11, Iraq-era audience.

This remake covers many of the same plot points as the original Frank Sinatra-Laurence Harvey film, but for the obvious need to change the agenda and the identity of the conspirators. Once again, heroic Army veteran Raymond Shaw (Liev Schreiber) stands on the cusp of history, ready to embark on a promising political career. The heir to a powerful political family — the son of the late Senator Tyler Prentice (William Meisle) and Senator Eleanor Prentice Shaw (Meryl Streep) — Shaw is exactly the sort of candidate political parties and voters dream of. The handsome, erudite young politician is intelligent, charismatic, and flawlessly poised in the media spotlight — and a Congressional Medal of Honor–winning veteran of the first Gulf War. With a presidential campaign season in full swing, his party's nominee selects him as a vice-presidential running mate. The only problem, however, is that Shaw is the brainwashed puppet of a global business conspiracy.

As in the original John Frankenheimer film, Shaw's combat heroics are nothing more than false memories implanted through sophisticated mind control surgery. This time, though, the villains come in the form of the sinister Manchurian Global corporation. They have brainwashed Shaw into believing that he saved his platoon from an Iraqi ambush, and programmed the same false memories into every man serving with him. Those who begin to slip from the grip of the mind control operation feel like they're losing their sanity.

The one man able to deduce what had happened is former sergeant Bennett Marco (Denzel Washington). Although outwardly a model of perfect physical and mental health, Marco's internal world had been a carefully controlled state of chaos and obsession since the war. He had lived as a loner and recluse since the Gulf. His apartment, almost like Jerry Fletcher's in *Conspiracy Theory*, is a repository of mountainous piles of every shred of information he could find on Shaw. Marco just seems to instinctively know that his feelings, recollections, and the very words he uses to describe Shaw and the ambush are not his own. Sometimes he is plagued by nightmares that tell him there was more to the Gulf War incident than what he is capable of remembering. After discovering a similar collection of news clippings and unhinged writings in the apartment of a dead "lost patrol" comrade (Jeffrey Wright), Marco suspects that all have been brainwashed.

Aside from a few plot modifications at the end, the new *Manchurian Candidate* proceeds through its conspiracy storyline just like its namesake. The presidential candidate has to die at the film's climax, just as in the original, and Shaw is able to foil the plot because he and Marco had discovered the truth. Then, just as in the original, Shaw winds up dead.

Although the Demme *Manchurian Candidate* hits all the plot points of the original and does it skillfully, the details of the conspiracy are too vague for the film to make as much of an impact as the original or the Richard Condon novel. In the novel and in the first film, the aims of the North Korean communists and the Soviet bloc were strong enough a cultural pressure point for the story to function without dwelling too deeply on the aims of the conspirators. Readers in the '50s and moviegoers in 1962 could understand what was at stake in a story about a communist foreign power's control of an American president. Those audiences, therefore, could accept the plot as either a straight thriller or a finely layered political satire. That sort of subtlety, however, does not work quite as well in the new film. The Demme film does not even pull off the same double duty of satire *and* straight thriller the way author Condon and director Frankenheimer did in their respective works. Demme's film is a serviceable thriller, yet one that does not go far enough in conveying the gravity of what is at stake. The villains of the new film, a global corporation heavily involved in international arms sales, is attempting to completely control the American president. They want to control him literally and absolutely by placing a single phone call and reducing the chief executive to a mindless puppet by way of hypnotic code words. Such power would certainly be much more efficient than the time- and money-consuming process of lobbying and cajoling through donations and junkets. However, the access of special interest lobbyists to lawmakers is already a reality of the political game. Audiences know this very well. For the film to have functioned more effectively, Manchurian Global should have had some clearly articulated and very extreme agenda. For thriller aficionados who might be familiar with the original versions of *The Manchurian Candidate*, the 2004 film feels incomplete. The filmmakers appear to be too timid to explore the full implications of the business conspiracy scenario they created. They could have made a harder, clearer statement about the tainting of the political process by money and special interests. This could have been either done straight — the tone Demme and screenwriter Daniel Pyne clearly settled on for the entire film — or they could have used Condon's and Frankenheimer's approach for understated satire. Moreover, despite Demme's and Pyne's liberal political orientation to the story, they are unwilling to take advantage of the heightened fear, distrust, and prejudice against Arabs after September 11 for the sake of critical commentary. The original *Manchurian Candidate* had, after all, condemned red-baiting as a means of political opportunism. Demme and Pyne could have made a similar statement condemning racial profiling and anti–Arab paranoia in their film.

In the plausible, real-world school of conspiratorial filmmaking in the 2000s, the worlds of high finance and global corporations would continue to be sources of villainy. Several major Hollywood films also drew even more obvious parallels between their plots and Washington's military and economic policies.

One of the films with the most overtly anti–Bush and anti-corporate sentiments is the 2007 Mark Wahlberg action thriller *Shooter*. Very loosely based on film critic and novelist Stephen Hunter's first book *Point of Impact* (1992), the story is a *Parallax View*–and *The Package*–style adaptation of the making-of-an-assassination-fall-guy plot. Former sniper-ace Bob Lee Swagger (Wahlberg) is deceived into becoming a Lee Harvey Oswald–type patsy in an assassination conspiracy. Swagger, a reclusive mountain man since the death of his sniper partner on a peacekeeping mission in Ethiopia, is approached by government operatives to consult on a security mission. There is good reason to believe, Swagger is told, that an attempt will be made on the president's life during a series of speaking engagements. The most skilled sniper alive is asked to figure out where the assassin is most likely to take a shot. Swagger, an old-fashioned, country-boy patriot, cannot refuse. But it's a set-up: Swagger is accused of murdering the president's guest, an African archbishop, during a speaking engagement. After the wounded Swagger escapes, he unravels a conspiracy that leads to corrupt security contractors, oil companies, and Capitol Hill. The archbishop, he finds out, was on the verge of rallying protests against the massacre of a village in Africa — a massacre carried out at the behest of an American oil company that needed an uncooperative tribe removed from a potential drilling area.

According to Thomas de Zengotita's assessment of the film for *The Huffington Post*, *Shooter*, at face value, is the most obvious sort of left-wing "propaganda." Although de Zengotita agrees with the film's politics and calls *Shooter* "a must see movie," the story wears its polemic very prominently on its sleeve. The shotgun-totting, truck-driving, down-home Swagger character, de Zengotita writes, is a stand-in for conservatives and "all those brave men who got snookered into this war" by the Bush administration's post–9/11 rhetoric of patriotism. Only once they — and the fashionably patriotic, flag-waving, and flag-wearing country, by extension — were in the middle of an ill-conceived and dishonestly sold military campaign, did they realize the sort of danger the entire nation and a generation of people who had gone to fight were in.[19]

The most insidious business conspiracy in the recent batch of cinematic offerings came in the Clive Owen-Naomi Watts thriller *The International* (2009). Nominally based on the downfall of the scandal- and corruption-ridden Bank of Credit and Commerce International (BCCI), *The International* is a paranoid, fast-paced, good-looking, but often highly implausible thriller about one of the most corrupt banks in the world. The film's fictional International Bank of Business and Credit is not so much a worldwide financial institution as a massive criminal conglomerate, involved in financial and political conspiracies in every corner of the globe. They bribe government officials, they steal, defraud, and manipulate financial markets, sell arms to terrorists, and assassinate anyone who stands in their way. The plot involves a rather standard investigation by a dashing, driven, and idealistic INTERPOL agent (Owen) and a beautiful New York district attorney (Watts). Much of the action is routine and unremarkable; the film's most effective moments actually come after the climax. The Owen and Watts characters are ultimately denied their shot at bringing the IBBC villains to justice when the vengeful sons of an Italian politician (murdered by a bank hitman) take the law into their own hands. The massive bank, however, suffers no great consequences. The bank is too vast, too complex, and intertwined with the political and financial framework of too many of the world's countries to ever be completely dismantled. The IBBC, simply, is too big to be allowed to fail. This frustrating conclusion, however, is a perfect reflection of the frustrations of Americans who had seen a financial crisis sweep the globe in 2008 and 2009. Just as in the film, global financial institutions had run on corruption, mismanagement, and, more than anything, unalloyed greed. In the eyes of many, insult had been added to injury when the United States had no choice but to spend billions of dollars in bailouts and stimulus packages for massive conglomerates that were "too big to fail."

Even the worlds of the most whimsical and hyperbolic action films of the decade had heroes contending with murderous, intricate conspiracies that threatened world peace and stability. It is notable that a conspiracy theory implicating the British and American governments would turn up in James Bond films. In *Quantum of Solace* (2008), Bond (Daniel Craig) discovers the true nature of an international criminal organization named Quantum. Although he had only dealt with members of this outfit when on an assignment to investigate a corrupt casino serving as a bank for terrorist organizations in the previous film, *Casino Royale* (2006), Bond uncovers the true subversive and corrupting power of Quantum when attempting to track down the people responsible for a lover's murder. Quantum is a massive criminal subcontracting group, selling its specialties of mayhem, assassination, and political destabilization to the highest bidders. Unfortunately, he comes to learn that Quantum's reach extends to the tops of financial institutions around the world and even into the British government. The secretary to the prime minister, in fact, is a Quantum member. Moreover, the United States government is not always entirely ignorant of what Quantum is up to or who they are selling their services to. When it benefits U.S. interests, Washington is willing to look the other way or even protect Quantum.

Such a dark and paranoid tone is remarkable in the Bond series since the films had always been among the most conservative of action franchises. As discussed in Chapter 1, the Bond films had always been about the defense of the Western status quo. Even though 007 usually dealt with fictional criminal organizations like SPECTRE or independent megalomaniacs who wanted to use super-weapons to destroy, extort, or rule the world, most of the films had been Cold War allegories. Bond's nemeses were agents of dictatorial repression, stand-ins for the Soviet Union. Plus, although Bond himself might have been at odds with superiors on a rare occasion, he knew he was on the side of right. In the worlds of *Casino Royale* and *Quantum of Solace,* however, it was no longer easy to tell the good guys from the bad.

Even the attempt at an American version of James Bond took a sudden and even more radical turn into conspiracy theory territory. The *xXx* series, launched in 2002, was an attempt to put a uniquely American spin or a story of glamourous, tongue-in-cheek, and hyperbolic international espionage action-adventure. With Vin Diesel in the lead role, the franchise appeared to have been envisioned as a multi-ethnic, extreme-sports-inspired version of a typical Bond plot crossed with the premise of *The Dirty Dozen.* Diesel plays Xander Cage, an adrenaline junkie who stages illegal stunts and posts the videos on the Internet. Once he is caught, he is given a chance to redeem himself by going on a high-risk mission for the U.S. government and track down an anarchistic Russian gangster who plans to detonate biological weapons over Prague. By the end of the film, of course, Cage comes to see the sort of threats faced by the country and the world every day. Although he is eventually given his freedom, the film suggests that he will remain a top secret agent, fighting the enemies of freedom and peace. By the sequel, *xXx: State of the Union,* however, the threats are coming from within the U.S. government itself.

The *xXx* sequel plays something like a hip hop remake of *Seven Days in May.* This time starring former rapper Ice Cube (after Diesel walked away from the franchise due to a salary dispute), the plot retains the cornered criminal concept from the first film. Ice Cube is a former Navy SEAL who is recruited out of prison for a near-impossible mission. The antagonists he needs to stop are right-wing military operatives conspiring to assassinate a liberal president (Peter Strauss) who is about to announce a radical new approach to foreign policy and the War on Terror. The president believes that the military posturing and defense buildup of the past is provoking terrorists into wanting to destroy the United States. The answer, he believes, is drastic defense cuts and disarmament. This gesture, he explains to the country, will show all would be enemies of the U.S. that they have nothing to fear and that peace is achievable. Just like the Pentagon conspirators of *Seven Days in May,* a conspiracy within the military is convinced that the disarmament plan will lead to the country's destruction. Their only option to save the nation, they calculate, is to remove the president from his office by force.

The Hidden Hand

The ancient society conspiracy theories that found such spectacular success in literature in the early half of the decade were discovered by Hollywood quickly enough. While some of these films had strong elements of the supernatural and others the fast-paced, special-effects-driven adrenaline of action-adventure films, they were all faithful to the concept of ancient secret society conspiracism. The key to the present state of the world lay in the subterfuge of the ancient world and among private cabals of immensely influential and secretive power brokers.

In 2006 and 2009, Dan Brown's standard-setting Robert Langdon novels were adapted to the big screen by director Ron Howard. Starting with *The Da Vinci Code*— as that book had attained worldwide phenomenon-status first — the filmmakers took a very faithful route to bringing the Vatican conspiracy to the movies. Tom Hanks played the lead role, supported by French star Audrey Tautou as Sophie Neveu and Ian McKellen as Sir Leigh Teabing.

Some of the minor alterations to the character development — to the film's benefit — come by way of making Langdon skeptical of the claims that there really existed a conspiracy to cover up Jesus' bloodline as part of a political ploy by the First Council of Nicaea. In the course of the movie, Langdon comes to find confirmation of the conspiracy theory, rather than confirmation of what he had firmly believed as fact. Although a solid success in both its American and worldwide release, grossing $758,239,851 in total, the *Da Vinci Code* film was not enough of a box-office phenomenon to match its runaway success at the bookstores. As the tepid critical reviews suggested, the film might have played it too conservative and close to the vest to stand much of a chance of becoming a true record-breaking blockbuster.

Much like the book, the movie received a measure of condemnation by conservative Christians. At one point, there was speculation that distributors Sony and Columbia Pictures and director Ron Howard might play it *too* safe and tone down some of the book's more obviously critical passages about Jesus and Mary Magdalene's union, church history, and the Opus Dei order. With the worldwide success of the book, the filmmakers decided that there was no reason to placate the critics.

Prior to the *Da Vinci Code* splash, on March 31, 2000, Universal released its Ivy League conspiracy film *The Skulls*. Based on the very real conspiratorial speculation surrounding the Skull and Bones fraternal organization at Yale University, it attempted to draw an audience of conspiracy fans *and* cash in to the late '90s "youth quake" trend in popular culture. The film starred Joshua Jackson from the popular *Dawson's Creek* teen-oriented television series. Unfortunately, as far as conspiracy theories and speculations about the nefarious plots of hidden power brokers were concerned, *The Skulls* was the least imaginative of all conspiracy-centered films of the new millennium.

The real Skull and Bones order is rich enough in paranoid lore, though, to have given the filmmakers enough material to work with. The group was conceived in 1833 by Yale student William Russell after a trip to Germany, and based in part on his studies of European fraternal organizations mimicking the original eighteenth century Illuminati. Returning to Yale, Russell and friend Alfonso Taft — father of future president William Howard Taft — organized their secret society, calling it "The Brotherhood of Death." Later it was formally named "The Order of the Skull and Bones." The group initiates fifteen new members into its order every year. One becomes a candidate only by invitation. Skull and Bones maintains that it always invited the most active and most accomplished members of the Yale student body. Members of the organization are called "Bonesmen." However, the group's exclusivity, along with its allegedly bizarre, death-iconography-focused initiation rights, have attracted the attention of conspiracy theorists.[20]

At best, the organization's critics argue, Skull and Bones is an "old boys' club." Hardly just recruiting Yale's best and brightest, the critics claim, the club actually tries to collect members of the most influential, economically and politically connected families in the country. When these children of wealth and privilege set out career-wise, they get their start through their connections to other former Bonesmen. Essentially, observers have said, Skull and Bones is a networking organization for the country's power elite that assures that positions of influence remain in the hands of the same small, exclusive clique of families and their cronies.

Fanciful conspiracy theorists have linked Skull and Bones to everything from the most ancient secret societies to the Kennedy assassination, to a Satanic plot to destroy religion, usher in the New World Order, and the reign of the Antichrist. For example, William Russell's interest in European secret societies and the Illuminati has inspired conspiracy theorists to name Skull and Bones an "offshoot" of the Illuminati (this despite the fact that no evidence exists to prove that the Illuminati have even been active past 1785). Once the Bonesmen graduate from Yale and take their positions of power in the country, their conspiratorial critics charge, they begin the implementation of the Skull and Bones' and, by extension, the Illuminati's master plan for America and the world. The Skull and Bones, some JFK assassination theorists charge, were the economic elites who felt threatened by the young president's progressive agendas. Other conspiracy theorists have focused on the group's apparent fixation on occult and death symbolism. To these theorists, the group looks suspiciously Satanic. Satanism, they claim, was the ultimate objective of both the Illuminati and the Masons. Some of the most illustrious members of the Skull and Bones society have been Prescott Bush, his son George H.W. Bush and grandson George W. Bush, William Howard Taft, Averell Harriman, McGeorge Bundy, Henry Luce, David Boren, John Kerry, and members of the Rockefeller family.

The Skulls does not focus its plot on any such twisty, byzantine conspiracy theories. The film appears content to spend its long 102-minute running time on a rather pedestrian murder mystery. The plot involves poor (but driven and hard-working) Yale undergraduate student Luke McNamara (Joshua Jackson) being invited to join a Skull and Bones–like order, the Skulls. Although the invitation might be the networking opportunity of a lifetime for Luke, it immediately hurts his current friendships. His girlfriend Chloe (Leslie Bibb) and best friend Will (Hill Harper), a liberal, muck-raking African American student journalist, are not happy with Luke's intentions of joining the club. They both see the Skulls as a collection of rich, privileged, white snobs. Will, in fact, is working on a story attempting to expose the Skulls' secrets. After breaking into the Skulls' headquarters, he gets into a fight with one of the student members, injuring himself very badly and falling unconscious. To cover up, one of the henchmen working for the villainous Litten Mandrake (Craig T. Nelson), father of one of Luke's Skulls friends, murders Will and disposes of the body. The film become a series of cat-and-mouse chases, frame-up attempts, and confrontations between Luke and the Skulls as he tries to get to the bottom of Will's death.

The film ends with a quasi-exoneration of the Skulls as Luke uncovers the truth behind Will's murder and realizes that Mandrake was but one bad apple among the group. Although the rest of the brotherhood's senior leadership tell him that they realize that changes need to be made, Luke still walks away from the group. He has solved his friend's murder and regained his girlfriend's respect after his momentary flirtation with the skulls.

The film is extremely unsatisfying. Its standard murder mystery denouement and the down-to-earth hero's rejection of the Skulls' elitism are generic plot points. The very appeal of a Skull and Bones–type film is the promise that the filmmakers will address some of the allegations leveled against one of the most obsessively secretive organizations around. A fan of thrillers and conspiracy theories might hope that *The Skulls*' creative team could present their own ideas of what secrets are hidden in such an organization's vaults. Are people like the Skulls truly hatching plots to rule the world, to assassinate world leaders, start wars, hide aliens, or pave the way for the coming of the Antichrist? Or, on the other hand, the film could just as well have been an anti-conspiracy film. It could have attempted to prove the absurdity of so many grand conspiracy theories. It could have revealed that secretive collegiate fraternities are what *Time* magazine characterized the real Skull and Bones as: "a laughably juvenile club for Dungeons-and-Dragons geeks."[21] Such a creative direction could have cast the Skulls—and their real-life counterparts—in the light of modern-day Wizards of Oz, private clubs of over-pampered rich kids whom conspiracy theorists have made out to be much more mysterious and influential than they really are. *The Skulls* takes neither of these approaches. Instead, the film remains a shaggy dog story that promises a lot but delivers very little. Nevertheless, *The Skulls* was successful enough in its theatrical run to prompt the production of two direct-to-DVD sequels. In 2002, *Skulls II* was released, then in 2004 *Skulls III*.

A much more whimsical approach to ancient secret society conspiracies was taken by the first of the Lara Croft film adaptations. Based on the video games about a buxom female relic collector, or "Tomb Raider," the Angelina Jolie film *Lara Croft: Tomb Raider* (2001) attempted to combine computer-enhanced hyperbolic action and shootout set pieces with an Indiana Jones–esque plot about an Illuminati master plan, time distortions, and the apocalypse. Lara Croft (Jolie) must retrieve the two halves of a mystical triangle before the Illuminati can use them in conjunction with a timepiece hidden in Siberia for the express purpose of destroying the world at the time of a certain planetary alignment.

While a majority of the critics argued that the plot made little sense underneath the quasi-Hong Kong-style shootout action, the basics of the secret society conspiracy mythology were retained within the mayhem. The fate of the present and the future are hinging on the proper use or abuse of items from the past. The battle with an evil order must be waged in secret, in exotic locales far removed from the eyes of the rest of the world. Ultimately, however, the conspiracy and the Illuminati are but the plot "McGuffins" of the Hitchcockian film lexicon, existing only to move the story from one action sequence to the next. The Illuminati, as an organization, are not presented as any sort of a group with a clear and distinct agenda, vision, or comprehensible goal. They exist as the film's bad guys because the conspiracy theory community and popular culture have already defined them as bad guys. They are, ultimately, one-dimensional and cartoonish in much the same way as the Nazi villains of the *Indiana Jones* films.

The *Indiana Jones* films became modern action classics because of an engaging, roguish, slightly rumpled character, and Harrison Ford's capable, tongue-in-cheek interpretation of the role and the absurd scenarios; the *Lara Croft* franchise did not fare as well. Despite trying to match the *Indiana Jones* films in special effects and adrenaline, as well as relics that possessed very real mystical properties, the series died with 2003's *Lara Croft: Cradle of Life*. Perhaps the reason behind audiences' fading interest lay less in the over-the-top secrets and conspiracies than in the Croft character herself. Complicated, layered conspiracies and secrets are the required plot archetypes for films like these and the *Lara Croft* films deliver complications in spades. The films, however, also suffer from a superwoman complex that tended to bedevil a lot of the female action films and superheroine films of the late '90s and early 2000s. Conspiracy film protagonists, when conceived and performed well, are harried underdogs. A compelling hero of a conspiracy theory film is someone who looks like a long shot, unlikely to overcome spectacular odds and obstacles stacked against him (or her) by an all-powerful, and unseen enemy. Such characters are not quite so compelling when they are larger-than-life superheroes with no weaknesses. Such perfection, unfortunately, is the problem of the *Lara Croft* movies. The main character is athletic, strong, virtually unbeatable in any confrontation, brilliant, beautiful, and so wealthy as to live in a opulent mansion with a vast fortune at her disposal to pursue adventures around the world for the sheer fun of it. Try as capable actress Angelina Jolie might to humanize a character like that, there is no way of getting around the fact that the screenwriters were unwilling to stray too far from the one-dimensional video game origins of Lara Croft. She is like so many of the female superheroine characters of the time—characters like Jennifer

Garner's Electra or Halle Berry's Cat Woman: a flawlessly, inhumanly perfect caricature that, ultimately, no one can relate to on any level. These characters feel like compensatory feminist fantasies rather than actual flesh and blood, three-dimensional heroines. They feel like they were created with an agenda to make up for a history of weak female characters in the action genre. In the conspiracy theory genre, however, such perfection is just not very interesting.

A much more coherent attempt at fusing *Da Vinci Code*–style ancient mysteries with *Indiana Jones*' action was presented by producer Jerry Bruckheimer and director Jon Turteltaub in the 2004 Nicolas Cage film *National Treasure*. It could be argued that the film's success might have been because it was doing most of its cribbing from Dan Brown rather than *Indiana Jones*. Although adorned with several breakneck-paced action scenes, the film concentrates on the clues and mysteries rather than just the stunts and special effects.

National Treasure follows Benjamin Franklin Gates (Cage), a cerebral hero in the mold of Robert Langdon. Gates has degrees in mechanical engineering from MIT and American history from Georgetown. He is also a maverick historian, obsessed with finding the lost treasure of the Templars and the Freemasons. A clue to its whereabouts has been passed along from generation to generation in his family, with a long line of Gateses attempting to find a fabled cache of gold the Masons hid somewhere in America. The quest for the treasure had led to a falling-out between Gates and his father Patrick (Jon Voight). His father had long abandoned the treasure hunt, convinced that the fabled gold is nothing but an empty legend. Their quest to find it has brought nothing but ridicule from the academic establishment. But Ben marches to the tune of his own idealism, hoping to find the treasure and restore the family's reputation.

In the arctic wilderness, Gates and his financier, Ian Howe (Sean Bean), discover clues to the location of a treasure map on the back of the Declaration of Independence. Realizing that the only way they could ever get hold of the map would be to steal it, Gates decides that the treasure might as well stay lost forever. Knowing that Gates would not only refuse to help steal the map but try to thwart anyone else's attempt, Howe tries to kill Gates and his computer-expert friend, Riley Poole (Jason Bartha). Surviving the murder attempt, Gates and Poole team up with Patrick and Dr. Abigail Chase (Diane Kruger) from the National Archives to steal the Declaration of Independence first and thus prevent Howe from destroying it and getting the treasure.

The movie's most interesting aspect is its idealized portrayal of the Masons and the Templars. According to the film, the Templars had eventually become the Masons and they hid a vast treasure they discovered under King Solomon's temple to protect it from all the unscrupulous ends such wealth could be used for. In America, the Masons eventually put their ideals into action by founding a new country based on the tenets of democracy, freedom, and justice. They viewed government power much the way they viewed the Templar treasure: something that could become destructive and oppressive when concentrated in a few hands. In fact, once Gates and his group finds the treasure in a vast cavern under New York City, he realizes that he needs to treat it as the original Masons would have. He decides to split it into several donations to various national museums.

In the 2007 sequel *National Treasure 2: Book of Secrets*, Ben and his father need to protect the family name by proving that an ancestor was not part of the conspiracy to assassinate Abraham Lincoln. In fact, the family history said that Thomas Gates (Joel Gretsch), a puzzle specialist, died a hero trying to *stop* the conspirators. But suddenly a shadowy businessman,

Mitch Wilkinson (Ed Harris), approaches the Gateses and challenges their version of the events. He claims that he has some of the missing pages torn from John Wilkes Booth's diary that implicate Thomas Gates in the assassination. Taking this as a personal affront, Ben teams with Riley Pool, his father, and now-estranged girlfriend Abigail to examine the rest of Booth's diary, find barely legible remnants of a code that Thomas Gates was manipulated into nearly solving for the Lincoln conspirators, and try to figure out what really happened on the evening of the president's death. What they find, with the help of Ben's mother Emily (Helen Mirren), one the world's preeminent scholars of pre–Columbian civilizations, is another series of clues to a legendary Native American city of gold. The Confederate conspirators had originally tried to find the immense gold deposit to fund their war against the Union. Today, however, the murderous Wilkinson and his group of mercenaries is attempting to follow Gates and his group to the gold, then lay claim to the discovery.

Just as in the previous film, *National Treasure 2* attempts to be one of the most overtly patriotic ancient-conspiracy films ever made. As director Turteltaub discusses in the film's DVD commentary, an intended message of the film is "to dignify the pleasure of enjoying the past of your own country." He wanted to tie the key plot points of both films to historical national monuments to encourage people to visit them and ponder the history of the United States. Those "national treasures" should be seen as reminders of the lengths great men went to in order to create a great country. In both *National Treasure* films, as a matter of fact, the past and the present has been shaped by multifaceted conspiracies. There were both good and evil conspirators. There was the conspiracy of the Freemasons of the first film that attempted to bring about freedom and democracy. In order to achieve this, they had to plot in secret and carry out a rebellion against the British government. In *National Treasure 2*, the evil conspirators were allied with the Confederate system. They were a secret order named the Knights of the Golden Circle, devoted to preserving slavery and going to any lengths necessary to steal a vast native American treasure to finance their agenda.

Another fascinating twist in *National Treasure 2* is the titular Book of Secrets, a volume that supposedly each president has recorded the country's biggest secrets in. At one point, Ben needs to get hold of this book because it contains a vital clue to the location of the city of gold. Instead of becoming a hindrance, the current president (Bruce Greenwood) helps Gates take a look at the book. This, however, comes in yet another of the film's optimistic departures from genre conventions. Gates attempts to get the book by kidnapping the president. But once Gates is able to explain the vital importance of finding the gold before Wilkinson can, the president willingly cooperates and *helps* Gates steal it from a hidden compartment at the Library of Congress. This head of the government is not a self-interested member of some power elite using his resources to subvert the truth and democracy. He wants to see Gates and his team succeed because their cause is just.

An interesting final note of ambiguity is allowed to creep into the film when it comes to the exact nature of the Book of Secrets. Why would an office like that of the president of the United States even *have* something like the Book of Secrets? Moreover, this book is clearly shown to have hidden information about such conspiratorial objects of obsession as the Kennedy assassination and Roswell. Why would the government hold onto such secrets, information that is, essentially, linked to one of the biggest crimes in America?

Conspiracy Remains in the Popular Culture on Screens Big and Small

While conspiracy theory films proved to be as resilient and popular as ever in the turbulent social climate of the 2000s, the genre also retained its popularity on television. In 2002, for example, the Sci-Fi Channel aired its mammoth ten-part miniseries *Taken*. Produced by Steven Spielberg, the program was a dramatization of the entire history of the UFO phenomenon and its antecedent conspiracy theories. In fact, one of the most influential television programs of the decade would turn out to be based on the very concepts of conspiracism: hidden secrets, the manipulation of the individual by unseen organs of power, the imposition of a false consciousness for the purposes of control and exploitation, and world-altering struggles between forces of good and evil unfolding just outside of the perception of ordinary people.

The fall of 2001 saw the debut of two spy-oriented series just as the entertainment industry was trying to determine what the September 11 attacks would mean for the national psyche and, in turn, for action and suspense entertainment. But as the video rentals of action films like *Die Hard* and *Rambo* proved, the public consumption of action films and television programs would not be significantly affected. ABC's *Alias* and Fox's *24* both proved to be unqualified hits. *24*, however, did play it safe on its November 6 premiere, removing a visual effect of an exploding plane.

In terms of conspiracism, *Alias* had more prominent storylines about secret societies, double and triple agents within the CIA and the U.S. government, ancient codes and apocalyptic prophecies, mind control, plagues, and various plot twists about people in covert government work not being what they appeared to be. *Alias,* however, was always well-rooted in the world of fantasy and hyperbole. It was more of a reminder of such stylized television spy fare as the whimsical 1960s series *The Man from U.N.C.L.E.*

24, on the other hand, was firmly rooted in the real world, focusing many of its storylines on assassinations and terrorist plots. The show's novel premise was that it unfolded in real time. Each season covered one day in the life of Counter Terrorist Unit agent Jack Bauer (Kiefer Sutherland) as he raced the clock to avert a disaster in 24 hours. Of the two series, *24* turned out to be the more controversial. The show's violence, especially numerous episodes where Bauer beat and tortured suspects for information, raised the ire of liberal television critics.

Then, in 2004, the USA Network, along with Francis Ford Coppola's American Zoetrope, created *The 4400,* the first television program conceived as a symbolic reflection of a world irrevocably changed by a single event. Its premise was that over the past 60 years, 4400 people have vanished from around the world after witnessing strange, blinding flashes of light in the sky. They have been of all ages, genders and walks of life. With no apparent connections, they disappeared, never to be seen again.

In 2004, however, they return.

What appears to be an asteroid is detected heading toward the Earth. This becomes public knowledge and many around the globe await the Apocalypse. Then, for all the world to see, the asteroid suddenly changes course, heading toward the United States—specifically, the Mt. Rainier area of the Pacific Northwest.

The Seattle branch of the National Threat Assessment Command (NTAC) of the Department of Homeland Security is tasked with responding to whatever will land in the nearby wilderness. By now, it has become obvious that something more spectacular than an asteroid will make contact with Earth. Something under intelligent guidance is descending toward Washington state and the first close encounter with an otherworldly emissary is about to take place.

What takes place, instead, is the appearance of a ball of energy depositing 4400 people. They are all from Earth, and had all been reported missing at some point. Some have vanished as little as a year ago and others have been gone for decades. None appear to have aged a day and none of them can remember where they have been.

The U.S. government initially quarantines the returnees, questioning them about their missing time and determining if they are contaminated by any communicable diseases. Once the returnees are deemed to pose no threat, they are all released, some to reunite with family, others to reintegrate into an a world that has passed them by.

From this point, *The 4400* became an ambitiously complex series of intertwining subplots. It involves the group of returnees (dubbed "4400s"), government investigators and the relatives and friends of various 4400s attempting to cope with the upheaval in their lives.

The Seattle NTAC office is headed by Dennis Ryland (Peter Coyote); the bureau's two chief investigators are Tom Baldwin (Joel Gretsch) and Diana Skouris (Jacqueline McKenzie). Baldwin's nephew, Shawn Farrell (Patrick Flueger), is a 4400. Abducted on April 22, 2001, Shawn was on a camping trip with Baldwin's son Kyle (Chad Faust) when there was an explosion of light above their heads. Shawn was abducted, while Kyle was knocked unconscious. Ever since, Kyle has been in a coma.

Diana quickly forms a bond with a young girl abductee. Eight-year-old Maia Rutledge (Conchita Campbell) was taken from a family picnic in 1946. She has no living relatives who can be found; NTAC attempted to place Maia with a foster family, but they returned her within a day, setting up what will become one of the show's key plot lines.

Some of the 4400s have telekinetic abilities. Others can read minds. Some have superhuman strength and some can release killer plagues when they touch people. Others can take over minds, implant memories or draw them out of those who have forgotten their pasts. But the most spectacular of these abilities manifests itself in Shawn. He can heal any disease with a touch, or he can drain the life out of any living being when provoked to anger. Maia's ability is precognition. After telling her foster father that she had visions of his death, the shaken family quickly returns Maia to NTAC headquarters. At that point, Diana petitions to adopt Maia.

The 4400s' paranormal abilities puts several conspiracy subplots into action. Splinter groups within several governments begin to fear the impact the abductees might have on the world. In turn, various 4400s, fearing prejudice and hostility, start forming factions. Some 4400s merely want to protect themselves, but others plan on using their abilities to influence the world to their own benefit.

The purpose for the 4400s' abduction is revealed by Kyle Baldwin. Having been raised from his coma by Shawn, Kyle is drawn back to the site of the 4400s' return. There, he is momentarily taken by tendrils of light, then returned to his father. The 4400s were not abducted by aliens, Kyle reveals, but they were taken into the future. The future has been ravaged by great cataclysms and almost completely destroyed. Our world today is quickly approaching the crossroads that can either lead to salvation or destruction. The 4400 have been taken through time, given new abilities, then returned to that point in history where they will be prepared to meet the coming disasters. The 4400, according to Kyle, are the only hope for the survival of the future.

The 4400 was a particularly effective addition to the canon of nervous popular culture mythology. Its motif was the fear that the world might be quickly spiraling into oblivion. Exactly how it will all be destroyed, we can't be sure. The details are being kept from us by various underhanded cabals of conspirators. Unlike in, say, the Cold War, the enemy is not out in the open. Instead, threats, fanatics, genocidal thugs, terrorists and their zealous minions can be just about anywhere. Their sleeper cells, their allies and sympathizers might be living just across the street. The definitions of allies and enemies also swiftly shift. You can't trust anyone. The future is up for grabs. But it doesn't look promising at all.

Two out of the three men mainly responsible for crafting the show came from *Star Trek*, generally considered the most optimistic science fiction series ever produced. However, at least one of them had often been publicly candid about his dissatisfaction with the world-view — or future view — of science fiction in the *Star Trek* mold. A future in the balance, on the brink of complete collapse and chaos, is better in line with the state of mind of modern audiences. "To me, *Star Trek* was always like what Long Island seemed like when I was growing up in New York," explained *4400* executive producer Ira Steven Behr. "It's white bread. It's safe. It's boring … I hated it."[22]

Behr was a writer for *Star Trek: The Next Generation* in its 1989–90 season, then a writer and producer for the *Deep Space Nine* spin-off for seven years. *Star Trek's* driving philosophy had always been to present the future as a place where people overcame their differences, lived in peace, acceptance and harmony, where science, technology and rationality gave a better life to all. Creator Gene Roddenberry summed up the world of *Trek* as "a world without hate and without greed, and where every child had enough to eat."

These were certainly admirable goals, except how they could be reached fostered some of the dissent among the *Trek* series' new generation of writers. In their view, *Star Trek* had become too short-sighted in its treatment of technology and dismissive of the dangers it might unleash on humanity. The Roddenberry vision, in Behr's opinion, had become an unrealistically single-minded endorsement of science. Such a vision had been uncritical of technology and its potential dark side. In the perfect world of *Trek*, there was no corruption and there were no conspiracies (but for the theatrical film *Star Trek VI*, which Roddenberry had no control over — and did not approve of).

In *The 4400*, on the other hand, the future is a near wasteland, it is hinted, either because of warfare or environmental devastation. There is only one city left according to one of the 4400s in the episode "Terrible Swift Sword." This city is ruled by a rigid, dictatorial technocracy that wields its knowledge, its science and technology like a weapon, as a means for repression, rather than as a tool to serve and enlighten. Here they conspire and hoard all of the world's remaining resources while the rest of humanity is dying out. *The 4400* ran for three summer seasons, boasting solid ratings for USA. Meanwhile, one of the most influential television series of the decade premiered on September 22, 2004. Created by *Alias* producer J.J. Abrams, ABC's *Lost* was one of the true television phenomena of the 2000s.

Lost told the story of a group of survivors of Oceanic Flight 815, an airliner that crashed on an uncharted, apparently uninhabited island in the Pacific Ocean. As the survivors begin their struggle to stay alive, they start noticing that the island seems to be a place where the laws of nature and physics do not function as they should. Strange occurrences take place with more and more frequency. Some of them are just perplexing, like the appearance of a polar bear in the middle of the tropical jungle. But others seem to be entirely otherworldly. A sentient column of smoke attacks and kills. The emerging leader of the group, Dr. Jack Shepard (Matthew Fox), and others see visions of their dead loved ones. For some, like John

Locke (Terry O'Quinn), a former salesman who gradually starts asserting himself as a challenger to Jack's authority, the island becomes a place of miraculous renewal. Before crashing on the island, Lock had been confined to a wheelchair. The moment he awoke in the downed wreckage, however, he had full use of his legs once again.

The true nature of the island, revealed only in the show's last season in the spring of 2010, was, indeed, supernatural. It was a place that traveled back and forth in time at random intervals. It was a well of an ancient power source that had at one time been harnessed by mysterious, unnamed inhabitants. But it was also a place where two brothers, both imbued with various degrees of supernatural abilities and apparent immortality, were engaged in an ongoing struggle of wills. One of the brothers had become evil incarnate, bent on escaping the island and either dominating or destroying the world. The other one had become the embodiment of angelic, messianic goodness, devoting himself to keeping his sibling imprisoned.

Another problem that bedeviled the survivors of Oceanic 815 was the discovery of clues to the fact that there were people on the island besides themselves (and the supernatural brothers). The island seemed to be inhabited by several factions of "others," led by a duplicitous figure named Ben Linus (Michael Emmerson), of ever-changing identities and loyalties. The others, in turn, represented a corporate or scientific organization called the Dharma Initiative, apparently embedded on the island for decades and tasked with unraveling the secrets of its power source. The man behind the Dharma Initiative's expedition was Charles Widmore (Alan Dale), a business titan in the true mold of the conspiracy film's generic antagonist. He was a ruthless and single-minded power broker who commanded vast resources and had the ability to subvert and manipulate anyone and any organization in order to achieve his ends.

While the conclusion of *Lost* was controversial among its fans because it offered frustratingly few explanations about the power, origins, and nature of the island (not to mention the ultimate fate of the Oceanic survivors), the show was one of the most influential of the decade. In its wake, all of the major broadcast networks, as well as cable networks like the Sci-Fi Channel, premiered their own shows with ongoing storylines about supernatural manifestation entangled in vast corporate and governmental conspiracies. ABC attempted to repeat the formula with *Invasion*, a show that was something of a serialized adaptation of the premise of *Invasion of the Body Snatchers*. That same season, NBC premiered *Surface*, a program that could have been called a cross between the plot elements of *Close Encounters of the Third Kind* and *E.T.* In it, a scientist (Lake Bell) and a recreational fisherman (Jay R. Ferguson) become aware of enormous reptilian creatures in the oceans. They begin to suspect a vast international conspiracy. CBS unrolled *Threshold*, about a covert government program investigating an alien presence on Earth and the manipulation of human DNA to alter the entire human race. NBC's successful *Heroes* was a *4400*–esque thriller about people suddenly exhibiting superpowers; CBS's *Jericho* concerned a Washington D.C. group detonating nuclear bombs across the country in an effort to suspend civil liberties and take over the government; Fox's *Fringe* focused on a looming interdimensional war; and ABC's *FlashForward* was about a mysterious global blackout. In the fall of 2009, cable's TruTV ran a series called *Conspiracy Theory with Jesse Ventura*; the former Minnesota governor investigated conspiracy theories (September 11, Denver International Airport, etc.).

In the 2009–10 television season, Kenneth Johnson's cult science fiction story *V* was resurrected by ABC. Following Johnson's publication of the novel *V: The Second Generation*, ABC decided to remake the old TV film, updating it into a post–9/11 world of terrorism.

Produced by the creative team behind *The 4400*, the new version of *V* took the story much further into the territory of conspiracy theories than Johnson ever did; the new incarnation almost appeared to take many of its cues from the conspiratorial world of David Icke. Here, the reptilian invaders have been on Earth for years, if not decades, before they revealed themselves in their fleet of gigantic mother ships. Just as in Icke's yarns, the Visitors have infiltrated all the governments of the world. They have been manipulating economies, engineering periods of prosperity and recession, fomenting disorder and bringing about wars.

Despite the fact that American culture appeared to temporarily cool to the concept of conspiracy entertainment in the first days of the new millennium, it is inconceivable that this genre would not have reasserted itself as the rest of the decade brimmed with turbulence, fear of long, costly foreign wars, the everpresent threat of terrorism, and a severe economic downturn. Conspiracy theories, after all, speak to the anxieties about uncertainty.

CHAPTER 10

Conclusions

Conspiracy Theories — The Good and the Bad?

Conspiracy entertainment, in one form or another, will always be appealing. It should perhaps be argued that conspiracy theory films need to be recognized as being as quintessentially American as the Western or the gangster film. They embody the democratic impulse to question authority, to challenge organs of power, and voice skepticism of the status quo. But, as so many conspiratorially oriented forms of entertainment deal in ever more corrosive, hostile, and nihilistic cynicism, one might wonder if so much paranoia is healthy for a society. Do we need to be concerned about a real dark side to conspiracism? The answer itself might be murky. In a way, a cultural critic needs to hedge his or her bets and say that the answer might be both "yes" and "no."

If today, at the start of the second decade of the twenty-first century, we try and draw a parallel between cultural anxieties, some of the very deep political and ideological divisions in the country, and conspiracy theories, we find a lot of the same conspiracy entertainment appealing to a broad cross-section of Americans. The resistance to authority that conspiracism embodies is still attractive to everyone from the most liberal to the most conservative and every other political orientation in between. We all really love a good conspiracy theory. The way such a large segment of the culture has kept this paranoid genre so successful gives evidence to the power of the genre to speak to so many anxieties and fears. One of the most interesting examples of an ideologically diverse audience co-opting a single piece of conspiracy entertainment could be seen in the controversy surrounding the ABC-TV's remake of Kenneth Johnson's *V*.

It premiered on November 3, 2009, following intense marketing hype, wild anticipation in the science fiction fan community, and a highly successful preview of the pilot episode at the 2009 Comic-Con fan convention in San Diego. (Of all the new television series previewed at the convention, *V* received the most excited reception and the most positive reviews by attendees.) But controversy soon followed.

As reimagined by *4400* creator Scott Peters, *V* attempted to be relevant in the post–September 11, Afghanistan-Iraq era. When the gigantic alien mother ships ominously hovering above the world's major cities, much the way they did in the 1983 miniseries, the United States government and its law enforcement agencies are contending with terrorist cells hiding in America. The main protagonist, in fact, is FBI agent Erika Evans (Elizabeth Mitchell), investigating terrorists in the New York area. Just before the arrival of the aliens—once again calling themselves "Visitors"— Erika and her partner Dale Maddox (Alan Tudyk) had been investigating an increase in terrorist activities. As the Visitors reveal themselves to be attractive, athletic human beings, and promise marvelous cures for much of society's ills in return for access to Earthly chemicals that can help save the dying alien home world, some of the people suspected of being terrorists attempt to reach out and recruit others into the ranks of what they claim is a resistance army. Calling themselves the "Fifth Column," these alleged terrorists claim to know something about the true nature of the Visitors that nobody else does. When Erika and Dale infiltrate one of the New York Fifth Column cells, they hear its members tell a wild tale of the Visitors being reptilian invaders bent on the extermination of the human race. Moreover, the Fifth Column claims, the Visitors have been on Earth for decades. They have long infiltrated and manipulated all our governments and institutions of power. Then, as mechanized Visitor drones attack the meeting, Dale is revealed to be an alien himself. Erika even finds out that the Visitors are reptilians in human disguise, just like the Fifth Column said.

The original *V* operated in a much less complicated political environment than that of the 2009 remake, and used its Visitor invaders as stand-ins for modern-day Nazis; it did not court controversy. The new iteration, however, could not escape a much more contentious and sensitive issue: It told a story about the Earth being invaded and occupied by an evil, exploitive invasion force at the time the United States had invaded and was occupying two foreign countries. Some in the fan communities wondered if *V* was going to side with a faction of its left-wing fans, equating its invaders with the Bush administration and the attempted conquest of Earth with the invasions of Afghanistan and Iraq. Proving audience activity and the often idiosyncratic interpretive powers of viewers to be ever unpredictable, *V* actually created an entirely different sort of controversy in its pilot episode. Far from being accused of being an anti–Bush, anti–Iraq statement from the left, *V* was seen by some viewers as a *right*-wing parable about the new Obama administration.

The pilot, and much of the subsequent first season of the show, put a great deal of emphasis on the mass media's unquestioning, uncritical acquiescence to the Visitors' demand for positive coverage. The news, personified by ambitious reporter Chad Decker (Scott Wolf), swiftly builds a personality cult around the Visitors, especially their alluring leader, Anna (Morena Baccarin). For critics of the real news media's coverage of candidate Barack Obama — who had been labeled a "rock star" of politics by some publications and even had a comic book based on him, depicting him as a costumed superhero saving America — the show's storyline of the blind adoration of the Visitors looked like a critique of the media's relationship with the charismatic Obama. But when one of the Visitors' benevolent promises to the people of the world is "universal health care," a large contingent of fans read the show as a definite critical commentary on the policies of the Obama administration. Even *V* fan, science fiction author, and Fordham University communication professor Paul Levinson (*The Silk Code, The Plot to Save Socrates*), an outspoken Obama supporter, commented about his need to balance his appreciation of a lot of the writing, plotting, and character development in *V* with what he saw as an unnecessary dig at the president with the "universal health care" plot.[1] On the other hand, Ilana Rapp, who had started one of the most successful *V* fan clubs in the world in 1985, argued that the social commentaries of both incarnations of *V* might be very much in the eyes of the audiences and not merely in the content on the screen. "You can replace World War II with Iraq," she writes,

> you can replace the attacks on humans with 9/11 ... I've found over the years that *V* fans, in general, are brilliant. Each fan has his or her own reason for clutching onto *V*. Sometimes fans go to extremes in trying to interpret things that are just coincidence. It makes for wonderful conversation and debates. I think if fans want to find a relation in *V* to today's politics, or anything else for that matter, let them. It may or

may not have anything to do with *V* but people search for connections that are dear to them, and if the fans want to make such connections to *V*, I say go for it.[2]

What is key in both the conservative and the liberal interpretations of the conspiratorial plots of *V* is the fact that audiences see stories of subterfuge, official dishonesty, and media manipulation as very accurate representations of the state of the modern world.

It is also arguable that the quintessential conspiracy theory protagonists are the most quintessentially American fictional heroes. They are individualists in every sense. They are proud geeks and nerds; they are outsiders who brave being mocked by the majority. From the slightly eccentric Fox Mulder of *The X-Files* to the neurotic Jerry Fletcher of *Conspiracy Theory*, or Richard Dreyfuss' childlike Roy Neary character in *Close Encounters of the Third Kind*, conspiracy theorists are not afraid to live on the fringes of society, to subject themselves to the ridicule and scorn of their peers once they commit themselves to uncovering "the truth." In a world more and more Americans see as oppressed by an air of conformity, cultural and artistic homogenization, by commercialism, P.R. spin, and the obsessive hunger to be accepted, popular, and hip, the conspiracy theorist makes for the most appealing sort of fantasy hero. The conspiracy theorist does not go along with the proverbial flow, and even suggests that the "flow" might somehow be deceiving, exploiting, and harming its masses of unquestioning followers.

Nonetheless, one must also finally wonder about any possible problems and potential dangers a society might face when one of its most popular forms of entertainment is founded on paranoia, distrust, and aggressive cynicism. Is it healthy for a society to be fixated on so much bleak, angry nihilism? Once again, the answer might be *both* "yes" and "no."

Mass entertainment reflects the culture that produces it. Certainly, screenwriters, producers, directors, and even star actors who have the clout to shape the content of a film might have their own personal agendas or statements they want a film to make. These people can all try to influence an audience. But whether or not that audience will *buy* the message is another matter. As director Alan J. Pakula (*All the President's Men*) remarked, every time he used his movies to deliver a message, there would be about half the people in the audience who would willfully ignore it.[3] A movie cannot turn a Republican into a Democrat. A conspiracy thriller will not send its audiences into paroxysms of fear and suspicion. As the theory of media agenda-setting argues, the media can tell audiences what to think about, but not necessarily what to think.[4] The success of conspiracy theory entertainment is a sign that a certain level of paranoia is already part of the culture. Nevertheless, if the entertainment business keeps suspicion, distrust, and cynicism a part of its agenda, what sort of a worldview might it help keep alive in the American national psyche?

On the one hand, one could argue that a very important worldview is kept alive by these films and TV shows. This sort of entertainment implores its fans not to take the "official" version of events at face value, to be wary of all the ways power and privilege can be abused. Conspiracy theory films insist that people keep asking who is in charge, what these people are doing, what they have to gain from it, and, most importantly, is it really for the benefit of the average American on the street? If anything, the ongoing popularity of conspiracy theory entertainment might be an important cultural bellwether. The resonance of these films might indicate that Americans do feel like they are losing more control, freedom, and influence over their lives every day.

But, on the other hand, it is not unreasonable to worry about a culture's obsession with cynicism and paranoia. Can conspiracism have a dark side? It is certainly tempting to say so when one reads some of the low levels of "social capital" exercised by so many Americans. As Harvard University political science professor Robert D. Putnam discussed in a 1995 essay, then his 2000 book *Bowling Alone: The Collapse and Revival of American Community*, social capital refers to the level of civic involvement a group of people engage in. Social capital is the involvement in community organizations, neighborhood groups, or just simply spending time with other people in one's community and making sure that strong bonds among people are maintained. This is important, Putnam argues, because it is the key to civic and political activity, to people coming together and affecting change in their world. Civic activity usually declines when people feel like they don't have any real power to affect change, or if they just don't care enough about their community and fellow citizens. Putnam's work is controversial and has been very strongly criticized on the grounds that he might be ignoring the way new media like the Internet might simply be changing the way people interact with others and build communities. But concern over levels of social activity is still valid. Perhaps the simplest, yet most important, civic activity Americans can take part in is voting, yet statistics still show that a large majority of people do not even bother to do that much. Thus, one might wonder if this sort of civic apathy might in any way have a connection to an entertainment environment that so relentlessly bombards its audiences with the message that the American system is hopelessly rigged in favor of the so-called power elites.

This, however, is not to imply that there is a reason to suspect a causal connection. There are simply no data to reach that conclusion. An apathetic culture that feels disconnected from institutions of power might flock to conspiracy theory films. It is not known whether people who feel more disenfranchised make up a greater percentage of the conspiracy-film-viewing audience either.

But conspiratorial thinking and conspiratorial rhetoric have also often had a disturbingly close relationship with the unscrupulous, the antisocial, and the homicidally violent.

When political dissent turns into terroristic violence, the justifications have historically proven to be similar to a lot of the logic of today's conspiracy theorists. For example, radical urban terrorists of the 1960s have justified murderous attacks on the police, the government, and even innocent bystanders who happened to get caught in a shootout or wound up as collateral damage in a draft-office bombing, through conspiratorial rhetoric. The system, the radicals argued, was run by international cabals of bankers and industrialists who prevented true social change from ever taking place. By the same token, right-wing militias and hate groups of the 1990s espoused anti-government violence through conspiratorial arguments. The U.S. government and the world, they claimed, was run by a New World Order conspiracy of Jewish financial elites bent on subjugating and exploiting the white race. This conspiracy, ultra right-wingers said, was so powerful that the only way "Christian patriots" could protect their freedoms and to protect the white race was the violent overthrow of the government. Oklahoma City bombers Timothy McVeigh and Terry Nichols, who murdered 168 people in their April 19, 1995, attack on the Murrah Federal Building, believed they were fighting a war against this international Jewish cabal.[5]

Over the past two decades, conspiracy theories have also been used as selling tools for various health, diet, and nutritional claims. Doctors and medical researchers, understandably, have been growing increasingly leery of the practice. Those who sell exotic diets, herbal and holistic treatment methods and supplements, or make claims to dramatically life-altering and life-extending "natural" and "alternative" cures came to use the language of conspiracy to sell their products. Simple and cheap natural cures for everything from obesity, the common cold, and all the way to cancer, diabetes, and heart disease, some claim, exist, but have been suppressed by a conspiracy of big pharmaceutical companies and the Food and Drug Administration.

Two of the most outspoken of these natural diet-cure advocates have been Kevin Trudeau and former television star Suzanne Somers (*Three's Company, Step by Step*). Trudeau — who has sold everything from the secrets of natural diets to memory enhancement and debt relief — has been the most aggressively conspiratorial. He includes the word "they" in the title of most of his self-published books, referring to the forces of the government and big business that are keeping life-saving health information from the masses.[6] So does Somers, who claims to have overcome breast cancer and reduced the symptoms of menopause with various natural diets, supplements, and hormone therapy.[7] With the tremendous successes they have had in their multimedia businesses, though, they have both attracted the attention of the scientific establishment and often drawn blistering criticism for making unsubstantiated, spurious claims.

With only a high school education, Trudeau has made millions criticizing the medical profession, the FDA, and pharmaceutical research, and claiming to have discovered natural cures to virtually all major diseases. His critics, including the Federal Trade Commission and various attorneys general, claim that Trudeau has discovered the secrets to bilking gullible people out of millions of dollars. In fact, Trudeau's history since the early 1990s includes a long list of run-ins with the law and federal regulators. He served two separate prison terms for fraud. He settled with seven states in charges of operating pyramid schemes, and he was banned from operating a business in Michigan. In 2004, he agreed to a lifetime ban by the FTC from the promotion of products in television infomercials. However, that move merely gave Trudeau the opportunity to become a bestselling, multimillionaire author. He has since taken to marketing his books, like *Natural Cures "They" Don't Want You to Know About* (2006), on his infomercials. What the books reveal are instructions for going to Trudeau's websites that can only be accessed after the payment of subscription fees. The enticements in the book include promises that everything from cancer to multiple sclerosis, muscular dystrophy, arthritis, and diabetes can be cured through natural diets. He writes that sunscreen lotion, not ultraviolet radiation, cause cancer, and that AIDS is a hoax. Trudeau's books and webpages are filled with extensive lists of unsubstantiated claims, vague anecdotal evidence, and nebulous references to "leading experts" and "groundbreaking" research that prove his claims about the body's major maladies being caused by toxins, stress, and "electromagnetic chaos." Nowhere does he cite the actual studies, their authors, or journals of publication. He is, however, very prolific in spinning overwrought yarns about being personally targeted by government disinformation campaigns. He even claims to have been a government operative who stumbled onto the FDA's dirty secret of colluding with the medical profession in a vast conspiracy to produce useless drugs that will never cure illnesses. Trudeau claims (in long diatribes reminiscent of Lenny Bruce decrying his harassment by the police and prosecutors) that the government has been committed to publicly maligning him and destroying his businesses. Trudeau often said that he saw himself as a revolutionary struggling to change the world for the better, a crusader in the traditions of Rosa Parks, Cesar Chavez, Gandhi, and Martin Luther King.[8]

Further pointing to the pernicious effects of conspiratorial paranoia on the public health, doctors warn of an impending health crisis in the wake of fears over a causal link between childhood vaccinations and autism. Although no empirical evidence of this has yet been found by researchers — or if there really is a greater incidence of autism today than at any time in the past — thousands of Internet conspiracy theories and celebrity activists like Jenny McCarthy say otherwise. Vaccines, these theories claim, have led to thousands of cases of autism; the government and the pharmaceutical companies know about it, yet they are keeping the data hidden to protect themselves and their profits. But the real threats, doctors argue, now comes from thousands of fearful parents who will allow their children to contract and spread diseases like whooping cough and measles, all out of a misguided paranoia over vaccines.[9]

Conspiracy theories, whether on the Internet, in speculative literature, on television, in bestselling novels, or the movies are here to stay. They are a natural byproduct of an ever more complex, bureaucratic, often overwhelming modern world. In many ways, conspiracy theory entertainment and the critical thinking it can inspire, *should* be a part of the culture. But perhaps when conspiratorial thinking permeates every part of our culture and our everyday lives, we would be well-advised to always seek that prize which *fictional* conspiracy theorists always find: the smoking gun.

Chapter Notes

Introduction

1. Michael Baigent, Richard Leigh, and Henry Lincoln, *Holy Blood, Holy Grail* (New York: Dell, 1983).
2. Ibid., 47–48.
3. Michael Baigent and Richard Leigh, *The Temple and the Lodge* (New York: Arcade, 1991).
4. Jim Marrs, *Rule by Secrecy: The Hidden History That Connects the Trilateral Commission, the Freemasons, and the Great Pyramids* (New York: HarperPerennial, 1999), 239.
5. Charles Upton, *Legends of the End: Prophecies of the End Times, Antichrist, Apocalypse, and Messiah from Eight Religious Traditions* (Hillsdale, NY: Sophia Perennis, 2005).
6. Jack Lambert and Norman Polmar, *Defenseless: Command Failure at Pearl Harbor* (Osceola, WI: Zenith Press, 2003).
7. Gary Webb, *Dark Alliance: The CIA, the Contras and the Crack Cocaine Explosion* (New York: Seven Stories Press, 1998).
8. Conspiracy theories about the American government's creation of AIDS are discussed in Peter Knight, *Conspiracy Nation: The Politics of Paranoia in Postwar America* (New York: New York University Press, 2002), and Alan Cantwell, *AIDS and the Doctors of Death: An Inquiry Into the Origins of the AIDS Epidemic* (Los Angeles: Aries Rising Press, 1992).
9. Marrs, *Rule by Secrecy*, 3.
10. Jane Parish and Martin Parker, *The Age of Anxiety: Conspiracy Theory and the Human Sciences* (Boston: Blackwell/Sociological Review, 2001).
11. Nina Schwartz, "Itsy-Bitsy Spiders and Other Pieces of the Real in Dead Calm," *Camera Obscura* 51, Volume 17, November 3, 2002, 151.
12. Nicholas Hagger, *The Secret History of the West: The Influence of Secret Organizations on Western History from the Renaissance to the 20th Century* (New York: O Books, 2005).
13. A look at the conspiracy theories surrounding wealthy collegiate fraternal organizations and secretive social clubs can be found in Kris Millegan, *Fleshing Out Skull & Bones: Investigations Into America's Most Powerful Secret Society* (Watterville, OR: Trine Day, 2005); Alexandra Robbins, *Secrets of the Tomb: Skull and Bones, the Ivy League and the Hidden Paths of Power* (Boston: Back Bay Books, 2003); and Steve Sora, *Secret Societies of America's Elite: From the Knights Templar to Skull and Bones* (Shippensburg, PA: Destiny Books, 2003).
14. Marrs, *Rule by Secrecy*, 12.
15. Ibid.
16. Ibid., 13.
17. Ibid.
18. J. Allen Hynek. *The UFO Experience: A Scientific Inquiry* (New York: Marlowe, 1998), 52.
19. Jacques Vallée. *Revelations: Alien Contact and Human Deception* (New York: Ballantine Books, 1991).

Chapter 1

1. Leo Braudy, "Genre: The Conventions of Connection," in *Film Theory and Criticism*, edited by Gerald Mast, Marshall Cohen and Leo Braudy (New York: Oxford University Press, 1976), 435.
2. Paul Schrader, "Notes on Film Noir," in *Film Genre Reader*, edited by Barry Keith Grant (Austin: University of Texas Press, 1986), 84.
3. Alain Silver and James Ursini, *Film Noir* (Los Angeles: Taschen, 2004).
4. Jans B. Wager, *Dames in the Driver's Seat: Rereading Film Noir* (Austin: University of Texas Press, 2005), and E. Ann Kaplan, *Women in Film Noir* (London: British Film Institute, 1998) give very thorough discussions of the complex roles women played in the *film noir* genre.
5. Gregory D. Black, *Hollywood Censored: Morality Codes, Catholics, and the Movies* (New York: Cambridge University Press, 1996).
6. Tom Wolfe, *The Right Stuff* (New York: Bantam, 1979), x.
7. Jerome Clark, *Unexplained!* (Detroit: Visible Ink Press, 1993).
8. David Lavery, Angela Hague, and Marla Cartwright, *Deny All Knowledge: Reading the X-Files* (Syracuse: Syracuse University Press, 1996).

Chapter 2

1. John M. Broder, "Greatness in Eye of Beholder?" *Los Angeles Times*, November 22, 1993.

2. Arthur M. Schlesinger, Jr., *Robert Kennedy and His Times* (New York: Mariner, 2002).

3. Black, *Hollywood Censored*.

4. James Gilbert, *A Cycle of Outrage: America's Reaction to the Juvenile Delinquent in the 1950s* (New York: Oxford University Press, 1986).

5. In his book *Reclaiming History: The Assassination of President John F. Kennedy* (New York: W.W. Norton, 2007), Vincent Bugliosi lists 214 prominent people who have, at one point or another, been accused of being a part of the JFK assassination. The list includes the likes of George H.W. Bush, Joe DiMaggio, Jimmy Hoffa, Howard Hughes, Nikita Khrushchev, Richard Nixon, Aristotle Onassis, Arlen Specter, Adlai Stevenson, and Abraham Zapruder.

6. Ibid., 990.

7. While explorations of the dark sides and indiscretions of the most prominent figures of the Kennedy family are voluminous, notable books about John F. Kennedy's private life, character, and behavior which, according to a consensus of historians, could have jeopardized his function as president, if not the very nation's foreign policy and security, include works by Nigel Hamilton, *JFK: Reckless Youth* (New York: Random House, 1995); Seymour M. Hersh, *The Dark Side of Camelot* (Boston: Back Bay Books, 1997); and Thomas Reeves, *A Question of Character: A Life of John F. Kennedy* (New York: Prima, 1997).

8. Michael John Sullivan, *Presidential Passions: The Love Affairs of America's Presidents: From Washington and Jefferson to Kennedy and Johnson* (New York: S.P.I. Books, 1994), 22.

9. James Spada, *Peter Lawford* (New York: Bantam, 1992).

10. J. Randy Taraborrelli, *The Secret Life of Marilyn Monroe* (New York: Grand Central, 2009).

11. According to Kennedy conspiracy lore, both the FBI and CIA had been particularly antagonistic to JFK and FBI director J. Edgar Hoover maintained an active surveillance of the Kennedy family and their associates. The FBI has admitted to watching influential celebrities, especially ones feared to harbor radical left-wing sympathies. In an August 1, 2006, episode of *CBS News 48 Hours Mystery*, "The Marilyn Tapes," it was disclosed that the FBI kept Monroe under surveillance since her March 1962 visit to Mexico, where she socialized with Americans who were admitted communists.

12. Ronald Kessler, *The Sins of the Father: Joseph P. Kennedy and the Dynasty He Founded* (New York: Warner Books, 1996).

13. George Robert Blakey, *The Plot to Kill the President* (New York: Times Books, 1981).

14. Church Committee, *Intelligence Activities and the Rights of Americans: 1976 U.S. Senate Report on Illegal Wiretaps and Domestic Spying by the FBI, CIA, and NSA* (St. Petersburg, FL: Red and Black, 2008).

15. Jonathan Vankin and John Whalen, *60 Greatest Conspiracies of All Time* (New York: Citadel Press, 1996).

16. Gerald Posner, *Case Closed: Lee Harvey Oswald and the Assassination of JFK* (New York: Random House, 1993).

17. Marina Oswald's past and connections to Russian officialdom are usually a point of interest for conspiracy theorists and her uncle is often incorrectly identified as a colonel in the KGB. In fact, he was a lumber industry expert in the Ministry of Internal Affairs, as discussed by Priscilla Johnson McMillan in *Marina and Lee* (New York: Random House, 1980).

18. Posner, *Case Closed*.

19. Jim Marrs, *Crossfire: The Plot That Killed Kennedy* (New York: Carroll & Graf, 1989).

20. Bugliosi, *Reclaiming History*, 991.

21. Ibid.

22. Conrad Black, *Richard M. Nixon: A Life in Full* (New York: PublicAffairs, 2007).

23. Ibid.

24. David Rudenstine, *The Day the Presses Stopped: A History of the Pentagon Papers Case* (Berkley: University of California Press, 1998).

25. Daniel Ellsberg, *Secrets: A Memoir of Vietnam and the Pentagon Papers* (New York: Viking Penguin, 2002).

26. Ibid.

27. Ibid.

28. Neil Sheehan, *The Pentagon Papers: The Secret History of the Vietnam War* (New York: Bantam Books, 1971).

29. Randal Bezanson, *How Free Can the Press Be?* (Champaign: University of Illinois Press, 2003).

30. Carl Bernstein and Bob Woodward, *All the President's Men* (New York: Simon & Schuster, 1974).

31. Athan Theoharis, *Spying on Americans: Political Surveillance from Hoover to the Huston Plan* (Philadelphia: Temple University Press, 1978).

32. Gerald P. Koocher and Patricia Keith-Spiegel, *Ethics in Psychology and the Mental Health Professions: Standards and Cases (Oxford Textbooks in Clinical Psychology)*, (New York: Oxford University Press, 2008).

33. Two good overviews of the late 19th century airship mysteries can be found in Daniel Cohen, *The Great Airship Mystery: A UFO of the 1890s* (New York: Dodd, Mead, 1981), and Jerome Clark, *Unexplained* (Detroit: Visible Ink Press, 1993).

34. David M. Jacobs, *The UFO Controversy in America* (Bloomington: Indiana University Press, 1975).

35. Jerome Clark, *The UFO Book: Encyclopedia of the Extraterrestrial* (Detroit: Visible Ink Press, 1997).

36. Richard M. Dolan, *UFOs and the National Security State: Chronology of a Cover-up 1941–1973* (Charlottesville, VA: Hampton Roads, 2002).

37. Jerome Clark, *Strange Skies: Pilot Encounters With UFOs* (New York: Citadel Press, 2003).

38. Ibid.

39. Hynek, *The UFO Experience*.

40. Jacobs, *The UFO Controversy in America*.

41. Dolan, *UFOs and the National Security State*, 98.

42. Curtis Peebles, *Watch the Skies! A Chronicle of the Flying Saucer Myth* (New York: Berkley Books, 1995), 217.

43. Hynek, *The UFO Experience: A Scientific Inquiry*, 195.

44. Ibid.

45. Clark, *Unexplained!* 396.

46. George Adamski, *Inside the Space Ships* (New York: Abelard-Schuman, 1955).

47. Jerome Clark, *The Emergence of a Phenomenon: UFOs from the Beginning Through 1959 — The UFO Encyclopedia, Volume 2*, (Detroit: Omnigraphics, 1992).

48. Hilary Evans, *Gods, Spirits, Cosmic Guardians: A Comparative Study of the Encounter Experience* (Wellingborough, Northamptonshire, England: Aquarian Press, 1987).

49. Although very cautious in endorsing conspiracy theories, Jacques Vallée argues this form of a conspiracy in his book *Revelations*.

50. *An Alien History of Planet Earth*, History Channel Documentary (10/13/05).

51. The most comprehensive overviews of the UFO abduction phenomenon can be found in Budd Hopkins' *Intruders: The Incredible Visitations at Copley Woods* (New York: Random House, 1987), David M. Jacobs' *Secret Life: First Hand Accounts of UFO Abductions* (New York: Simon & Schuster, 1992), John E. Mack's *Abduction: Human Encounters with Aliens* (New York: Ballantine Books, 1994), and Jacobs' *The Threat* (New York: Simon & Schuster, 1998).

52. John G. Fuller, *The Interrupted Journey: Two Lost Hours Aboard a Flying Saucer* (New York: Dial Press, 1966).

53. Jacobs, *The Threat*, 258.

54. The most prominent figure in the animal mutilation mystery is Linda Moulton Howe. Her book *Alien Harvest: Further Evidence Linking Animal Mutilations and Human Abductions to Alien Life Forms* (self published, 1989) is one of the key texts on mutilation.

55. Tony Edwards, "End of the Road for Car That Ran on Water," *The Sunday Times*, December 1, 1996.

56. Jonathan Eisen, *Suppressed Inventions and Other Discoveries* (New York: Perigee, 1999).

57. Jim Keith, *Mind Control and UFOs: Casebook on Alternative 3* (Kempton, IL: Adventures Unlimited Press, 2005).

Chapter 3

1. Black, *Hollywood Censored*.

2. Ernest F. Martin, "Five," in *Nuclear War Films*, edited by Jack G. Shaheen and Marshall Flaum (Carbondale: Southern Illinois University Press, 1978), 11–16.

3. Tony Shaw, *Hollywood's Cold War* (Edinburgh: Edinburgh University Press, 2007), 157.

4. Frank W. Oglesbee, "The World, the Flesh, and the Devil," in Shaheen and Flaum, 25.

5. Roger Ebert discusses this in his liner notes to the 40th anniversary special edition DVD of *Dr. Strangelove*.

6. This transformation of the Peter George novel into the satirical film is discussed in the DVD documentary *No Fighting in the War Room: Or Dr. Strangelove and the Nuclear Threat*.

7. Linda Hunt, *Secret Agenda: The United States, Nazi Scientists, and Project Paperclip, 1945 to 1990* (New York: St. Martin's Press, 1991).

8. Joseph P. Farrell, *The SS Brotherhood of the Bell: NASA's Nazis, JFK, and Majic-12*, (Kempton, IL: Adventures Unlimited Press, 2006).

9. Dick Lochte, "Warren Murphy and His Heroic Oddballs," in *Murder Off the Rack: Critical Studies of Ten Paperback Masters*, edited by John L. Breen and Martin Harry Greenberg (Metuchen, NJ: Scarecrow, 1989), 162.

10. The difficulties of getting the film project off the ground are discussed by Redford in his audio commentary on the film's DVD.

11. Bill Carter, "Springer Quits News Show, Citing Attacks," *New York Times*, May 9, 1992.

12. Ben H. Bagdikian, *The New Media Monopoly* (Boston: Beacon Press, 2004).

13. A thorough discussion of *The Day the Earth Stood Still*'s controversial ending can be seen on the documentary *Making the Earth Stand Still*, on the film's DVD.

14. Lyndon W. Joslin, "Cosmic Frames and Cover-ups: *Invasion of the Saucer Men* and the UFO Conspiracy of Silence," in *Science Fiction America: Essays on SF Cinema*, edited by David J. Hogan (Jefferson, NC: McFarland, 2006), 138.

15. Gray Barker, *They Knew Too Much About Flying Saucers* (New York: University Books, 1956). Barker's work is largely credited with popularizing the Men in Black mythos, but not without a great deal of controversy. Throughout the years, he had been accused of taking part in perpetrating UFO hoaxes and repeating allegations of alien contact he knew to be fraudulent. He is the subject of the 2010 documentary *Shades of Gray*.

16. John Keel, in his *Mothman Prophecies*, has focused his speculation on the otherworldly aspects of the Men In Black. The MIBs, he argues, just like UFOs themselves, might be extradimensional beings rather than extraterrestrials or clandestine government operatives.

17. Robert Tinnell, "*Logan's Run* to Relevance," in Hogan.

18. The Discovery Channel's *Mythbusters* series also ran its *NASA Moon Landing* episode on August 27, 2008, refuting each of the major moon landing hoax arguments.

19. The plot of *The Island* was so similar to *The Clonus Horror* that the original film's screenwriter sued Dreamworks studios for copyright infringement. Dreamworks settled the case out of court. Daniel Fireman, "Attack of the Clones," *Entertainment Weekly*, July 22, 2005.

20. Leon R. Kass, *Human Cloning and Human Dignity: The Report of the President's Council on Bioethics* (New York: PublicAffairs, 2002).

Chapter 4

1. Kevin D. Randle and Donald R. Schmitt, *UFO Crash at Roswell* (New York: Avon Books, 1991).
2. Ibid., 68.
3. Vallée, *Revelations*.
4. Greg Bishop, *Project Beta: The Story of Paul Bennewitz, National Security, and the Creation of a Modern UFO Myth* (New York: Pocket Books, 2005).
5. Vallée, *Revelations*, 125.
6. Clark, *The UFO Book*.
7. Joe Nickell and John F. Fischer, "The Crashed Saucer Forgeries," *The International UFO Reporter*, March 1990.
8. Denna Allen and Janet Midwinter, "Michelle Remembers: The Debunking of a Myth," *The Mail on Sunday*, September 30, 1990.
9. Paul Eberle and Shirley Eberle, *The Abuse of Innocence: The McMartin Preschool Trial* (Amherst, NY: Prometheus Books, 2003).
10. Debbie Nathan, *Satan's Silence: Ritual Abuse and the Making of a Modern American Witch Hunt* (New York: Basic Books, 1995).
11. John E. B. Myers, *Child Protection in America: Past, Present, and Future* (New York: Oxford University Press, 2006).
12. May de Young, *The Ritual Abuse Controversy: An Annotated Bibliography* (Jefferson, NC: McFarland, 2002).
13. Eberle and Eberle, *The Abuse of Innocence*.
14. For two strong sociological and historical analyses of the Satanic abuse panic, see David Frankfurter, *Evil Incarnate: Rumors of Demonic Conspiracy and Satanic Abuse in History* (Princeton, NJ: Princeton University Press, 2006), and Jeffrey S. Victor, *Satanic Panic: The Creation of a Contemporary Legend* (Chicago: Open Court, 1993).
15. In his book about the Manson family's killing spree and the subsequent trial, *Helter Skelter: The True Story of the Manson Murders* (New York: W.W. Norton, 1994), Vincent Bugliosi discusses the media's casting of Manson as the diabolical figure who brought an end to the era of hippies. He argues that this is not entirely accurate because the hippie movement was already in decline by the time of the trials. Moreover, the peace, non-violence, and love ethos of true hippies—as opposed to the more aggressive factions of the counter culture like the Weathermen and other far-left radical organizations—was completely antithetical to Manson's desire to ignite a race war and destroy the status quo. Bugliosi, instead, writes that Manson's dark allure might be rooted in his sheer strangeness and the bizarre hold he had over his followers. There is something frightening, Bugliosi writes, in the way a figure like Manson seemed to be able to brainwash others and make them do his murderous bidding. The dread fear of such a manipulative psychopath is similar to the instinctive fascination and repulsion people feel toward figures like Jim Jones or David Koresh or any such charismatic cult leaders. Nevertheless, for the very conservatively inclined, those who already harbored a resentment of everything the counter culture movement stood for, Manson is still a favorite—if perhaps misplaced—emblem of that movement.
16. Dionne Searcey, "Behind the Music: Sleuths Seek Messages in Lyrical Backspin," *Wall Street Journal*, January 9, 2006.
17. Clyde Wilcox and Carin Robinson, *Onward Christian Soldiers? The Religious Right in American Politics (Dilemmas in American Politics)* (Boulder, CO: Westview Press, 2000).
18. Victor, *Satanic Panic*.
19. Ibid.
20. Eberle and Eberle, *The Abuse of Innocence*.
21. Louis-Georges Tin and Marek Redburn, *Dictionary of Homophobia: A Global History of Gay & Lesbian Experience* (Vancouver, BC: Arsenal Pulp Press, 2008).
22. Katy Burns, "Jerry Falwell's Greatest Hates," *Concord Monitor*, May 17, 2007.
23. Victor, *Satanic Panic*.
24. Eberle and Eberle, *The Abuse of Innocence*.
25. Robert D. Hicks, *In Pursuit of Satan: The Police and the Occult* (Amherst, NY: Prometheus Books, 1991).
26. Allen and Midwinter, "Michelle Remembers."
27. Chris Mathews, *Modern Satanism: Anatomy of a Radical Subculture* (Westport, CT: Praeger, 2009).
28. John E.B. Myers, *The Backlash: Child Protection Under Fire* (Thousand Oaks, CA: Sage, 1994).
29. Two of the most lengthy conspiratorial perspectives on the Council on Foreign Relations are given by Jim Marrs in *Rule by Secrecy*, and James Perloff in *The Shadows of Power: The Council on Foreign Relations and the American Decline* (Appleton, WI: Western Islands, 2000).
30. A concise, non-conspiratorial history of the Council on Foreign relations can be read in Peter Grose's *Continuing the Inquiry: The Council on Foreign Relations from 1921 to 1996* (New York: Council on Foreign Relations Press, 1996).

Chapter 5

1. David Denby, "Movies: The Last Angry Men," *New York*, January 16, 1984.
2. Vallée, *Revelations*, 20–25.
3. Ibid., 28.
4. Timothy Good, *Alien Contact: Top Secret UFO Files Revealed* (New York: Quill, 1993), 79.
5. Ibid., 81.

6. Ibid.

7. Peter Biskind's exhaustive work on the late 1960s and early 1970s era of young filmmakers, *Easy Riders, Raging Bulls: How the Sex-Drugs-and-Rock 'n' Roll Generation Saved Hollywood* (New York: Simon & Schuster, 1998) argues that the edgy, counterculture sensibilities of Baby Boomer filmmakers rescued Hollywood from a string of big-budget box office failures that had been a result of an industry out of touch with the culture. Then, a new era of late '70s blockbusters threatened to undermine personal filmmaking for decades to come.

8. Roger Ebert, "Rambo: First Blood Part II," review of *Rambo: First Blood Part II* in *Roger Ebert's Home Movie Companion* (Kansas City: Andrews McMeel, 1992), 115.

9. Frank Sanello, *Stallone: A Rocky Life* (Edinburgh: Mainstream, 1998), 148.

10. Ibid.

11. Susan Faludi, *Stiffed: The Betrayal of the American Man* (New York: William Morrow, 1999).

12. Ibid.

13. Susan Jeffords, *Hard Bodies: Hollywood Masculinity in the Reagan Era* (New Brunswick, NJ: Rutgers University Press, 1994).

14. Richard Corliss, "Seagal Under Siege," *Time*, July 5, 1993.

15. Webb, *Dark Alliance.*

Chapter 6

1. Katherine Ramsland, *Piercing the Darkness: Undercover with Vampires in America Today* (New York: HarperPrism, 1998), 348.

2. Ibid., 347.

3. Faludi, *Stiffed.*

4. J. Gordon Melton, "Vampire Games," *The Vampire Book: The Encyclopedia of the Undead* (Detroit: Visible Ink Press, 1999), 273–282.

5. John D. Morrocco, "Multiple Sightings of Secret Aircraft Hint at New Propulsion, Airframe Designs," *Aviation Week and Space Technology*, October 1, 1990, 22–23.

6. Good, *Alien Contact.*

7. David Darlington, *Area 51: The Dreamland Chronicles* (New York: Owl Books, 1997).

8. Emenegger also discusses the incident in his book *UFOs: Past, Present and Future,* (New York: Ballantine, 1974).

9. Vallée, *Revelations*, 62.

10. Darlington, *Area 51*, 61.

11. Marrs, *Alien Agenda.*

12. Darlington, *Area 51.*

13. Good, *Alien Contact.*

14. Ibid., 171–172.

15. Darlington, *Area 51.*

16. Vallée, *Revelations*, 227.

17. Despite publishing *UFO* magazine, William J. Birnes does not enjoy the highest regard among UFO researchers with academic credentials. Many, like Temple University historian David M. Jacobs, dismiss him simply as a businessman, a showman out to turn a profit by providing a segment of the UFO-enthusiast community as many sensational stories about conspiracies and alien encounters as possible. They accuse him of never having met a conspiracy theory or a colorful alien story he did not endorse.

18. William J. Broad, "Senator Regrets Role in Book on Aliens," *New York Times*, June 5, 1997.

19. Vallée, *Revelations*, 67.

20. For a sample of conspiratorial discussions of the tunnels at DIA, see http://newsflavor.com/opinions/mystery-surrounding-denver-international-airport/.

21. Patricia Calhoun, "The Art at DIA Keeps Rumors Flying," *Denver Westword News*, July 6, 2010.

22. For a full text of Bush's speech, see www.historyplace.com/speeches/bush-war.htm.

23. For several books prescribing to the demonic-alien and Nephilim interpretations of the UFO phenomenon, see Hugh Ross, *Lights in the Sky and Little Green Men: A Rational Christian Look at UFOs and Extraterrestrials* (Colorado Springs: NavPress, 2002); Chuck Missler and Mark Eastman, *Alien Encounters: The Secret Behind the UFO Phenomenon* (Coeur d'Alene, ID: Koinonia House, 2003); and J.C., *Mysteries of the Universe: A Revolutionary Commentary on UFOs, Aliens, Angels, Pyramids, Bible Codes, Reincarnation, the Antichrist…* (Longwood, FL: Xulon Press, 2004).

24. Thomas Michael Alleman, "25 Most Influential Evangelicals in America," *Time*, September 8, 2007.

25. Robert Dreyfus, "Reverend Doomsday: According to Tim LaHaye, the Apocalypse is Now," *Rolling Stone*, January 28, 2004.

26. Michelle Goldberg, "Fundamentally Unsound," *Salon.com*, July 29, 2007.

Chapter 7

1. Luis Murillo, *The Noriega Mess: The Drugs, the Canal, and Why America Invaded* (Berkeley: Video-Books, 1995).

2. John Leo, "Twisted History," *Newsweek*, December 23, 1991, 47.

3. Ibid.

4. Ibid., 48.

5. Patricia Lambert critiques the film in her book *False Witness: The Real Story of Jim Garrison's Investigation and Oliver Stone's Film* JFK (New York: M. Evans, 1998).

6. Ted Edwards, X-Files *Confidential: The Unauthorized X-Philes Compendium*, (Boston: Little, Brown, 1997).

7. Ibid., xv.

8. Ibid., 134.

9. Ibid.

10. Ibid., 81–82.

11. Ibid., 135.

12. Ibid.

13. Ibid., 135.

14. Ibid.

15. Read Mercer Schuchardt, "What Is the Matrix?" in *Taking the Red Pill: Science, Philosophy and Religion in* The Matrix, edited by Glenn Yeffeth (Dallas: Benbella, 2003), 5.

Chapter 8

1. Jason Davis, "Tune in for the 'Truth': Carter and Spotnitz Revisit *The X-Files* TV Series," *Creative Screenwriting*, July/August, 2008.

2. *Revealed*, "The Man Behind the Da Vinci Code" (6/10/06).

3. Laura Miller, "The Last Word; The Da Vinci Con," *New York Times*, February 22, 2004.

4. Ibid.

5. *60 Minutes*, "The Secret of the Priory of Sion" (4/30/06).

6. Tim Wu, "Holy Grail Wars: The Latest Battle Over *The Da Vinci Code*," *Slate*, March 13, 2006.

7. An overview of the post–9/11 Nostradamus hoaxes and examples of some of the most commonly circulated e-mails can be read on the urban legends web site About.com: Urban Legends.

8. Erika Cheetham, *The Further Prophecies of Nostradamus: 1985 and Beyond* (New York: Perigee Books, 1985), 194.

9. In *The Further Prophecies of Nostradamus*, Erika Cheetham interprets that "the advent of the Third World War, according to Nostradamus, will be heralded by an attack on New York—city and state—through both bombs and chemical warfare" (194).

10. Brendan McKay, Dror Bar-Natan, and Maya Bar-Hillel, "Solving the Bible Code Puzzle," *Statistical Science*, Vol. 14, 1999.

11. Robert Aumann, Dror Bar-Natan, Hillel Furstenberg, Isaak Lapides, and Elihu Rips, "Analyses of the 'Gans' Committee Report," Report presented to the Center for the Study of Rationality, 1996, 2.

12. Jon Ronson, *Them: Adventures with Extremists* (New York: Simon & Schuster, 2002).

13. Ibid.

14. David Icke, *And the Truth Shall Set You Free* (self published, 2004), 120–121.

15. Paul Brown, "Ex-Nutter Icke Rails at the New World Order Mind Benders," *The Guardian*, May 19, 1995.

16. Michael Barkun, *A Culture of Conspiracy: Apocalyptic Visions in Contemporary America (Comparative Studies in Religion and Society)* (Berkeley: University of California Press, 2003).

17. For three of the most comprehensive works on the build up to, invasion of, and aftermath of Iraq, see Bob Woodward's *Plan of Attack* (New York: Simon & Schuster, 2004), Thomas E. Ricks' *Fiasco: The American Military Adventure in Iraq* (New York: Penguin Press, 2006), and Michael R. Gordon and Bernard E. Trainor's *Cobra II: The Inside Story of the Invasion and Occupation of Iraq* (New York: Vintage Books, 2007).

18. Valerie Plame Wilson and Laura Rozen, *Fair Game: How a Top CIA Agent Was Betrayed by Her Own Government* (New York: Simon & Schuster, 2007).

19. Bruce Crumley, "Conspiracy Theory," *Time*, May 13, 2002.

20. Ibid.

21. Cinamon Stillwell, "The Truth About 9/11 Conspiracy Theories," *San Francisco Chronicle*, August 19, 2006.

22. Jason Kane, "PPC Backs away From 9/11 Conspiracy Book," *Presbyterian News Service*, November 28, 2006.

23. Michelle Goldberg, "Truther Consequences," *The New Republic*, October 7, 2009.

24. Zdenek P. Bazant and Mathieu Verdure, "Mechanics of Progressive Collapse: Learning from World Trade Center and Building Demolitions," *Journal of Engineering Mechanics*, March 2007.

25. John Gravois, "Professors of Paranoia?" *Chronicle of Higher Education*, June 23, 2006.

26. Jones' paper can be found at http://web.archive.org/web/20051124011753/http://www.physics.byu.edu/research/energy/htm7.html.

27. Tad Walch, "BYU Professor in Dispute Over 9/11 Will Retire," *Deseret News*, October 22, 2006.

28. Gretchen Ruethling, "A Skeptic on 9/11 Prompts Questions on Academic Freedom," *New York Times*, August 1, 2006.

29. Matt Taibi, *The Great Derangement: A Terrifying True Story of War, Politics, and Religion at the Twilight of the American Empire* (New York: Spiegel & Grau, 2008).

30. All the theories and claims forwarded by *Scholars for 9/11 Truth* can be found on their webpage: www.scholarsfor911truth.org.

31. All the theories and claims forwarded by *Scholars for 9/11 Truth and Justice* can be found at http://stj911.org.

32. Claims made by *Architects and Engineers for 9/11 Truth* can be found on their web page: www.ae911truth.org.

33. Stephen Lemons, "The Yoda of 9/11," *Phoenix NewTimes*, August 9, 2007.

34. The *Loose Change* online documentaries and their producers were profiled in the August 20, 2007, History Channel documentary *The 9/11 Conspiracies: Fact or Fiction.*

35. Matt Mitovich, "Charlie Sheen to Give Voice to 9/11 Conspiracy Theorists After All ... Maybe," *TV Guide*, June 1, 2007.

36. Taibi, *The Great Derangement*, 212.

37. Tad Walch, "Controversy Dogs Y's Jones," *Deseret News*, September 11, 2006.

Chapter 9

1. *The Lone Gunmen*'s creative team's recollections of their reaction to September 11 are compiled on the 9/11 conspiracy webpage *Killtown*. They can be accessed at http://killtown.911review.org/lonegunmen.html.

2. Ibid.

3. Ibid.

4. Jones' analysis of *The Lone Gunmen* pilot episode can be read at http://www.prisonplanet.com/multimedia_prior-knowledge_lonegunmen.html.

5. Cesar G. Soriano, "Politics Creates a Disturbance in the Force," *USA Today*, May 17, 2005.

6. Biskind, *Easy Riders, Raging Bulls.*

7. Ibid.

8. Ibid., 318.

9. Ibid., 330.

10. *Left Behind*, www.imdb.com/title/tt0190524/.

11. *Left Behind: World at War*, www.imdb.com/title/tt0443567/.

12. Josh Kimball, "Settlement Brings End to 9-Year 'Left Behind' Dispute," *Christian Post*, August 15, 2008.

13. Ibid.

14. Bradford W. Wright, *Comic Book Nation: The Transformation of Youth Culture in America* (Baltimore: Johns Hopkins University Press, 2003).

15. Stephen Knight, *Jack the Ripper: The Final Solution* (Detroit: Treasure Press, 1984).

16. Moore discusses his work and his impressions of Hollywood film making in an interview for *MTV.com*. The piece can be accessed at www.mtv.com/shared/movies/interviews/m/moore_alan_060315.

17. Nicholas Goodrick-Clarke, *Black Sun: Aryan Cults, Esoteric Nazism and the Politics of Identity* (New York: New York University Press, 2002).

18. Alexandra Bruce, *2012: Science or Superstition (The Definitive Guide to the Doomsday Phenomenon)* (New York: Disinformation Company, 2009).

19. Thomas de Zengotita, "Must See Movie: Shooter," *The Huffington Post*, April 2, 2007.

20. Robbins, *Secrets of the Tomb.*

21. M.J. Stephey, "The Skull and Bones Society," *Time*, February 23, 2009.

22. Behr discussed his views of the shortcomings of *Star Trek* in the November 13, 2005, History Channel documentary *How William Shatner Changed the World.*

Chapter 10

1. Levinson's media commentary can be read at his "Paul Levinson's Infinite Regress" blog: www.paullevinson.blogspot.com.

2. Ilana Rapp's writings about the old and new incarnations of *V* can be found at www.ilanasVsite.com.

3. *Telling the Truth About Lies: The Making of All the President's Men* documentary for *All the President's Men* DVD.

4. Maxwell McCombs and Donald Shaw, "The Evolution of Agenda-Setting Theory: 25 Years in the Marketplace of Ideas," *Journal of Communication*, 43 (1993): 58–66.

5. McVeigh and Nichols specifically claimed that they planned and carried out the bombing to avenge the 1992 raid on white separatist Randy Weaver's property at Ruby Ridge, Idaho, and the 1993 raid on the Branch Davidian compound in Waco, Texas. However, both men believed, just as the militia movement does, that a New World Order run by Jews was secretly controlling the American government and much of the world.

6. Trudeau's books are identified as being published by Alliance Publishing. The organization is, in fact, Trudeau's own self-publishing company.

7. Jocelyn Noveck, "Somers' New Target: Conventional Cancer Treatment — Suzanne Somers' New Book on Alternative Cancer Remedies; Latest Attack on Mainstream Med," *Associated Press*, October 19, 2009.

8. Christopher Dreher, "What Kevin Trudeau Doesn't Want You to Know," *Salon.com*, July 29, 2005.

9. Paul A. Offit, *Autism's False Prophets: Bad Science, Risky Medicine, and the Search for a Cure* (New York: Columbia University Press, 2008).

Bibliography

Books and Articles

Adamski, George *Inside the Space Ships*. New York: Abelard-Schuman, 1955.

Alleman, Thomas Michael. "25 Most Influential Evangelicals in America." *Time*, September 8, 2007.

Allen, Denna, and Janet Midwinter. "Michelle Remembers: The Debunking of a Myth." *The Mail on Sunday*, September 30, 1990.

Aumann, Robert, Dror Bar-Natan, Hillel Furstenberg, Isaak Lapides, and Elihu Rips, "Analyses of the 'Gans' Committee Report." Report presented to the Center for the Study of Rationality, 1996.

Bagdikian, Ben H. *The New Media Monopoly*. Boston: Beacon Press, 2004.

Baigent, Michael. *The Jesus Papers: Exposing the Greatest Cover-Up in History*. New York: HarperCollins, 2006.

_____. *Racing Toward Armageddon: The Three Great Religions and the Plot to End the World*. New York: HarperOne, 2009.

Baigent, Michael, Richard Leigh, and Henry Lincoln. *Holy Blood, Holy Grail*. New York: Dell, 1983.

_____. *The Masonic Legacy*. New York: Henry Holt, 1987.

Baigent, Michael, and Richard Leigh. *The Temple and the Lodge*. New York: Arcade, 1991.

_____. *The Elixir and the Stone: The Tradition of Magic and Alchemy*. New York: Arrow, 2005.

Barker, Gray. *They Knew Too Much About Flying Saucers*. New York: University Books, 1956.

Barkun, Michael. *A Culture of Conspiracy: Apocalyptic Visions in Contemporary America (Comparative Studies in Religion and Society)*. Berkeley: University of California Press, 2003.

Bazant, Zdenek P., and Mathieu Verdure. "Mechanics of Progressive Collapse: Learning from World Trade Center and Building Demolitions." *Journal of Engineering Mechanics*, March 2007.

Benchley, Peter. *Jaws*. New York: Doubleday, 1974.

Berlitz, Charles, and William Moore. *The Philadelphia Experiment: Project Invisibility*. New York: Fawcett, 1979

_____. *The Roswell Incident*. New York: MJF Books, 1980.

Bernstein, Carl, and Bob Woodward. *All the President's Men*. New York: Simon & Schuster, 1974.

Berry, Steve. *The Amber Room*. New York: Ballantine Books, 2003.

Bezanson, Randal *How Free Can the Press Be?* Champaign: University of Illinois Press, 2003.

Bishop, Greg. *Project Beta: The Story of Paul Bennewitz, National Security, and the Creation of a Modern UFO Myth*. New York: Pocket Books, 2005.

Biskind, Peter. *Easy Riders, Raging Bulls: How the Sex-Drugs-and-Rock 'n' Roll Generation Saved Hollywood*. New York: Simon & Schuster, 1998.

Black, Conrad. *Richard M. Nixon: A Life in Full*. New York: PublicAffairs, 2007.

Black, Gregory D. *Hollywood Censored: Morality Codes, Catholics, and the Movies*. New York: Cambridge University Press, 1996.

Blakey, George Robert. *The Plot to Kill the President*. New York: Times Books, 1981.

Braudy, Leo. "Genre: The Conventions of Connection." In *Film Theory and Criticism*. Edited by Gerald Mast, Marshall Cohen & Leo Braudy. New York: Oxford University Press, 1976. 435–452.

Broder, John M., "Greatness in Eye of Beholder?" *Los Angeles Times*, November 22, 1993.

Brown, Dale. *Storming Heaven*. New York: Putnam, 1992.

Brown, Dan. *Digital Fortress*. New York: Thomas Dunne Books, 1998.

_____. *Angels and Demons*. New York: Pocket Books, 2000.

_____. *The Da Vinci Code*. New York: Doubleday, 2003.

_____. *The Lost Symbol*. New York: Doubleday, 2009.

Brown, Paul. "Ex-Nutter Icke Rails at the New World Order Mind Benders." *The Guardian*, May 19, 1995.

Bruce, Alexandra. *2012: Science or Superstition (The Definitive Guide to the Doomsday Phenomenon)*. New York: Disinformation Company, 2009.

Buchanan, Thomas G. *Who Killed Kennedy?* New York: Putnam, 1964.

Bugliosi, Vincent. *Helter Skelter: The True Story of the Manson Murders*. New York: W.W. Norton, 1994.

_____. *Reclaiming History: The Assassination of President John F. Kennedy*, New York: W.W. Norton, 2007.

Burns, Katy. "Jerry Falwell's Greatest Hates." *Concord Monitor*, May 17, 2007.

Calhoun, Patricia. "The Art at DIA Keeps Rumors Flying." *Denver Westword News*, July 6, 2010.

Cantwell, Alan. *AIDS and the Doctors of Death: An Inquiry Into the Origins of the AIDS Epidemic.* Los Angeles: Aries Rising Press, 1992.

Carter, Bill. "Springer Quits News Show, Citing Attacks." *New York Times,* May 9, 1992.

Cheetham, Erika. *The Further Prophecies of Nostradamus: 1985 and Beyond.* New York: Perigee Books, 1985.

Church Committee. *Intelligence Activities and the Rights of Americans: 1976 U.S. Senate Report on Illegal Wiretaps and Domestic Spying by the FBI, CIA, and NSA.* St. Petersburg, FL: Red and Black, 2008.

Clancy, Tom. *Debt of Honor.* New York: Putnam, 1994.

_____. *The Sum of All Fears.* New York: Putnam, 1990.

Clark, Jerome. *The Emergence of a Phenomenon: UFOs From the Beginning Through 1959 — The UFO Encyclopedia, Volume 2.* Detroit: Omnigraphics, 1992.

_____. *Strange Skies: Pilot Encounters with UFOs.* New York: Citadel Press, 2003.

_____. *The UFO Book: Encyclopedia of the Extraterrestrial.* Detroit: Visible Ink Press, 1997.

_____. *Unexplained!* Detroit: Visible Ink Press, 1993.

Coale, Samuel. *Paradigms of Paranoia: The Culture of Conspiracy in Contemporary American Fiction.* Tuscaloosa: University of Alabama Press, 2005.

Cohen, Daniel. *The Great Airship Mystery: A UFO of the 1890s.* New York: Dodd, Mead, 1981.

Condon, Richard. *The Manchurian Candidate.* New York: McGraw-Hill, 1959.

Crumley, Bruce. "Conspiracy Theory." *Time,* May 13, 2002.

Darlington, David. *Area 51: The Dreamland Chronicles.* New York: Owl Books, 1997.

David, James F. *Ship of the Damned.* New York: Tor Books, 2000.

Davis, Jason. "Tune in for the 'Truth': Carter and Spotnitz Revisit *The X-Files* TV Series." *Creative Screenwriting,* July/August 2008.

Denby, David. "Movies: The Last Angry Men." *New York,* January 16, 1984.

de Sede, Gerard. *Le Tresor Maudit de Rennes-le-Chateau.* Paris: J'ai Lu, 1969.

de Young, May. *The Ritual Abuse Controversy: An Annotated Bibliography.* Jefferson, NC: McFarland, 2002.

Dolan, Richard M. *UFOs and the National Security State: Chronology of a Cover-up 1941–1973.* Charlottesville, VA: Hampton Roads, 2002.

Dreher, Christopher. "What Kevin Trudeau Doesn't Want You to Know." *Salon.com,* July 29, 2005.

Dreyfus, Robert. "Reverend Doomsday: According to Tim LaHaye, the Apocalypse is Now." *Rolling Stone,* January 28, 2004.

Dunbar, David, and Brad Reagan. *Debunking 9/11 Myths: Why Conspiracy Theories Can't Stand Up to the Facts.* New York: Hearst Books, 2006.

Eberle, Paul, and Shirley Eberle. *The Abuse of Innocence: The McMartin Preschool Trial.* Amherst, NY: Prometheus Books, 2003.

Ebert, Roger. *Roger Ebert's Home Movie Companion.* Kansas City: Andrews McMeel, 1992.

Edwards, Ted. The X-Files *Confidential: The Unauthorized X-Philes Compendium.* Boston: Little, Brown, 1997.

Edwards, Tony. "End of the Road for Car That Ran on Water." *The Sunday Times,* December 1, 1996.

Eisen, Jonathan. *Suppressed Inventions and Other Discoveries.* New York: Perigee, 1999.

Ellsberg, Daniel. *Secrets: A Memoir of Vietnam and the Pentagon Papers.* New York: Viking Penguin, 2002.

Emenegger, Robert. *UFOs: Past, Present and Future.* New York: Ballantine, 1974.

Evans, Hilary. *Gods, Spirits, Cosmic Guardians: A Comparative Study of the Encounter Experience.* Wellingborough, Northamptonshire, England: Aquarian Press, 1987.

Faludi, Susan. *Stiffed: The Betrayal of the American Man.* New York: William Morrow, 1999.

Farrell, Joseph P. *The SS Brotherhood of the Bell: NASA's Nazis, JFK, and Majic-12.* Kempton, IL: Adventures Unlimited Press, 2006.

Fireman, Daniel. "Attack of the Clones." *Entertainment Weekly,* July 22, 2005.

Frankfurter, David. *Evil Incarnate: Rumors of Demonic Conspiracy and Satanic Abuse in History.* Princeton, NJ: Princeton University Press, 2006.

Fuhrman, Mark. *A Simple Act of Murder: November 22, 1963.* New York: William Morrow, 2006.

Fuller, John G. *The Interrupted Journey: Two Lost Hours Aboard a Flying Saucer.* New York: Dial Press, 1966.

George, Peter. *Red Alert.* London: T.V. Boardman, 1958.

Gilbert, James. *A Cycle of Outrage: America's Reaction to the Juvenile Delinquent in the 1950s.* New York: Oxford University Press, 1986.

Goldberg, Michelle. "Fundamentally Unsound." *Salon.com,* July 29, 2007.

_____. "Truther Consequences." *The New Republic,* October 7, 2009.

Good, Timothy. *Above Top-Secret: The Worldwide UFO Cover-Up.* New York: William Morrow, 1988.

_____. *Alien Contact: Top-Secret UFO Files Revealed.* New York: Quill, 1993.

Goodrick-Clarke, Nicholas. *Black Sun: Aryan Cults, Esoteric Nazism and the Politics of Identity.* New York: New York University Press, 2002.

Gordon, Michael R., and Bernard E. Trainor, *Cobra II: The Inside Story of the Invasion and Occupation of Iraq.* New York: Vintage Books, 2007.

Gravois, John. "Professors of Paranoia?" *Chronicle of Higher Education,* June 23, 2006.

Griffin, David Ray. *Christian Faith and the Truth Behind 9/11: A Call for Reflection and Action.* Louisville, KY: Westminster John Knox Press, 2006.

_____. *Debunking 9/11 Debunking: An Answer to Popular Mechanics and Other Defenders of the Official Conspiracy Theory.* Northampton, MA: Olive Branch Press, 2007.

_____. *The New Pearl Harbor: Disturbing Questions About the Bush Administration and 9/11.* Northampton, MA: Interlink Books, 2004.

_____. *The 9/11 Commission Report: Omissions and Distortions.* Northampton, MA: Olive Branch Press, 2005.

Grisham, John. *The Firm.* New York: Dell, 1992.

Grose, Peter. *Continuing the Inquiry: The Council on Foreign Relations from 1921 to 1996.* New York: Council on Foreign Relations Press, 1996.

Hagger, Nicholas. *The Secret History of the West: The Influence of Secret Organizations on Western History from the Renaissance to the 20th Century.* New York: O Books, 2005.

Hamilton, Nigel. *JFK: Reckless Youth.* New York: Random House, 1995.

Hersh, Seymour M. *The Dark Side of Camelot.* New York: Back Bay Books, 1997.

Hicks, Robert D. *In Pursuit of Satan: The Police and the Occult.* Amherst, NY: Prometheus Books, 1991.

Hopkins, Budd. *Intruders: The Incredible Visitations at Copley Woods.* New York: Random House, 1987.

Howe, Linda Moulton. *Alien Harvest: Further Evidence Linking Animal Mutilations and Human Abductions to Alien Life Forms.* Self published, 1989.

Hunt, Linda. *Secret Agenda: The United States, Nazi Scientists, and Project Paperclip, 1945 to 1990.* New York: St. Martin's Press, 1991.

Hynek, J. Allen. *The UFO Experience: A Scientific Inquiry.* New York: Marlowe, 1998.

Icke, David. *Alice in Wonderland and the World Trade Center Disaster: Why the Official Story of 9/11 Is a Monumental Lie.* Self published, 2002.

_____. *And the Truth Shall Set You Free.* Self published, 2004.

_____. *The Biggest Secret: The Book That Will Change the World.* Self published, 1999.

_____. *Children of the Matrix: How an Interdimensional Race has Controlled the World for Thousands of Years — and Still Does.* Self published, 2001.

_____. *The David Icke Guide to the Global Conspiracy (And How to End It).* Self published, 2007.

_____. *Infinite Love is the Only Truth: Everything Else is Illusion.* Self published, 2005.

_____. *Tales From the Time Loop: The Most Comprehensive Expose of the Global Conspiracy ever Written and All You Need to Know to Be Truly Free.* Self published, 2003.

Jackson, Devon. *Conspiranoia: The Mother of All Conspiracy Theories.* New York: Plume, 1999.

Jacobs, David M. *The UFO Controversy in America.* Bloomington: Indiana University Press, 1975.

_____. *Secret Life: First Hand Accounts of UFO Abductions.* New York: Simon & Schuster, 1992.

_____. *The Threat.* New York: Simon & Schuster, 1998.

J.C. *Mysteries of the Universe: A Revolutionary Commentary on UFOs, Aliens, Angels, Pyramids, Bible Codes, Reincarnation, the Antichrist....* Longwood, FL: Xulon Press, 2004.

Jeffords, Susan. *Hard Bodies: Hollywood Masculinity in the Reagan Era.* New Brunswick, NJ: Rutgers University Press, 1994.

Joesten, Joachim. *Oswald: Assassin or Fall Guy?* New York: Marzani & Munsell, 1964.

Johnson, Kenneth. *V: The Second Generation.* New York: Tor Books, 2008.

Jones, Alex. *9/11: Descent Into Tyranny.* Joshua Tree, CA: Progressive Press, 2002.

Joslin, Lyndon W. "Cosmic Frames and Cover-ups: *Invasion of the Saucer Men* and the UFO Conspiracy of Silence." In *Science Fiction America: Essays on SF Cinema.* Edited by David J. Hogan. Jefferson, NC: McFarland, 2006. 138–150.

Kane, Jason. "PPC Backs away From 9/11 Conspiracy Book." *Presbyterian News Service,* November 28, 2006.

Kaplan, E. Ann. *Women in Film Noir.* London: British Film Institute, 1998.

Kass, Leon R. *Human Cloning and Human Dignity: The Report of the President's Council on Bioethics.* New York: PublicAffairs, 2002.

Kaysing, Bill. *We Never Went to the Moon: America's Thirty Billion Dollar Swindle.* Self published, 1974.

Keel, John A. *The Mothman Prophecies.* New York: E.P. Dutton, 1975.

_____. *UFOs: Operation Trojan Horse.* New York: Putnam, 1970.

Keith, Jim. *Mind Control and UFOs: Casebook on Alternative 3.* Kempton, IL: Adventures Unlimited Press, 2005.

Kessler, Ronald. *The Sins of the Father: Joseph P. Kennedy and the Dynasty He Founded.* New York: Warner Books, 1996.

Keyhoe, Donald E. *Aliens From Space: The Real Story of Unidentified Flying Objects.* New York: Doubleday, 1973.

_____. *Flying Saucers From Outer Space.* New York: Henry Holt, 1953.

Khoury, Raymond. *The Last Templar.* New York: Signet, 2006.

Kimball, Josh. "Settlement Brings End to 9-Year 'Left Behind' Dispute." *Christian Post,* August 15, 2008.

King, Neal. *Heroes in Hard Times: Cop Action Movies in the U.S.* Philadelphia: Temple University Press, 1999.

Knight, Peter. *Conspiracy Nation: The Politics of Paranoia in Postwar America.* New York: New York University Press, 2002.

Knight, Stephen. *Jack the Ripper: The Final Solution.* Detroit: Treasure Press, 1984.

Koocher, Gerald P., and Patricia Keith-Spiegel. *Ethics in Psychology and the Mental Health Professions: Standards and Cases (Oxford Textbooks in Clinical Psychology).* New York: Oxford University Press, 2008.

Koontz, Dean. *From the Corner of His Eye.* New York: Bantam, 2001.

LaHaye, Timothy, and Jerry B. Jenkins. *Left Behind: A Novel of the Earth's Last Days.* Carol Stream, IL: Tyndale House, 2000.

Lambert, Jack, and Norman Polmar. *Defenseless: Command Failure at Pearl Harbor.* Osceola, WI: Zenith Press, 2003.

Lambert, Patricia. *False Witness: The Real Story of Jim Garrison's Investigation and Oliver Stone's Film JFK.* New York: M. Evans, 1998.

Lavery, David, Angela Hague, and Marla Cartwright. *Deny All Knowledge: Reading* The X-Files. Syracuse: Syracuse University Press, 1996.

Lemons, Stephen. "The Yoda of 9/11." *Phoenix NewTimes,* August 9, 2007.

Leo, John. "Twisted History." *Newsweek,* December 23, 1991.

Levinson, Paul. *The Plot to Save Socrates*. New York: Tor Books, 2006.

_____. *The Silk Code*. New York: Tor Books, 1999.

Lewis, Sinclair. *It Can't Happen Here*. New York: Dell, 1935.

Lindsey, Hal, and Carole C. Carlson. *The Late, Great Planet Earth*. Grand Rapids: Zondervan, 1970.

Lochte, Dick. "Warren Murphy and His Heroic Oddballs." In *Murder Off the Rack: Critical Studies of Ten Paperback Masters*. Edited by John L. Breen and Martin Harry Greenberg. Metuchen, NJ: Scarecrow, 1989. 145–165.

Mack, John E. *Abduction: Human Encounters with Aliens*. New York: Ballantine Books, 1994.

Marrs, Jim. *Crossfire: The Plot That Killed Kennedy*. New York: Carroll & Graf, 1989.

_____. *Inside Job: Unmasking the 9/11 Conspiracies*. San Rafael, CA: Origin Press, 2004.

_____. *PSI Spies: The True Story of America's Psychic Warfare Program*. Franklin Lakes, NJ: New Page Books, 2002.

_____. *The Rise of the Fourth Reich: The Secret Societies That Threaten to Take Over America*. New York: William Morrow, 2008.

_____. *Rule by Secrecy: The Hidden History that Connects the Trilateral Commission, the Freemasons, and the Great Pyramids*. New York: HarperPerennial, 1999.

_____. *The Terror Conspiracy: Deception, 9/11, and the Loss of Liberty*. New York: Disinformation Company, 2006.

_____. *The Trillion Dollar Conspiracy: How the New World Order, Man-Made Diseases, and Zombie Banks are Destroying America*. New York: William Morrow, 2010.

_____. *The War on Freedom: The 9/11 Conspiracies*. ARES Publishing, 2003.

Martin, Ernest F. "Five." In *Nuclear War Films*. Edited by Jack G. Shaheen and Marshall Flaum. Carbondale: Southern Illinois University Press, 1978. 11–16.

Mathews, Chris. *Modern Satanism: Anatomy of a Radical Subculture*. Westport, CT: Praeger, 2009.

McCombs, Maxwell, and Donald Shaw. "The Evolution of Agenda-Setting Theory: 25 Years in the Marketplace of Ideas." *Journal of Communication*, 43 (1993): 58–66.

McKay, Brendan, Dror Bar-Natan, and Maya Bar-Hillel. "Solving the Bible Code Puzzle." *Statistical Science*, Vol. 14, 1999.

McMillan, Priscilla Johnson. *Marina and Lee*. New York: Random House, 1980.

Meehan, Paul. *Saucer Movies: A UFOlogical History of the Cinema*. Lanham, MD: Scarecrow, 1998.

Melton, J. Gordon. "Vampire Games." *The Vampire Book: The Encyclopedia of the Undead*. Detroit: Visible Ink Press, 1999, 273–282.

Meyssan, Thierry. *L'Effroyable Imposture*. London: Carnot, 2002.

_____. *LePentagate*. London: Carnot, 2002.

Millegan, Kris. *Fleshing Out Skull & Bones: Investigations Into America's Most Powerful Secret Society*. Walterville, OR: Trine Day, 2005.

Miller, Laura. "The Last Word; The Da Vinci Con." *New York Times*, February 22, 2004.

Missler, Chuck, and Mark Eastman. *Alien Encounters: The Secret Behind the UFO Phenomenon*. Coeur d'Alene, ID: Koinonia House, 2003.

Mitovich, Matt. "Charlie Sheen to Give Voice to 9/11 Conspiracy Theorists After All ... Maybe." *TV Guide*, June 1, 2007.

Moore, Alan, and Eddie Campbell. *From Hell*. Marietta, GA: Top Shelf Productions, 1989.

Moore, Alan, and Dave Gibbons. *Watchmen*. New York: DC Comics, 1987.

Moore, Alan, and David Lloyd. *V for Vendetta*. New York: DC Comics, 1990.

Morrell, David. *First Blood*. New York: Warner Books, 1997.

Morrocco, John D. "Multiple Sightings of Secret Aircraft Hint at New Propulsion, Airframe Designs." *Aviation Week and Space Technology*, October 1, 1990, 22-23.

Murillo, Luis. *The Noriega Mess: The Drugs, the Canal, and Why America Invaded*. Berkeley: Video-Books, 1995.

Myers, John E.B. *Child Protection in America: Past, Present, and Future*. New York: Oxford University Press, 2006.

Nathan, Debbie. *Satan's Silence: Ritual Abuse and the Making of a Modern American Witch Hunt*. New York: Basic Books, 1995.

Newcomb, Horace, and Robert Alley. *The Producer's Medium: Conversations with Creators of American TV*. Oxford: Oxford University Press, 1983.

Nickell, Joe, and John F. Fischer. "The Crashed Saucer Forgeries," *The International UFO Reporter*, March 1990.

Noveck, Jocelyn. "Somers' New Target: Conventional Cancer Treatment — Suzanne Somers' New Book on Alternative Cancer Remedies; Latest Attack on Mainstream Med." *Associated Press*, October 19, 2009.

Offit, Paul A. *Autism's False Prophets: Bad Science, Risky Medicine, and the Search for a Cure*. New York: Columbia University Press, 2008.

Oglesbee, Frank W. "The World, the Flesh, and the Devil." In *Nuclear War Films*. Edited by Jack G. Shaheen and Marshall Flaum. Carbondale: Southern Illinois University Press, 1978. 25–30.

Parish, Jane, and Martin Parker. *The Age of Anxiety: Conspiracy Theory and the Human Sciences*. Boston: Blackwell/Sociological Review, 2001.

Peebles, Curtis. *Watch the Skies! A Chronicle of the Flying Saucer Myth*. New York: Berkley Books, 1995.

Perloff, James. *The Shadows of Power: The Council on Foreign Relations and the American Decline*. Appleton, WI: Western Islands, 2000.

Posner, Gerald. *Case Closed: Lee Harvey Oswald and the Assassination of JFK*. New York: Random House, 1993.

Putnam, Robert D. *Bowling Alone: The Collapse and Revival of American Community*. New York: Simon & Schuster, 2000.

Ramsland, Katherine. *Piercing the Darkness: Undercover With Vampires in America Today*. New York: HarperPrism, 1998.

Randle, Kevin D. and Donald R. Schmitt. *UFO Crash at Roswell*. New York: Avon Books, 1991.

Reeves, Thomas. *A Question of Character: A Life of John F. Kennedy*. New York: Prima, 1997.

Ricks, Thomas E. *Fiasco: The American Military Adventure in Iraq*. New York: Penguin, 2006.

Robbins, Alexandra. *Secrets of the Tomb: Skull and Bones, the Ivy League and the Hidden Paths of Power*. Boston: Back Bay Books, 2003.

Robinson, John. *Proofs of a Conspiracy Against All the Religions and Governments of Europe Carried out in the Secret Meetings of the Free Masons, Illuminati, and Reading Societies*. New York: George Forman, 1798.

Ronson, Jon. *Them: Adventures with Extremists*. New York: Simon & Schuster, 2002.

Ross, Hugh. *Lights in the Sky and Little Green Men: A Rational Christian Look at UFOs and Extraterrestrials*. Colorado Springs: NavPress, 2002.

Rudenstine, David. *The Day the Presses Stopped: A History of the Pentagon Papers Case*. Berkley: University of California Press, 1998.

Ruethling, Gretchen. "A Skeptic on 9/11 Prompts Questions on Academic Freedom." *New York Times*, August 1, 2006.

Ruppelt, Edward J. *The Report on Unidentified Flying Objects*. Garden City, NY: Doubleday, 1956.

Sanello, Frank. *Stallone: A Rocky Life*. Edinburgh: Mainstream, 1998.

Schlesinger, Arthur M. *Robert Kennedy and His Times*. New York: Mariner, 2002.

Schrader, Paul. "Notes on Film Noir." In *Film Genre Reader*. Edited by Barry Keith Grant. Austin: University of Texas Press, 1986.

Schuchardt, Read Mercer. "What is the Matrix?" In *Taking the Red Pill: Science, Philosophy and Religion in* The Matrix. Edited by Glenn Yeffeth. Dallas: Benbella, 2003. 5–21.

Schwartz, Nina. "Itsy-Bitsy Spiders and Other Pieces of the Real in Dead Calm." *Camera Obscura*, 51, Volume 17, November 3, 2002, 149–179.

Searcey, Dionne. "Behind the Music: Sleuths Seek Messages in Lyrical Backspin." *Wall Street Journal*, January 9, 2006.

Shaw, Tony. *Hollywood's Cold War*. Edinburgh: Edinburgh University Press, 2007.

Sheehan, Neil. *The Pentagon Papers: The Secret History of the Vietnam War*. New York: Bantam Books, 1971.

Silver, Alain, and James Ursini. *Film Noir*. Los Angeles: Taschen, 2004.

Sora, Steve. *Secret Societies of America's Elite: From the Knights Templar to Skull and Bones*. Shippensburg, PA: Destiny Books, 2003.

Soriano, Cesar G. "Politics Creates a Disturbance in the Force." *USA Today*, May 17, 2005.

Spada, James. *Peter Lawford*. New York: Bantam, 1992.

Stephey, M.J. "The Skull and Bones Society." *Time*, February 23, 2009.

Stillwell, Cinamon. "The Truth About 9/11 Conspiracy Theories." *San Francisco Chronicle*, August 19, 2006.

Sullivan, Michael John. *Presidential Passions: The Love Affairs of America's Presidents: From Washington and Jefferson to Kennedy and Johnson*. New York: S.P.I. Books, 1994.

Sutton, Anthony C. *America's Secret Establishment: An Introduction to the Order of Skull and Bones*. Walterville, OR: Trine Day, 2004.

Taibi, Matt. *The Great Derangement: A Terrifying True Story of War, Politics, and Religion at the Twilight of the American Empire*. New York: Spiegel & Grau, 2008.

Taraborrelli, J. Randy. *The Secret Life of Marilyn Monroe*. New York: Grand Central, 2009.

Theoharis, Athan. *Spying on Americans: Political Surveillance From Hoover to the Huston Plan*. Philadelphia: Temple University Press, 1978.

Tin, Louis-Georges, and Marek Redburn. *Dictionary of Homophobia: A Global History of Gay & Lesbian Experience*. Vancouver, BC: Arsenal Pulp Press, 2008.

Tinnell, Robert. *"Logan's Run* to Relevance." In *Science Fiction America: Essays on SF Cinema*. Edited by David J. Hogan. Jefferson, NC: McFarland, 2006. 217–224.

Trevanian. *The Eiger Sanction*. New York: Avon, 1973.

Trudeau, Kevin. *Natural Cures "They" Don't Want You to Know About*. Alliance Publishing, 2006.

Upton, Charles. *Legends of the End: Prophecies of the End Times, Antichrist, Apocalypse, and Messiah from Eight Religious Traditions*. Hillsdale, NY: Sophia Perennis, 2005.

Vallée, Jacques. *The Invisible College: What a Group of Scientists Has Discovered About UFO Influences on the Human Race*. New York: E.P. Dutton, 1975.

_____. *Messengers of Deception: UFO Contacts and Cults*. Berkeley: Ronin Publishing, 1979.

_____. *Passport to Magonia: From Folklore to Flying Saucers*. Chicago: Henry Regnery, 1969.

_____. *Revelations: Alien Contact and Human Deception*. New York: Ballantine Books, 1991.

Vankin, Jonathan, and John Whalen. *60 Greatest Conspiracies of All Time*. New York: Citadel Press, 1996.

Victor, Jeffrey S. *Satanic Panic: The Creation of a Contemporary Legend*. Chicago: Open Court, 1993.

von Bulow, Andreas. *The CIA and September 11*. Munich: Piper, 2003.

von Däniken, Erich. *Chariots of the Gods?* New York: Berkley Books, 1969.

Wager, Jans B. *Dames in the Driver's Seat: Rereading Film Noir*. Austin: University of Texas Press, 2005.

Walch, Tad. "BYU Professor in Dispute Over 9/11 Will Retire." *Deseret News*. October 22, 2006.

_____. "Controversy Dogs Y's Jones." *Deseret News*, September 11, 2006.

Webb, Gary. *Dark Alliance: The CIA, the Contras and the Crack Cocaine Explosion*. New York: Seven Stories Press, 1998.

Wells, H.G. *The War of the Worlds*. Naperville, IL: Sourcebooks, 2005.

Wilcox, Clyde, and Carin Robinson. *Onward Christian Soldiers? The Religious Right in American Politics (Dilemmas in American Politics)*. Boulder, CO: Westview Press, 2000.

Wilson, Valerie Plame, and Laura Rozen. *Fair Game: How a Top CIA Agent Was Betrayed by Her Own Government*. New York: Simon & Schuster, 2007.

Wisnewski, Gerhard. *Operation 9/11*. Munich: Droemer/Knaur, 2003.
Woodward, Bob. *Plan of Attack*. New York: Simon & Schuster, 2004.
Wolfe, Tom. *The Right Stuff*. New York: Bantam, 1979.
Wright, Bradford W. *Comic Book Nation: The Transformation of Youth Culture in America*. Baltimore: Johns Hopkins University Press, 2003.
Wu, Tim. "Holy Grail Wars: The Latest Battle Over *The Da Vinci Code*." *Slate*, March 13, 2006.

Documentaries

An Alien History of Planet Earth. History Channel Documentary (10/13/05).
Carter, Chris. The X-Files: *Fight the Future* DVD commentary.
CBS News 48 Hours Mystery. "The Marilyn Tapes." CBS News Documentary (8/1/06).
Conspiracy Theory: Did We Land on the Moon? Fox Network Documentary (2/15/01).
Coppola, Francis Ford. *The Conversation* DVD commentary.
del Toro, Guillermo. *Hell Boy* DVD commentary.
How William Shatner Changed the World. History Channel Documentary (11/13/05).
King, Stephen. *Storm of the Century* DVD commentary.
Making the Earth Stand Still. Documentary for *The Day the Earth Stood Still* DVD.
Mythbusters: NASA Moon Landing. Discovery Channel (8/27/08).
The 9/11 Conspiracies: Fact or Fiction. History Channel Documentary (8/20/07).
No Fighting in the War Room: Or Dr. Strangelove and the Nuclear Threat. Documentary for *Dr. Strangelove* DVD.
Redford, Robert. *All the President's Men* DVD commentary.
Revealed: The Man Behind the Da Vinci Code. CNN (6/10/06).
Shades of Gray. Seminal Films Documentary (6/15/10).
60 Minutes: The Secret of the Priory of Sion. CBS (4/30/06).
Sullivan, Bob. *Parts: The Clonus Horror* DVD commentary
Telling the Truth About Lies: The Making of All the President's Men. Documentary for *All the President's Men* DVD.
Turteltaub, Jon. *National Treasure 2: Book of Secrets* DVD commentary.

Internet

Architects and Engineers for 9/11 Truth. <www.ae911truth.org>
Corliss, Richard. "Seagal Under Siege." *Time*, July 5, 1993. <www.time.com>
Debunking 9/11 Conspiracy Theories. <www.debunking911.com>
Denver International Airport Mystery. <http://newsflavor.com/opinions/mystery-surrounding-denver-international-airport/>
de Zengotita, Thomas. "Must See Movie: Shooter." *The Huffington Post*, April 2, 2007. <www.huffingtonpost.com/thomas-de-zengotita/must-see-movie-shooter_b_45406.html>
Ebert, Roger. "Fire in the Sky." Review of *Fire in the Sky*. March 15, 1993. <http:www.rogerebert.suntimes.com>
"Ilana's V Page" www.ilanasVsite.com/.
Jones, Alex. "*The Lone Gunmen*: Pilot Episode of *X-Files* Spin Off an Insider 9/11 Warning or Sick Conditioning? <www.prisonplanet.com/multimedia_priorknowledge_lonegunmen.html>.
Jones, Steven E. "Why Indeed Did the World Trade Center Building Completely Collapse." <http://we.archive.org/web/20051124011753/http://www.physics.byu.edu/research/energy/htm7.html>
Journal of Debunking 911 Conspiracy Theories. <www.jod911.com>
Left Behind. <www.imdb.com/title/tt0190524/>
Left Behind: World at War. < www.imdb.com/title/tt0443567/>
The Lone Gunmen's pilot episode discussion.<http://killtown.911review.org/lonegunmen.html>
Moore, Alan. *MTV.com* interview. <www.mtv.com/shared/movies/interviews/m/moore_alan_060315>
"Paul Levinson's Infinite Regress." <www.paullevinson.blogspot.com>
President George Bush Announcing War Against Iraq. <www.historyplace.com/speeches/bush-war.htm>
Scholars for 9/11 Truth. <www.scholarsfor911truth.org>
Scholars for 9/11 Truth and Justice. <http://stj911.org>

Index